J. Revell Carr

J. Revell Carr was for thirty-one years curator and then director of Mystic Seaport, the American maritime museum, and had responsibility for the *Anglo-Saxon*'s jolly boat for more than twenty-five years. During his years at Mystic Seaport he served on numerous national and international committees and was elected president of both the Council of American Maritime Museums and the International Congress of Maritime Museums. He retired in 2000 and lives on the coast of Maine.

J. Revell Carr

ALL BRAVE SAILORS

THE SINKING OF THE *ANGLO-SAXON*,
21 AUGUST 1940

HODDER

Copyright © 2004 by J. Revell Carr

First published in Great Britain in 2004 by Hodder and Stoughton
A division of Hodder Headline

Grateful acknowledgement is made to the following sources for photographs reproduced
here: Arthur K. Blood: 7, 19; Bundesarchiv: 5; Bundesarchiv, Freiburg: 6;
J. Revell Carr: 17; John Clarkson: 1, 2; Betty McAteer: 8; Ted Milburn: 9, 11, 21, 22:
Ted Milburn and Desmond Denny: 3, 12, 13; Ted Milburn and the Penny family: 14:
Newcastle *Evening Chronicle and Journal*: 10, 11; Garnett Thompson: 18; Stanley Toogood,
courtesy of Michael Toogood: 15, 16, 20; W. Z. Bilddienst, Wilhelmshaven: 4.

A Coronet paperback

1 3 5 7 9 10 8 6 4 2

A CIP catalogue record for this title
is available from the British Library

ISBN 0 340 82578 2

Typeset in Requiem by Palimpsest Book Production Limited, Polmont, Stirlingshire

Printed and bound by
Mackays of Chatham Ltd, Chatham, Kent

Hodder Headline's policy is to use papers that are natural, renewable and recyclable
products and made from wood grown in sustainable forests. The logging
and manufacturing processes are expected to conform to the environmental
regulations of the country of origin

Hodder and Stoughton
A division of Hodder Headline
338 Euston Road
London NW1 3BH

Acknowledgments

There are many people who contributed to this book, and I am indebted to them all, and could not have written it without them. There are several, however, who have been exceptionally helpful and who made the creation of this book the most pleasurable of tasks. In England, Ted Milburn and Anthony Smith generously shared their knowledge. Ted made available his remarkable archive on the *Anglo-Saxon*, his father, and others involved with the ship. His help and friendship have been invaluable and are most appreciated. In the United States, George Duffy, who was on the receiving end of a Ruckteschell attack, related his firsthand experiences and introduced me to two former officers who served with Ruckteschell. In Germany, those two officers, Konrad Hoppe and Jürgen Herr, welcomed me into their homes and were hospitable, open, and generous with their information. The assistance from these two men has also been invaluable. I have been the beneficiary of superb assistance from a brilliant young scholar, Olaf Griese. His careful translations of German texts have been essential during this effort, and his insightful notes and comments have often clarified important points and given me a perspective that would otherwise have been difficult to achieve.

Also deserving of my thanks are Ruth and Lawson Willard, who, in addition to providing the most comfortable of "homes away from home" on numerous occasions, are among many friends who have been encouraging listeners throughout the process.

There are many institutions and individuals in Great Britain who have assisted, supported, and encouraged this project. Among the institutions that have been sources of information are: The Public Records

Office in Kew, with its very helpful staff; The Admiralty Library and Iain MacKenzie; The House of Lords Record Office and Ms. K. V. Bligh; The Merseyside Maritime Museum Library and Tony Tibbles; The Imperial War Museum and David Penn; The Family Records Center; The British Library Newspaper Library; The Glamorgan Record Office in Cardiff; and The Cardiff Central Library.

Among the individuals in Great Britain who gave spirit to this book, in addition to Ted Milburn and Anthony Smith, are relatives and friends of men in the *Anglo-Saxon,* including: Bob Tapscott's widow, Norma Tapscott, and their daughter, Diane Tapscott Terrazino (a resident of Belgium); Jim Fowler's niece, Betty McAteer and her daughter, Leslie Grant; the daughter of Roy Widdicombe's widow, Cynthia, Sue Irvine; Captain Flynn's nephew, Dr. Desmond Flynn; Roy Pilcher's friend Cliff Walder and his cousins, Frank H. Bacon and James R. Bacon. Two of Bob Tapscott's shipmates, Phil Hayden and Harry Griffin offered insight. Several people provided research leads: Jak Showell on U-boats, Brian Boyd on the Tweedsmuir Camp, and Carol Souter in Bury St. Edmunds.

Within the Bahamas a number of organizations and people were of assistance. In Nassau they include: The Bahamas Department of Archives, its Director, Gail Saunders, and particularly Mrs. Sherilee Strachan; The Nassau Public Library and Mrs. Winifred Murphy; The Office of the Registrar General; Dr. Michael M. Gerassimos; Miss Gwen French; Tiffany Sullivan; Mallie Lightbourn (living in London but in Nassau while the survivors were there); Richard Lightbourn; Andrew McKinney; Michael Toogood; and Montague Higgs. On Eleuthera, the Haynes Library and its Director, Rosalind Seyfert; Loraine and Joy Pyfrom; Rev. Samuel B. Pinder; former Constable Elijah Mackey; and Garnett Thompson.

In addition to the National Archive of Canada, the following people in Canada were of assistance: Roy Pilcher's friend, Marion Wastell Blake; Provost Sergeant at the Tweedsmuir Camp, B. J. Keegan; and Miss Ella May Sim.

In Germany, in addition to Jürgen Herr, Konrad Hoppe, and Olaf Griese, assistance came from the Deutsches Marinearchiv, the Bundesarchiv Militararchiv; The U-boot Archiv; Horst Schwenk; and Dr. Gerhardt Kaufmann.

In Sweden, I am indebted to the Director of the Gothenburg Maritime Museum, Thomas Thieme, for putting me in touch with the fine researcher Christer Johansson, who was thorough in his research into Ruckteschell and his crew in Sweden. Christer drew on the following sources for his information: the Goteborg Poliskammare; the Landskansliet Goteborg och Bohuslan; Kurs-och Tidningsbiblioteket Goteborg; and the Landsarkivet Goteborg.

In France, I was aided by the Director of the Musée de la Marine, Admiral Georges Prud'homme, and by Franck Genestoux.

Within the United States, several institutions have been of great help. These include: The New York Public Library; The Boston Public Library; The Seamen's Church Institute and Lana Parr; The Nantucket Atheneum and their very helpful reference librarian, Sharon Carlee; Mystic Seaport's G. W. Blunt White Library and its fine staff under the direction of Paul O'Pecko; The Director of The Williams College/Mystic Seaport Maritime Studies Program, Dr. Jim Carlton; and from Mystic Seaport staff members, Phil Budlong, Dana Hewson, Peggy Tate Smith, Mary Anne Stets, Don Treworgy, Peter Vermilya, and Rodi York. I would also like to thank Dr. Aphrodite Matsakis for her insights into posttraumatic stress disorder and Dr. Bill Dudley, Director of the Naval Historical Center, for his advice.

My most sincere thanks go to a number of people who have been of extraordinary help in bringing this book into existence. At Simon & Schuster, my editor, the remarkable Alice Mayhew, has made the entire process a pleasure. Her team of Associate Editors, Emily Takoudes and Anja Schmidt, and assistants Jonathan Jao and Hui Xie, kept everything moving effortlessly. The rest of the Simon & Schuster crew, particularly Gypsy da Silva and Elizabeth Hayes, has been equally efficient and helpful.

From the very beginning of this project, my literary agent, Stuart Krichevsky, has been my advocate, mentor, confidant, motivator, and friend. I have nothing but admiration and respect for Stuart and the team at the Stuart Krichevsky Literary Agency, including Shana Cohen, Elizabeth Fisher, and Schuyler Gilmore.

Particular thanks go to Nat Philbrick of Nantucket, who has been an inspiration, guide, tutor, and valued friend.

Lastly, my special thanks go to my family. Rev, Geordie, and Lisa, my children, gave their enthusiastic encouragement. My greatest appreciation goes to my wife, Barbara, for her consistent support, full participation, and faith as well as the tears of sympathy she shed for those of the *Anglo-Saxon* during her readings and first edit of the manuscript. I thank her for all her contributions and sharing the joys and trials of this endeavor.

New Harbor, Maine
June 2003

To my wife
Barbara
who is precious to me.

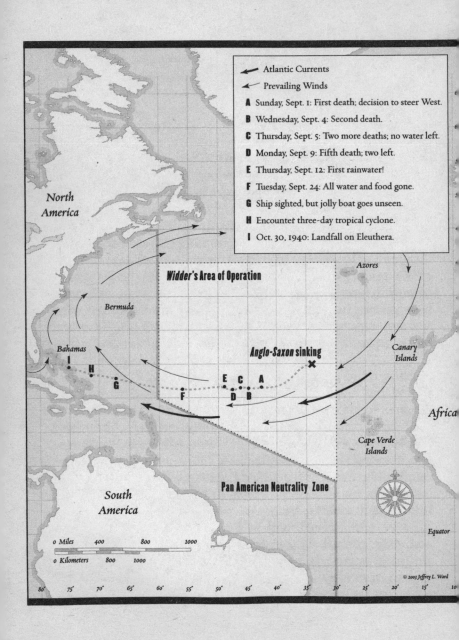

Atlantic Currents
Prevailing Winds

A Sunday, Sept. 1: First death; decision to steer West.
B Wednesday, Sept. 4: Second death.
C Thursday, Sept. 5: Two more deaths; no water left.
D Monday, Sept. 9: Fifth death; two left.
E Thursday, Sept. 12: First rainwater!
F Tuesday, Sept. 24: All water and food gone.
G Ship sighted, but jolly boat goes unseen.
H Encounter three-day tropical cyclone.
I Oct. 30, 1940: Landfall on Eleuthera.

North
America

Widder's Area of Operation

Azores

Bermuda

Anglo-Saxon sinking

Canary
Islands

Bahamas

E C A
D B
F

Africa

Pan American Neutrality Zone

Cape Verde
Islands

South
America

Equator

0 Miles   400   800   1000
0 Kilometers   800   1000

© 2003 Jeffrey L. Ward

80° 75° 70° 65° 60° 55° 50° 45° 40° 35° 30° 25° 20° 15° 10°

Contents

Flaunt out O Sea, your separate flags of nations!

Flaunt out, visible as ever, the various ship-signals!

But do you reserve especially for yourself, and for the soul of man, one flag above all the rest,

A spiritual woven Signal, for all nations, emblem of man elate above death,

Token of all brave captains, and all intrepid sailors and mates,

And all that went down doing their duty;

Reminiscent of them—twined from all intrepid captains, young or old;

A pennant universal, subtly waving, all time, o'er all brave sailors,

All seas, all ships.

—*from "Song for All Seas, All Ships" by Walt Whitman*

ALL BRAVE SAILORS

Author's Note

The history museums of the world preserve and exhibit an incredible range of items, which, when taken together, tell the story of civilization. Some of these items are minor curiosities, while others are powerful pieces that evoke a full range of emotions. For most Americans, entering the Smithsonian Institution's National Museum of American History is an awesome experience. There they encounter a huge flag, the Star-Spangled Banner, that inspired the national anthem of the United States. This flag was not conceived with this august future role in mind; it was simply a large garrison flag for Fort McHenry, the fortress protecting Baltimore Harbor, in Maryland. It was stitched together by Mary Pickersgill and her helpers, who had been hired to construct the flag as the United States found itself at war once again with Britain. Ironically, English woolen bunting was used on the 30-by-42-foot flag, which took shape on the floor of a brewery. On September 13, 1814, the flag conspicuously waved over the fort as the British attacked. Witnessing the battle was an amateur poet, Francis Scott Key. The following morning, inspired by the sight of the flag still boldly flying after more than twenty-five hours of heavy bombardment, he hastily penned a four-verse poem in tribute to the flag and the valiant fight he had witnessed. Within days, the poem was published and its popularity increased over decades until it officially became the national anthem in 1931. Being in the presence of that flag today is a moving experience that inspires awe and pride.

The British, with their rich heritage, have innumerable objects that might create the same effect. One of the simplest yet most powerful is a small coat. In the center of the Nelson gallery of the National Maritime

Museum, in Greenwich, there is a naval officer's coat with a stark bullet hole in the left shoulder. When you see that coat, you are transported back in time to the deck of HMS *Victory* as Vice Admiral Horatio Nelson led the British fleet into battle off Cape Trafalgar in 1805. His great victory that day against a combined French and Spanish fleet would be the greatest in his brilliant career and would cost him his life. To inspire his men in the thick of this fierce naval battle, he walked the deck, resplendent in his admiral's uniform with numerous dazzling decorations, despite being warned that he was a conspicuous target. From the mizzen top of an enemy ship, the *Redoutable,* a sharpshooter found the Admiral in his sights, and his musket ball pierced the coat, ripped through Nelson's chest, and lodged itself in his spine. Mortally wounded, Nelson was carried below, where a few hours later he succumbed. It is hard to imagine an English man or woman who isn't touched to the core by the realization of what that coat represents and isn't proud of Nelson and the many other English heroes.

Another coat also inspires awe. When you enter the large central hall of the maritime museum in St. Petersburg, Russia, to your left is a very tall glass case with an enormous gray leather coat. It is made of elk hide and served as the foul-weather coat for Peter the Great, who stood so tall, literally and figuratively, among the Russians. When you look up at this great coat, you cannot help but feel the greatness of Czar Peter.

These coats and the flag are simple objects, utilitarian objects of their times, and yet they have acquired enormous power because of the history associated with them. This book was inspired by another simple object, preserved in a museum: a small boat.

In 1969, I began work as a Research Associate at Mystic Seaport, America's leading maritime museum, in Mystic, Connecticut. Within days of arrival, I came upon a sturdy wooden boat on exhibit on the grounds of this large outdoor maritime-history museum. I read the brief description of this jolly boat, which had come from an English freighter, and its remarkable voyage, and instantly had the feeling that here was one of those exceptionally powerful objects. Through this boat you can physically connect with people and events of the early days of World War II.

A year later, I was asked to take on the responsibilities of Chief Curator of Mystic Seaport, which included the care of the watercraft collection and this remarkable boat. Seven years later, I became the Director of the museum and had responsibility for all aspects of the museum's operation, including the jolly boat. For virtually all of my career at Mystic Seaport, I was conscious of this boat and her extraordinary story.

Toward the end of my time at Mystic, I was contacted by relatives of the men whose lives had been linked to this boat nearly sixty years before. Their request was for the return of the boat to her country of origin. It was clear that while the story surrounding this boat has resonance in virtually any country, the boat herself, with her powerful personal connections, belonged in England. After prolonged and complicated discussions and arrangements, this goal was achieved, and today the boat is the central object in the Battle of the Atlantic exhibition in London's Imperial War Museum.

I had been moved by the story in 1969 and was even more intrigued as I came to know relatives of the merchant mariners associated with the boat. My own grandfather was a merchant marine officer who had served in World War I, and I was aware of the vital role these sailors played in both world wars of the twentieth century. To me, this boat and the story of which it is a part are symbolic of the courage and sacrifice of dauntless merchant sailors and their families, and I hope that by telling this story in the broad context of the period leading up to the war, the war itself, and the time following up to the present to pay tribute to the Allied merchant mariners.

There is little doubt that the sailors and officers of the Allied merchant navies were true heroes of World War II. Yet their enormous contribution often goes unrecognized as the focus falls on the combat forces: the army, air corps, navy, marines, and their direct support. In no way should any of the praise and credit be withdrawn from these soldiers, airmen, sailors, and marines, but the full measure of the merchant mariners' contribution also should be taken, celebrated, and revered.

It is a simple yet sobering fact that for both the British and American merchant navies in World War II, a greater percentage of mariners were killed than in any other branch of service. One has to pause to contemplate this reality. More merchant sailors perished proportionately than soldiers, sailors, airmen, or marines. Your risk of losing your life was greater as a "civilian" merchant mariner than if you were a member of the British or American armed forces. The newspapers and newsreels were full of the terrible toll being taken on Allied shipping. Weekly statistics on shipping tonnage lost were published in the papers, and everyone knew that "tonnage" also meant sailors' lives. Yet the valiant merchant sailors continued to sign on to ships that would stand in harm's way on all the oceans of the globe, playing the essential role of movers of the goods and materials needed to sustain life and prosecute a global war.

For the British merchant mariners, the price paid was fearsome. John Slader, in the introduction to his book *The Red Duster at War*, summarizes the grim statistics. The conservative estimate of deaths among merchant mariners in British ships during World War II, as determined by the Registrar General of Shipping and Seamen, was almost 32,000! In addition, thousands more were wounded and additional thousands ended up in prisoner-of-war camps such as Milag Nord camp, in northern Germany.

In the early days of the war the brunt of the burden fell on the British merchant navy, but once the United States entered the war, following the attack on Pearl Harbor, the American merchant mariners bravely endured the same harrowing ordeal in fulfillment of their mission. The United States merchant marine quadrupled in number during the war. Of the more than 200,000 sailors, over 8,000 lost their lives, with an additional 11,000 wounded and over 600 in prisoner-of-war camps. The ratio of 1 of every 26 U.S. merchant mariners perishing meant that proportionately more merchant sailors were lost than were members of any other branch of the United States armed forces during World War II.

In wars stretching back for millennia, merchant ships have been subject to attack and capture by their enemies as a "prize of war." For many years, there was economic motivation to capture enemy ships, since the ships and cargos would be sold, with the proceeds going to the crew who made the capture. While prizes were taken during World War II, the economic incentive was not there in most cases, so it was easier and more efficient to simply sink the captured ships. This made the life of the merchant sailor much more dangerous.

To fully appreciate the valor of these seamen one has to contemplate what it took in simple courage and commitment to join a ship's crew and steam, motor, or sail off into the vast oceans that were teeming with danger. The life of the sailor has always been perilous, the mariner pitting his wit and strength against the natural hazards of rocks, shoals, and the fury of storms, squalls, and hurricanes. That peril is compounded when wartime conditions prevail. In World War II, the Allied sailors had to face a broad range of lethal weapons arrayed against them. The submarine demonstrated the full measure of its terrible effectiveness during the Second World War. In addition, both sides had deployed increasingly sophisticated mines, some anchored to the seafloor and ready to explode on contact with a ship. Aircraft had a longer range by the mid-twentieth century, adding a new threat to ships at sea. It is staggering to imagine facing this arsenal of weaponry day after day, month after month, year after year, as merchant sailors responded to the needs of their countries and the free world during the war. And yet they did. Sailors would complete a voyage on one ship and either immediately sign on for the next voyage or, after a brief time at home, sign on to another ship. In many instances, mariners had their ships sunk, were rescued, joined another ship, and were right back at sea again. There are numerous accounts, including this one, in which individuals had several ships shot out from under them.

Our world situation today, with its widespread terrorism, can help us understand the reasons why these sailors put themselves in that position time and time again. There are many, but at the core of the issue was a global threat to their freedom, their homes, and their way of life. They had the skills to respond to the most fundamental need in that war: supply. By early summer of 1940, England was an island nation standing alone against the onslaught of Nazi conquest just across the Channel and the North Sea. Merchant shipping was essential to supply raw materials for her defense and civilian industries, food and supplies for her people, and to carry her products to markets around the world. The merchant ships were also necessary to carry troops and supplies to all the theaters of combat across the globe. As the war expanded so did the reliance on the Allied merchant navies. Without the heroic service of the merchant mariners, the civilian populations and the troops would not have had the supplies needed to sustain the war effort until victory was achieved.

The mariners recognized the critical role they played. They assumed that role with patriotism and courage that exceeds measurement. There can be no doubt that they were all brave sailors.

The story that follows has as its primary focus one sinking, one of thousands during World War II, but it stands as typical of what the Allied merchant mariners faced around the world throughout the war.

Part I

FATE

Chapter 1

ATTACK

I n the darkness before dawn on the 21st day of August, 1940, an English tramp steamer was making her way south in the Atlantic Ocean toward a fateful rendezvous. When darkness fell at the end of that day, it brought the end of the ship and the end of the lives of most of her crew. It also brought the beginning of the remarkable voyage of a small boat that required enormous courage, sacrifice, and fortitude.

The English ship was the *Anglo-Saxon,* and she was doing what hundreds of other tramps did, carrying cargo to a far-distant port where, once it was discharged, they would take on another, perhaps very different, cargo for their next port. The *Anglo-Saxon* had been doing this work for over a decade; but now what had once been routine was linked to the very survival of her home country. England had been at war with Germany for almost a year. The first six months of that war were deadly at sea, with Allied shipping preyed upon by German submarines and warships. With the spring came the incredible advance of the German blitzkrieg sweeping across Holland and Belgium and into France. Denmark was occupied by its neighbor to the south, and Norway was invaded in April of 1940. England and her allies had endured the humiliating rout that called for the heroic rescue of more than 300,000 Allied troops from the beaches of Dunkirk, on the French northern coast. Nearly

1,000 vessels of every size and description were engaged. It was a herculean feat that ultimately enabled the Allies to reorganize, reequip, and redeploy their forces for victory; but in the summer of 1940 the picture remained grim.

The British had witnessed the collapse of one country after another in the path of the seemingly unstoppable Nazi war machine. With the fall of France in June, England found herself standing alone in the face of this fearsome military power. The British girded themselves for invasion, marshaling every available resource for the defense of their island. But seaborne invasion did not immediately come. Hitler had the greatest confidence in the man he had just promoted to Reichsmarschall, Hermann Göring, who by 1939 had developed the strongest air force in the world. Göring was certain of the effectiveness of his Luftwaffe, which had been used so decisively against the Poles, Norwegians, Dutch, Belgians, Danes, and French. The German invasion of England began with an air assault that the Nazi leaders incorrectly anticipated would bring England to her knees and make a land invasion a simple task.

The men of the *Anglo-Saxon* were intimately aware of the precarious position of their country, since the air attacks had begun in mid-June and the Battle of Britain raged in the skies as they prepared to depart. The sailors understood the dangers that awaited them and the critical importance of the role of the merchant navy. This was a fight for their families, their homes, and their country. Their duty was clear and their response resounding.

On that late August morning, however, the war and its dangers seemed remote and distant. The ship had departed England two weeks earlier in the relative safety of a convoy, protected by air cover and several small warships. The waters near England were infested with deadly German U-boats and the arrival and departure from these home waters was often the most dangerous part of a voyage. Once safely out of this danger zone, the *Anglo-Saxon* had chosen her own time to break off from the convoy and head on a more southerly course toward her own destination in South America.

As the sun rose on the 21st, the cold of the North Atlantic had been left behind and the crew felt the warmth of the sun as they neared the Tropic of Cancer. While there were still threats, each mile they steamed away from the seat of conflict would ease their minds. The U-boat menace was largely focused on the shipping lanes of the northern Atlantic, and the ship was also beyond the range of land-based aircraft that might attack. With literally miles of water between them and the ocean floor, this was not an area where mines were a danger. There was, of course, the possibility of attack by a German war ship, but the relatively few cruisers and pocket battleships the Kriegsmarine possessed were being challenged by Britain's Royal Navy. Even the natural threats seemed remote, since the ship was more than 800 miles from land and there was no danger from reefs or shoals. Although it was the hurricane season, she was close enough to Africa, where these storms spawn, that tropical depressions had little chance to develop into serious trouble for a seaworthy ship like the *Anglo-Saxon*. The strain was obviously reduced.

The daily routine was by then exactly that. The new crew was settled in and days took on a typical similarity. The engineers expertly tended the massive quadruple-expansion steam engine and its attendant boilers, valves, and pumps that moved them steadily forward at about 10 knots. The deck crew stood their watches in the wheelhouse or as lookouts around the clock. During the day they attended to all the endless maintenance tasks, large and small, needed to keep their 426-foot ship and her deck machinery functioning. There was the windlass used to raise the huge anchors, the winches, cables, and cranes used for cargo handling, the life rafts and lifeboats and the equipment to launch them. The ship's hull and superstructure, with continuous exposure to the sea and the elements, needed constant attention. By midmorning the day's work would be well under way.

That day's work would also be under way on another ship nearby, heading in the opposite direction. This appeared also to be a merchant ship, from a neutral country. Instead of persistently heading in the direction of her next port with her cargo, this other ship reversed course at 10:30 that morning. Her lookouts, perched as high as possible on the cargo masts, had spotted the *Anglo-Saxon* five minutes earlier, and the response was immediate. Within another five minutes the two ships were on almost parallel southerly courses.

The *Anglo-Saxon*'s new companion behaved strangely for a merchant ship. Instead of the purposeful, focused steaming from one port to another, this ship had been ominously meandering in the mid-Atlantic for three months, never entering any port. Disguised as the neutral Swedish freighter *Narvik,* the ship had entered the Atlantic in May. Beneath this disguise was just the ship that the *Anglo-Saxon* dreaded: a well-armed, powerful warship of Germany's Kriegsmarine. In an age-old tactic of sea warfare, she masked her identity and flew false colors. The ship was in fact one of a small fleet of aggressive surface raiders that would wreak havoc on Allied shipping and achieve successes far beyond those anticipated by the senior officers who had sent them to sea. The 477-foot vessel masquerading as the *Narvik* carried the actual name of *Widder.*

Throughout June and into July, traveling as the *Narvik,* she had cruised through her assigned area of operation, overwhelming the unsuspecting merchant ships that happened upon her as they trudged across the seas laden with their cargo. Upon spotting a potential victim, the *Narvik* would casually steer a course that would gradually intersect the course of her target. On the ship that was her intended prey, the crew would see what appeared to be another merchant vessel heading on a course that would at some point cross their own. On the lonely ocean, at least in prewar days, it was always interesting to see another ship at sea and come close enough for recognition, acknowledgment, and simple human contact.

When the *Narvik* was within firing range of her victim, her disguise would be dropped, her false colors hauled down, her true colors broken out, and her powerful guns would open fire. With this tactic the *Narvik* had claimed four victims, sinking three and taking one as a prize of war to send to Lorient in occupied France. As July came to an end, so did the false career of the *Narvik,* which in mid-ocean was transformed again, this time into a neutral Spanish freighter, the *El Neptuno* from Bilbao.

With her new persona came a new and terrifying tactic. In the first weeks of August the *El Neptuno* had used it twice with great success. So, it was the *Widder* as the *El Neptuno* that was on a parallel course with the *Anglo-Saxon.*

At the time of the initial sighting of the *Anglo-Saxon* at 10:25 in the morning, the two ships were approximately fifteen nautical miles apart. The crew aboard the *El Neptuno* had the distinct advantage of lookout stations near the tops of the two towering cargo masts. These stations were equipped with the finest-quality high-power binoculars, for which the Germans were world famous. This enabled the German sailors, who continually scanned the horizon for any hint of other ships, to catch a glimpse of a potential enemy vessel while virtually out of sight themselves. Due to the curvature of the earth, the horizon that is seen in the far distance at sea is only about 10 miles away. The taller the object, the farther away it can be seen. Therefore, when one ship is "hull down" over the horizon from another, a lookout on one ship will see the tops of the other ship's masts before seeing the ship herself. A lookout higher on the *El Neptuno* than on the *Anglo-Saxon* would see the other ship first.

For the officers and crew of the German ship, this was a critical advantage. They were the hunters, prowling the ocean ready to pounce on any Allied merchant ship that they could discover. However, they could easily become the hunted if the stranger just over the horizon turned out to be a fast Royal Navy warship. Seconds of advance warning could mean survival for a ship like the *El Neptuno,* as they might give her the chance to change course and steam away from an enemy warship without being seen. This was the very beginning of the era of radar. Land-based radar installations were playing a vital role in the Battle of Britain in the air over England at the very moment these ships were encountering each other, however, neither the German nor the English ship was equipped with the cumbersome and often unreliable early warning system. At this time the role of the lookouts was crucial, both to the success and the survival of these ships.

On board the *Anglo-Saxon* the lookout was stationed in the "eyes" of the ship, as far forward as possible. From this position the lookout had a clear, unobstructed view of the sea ahead and was able to give a warning if anything appeared in the ship's path. On the bridge of the *Anglo-Saxon,* the officer of the watch directed the ship's movements, executed by the sea-man on the helm steering the ship. The bridge was approximately 20 feet higher than the lookout on the bow and toward the middle of the ship. While having the advantage of greater height, those on the bridge had ample distractions that would have made it very unlikely that they would have spotted the thin wisps of the antennas and the lookout stations of the *El Neptuno* as she slipped briefly into view above the horizon. If they had spotted these masts during the day, while the ships were on parallel courses, the *El Neptuno* would certainly have appeared to be another mer-chant ship slightly ahead on a similar course that was making no threaten-ing movement toward the *Anglo-Saxon*.

In fact, the movements of the *El Neptuno* as the day went on were most threatening. After the officer of the watch immediately reversed the *El Neptuno*'s course, one of the enlisted men who had spotted the *Anglo-Saxon* was replaced aloft by an experienced officer who could monitor the movement of their quarry and actually control the ship, directing her course and speed, from his perch. He increased the *El Neptuno*'s speed to slightly more than the 9.5 knots of the *Anglo-Saxon* to increase the distance between the two ships and lessen the chance of being detected. After an hour, when the Germans were almost 19 miles away from their unknow-ing victim, they began very slowly to converge with her anticipated course. At 12:50 in the afternoon, after the crew had their midday meal, the *Anglo-Saxon* altered her course slightly, from 166 degrees to 178, almost due south. A little after 1:00 P.M., the *El Neptuno* altered her course again to reduce the convergence and settled on 180 degrees, straight south. With her slightly higher speed, the German ship stayed well ahead and positioned herself for the critical maneuver that would immediately pre-cede the attack, for there was little question at this point that the British freighter would steam into her trap.

In midafternoon the *Anglo-Saxon* made another slight course change, of 6 degrees east, certainly not an evasive move. The day went on with routine chores being attended to, and the officers shifted from their dark woolen uniforms to the cooler white tropical uniforms as confirmation of the pleasure of steaming into the warmth that lay ahead. It was a clear day, with the wind and the ocean swell decreasing and the temperature in the comfortable 70s Fahrenheit. The ship was in the mid-Atlantic, approximately equidistant from the island groups of the Azores, Canaries, and Cape Verdes, each approximately 800 miles away toward the northeast, east, and southeast respectively, and over 2,000 miles east of Florida. This combination of location and fair weather had to create a positive sense as the forty-one officers and men of the British crew went to their evening meal and looked forward to relaxation and sleep or their turn on the night watch.

On board the *El Neptuno,* her officers and men, nine times the number on the ship they were stalking, were also having their evening meal; but rather than anticipating relaxation, they were making the final preparations for their attack. While it would have its dangers, their new tactics had worked so well on two previous occasions that there was little fear of this being a sea battle. The English ship did have a single 4-inch naval gun mounted on her stern for defensive use and a single former Royal Marine as the gunlayer. The Germans, in their previous attacks, had not been fired upon and did not seriously anticipate return fire this evening. The German captain had developed his new and effective tactic with two key elements: complete surprise and overwhelming force. The *El Neptuno* was now, at ten minutes past seven in the evening in the last rays of daylight, perfectly positioned for the assault. At that moment, while still nearly 20 miles ahead and to the west of the *Anglo-Saxon,* their commanding officer gave the order to turn sharply to the east to a course and speed that would bring them directly to the prey in less than an hour. With both ships now on courses toward each other and with a closing speed of over 20 miles per hour, there would be little reaction time to avoid collision or take evasive action. In the coming darkness it was no longer necessary for the *El Neptuno* to carry her disguise. Special tarpaulins were lowered over the sides to cover the large Spanish flags painted on the sides of the ship. The six heavy guns were unmasked, as were the rapid-fire cannons, and the deadly torpedo tubes emerged from the hull. The hundreds of well-trained and experienced German sailors were at their battle stations. The *El Neptuno* was gone and the fierce *Widder* was on the attack!

The governing factor for the attacking captain that night was moonrise. He wanted to attack in the pitch black to maximize the element of surprise and avoid the enemy making evasive moves. The moon was going to rise at 8:18 that night and with complete darkness occurring only at 8:00, there was only a twenty-minute window for the final closing with the British ship, which remained unaware of the presence of her completely darkened foe. Just before 8:00, with another course change, the final meticulously calculated run into the target began.

Within minutes the *Anglo-Saxon* loomed out of the darkness at a distance of less than a mile and a half. Moments later, the order to open fire was given. On board the *Anglo-Saxon* the watch had just changed and those at their posts were settling in for four hours of tranquil steaming on a soon-to-be-moonlit night. The first hint of the impending disaster for those on the freighter's bridge was the flash and report as guns fired out of the darkness from the *Widder*'s starboard bow. Instantly, the shells from the attacker struck their target and a devastating explosion ripped through the stern of the ship, destroying the ship's only defensive gun. Every weapon that the Germans could bring to bear began firing. They had achieved complete surprise and now were pouring gunfire into the shocked and wounded ship. Four heavy 15cm guns poured salvo after salvo into the English ship at close range. Each of these shells had a diameter of almost 6 inches and was packed with explosives. The shells penetrated the relatively thin steel of the *Anglo-Saxon*'s hull and superstructure and exploded, ripping men and materials to shreds. With the stern gun of the freighter destroyed, firepower was directed at other key targets: the navigational bridge to destroy the ship's controls, and particularly the radio room to prevent warnings and distress signals getting out.

By then the deck of the *Anglo-Saxon* was alive with men, startled from their sleep, relaxation, or duty. Only one minute after the heavy guns opened fire, the smaller but equally fearsome rapid-fire weapons joined the fusillade. The twin-barreled 37mm cannon pumped round after round into the target with a rhythm and precision that destroyed every-thing in its sights. The smallest guns, two rapid-fire 20mm anti-aircraft guns, sprayed their explosive projectiles, each 3/4 of an inch in diameter and 3 inches long, back and forth across the deck and the superstructure of the ship. Among these bullets and shells were tracer rounds that glowed with ominous bright color as they traveled from muzzle to target, creating an incendiary effect on impact.

The scene was beyond imagination: the *Widder*, standing off at a safe distance, spreading withering gunfire from eight well-aimed guns into the bewildered freighter. On deck, the British mariners attempted to comprehend what had been brought upon them amid the terrible ca-cophony of exploding shells and the horror of seeing shipmates torn apart before their eyes. As it raked the deck fore and aft, the gunfire shat-tered equipment as well as bodies. There was no hope for the freighter against this extraordinary firepower wielded with such vehemence and precision. As they were being bludgeoned, those well-drilled merchant sailors who were still alive struggled through the rain of bullets to their assigned lifeboats. They scrambled to one then another, but the boats too had fallen victim to the shattering impact of bullets, shells, and lethal, fly-ing, jagged chunks of metal and wood torn from their ship. Both the star-board and port lifeboats hung shattered and useless from their davits.

One boat, however, had been sheltered from the destructive fire. An 18-foot utility boat, the ironically named "jolly boat," had been on the port side just below the bridge and one deck above the main deck and its carnage. With the attack coming from the starboard side, the superstruc-ture had absorbed all the fire and shielded this small boat. Quick-thinking men started to lower the boat into the dark water below. As she passed the main deck, two souls grasping the opportunity hurled them-selves in. The men who lowered the boat slid down the ropes into her, and a moment before they cast off, a fifth person slid down into the toss-ing boat. The ship was still moving forward and as the small boat drifted toward the stern, two more mariners leapt over the railing and landed among the stunned occupants of the jolly boat. The mangled, flaming wreck that had moments before been their ship and their home steamed on without them, still enduring the pounding and destruction of the gunfire. The men in the boat observed the scene in awe. For a moment they were encouraged when they saw lights in the water near the *Anglo-Saxon*. With both lifeboats destroyed, they thought the lights must have been men on some of the life rafts. Then they were horror-struck as they saw gunfire turned on those rafts, extinguishing the lights along with the lives of any on board.

With the fury and frustration of their impotence, they then witnessed the coup de grâce as the *Widder* sent a torpedo deep into her crippled victim. A huge explosion was heard and felt. In only forty minutes from the first salvo, the rugged tramp steamer had been transformed from a proud ship into a mortally wounded hulk that was quickly sinking into the sea and to the bottom over three miles below.

It was clear that their attacker was a tenacious enemy surface raider, and it was equally clear to those in the jolly boat that their persecutor wanted no one to survive to tell the story of that night. The small boat had already drifted some distance from the scene and, hoping to remain undetected, the sailors took up their oars to put more ocean between themselves and the raider. As soon as the *Anglo-Saxon* had slipped beneath the waves, and without searching for any survivors from the rafts, whose lights the Germans would have seen, the *Widder* turned east and departed the scene.

What lay ahead was a perilous time for the world and also for the seven men in the 18-foot boat in the middle of the Atlantic, who were about to begin an astonishing, epic voyage.

Anyone who has spent extended time at sea knows that each ship has her own character. Sometimes this is the result of the handling characteristics of the vessel, or the good or bad aspects of her propulsion system, but most often it is those who sail in the vessel that endow her with much of that individual character. Both the *Anglo-Saxon* and the *Widder* had distinct personalities, and it was from the ships' captains and the people who served with them that these developed. In both cases, they had competent captains. While the *Anglo-Saxon*'s skipper, Philip "Paddy" Flynn, was a firm leader, he was also a pure sailor, experienced and uncomplicated. The captain of the *Widder,* Hellmuth von Ruckteschell, on the other hand, was an extremely complex character, with naval training from another era, who would become internationally notorious.

Chapter 2

THE CATALYST

There can be no doubt that many lives were changed dramatically by Hellmuth von Ruckteschell while he moved steadily on his course through life. Nor can it be said that his life was ordinary. From his youth, through his early naval service in World War I, to the "simple" life he led between the wars, to his service in World War II, and finally to his postwar years, this man's life was a tangle of influences and attitudes that make him a truly fascinating character. To understand the central figure in this drama, his full story must be told, since each aspect of it builds upon the former and contributes to the complexity of this man. He was at once hero and villain, saint and sinner, but always a formidable foe for Allied merchant mariners.

Even his parentage represents a contrast. His mother, the Baroness Catharina Helene von Engelhardt, brought an aristocratic air into the home, while his father, Carl Nikolai Sergius von Ruckteschell, a doctor of theology, spent his life as a pastor. The Ruckteschell home was a place of intellectual, musical, and artistic stimulation that would be reflected in the lives of the children of the Baroness and the Pastor. The first decade of their marriage was spent in St. Petersburg, Russia, and their first child, Walter Alexander Moritz von Ruckteschell, who would be very influential in Hellmuth's life, was born in Russia in 1882. By 1888, Pastor Dr. von

Ruckteschell's evangelistic ministry attracted the animus of the authorities in a country not receptive to evangelism. Through his wife's friendship with the Czarina, he was spared arrest but had to leave Russia. He established his new home and ministry in Hamburg, Germany. Two years later, his wife and children joined him, and in March of 1890 the Baroness gave birth to Hellmuth. In all, there were fourteen children in this extraordinary household—eight sons and six daughters. Hellmuth's father was the Pastor of the Friedenskirche in the Eilbek area of Hamburg and held that position for twenty years, from the time of Hellmuth's birth until his own death in 1910 at the age of fifty-seven.

Hellmuth von Ruckteschell had the nurture of life at home only until age eleven, when he was sent to study at the Voss-Gymnasium in Eutin, 50 miles northeast of Hamburg. For two years, he studied in this community and lodged with Fräulein Jencus. When later asked what drew him to naval service, he said, "From the time I was very young I was related to the sea since the place of my birth was so near the sea and also my father loved the Navy and I chose the profession of a sailor because I liked it." On Easter of 1903, at about his thirteenth birthday, Hellmuth began his naval training by entering the Cadet Corps in Plön, on the lake known as the Plöner See. The school was located near Hamburg, Kiel, Lübeck, and Travemünde, and he grew up in the midst of some of Germany's great ports and naval centers.

At about this time, his older brother Walter began his military service in the infantry. Walter's artistic interests were strong, and he did not envision the military career that Hellmuth, eight years his junior, did. With a commission as a lieutenant in the reserves, Walter settled into art studies in Munich, while young Hellmuth entered the Main Cadet Institution in Berlin-Lichterfelde, steady on the course for what he hoped would be a brilliant career as a naval officer. Within two years, he passed his Seekadett examination and became a member of the Imperial German Navy, the Kaisermarine. From May 1909 until March of the following year on a training voyage on the cruiser *Hertha,* Seekadett von Ruckteschell cruised the Atlantic. He also made his first visits to South and North America, and a month after his return made the important step up-

ward to Fahnrich zur See. Instruction at the new Naval College at Flens-
burg-Mürwik followed, with special courses in naval artillery and torpedo
operations, skills that he would retain and use effectively during his career.

On the 1st of October, 1911, the bright, well-trained young midship-
man reported to his first vessel, the battle cruiser *Von der Tann*. It was on
this ship that he served as the war clouds of the First World War gathered
and the war erupted in 1914. He obviously served well since he was promoted to Leutnant zur See in less than a year and again to Oberleutnant
zur See in May of 1915; he received his first major decoration, the Iron
Cross 2nd Class, in October of that same year.

Ruckteschell was now twenty-five and virtually half his life had been
devoted to naval training and service. For a young naval officer, the fast
path to success was in command of a vessel. Major vessels such as the *Von
der Tann* were commanded by very senior officers; but a new, dynamic area
of naval warfare was tailor-made for an ambitious, intelligent young officer—submarines. In the spring of 1916, Ruckteschell had his opportunity.
In fact, he left the *Von der Tann* to begin the specialized training for the
submarine service only three months before that cruiser participated in
the famous Battle of Jutland. The British Grand Fleet, led by Admiral Sir
John Jellicoe, engaged the German High Seas Fleet, under the control of
the stern Admiral Reinhard von Scheer, off Jutland on the Danish coast.
While British losses were somewhat greater than the Germans', the battle was inconclusive and the British retained their dominance of the seas
when the German High Seas Fleet withdrew to its ports. Without their
warships ranging the oceans, the Germans began a strategy that would
provide opportunities for success and glory for young German officers, a
number of whom would be the leaders of the Navy of the Third Reich a
quarter of a century later. The plan was for unrestricted submarine warfare, a prospect that was intended to terrorize British and Allied merchant mariners.

The First World War produced several horrible new aspects of war,
including poison gas, the aerial bombardment of civilian populations
from the rigid airships developed by Count Zeppelin, and the hidden
threat of lurking submarine attacks. When this stealthy weapon was

turned against merchant ships, it was considered against the "laws of war and dictates of humanity." Before the war, in 1913, when the prospect of the use of submarines against merchant ships was raised in a report to Britain's First Lord of the Admiralty, Winston Churchill, he responded that while the report was excellent there were "a few points of which I am not convinced. Of these the greatest is the question of the use of submarines to sink merchant vessels. I do not believe this would ever be done by a civilized power."

The world had its rude awakening to this new reality in the early afternoon of May 7, 1915, off the beautiful village of Kinsale, on the Irish coast south of Cork. There for the first time, in a moment that was its era's Hiroshima, a torpedo from the German submarine *U-20* ripped into the majestic transatlantic passenger steamer *Lusitania,* which was nearing her destination. In twenty minutes, the ship had disappeared into the cold waters, taking with her 1,198 men, women, and children.

The news of this repellent act brought immediate response from the Allied nations and the United States, which had lost 128 of its citizens. The justification for the attack was that the *Lusitania* had been warned through advertisements in New York newspapers and other announcements that such ships were subject to attack. It was also asserted, and is still debated, that the *Lusitania* was carrying munitions and was therefore an appropriate target. Oberleutnant zur See Walther von Schweiger, however, who was in command of the *U-20,* would have had no way of knowing of the supposed munitions when he launched his torpedo at the liner and made his dubious mark on history.

For centuries, merchant ships had been fair targets in wartime, but there was a general acceptance that a merchant ship would be stopped and given an opportunity to abandon ship before the vessel was sunk. There were instances in World Wars I and II when vessels were allowed to proceed if they had no boats capable of holding the crew, on assurance that those released would not further participate in the war. In one instance, a ship was spared and directed to rescue sailors from a ship that had been sunk. However, this gallantry worked against the very nature of the submarine. This weapon was developed to disappear, penetrate enemy defenses, fire its deadly torpedoes at a target unaware of its presence, and slink away undetected: a truly ominous weapon. The fear of an unseen enemy is a powerful, unnerving weapon in itself.

After an initial period of unrestricted submarine warfare, strong protests were made by the United States. In the spring of 1916, not wanting to risk a break in diplomatic relations with the United States or, even worse, have the Americans enter the war, the German government curtailed the submarine offensive, much to the distress of the commanders of the submarine force. Their U-boats now had to function within the prize law regulations, which required the warning of a ship to stop, the examination of the ship's papers, cargo manifests, and the cargo itself, and the provision of safety for the ship's passengers and crew. The submarine captains were constrained, unable to use their most powerful asset, stealth, while the moral debate concerning submarine warfare was argued around the world. This was the complicated naval world that Hellmuth von Ruckteschell entered when he began his U-boat training at Eckernforde in March of 1916.

After four months of training as a submarine watch officer, he reported for duty on a new submarine, the U-57, on the day of her commissioning, July 6, 1916. For the next year, he would play a key role in her success. His tutor was Kapitänleutnant Carl Siegfried Ritter von Georg, who would become a hero in Germany through his sinking of almost 100,000 tons of enemy shipping, but whose aggressive tactics won him a spot on the British list of war criminals at the conclusion of the war. In his voyages into the North Sea and around the English coast, Georg took a serious toll and taught his star pupil well. Their submarine was the latest design, built in less than a year by one of the best shipyards, Weserwerft, in Bremen. Georg, Ruckteschell, and two other officers carried the responsibility for this vessel and her crew of 32. They were all crowded into a hull only 220 feet in length, which was also crammed with two large diesel engines for running on the surface and charging the batteries for the two electric motors used for underwater propulsion; spare torpedoes for the four torpedo tubes, situated two in the bow and two in the stern; all the fuel, spare parts, and munitions for the deck guns; provisions and supplies needed for the voyage; and bunks for approximately half the crew, since they would sleep in shifts and share bunks. It took a special breed of men to serve in submarines, particularly in these early days of development. The propulsion system could move them along smartly at 14.7 knots (almost 17 miles per hour) on the surface or 8.4 knots underwater, and Ritter von Georg would put this machinery to the test immediately.

Within two months of her commissioning, the U-57 was hard at work off the coast of England, an area patrolled by English guard ships. Georg was hobbled by the need to abide by the prize law regulations. On September 24, the U-57 sank four English trawlers and a small Norwegian freighter carrying contraband to England 40 miles east of Whitby. There were more ships to be taken, but night would make gunfire more visible, so Georg and Ruckteschell devised a clever scheme. In a commando-style raid, using the U-57's dinghy, Ruckteschell and his boarding party seized the trawler, the *Fisherprince,* and then quietly approached nine other trawlers, one after the other, taking their crews captive aboard the *Fisherprince.* Ruckteschell then went from one abandoned trawler to the next, opening their valves to the sea and silently sending them to the bottom without a sound or loss of life. The following morning, the men overwhelmed four more trawlers and added their crews to those already on the *Fisherprince.* Later in the day, they stopped another Norwegian freighter, which was not trafficking war materials and could not be sunk. Onto this ship they transferred the trawler crews, and then scuttled the *Fisherprince.* In twenty-four hours, through the daring of Ruckteschell, they had managed to destroy eighteen significant fishing vessels and a freighter.

While this episode was executed without the loss of life, that was not the case as the U-57 continued her war patrols. A month later, she sank an English gunboat with her crew of over 100 officers and men just south of Ireland. Despite raging winds and high seas so powerful that one of the German officers on the conning tower was killed, the U-57 managed to sink a large English freighter bringing war materials and food from North America and several smaller ships before limping back to the German submarine base of Heligoland with engine problems.

Early in 1917, reeling from the drain on materials and men in the

Battle of the Somme, which had lasted from July through November 1916 and claimed 1 million casualties on both sides, the German High Command considered lifting the restrictions on her submarine force. The choking Allied blockade of Germany was also taking a heavy toll and the country was being starved. The constraints were lifted and the *U-57*'s more aggressive, efficient work commenced in March and April of 1917, with Ruckteschell playing a key role. Many of the English merchant ships carried deck guns for self-defense against a submarine surface attack. No longer required to warn a target before attack, Ruckteschell was able to gain more experience on this voyage with the safer submerged torpedo attacks.

This patrol also brought Ruckteschell's first contact with an unusual type of English ship similar to the raiders he would later command. As the English sought to create a countermeasure to combat the successes of the U-boats, they developed and deployed "Q-ships." These were decoy ships that appeared to be unarmed merchantmen steaming alone, which hoped to draw the attack of a submarine on the surface. The Q-ship would absorb the first few rounds, luring the U-boat closer, before suddenly returning the fire and attempting to sink the submarine. These were well-armed ships, disguised to look benign, just as the *Widder* was in World War II. The significant difference was that the Q-ships were used exclusively for defensive purposes against warships. The German raiders were offensive weapons used against merchant ships, overwhelming their victims with far superior firepower. The *U-57* was lured into a surface attack by the Q-ship *Paxton* at the end of March. Using her deck gun, the submarine began to close in, when she was surprised by return fire. Before she could be hit, Georg ordered the *U-57* into a crash dive and she escaped. Another lesson for Ruckteschell.

May and early June of 1917 saw Georg and his submarine on the attack with increasing violence. By mid-May, the *U-57* sank the 2,642-ton English steamer *Refugio* in two hours, and then hit the nearly twice as large *Arlington Court* with a torpedo. She sank the English ships SS *Belgian* and SS *Jersey City* on May 24, and, homeward bound for Heligoland, sank the trawler *Teal*. The lessons Hellmuth von Ruckteschell learned were controversial, because the charges that brought Captain Carl-Siegfried Ritter von Georg onto the war crimes list included the sinkings of the *Refugio,* the *Arlington Court,* the *Jersey City,* and the *Teal.* In the eyes of Georg and his superior officers, however, Ruckteschell had proven himself. He earned the Iron Cross 1st Class and the opportunity he had been seeking, his own command.

During the spring of 1917, the focused, dedicated naval officer, now twenty-seven, developed an intimate personal relationship with a ballet dancer. Frieda Martha Agnes Schmidt found this lean, cultured, serious submariner a man to whom she could commit herself. Likely their relationship was severely strained, as were many other wartime romances. Ruckteschell's commitment and duty to his country were clear, and by the time he was ready for his next critical career move, this was his priority. He was unaware that Fräulein Schmidt was by then carrying his child.

He left the *U-57* in early August of 1917 and, after a month of special training for prospective commanding officers, proudly stepped aboard *his* submarine, the *UB-34.* His country was in increasingly difficult straits, with its High Seas Fleet essentially neutralized by Britain's Royal Navy, augmented by the United States Navy, which had entered the war in early April. A huge burden fell on the submariners, who were the only hope to cripple the Allied shipping effort that was keeping England and the Allied forces on the Continent supplied and fighting. Ruckteschell's strong feelings of nationalism motivated him as he assumed his first command.

Submarines carrying the UB designation were smaller than those designated by U and a number. Ruckteschell's new vessel was only 121 feet long, 100 feet shorter than the submarine in which he had been serving. She was slower, with only two torpedo tubes, located in the bow, and a single deck gun; but she was *his* submarine. With only one other officer to share responsibility for the vessel and her crew of 21, their task would be the dangerous coastal patrols off England's east coast. He had come to know these waters well from his earlier voyages in the *U-57.* Within days of Ruckteschell taking command, the *UB-34* was ordered to sea and made her way from her base in Heligoland to the coast of England, off Flamborough Head. Immediately upon arrival in this area of operations,

Ruckteschell torpedoed a 5,000-ton English freighter, the SS *Grelfryda*, with the most extraordinary result. As the freighter struggled to beach herself to keep from sinking, Ruckteschell in his submerged vessel peered into his periscope and was astonished to see a lone British sailor swimming in front of him and waving toward the periscope. In his decisive manner and considering his priorities, he abandoned the swimmer. He was faced with the choice of saving one enemy sailor or protecting his crew and ship from the patrol boats and aircraft that were coming. For Ruckteschell, there was no question.

The following day, the *UB-34* sank a Norwegian steamer and, with her torpedoes spent and two victories, headed back to base after a first patrol lasting only five days. Two weeks later, Ruckteschell sailed from his new home port of Bremerhaven, making a harrowing exit from the German Bight. The previous day, the British had laid a massive minefield of 434 mines anchored to the ocean floor north of the West Frisian island of Terschelling. While making his way to sea, Ruckteschell took the *UB-34* to a depth of about 90 feet and unknowingly entered the minefield. In twelve hours underwater, the boat picked her way through the jungle of mine cables, hearing them scrape down the sides and feeling occasional bumps against the fragile hull. This unemotional excerpt from the *UB-34*'s war diary gives a glimpse of the stressful experience: "Still at a depth of 30 meters. Heavy rumbling, especially in the stern section; the boat is vibrating a lot; there seem to be a series of distant explosions in quick succession. Objects are being thrown around in the stern section, but the boat maintains its depth. The boat is stopped for an audio sweep; no noises can be heard. Went deeper at slow speed. Something hooks onto the boat's hull; one feels a couple of weak punches and then a quite loud explosion above the boat. The boat lies on the bottom of the sea. Waiting for a while. All quiet. Continue the voyage at a depth of 30 meters. From time to time one can still hear the scratching of mines and anchor cables. Surfaced at 11.51 hrs. after having been submerged for 12 hours." They emerged from the minefield unscathed.

This, however, was not the crew's only close call on this short sortie. Two days after their brush with death in the minefield, they had another.

While submerged and running at a depth of 40 feet, they closed in on a target. A single torpedo was launched and found its mark, sinking the 5,143-ton freighter SS *Greltoria*. Moments after the torpedo streamed out of her bow tube, the UB-34's crew had the horrifying realization that they were about to be rammed by another steamer. Certain death was at hand, and the men trapped in their vulnerable steel cylinder awaited their fate. Amazingly, only the periscope was hit by what was probably the SS *Morocco* scraping over her. Feeling incredibly fortunate, the UB-34 headed back to her home base for repair.

On his next cruise, after sinking an oceangoing tug, the *Desire,* Ruckteschell saw an opportunity to attack a Dutch freighter near the dock in Sunderland. During the daring approach into the harbor for the attack, the UB-34 ran aground. Rather than retreat, Ruckteschell was able to maneuver his boat to launch his torpedo while still aground, sinking the freighter SS *Folmina*. He immediately came under attack from a British subchaser, and only by applying full power from his straining engines was he able to finally slide back into deeper water and escape. Two more small freighters fell victim to the sub before she turned for home, where Ruckteschell was commended for his daring attacks. At this time, he alerted his superiors to the increasing intensity of the antisubmarine forces along England's east coast. A frank exchange with his superiors became a hallmark of Ruckteschell's career. He had demonstrated the steady nerves needed in this aggressive new naval warfare, as well as the fervor needed to prosecute attacks against enemy shipping and lives.

It is probable that Agnes Schmidt followed Hellmuth von Ruckteschell when he shifted to Bremerhaven, but it is not known how long their relationship lasted. In March of 1918, as Ruckteschell made his long-sought move from a small UB boat to the prestige of a full U-boat, Fräulein Schmidt gave birth to her son, Hellmuth, in Wilhelmshaven, a short distance from Bremerhaven. By all accounts, Hellmuth von Ruckteschell never knew that his son existed. He never mentioned him to friends or shipmates, and later, when required to fill out biographical forms, Ruckteschell stated that he had no children, legitimate or illegitimate. One can only speculate at the poignancy of this experience for

Fräulein Schmidt. There is sadness also for Ruckteschell, who never had the satisfaction of knowing that he not only had a son, but one who also became a naval officer. For Hellmuth von Ruckteschell, it was duty calling once again, and this time it was to the U-54—a newer, faster submarine built by Germaniawerft, in Kiel, the port in which the *Widder* would be built a decade later.

Within a month of taking over the submarine on March 23, he and his crew were off on a voyage that would take them over the top of Scotland, down into the Irish Sea, and back again in a twenty-four-day period. Five days after departure, between the Orkney and Shetland Island groups, the U-54 made her first enemy contact under Ruckteschell's command. Although the Allied losses to U-boats had been greatly reduced by grouping ships together in convoys protected by warships, a system that had been in place for over a year, it was not unusual to see a lone, small freighter in this area. The U-54 carried out a textbook attack, and from periscope depth sent a torpedo into the ship. Although she wasn't listing, the Germans observed lifeboats being launched. While considering sur-facing to finish the ship off with the deck gun, the senior watch officer continued to observe the ship through the periscope and to his horror saw an ominous torpedo tube emerging from the hull of what he now rec-ognized was clearly a lethal Q-ship. Once again, Ruckteschell's life and vessel were in great peril as the steady English ship withstood his initial attack and only then commenced her own. The U-54 was unable to react in time and could not evade the British torpedo hissing toward her. Braced for the impact, explosion, and chaos that would follow, the sub-mariners felt and heard only a muffled thump. The torpedo had hit and failed to explode. Given this chance to escape, Ruckteschell turned, sped away, and dove to avoid the rain of shells coming from the fully manned guns of the Q-ship, HMS *Starmount*.

On his next foray, Ruckteschell encountered a target like none other he had seen, an ocean liner of over 30,000 tons, the size of the famous *Lusitania*. The prized ship, the *Justitia*, was being escorted in ballast with no passengers when she was attacked by another submarine, the UB-64, on July 18 and 19. The ship incredibly had absorbed four powerful torpedo impacts and stayed afloat, although crippled. She had been taken under tow, with an enormous protective screen of some eighteen destroyers in the outer ring of defense and sixteen trawlers in the inner ring. Due to damage sustained during her attacks, the UB-64 could not attack, but managed to shadow the armada.

Highly motivated to press an attack against daunting odds, Ruckteschell began a risky approach of going beneath the outer ring of destroyers. The British detected the intruding periscope and dropped sixty depth charges, forcing Ruckteschell to dive over 150 feet to avoid destruction. After carefully calculating his course and speed in relation to the movement of the ships above him, he rose to periscope depth and immediately launched two torpedoes from his stern tubes, the only ones he could bring to bear on the enormous target. As he launched his "fish," he could see escort vessels coming to attack the U-54. He evaded his pursuers and lay on the bottom for several hours to be certain it was safe to surface. The Justitia, hit by two torpedoes, capsized and sank during the afternoon. While many contemporary sources credit Ruckteschell with a portion of the honor for this sinking, there is later research that indicates that the two torpedoes that caused the sinking came from the UB-124, which had joined the attack at virtually the same time as Ruckteschell and fired from the other side. Whatever the truth, it has to be said that Ruckteschell did not hold back when confronted with a formidable escort fleet, but pressed the attack against extraordinary odds.

The U-54 returned to her base and made only two more patrols as the war finally ground to an end. However, during Ruckteschell's last patrol, there occurred an incident that would have far-reaching ramifications. On September 27, 1918, the Captain made this entry in the war diary of U-54: "Sank the French armed sailing vessel En Avant, 64 tons, with explosive charges after a brief artillery duel in the Western entrance of the English Channel. The ship was en route from Swansea to Boulogne with a cargo of 120 tons of coal." This encounter sounds like another routine victory for U-54, but it resulted in an astonishing war crimes allegation against Ruckteschell. The allegation of this atrocity, which did not emerge until after the war, came from one of Ruckteschell's own men,

Otto Wiedemann, who was Master's Mate in the *U-54*. He states that after the capture of the French sailing vessel, the French crew was gathered on the deck of the submarine, behind the conning tower. Ruckteschell then asked Wiedemann if he was prepared to close the hatch. Wiedemann realized this would only be done in preparation to submerge the U-boat and refused. He alleged that Ruckteschell then drew a pistol, ordered Wiedemann below, and then followed immediately with the gun still drawn. Ruckteschell then closed the hatch himself and ordered the boat to submerge, drowning the French crew. When they resurfaced thirty minutes later, there was no sign of the Frenchmen.

A year earlier, on April 8, 1917, one of Ruckteschell's compatriots, Kapitänleutnant Wilhelm Werner, in command of the *U-55*, had carried out a similar atrocity when he sank the British steamship *Torrington* and drowned 34 of her crew that he had gathered on his deck. In this case, members of the crew of the *U-55* stated that there were other similar acts. The conduct of Werner, who received the high award of the Pour le Mérite, may have inspired Ruckteschell or given him a sense of license to commit the crime.

At this time, the first hint of problems that would plague Ruckteschell throughout his life appeared. Two days after the heinous *En Avant* incident, Ruckteschell sank his last vessel of World War I. The ship's log then indicated that further attacks were discontinued "as a consequence of the commanding officer's bad health condition." Oberleutnant Hellmuth von Ruckteschell had shown that he was indeed human and vulnerable. Stress had taken its toll on the captain of the *U-54*, and it was a malady that would stay with him. Nevertheless, he had carried out numerous patrols in his two U-boats, stealthfully attacking and sinking many ships, while escaping death and destruction numerous times and never losing a man in his crew. His guile, guts, and good fortune had seen him and his crews through this war, and those same attributes would see him through the next. He had, however, the dark cloud of the *En Avant* attack hanging over him. Otto Wiedemann, repelled by what had occurred, went absent without leave as soon as he reached Wilhelmshaven in order to escape from Ruckteschell. It must have been extremely disturbing to

Ruckteschell that there was someone out there who could tell the world of the fate of those French sailors.

He returned from his last mission on October 15, 1918, and exactly a month later, four days after the armistice, relinquished his command of the U-54. Those were disheartening and bewildering times for a German naval officer and patriot. The exhaustion and deprivations from years of withering war made many Germans receptive to the cries of revolution that had been echoing on the Continent since October of 1917.

By September, it was clear that Germany had lost the greatest war the world had ever seen. U.S. President Woodrow Wilson refused to negotiate as long as Kaiser Wilhelm II remained on the throne, and he was forced to abdicate. Some senior members of the German military thought their country was being sold out by the politicians and that there was a need for one final, decisive battle. When rumor of this spread through Germany's proud but demoralized High Seas Fleet, mutiny began to foment and spread quickly. When the fleet was ordered to rendezvous near the naval base at Wilhelmshaven on October 29, the mutiny became a reality, spreading in only six days to every German naval base and port. One week later, at the eleventh hour of the eleventh day of the eleventh month, the armistice was signed. The war had ended, but a time of confusion, frustration, and anarchy lay ahead for Germany, and its loyal citizen Hellmuth von Ruckteschell.

Ten days later, the High Seas Fleet was surrendered to British Admiral David Beatty, who ordered that the German naval battle flag be lowered and not raised again. The once formidable fleet was interned in the massive basin of the British naval base at Scapa Flow, in the Orkney Islands, north of Scotland. No longer in command of a vessel, Ruckteschell sought what stability he could find with administrative assignments. Once a successful naval officer with significant military decorations, he now was struggling in a shattered country with virtually no Navy. Hellmuth's idolized, artistic older brother, Walter, who had served as adjutant to the remarkable General Paul von Lettow-Vorbeck in Africa throughout the war, would survive and come home, but his younger brother, Hans Ritter, had been killed in action on April 22, 1918, close to the end of the war. Another brother, Roland, would die during 1919. The von Ruckteschell family had felt the full impact and pain of this war and now the humiliation of defeat.

By June of 1919, some order was being made out of the chaos, and Ruckteschell was once again in command of a vessel. She was not, however, a majestic man-of-war, but a small 80-foot surface ship, the UZ-21, which had been used in minesweeping and sub-chasing operations and was now relegated essentially to police work. Ruckteschell and his small crew of former shipmates from his submarine commands patrolled the harbor of Kiel, looking for smugglers and black marketeers who would undermine the fragile new economy as it strained to get established. While there might have been some solace in being back in command of a vessel, Ruckteschell, for two reasons, was a very worried man. First was his angst over the plight of his country. In early May, the terms of the Treaty of Versailles, based on Woodrow Wilson's 14 Points, were announced, and Ruckteschell saw nothing but ignominy and humiliation in these conditions. Germany, in his opinion, was being stripped of her pride and dignity by the politicians who were about to sign this document at the formal surrender. Secondly, he had learned from Berlin that his name was on the list of war criminals.

Throughout the war, from 1914 onward, atrocities and war crimes were recorded by the Allies, for the time when, in victory, they could hold the perpetrators accountable. The Treaty of Versailles had provisions, in Articles 228 to 231, for the turning over and extradition of alleged war criminals for trial. The list at one point was enormous, with over 3,000 names. It would take years for the list to be reduced and actual trials to be held. For those on the list, there was real jeopardy. The subject of submarine warfare was a prime issue, particularly the attacks on merchant ships without warnings. As the list was refined it included the names of at least fifty U-boat captains, among them Kapitänleutnant Lothar von Arnauld de la Perière, the top "ace." Also listed was Erich Raeder, who appeared on the list because he had been Chief of Staff to Vice Admiral Franz von Hipper, the Navy's Commander in Chief. Raeder would eventually become Ruckteschell's supreme commander and the head of Hitler's Navy in World War II.

The list included admirals, generals, princes, and even the deposed Kaiser, but this illustrious company was no comfort to Ruckteschell. The people whose names were on the list had very personal decisions to make. Erich Raeder chose to stand fast and await what fate had in store for him. Others, like Oberleutnant Patzig, who was accused of sinking the hospital ship *Llandovery Castle* and firing on lifeboats, fled, leaving his junior officers to stand trial. Ruckteschell pondered his options and chose escape, but with a flare and drama that would make a statement and draw the attention of the press on both sides of the Atlantic.

As he planned his bold move, the representatives of Germany were preparing to sign the Treaty of Versailles on June 28. A week before the signing, the officers and sailors on board the interned ships of the High Seas Fleet made their own astonishing statement. Under the secret orders of Vice Admiral Ludwig von Reuter, on June 21 the crews were directed to open the sea cocks on all seventy-two of the interned ships. To the disbelief of everyone who was watching, from British officials and naval personnel on shore to schoolchildren on a boat trip to see the conquered fleet, the fleet disappeared before their eyes. After the ships had swung on their anchors for seven months, the sailors of the Kaisermarine had deprived the victors of their use. The world was aghast at this self-destruction that took lives as well as ships, and it was in this atmosphere that Ruckteschell went into action on a much smaller scale. His immediate superior, Oberleutnant Stoas, was sympathetic to Ruckteschell's plight as a member of the war crimes roster, and was fully aware of his plan. As darkness fell in Kiel on June 23, two days after the scuttling at Scapa Flow, Oberleutnant Hellmuth von Ruckteschell, proud German and officer of the Kaisermarine, hoisted a handmade version of the outlawed Kaisermarine battle flag and, with his small, bewildered crew, headed out to sea.

Since most of the thirteen men in the crew of the *UZ-21* had served with Ruckteschell in his U-boats during the previous three years, they knew and trusted him. Their voyage, however, was somewhat mysterious because they had removed the firing mechanisms of their guns and left them and their munitions behind in Kiel. As reported by the Associated Press news service and published on the front page of the *New York Times* on June 30, "Captain Ruckteschell did not divulge the destination of the craft upon leaving Kiel. When the UZ-21 reached the open sea, he told the crew that he would not return, as the honor and fortune of Germany had been lost in the Peace Treaty. He intended, he said, 'to proceed to South America, and asked the crew to accompany him, leaving the chaser at Gothenburg.' " Clearly, it was a matter of honor for this son of Germany, and this action reveals how strongly he felt the loss of Germany's "honor and fortune." However, he did have another motivation to leave. He was now a fugitive, on the run from those who wished to bring him to trial.

To keep their escape as inconspicuous as possible, the Captain and crew hugged the shore of the Jutland peninsula shared by Germany and Denmark, passed through the narrow strait of Lille Baelt that night, and then crossed over the top of the two large Danish islands of Fyn and Sjælland, heading for the Swedish coast. Because of its neutrality, Sweden seemed the ideal first stop on the way to South America. At midday on midsummer's day, June 24, people on the beach in the town of Mölle, 18 miles north of Helsingborg, were amazed to see a fast gray warship entering their harbor. When they hurried to the pier, the spectators found the confusing image of the ship's Captain dressed in civilian clothes but wearing his naval officer's cap. Ruckteschell took advantage of the confusion, filled his fuel tanks, and purchased a navigational chart of the region.

Before departing, he invited a reporter from a Stockholm paper aboard, and after offering the only libation he had, a glass of the Dutch liquor, genever, told him the essence of his plan and why he had left Germany. Thinking that he was speaking to the reporter in confidence, he revealed that if he had stayed in Germany he would probably have been handed over to the enemy for a war crimes trial. The story would promptly appear in the *Stockholms-Tidningen,* a Stockholm newspaper. With fuel and his chart, Ruckteschell and his small crew of thirteen put to sea again and headed north for the city of Gothenburg, about 100 miles away. Arriving off the approach to Gothenburg late that evening, they were stopped by the authorities from the Fortress Alvsborg. Upon inspecting the vessel and being assured that her weapons were inoperable, permission was given for the little warship to proceed into Gothenburg Harbor. The first part of Ruckteschell's escape plan had been executed perfectly.

During the voyage, the crew wrestled with the proposition their commanding officer had made. They all had been stung by Germany's defeat, and their prospects in Germany were grim. However, they all had relatives, some wives and children, they did not want to leave. Although Ruckteschell had been to South America on his training cruise nine years earlier, for most it was an exotic unknown. By the time the men reached Gothenburg, 6 of them chose to stay with their leader: an Oberleutnant zur See, a Leutnant zur See, 2 Fähnriche zur See, and 2 machinists. Ruckteschell had the ship quickly drop off those who chose to stay; then with the 8 remaining crew members under the command of Oberbootsman Huxoll, the ship headed immediately back to Kiel. The police arrived quickly, but since the UZ-21 was gone, there was no way to order the men out of the country. The Germans were taken to the police station, where they were questioned. They explained that they only wanted to stay a short time and then proceed on to South America, but they hoped to work temporarily, since they had only a small amount of money. The question, of course, arises of how Ruckteschell expected to transport himself and his crew to South America, but the answer is not evident in any of the accounts. There were groups established in Germany to help those on the war criminal list who wished to flee, but it is doubtful that such a group would assist crewmen who were not on the war crimes list to go halfway around the world. They may, however, have secretly helped Ruckteschell.

In order to stay in Sweden, the Germans had to apply for temporary visas, "permissions to sojourn." Once these were issued, it seems the plan for the group to depart for South America was abandoned (if it was ever a reality), and the men began to go in different directions. It is not known where these men went when they finally left Sweden after their "permissions to sojourn" expired, but it is assumed most returned to Germany. The leutnant and one of the Fähnriche z.S. left quite soon, on August 4; the Oberleutnant z.S. left in June of the following year; one of the machinists followed six months later; and the other machinist in January 1923. It is not known when the other Fähnriche z.S. departed.

After only four days in a hotel in Gothenburg, Ruckteschell moved to the town of Gunnebo, 10 miles away, where he must have had contacts. This had to have been planned in advance, perhaps by the group helping alleged war criminals, since Ruckteschell had stated on his temporary visa application that he intended to stay in Gunnebo and work during the time of his "sojourn." When his first "permission" expired at the end of July, the fugitive began a radically different chapter of his life. Instead of heading for the warmth of South America, he headed north from Gunnebo into the frigid vast wilderness of Lapland.

Chapter 3

THE BRITISH

A t the time Hellmuth von Ruckteschell evaporated into the wilds of Lapland, many of the people who would lose their lives as the result of his attack on the *Anglo-Saxon* were just beginning their lives and a few were yet unborn. Of course, a number were already seasoned veterans with their own experiences in the Great War. Of the 41 people whom fate would place on board the *Anglo-Saxon* that August night, 5 would be teenagers, 17 would be in their twenties, 8 would be in their thirties, 7 in their forties, and only 4 in their fifties. They were a microcosm of those who manned the British merchant fleet at that time, and a reflection of the residual effects of World War I.

When the Great War finally ground to a halt, all the countries involved were reeling from the grim impact of the war and the difficult aftermath they faced. It is calculated that the combined European and British death toll numbered over 10 million. In addition, the American loss was in excess of 100,000. The numbers are too enormous to comprehend, particularly when you extend the painful outreach from that staggering number to include the parents, wives, children, sweethearts, and siblings who were anguished by these losses. Then, of course, must be added the number of wounded, many maimed for life, who led lives with deep physical and psychological scars. As has been so often said, this war tore away the flower of Europe's youth and left a gaping hole in a genera-tion. It was not easy to imagine how those countries were going to recover from these wounds.

This loss of lives had an impact on all aspects of life in Britain, but it ripped through the merchant marine community with particular force. In the early months of the war, in 1914, the merchant ships of the British Empire suffered the loss of 252,736 tons of carrying capacity. This was a terrifying number, particularly when it was broken down into actual ships and the lives of crewmen. In 1915, the losses more than tripled. The fol-lowing year, the losses exceeded the first year's quarter-million tons by al-most 1 million tons. With the unrestricted submarine warfare of 1917, the merchant losses tripled again, from the 1.23 million tons of 1916 to 3.66 million tons lost in 1917. In the last year of the war, the losses were cut by more than half, but that still represented the second-worst year of the war, with over 1.6 million tons destroyed. These losses, of course, were primarily the work of submariners, who sank 4,837 ships, a startling 87.6 percent of the 5,516 vessels sunk. Ruckteschell and the other submarine commanders taught the world the lesson of how powerful a weapon the submarine could be when unfettered and in the hands of competent, dar-ing, aggressive naval officers.

What seems more amazing is that the British merchant mariners con-tinued to go to sea when faced with the realities they experienced every day, as they saw ships destroyed around them and watched as ships in the distance went down, taking friends and former shipmates with them. At the beginning of the war, there were so few U-boats that it was thought they could not make much impact on Britain's vast merchant fleet but rather might terrorize the sailors. The Germans hoped that the sudden fierce attacks from an unseen enemy would wither the courage of these mariners and they would refuse to sign on and go to sea. However, these theorists had failed to measure the courage and patriotism of the men who sailed under the "red duster," as the British merchant flag is affec-tionately known. As this nickname for their banner conveys, they were a self-deprecating lot, who recognized their duty to King and Country and marshaled the willpower and discipline to take voyage after voyage.

While the British Merchant Navy had been in the thick of the battle throughout World War I, the burden had been shared by the Allied merchant mariners, who also shared in the honor of the task they performed. In addition, numerous vessels from neutral countries were also attacked and sunk, so these sacrifices also need to be weighed in assessing the losses and recognition of all these individual mariners, all brave sailors. It is estimated that Allied and neutral losses between 1914 and 1918 totaled over 12.5 million gross registered tons. Ruckteschell's toll included numerous British vessels, but also Norwegian, French, Danish, and Dutch. Other U-boat commanders added Belgian, Italian, Russian, and, of course, American ships to their roster.

With the war over, England and her Allies now faced the task of rebuilding and manning their decimated merchant fleets. Before World War I, the United Kingdom imported nearly 53 million tons per year of commodities, including food, minerals, fibers for textiles, timber, and all the other items needed by this vibrant nation. Four years later, at the height of the unrestricted submarine warfare, those imports had been cut by 35 percent. The actual rebuilding of the fleets was relatively simple. The challenge was finding the funds. Allied shipyards had been in wartime production, so the infrastructure to rebuild the ships themselves was there. As the military services released their personnel, there was a ready supply of workers to move into the ship construction business, but it was a slow process in the shaky postwar economy. With regard to the mariners themselves, particularly the skilled able seamen, firemen, engineers, and deck officers, there was a solid core of manpower on which to build: the weathered, war-hardened merchant marine that had survived the fearful nights and anxious days of the war. They were people like Philip "Paddy" Flynn, who twenty years after the end of one world war would captain the *Anglo-Saxon* on the eve of the next.

Philip Limpenny Flynn is the classic example of the kind of lad who was drawn to the sea, followed his calling, and rose through the ranks to command. Although he was born in Plymouth and raised in Exeter, both maritime communities in southern Devon, Philip Flynn's family did not have a maritime orientation. It was through his own drive and initiative

that he pursued his successful maritime career. In this sense, his life par-
alleled that of Ruckteschell; but this seems to be the only area in which
the two men were alike. While Ruckteschell would take one logical, rigid,
disciplined step after the other along the path to his naval career and
command, Flynn, three years older, would steer a more casual course. He
was the oldest of three brothers whose father, also Philip, was a dental
surgeon. By the time young Philip reached his teens, the family had
moved to the London area, living in Croydon, a suburb 10 miles south of
London. As was often the case at that time, the senior Flynn envisioned
his oldest son following in his footsteps. Since formal academic or medical training was not required and the licensing of dental surgeons did not
come about until 1921, he took his son on as an apprentice when he was
thirteen. While the father anticipated a long and prosperous career of
tooth extractions for his son, young Philip had other ideas. Perhaps it was
his youth, spent on the Exe estuary, or his reading that first awakened
young Philip Flynn's enthusiasm for a life at sea; or perhaps it was the
prospect of a life of dental extractions. It will never be known, but something forced him to act decisively. After only a year of apprenticeship with
his father, he ran away to sea.

His early maritime adventures are not well documented, but it is clear
that he was motivated, learned quickly, and made his own way. By the
start of World War I, Philip Flynn, who by then was known as "Paddy,"
had thirteen years of sea experience. He was one of those merchant
sailors who constantly put his life at risk to sustain the flow of critically
needed supplies, and who, like so many others, was torpedoed. With the
armistice in 1918, Paddy Flynn was a veteran merchant mariner in his
early thirties, and, by 1925, an officer on his way to command. He had
achieved this status the hard way, with limited formal maritime training
and his education carried out under the most difficult of circumstances—
the Great War at sea. His experience served him well, in that he understood thoroughly what merchant service was like for both the sailor and
the officers. This would make him an admired and respected commanding officer.

Paddy Flynn served as Second and Third Mate in several ships before achieving the position of First Mate, second-in-command of the Lawther, Latta line ship *Anglo-Canadian* in 1928. He gained additional experience during his nine years in this position as he awaited his first command. Serving with him during the latter part of this period was a bright Second Mate twenty-two years his junior, Barry Denny. With Flynn's easy manner and good sense of humor and Denny's professionalism, a bond developed. Denny came from a family with deep maritime roots. That connection is easily recognized in his middle name, Collingwood. For five generations, members of the Denny family carried the famous name from its root in Barry's great-, great-, great-grandfather. Vice Admiral Cuthbert Collingwood was one of England's great naval heroes of the Napoleonic Wars and, with Nelson, a hero at Trafalgar. It was Admiral Collingwood, leading the leeward column of British ships in his flagship, the *Royal Sovereign,* who first engaged the combined French and Spanish fleet in this famous battle. It was he who drew Lord Nelson's admiration and praise: "See how that noble fellow, Collingwood, carries his ship into action!" This is the stock from which Barry Denny came. The name Collingwood was something very proud for any Englishman to carry, as Barry and both his brothers, Anthony and Desmond, did. It was also a name to live up to, which was Barry Collingwood Denny's intent.

It was not, however, the Royal Navy that attracted this Collingwood, but rather the distinguished service with traditions even older than the Navy—the merchant service. Cuthbert Collingwood Denny, who had served in the Essex Regiment, and his wife, Violet, sent their middle son, Barry, off for maritime training when he reached his early teens. He entered the training ship *Mercury,* built in 1878 as HM sloop *Gannet,* where he was immersed in maritime studies for three years. By the late twenties, he left the River Hamble and the *Mercury,* and assumed his first professional position as a cadet with the Lamport & Holt Line of Liverpool. His career would bring him to the *Anglo-African* as the Third Mate in 1934. In 1935, he served with Paddy Flynn on the *Anglo-Canadian,* as Second Mate, before joining his next ship, the *Anglo-Saxon.*

Far to the north of London where Denny had lived, another future key officer of the *Anglo-Saxon* was preparing for his merchant marine career.

This young man, Edward Ernest Milburn, found his way into the special-ized and well-paying field of marine engineering. The Milburns were "geordies" from northeast England and the River Tyne. With a father who was a plumber and sanitary health inspector and an uncle who was a fitter-engineer in the shipyards of the Tyne, it was not a leap for this hardwork-ing young man to seek an engineer's position in the merchant service.

Eddie Milburn's first employment, when he was fourteen, was as a uniformed telegraph messenger, and it was apparently while visiting ships in his "official capacity" of delivering telegrams that he had his first glimpse of the wondrous maze of a ship's engine room. The fascination with the engines and the "glamorous" life of the sailor that lay beyond his town of North Shields in Northumberland appealed to this lad.

There was no specific training program for marine engineers at this time, so an interested person had to work his way through a long appren-ticeship to acquire the skills and certifications to be a junior engineer at sea. For Milburn, it was a five-year apprenticeship, from 1917 to 1922, and when he was finally ready for work, the economic environment made it difficult to find a ship. He had always been a hard worker and found em-ployment with the London & North Eastern Railway until his break came. With virtually no notice, in May of 1926 he was informed that he had a berth as Fourth Engineer on the SS *Chertsey* and shifted from being a railway worker one day to ship's engineer the next. He left the *Chertsey* after two years at sea and, after a special course of study at Thorn's Ma-rine Engineering Academy, took his exams for Second-Class Engineer. This status now gave him the opportunity to marry, and he and Ethel May Hall became husband and wife in October of 1929—two weeks before the stock market crash in the United States, which impacted economies around the world. In this difficult Depression environment, the Mil-burns began their family. Their first son, Ted, was born in 1931 and, after Eddie obtained his first-class engineer certificate in February 1933, their second son, Derek, was born in December 1933. Eddie Milburn managed to continue his advancement at sea with periodic positions on the Lawther, Latta line ships and occasional trips to London in the famous "geordie colliers," carrying coal from Newcastle. By the late thirties, Milburn was a respected, well-qualified marine engineer who was ready for his Chief Engineer's assignment aboard the *Anglo-Saxon*.

While Eddie Milburn was at the high point of his career with this Chief Engineer's position, one of his junior engineers, who lived in the same region, would look to the chief for guidance as he began his own career. Lionel Henry Hawks was sixteen years younger than Milburn and had just turned one year old when Ruckteschell fled to Sweden. Hawks was born in Dudley near Newcastle, but his family soon moved to the Benton area of Newcastle upon Tyne. After study at Jesmond School and Oxford, his first assignment as Fourth Engineer, the lowest engineering officer position, was on the *Columbia Star*. He was pleased to take a step up the ladder and sign on as Third Engineer aboard the *Anglo-Saxon*, working under Milburn.

Another key officer of the *Anglo-Saxon*, who would be greatly admired for his fine character and exceptional courage, was younger still than Hawks. Roy Hamilton Pilcher was born three days before Ruckteschell left Gunnebo. He was born in Durham, not far from the Tyne and the homes of Milburn and Hawks, but by the time he was of school age he lived in Farncombe, in Surrey. From there he would travel by train to Guildford, where he attended the Royal Grammar School with his friend David Enticknap, who would also have a ship shot out from under him during World War II. In school, he put up with the nickname "Fish," derived from the closeness of his name to "pilchard," a kind of fish; but after the family moved to Canterbury, and through his teen years, he coped with the affectionate nickname of "Bun" without apparent protest. During his teen years, in the mid-1930s, he traveled from Canterbury to Shoreham on the Sussex coast to stay with his cousin Roderick's family, where he met Cliff Walder, who would be his friend for the remainder of his life. On those summer visits, they would swim, cycle, and generally enjoy life in the seaside community.

Roy's path to the *Anglo-Saxon* began with his decision to study radio, which led him to become a "wireless transmitting officer" at sea. In this, he was somewhat following his father's precedent, since Bernard Pilcher had been a telegraphist in the Army during the First World War and worked in that capacity for the postal service after the war. Roy obtained his training at the best source, the Marconi training facility on the Menai Strait, between northern Wales and the Isle of Anglesey. He must have done well, since he was employed by the Marconi company, which then placed him in various vessels. Through his friendship with Cliff Walder, he met Marion Wastell. It was easy for Marion to find this handsome, soft-spoken, well-read, and intelligent young man attractive. With their limited funds, going out on dates to restaurants was not possible, so Roy, Marion, Cliff, and Cliff's girlfriend, Daphne, often went to "the pictures," or, for excitement, out to the somewhat racy "Bungalotown," which had sprung up on the shingle bank of the shore. Trips to Shoreham became more rare as Marconi sent Roy to sea, first as the only radio officer on the *Salvonia*, a large North Sea trawler, and then on long voyages in the merchant ship *Beacon Grange*.

Another central figure in the *Anglo-Saxon* drama was born the same year as Pilcher, but had a very different background and would lead a very different life. While Pilcher was refined and self-deprecating, Wilbert Charles Roy Widdicombe was a brash and braggadocian young man. Born in Totnes, Devon, to Adam Widdicombe, a shipwright, and his wife, Lily, Roy's life changed drastically after the death of his mother when he was four. As Roy would later tell the story, with his flare for drama and fabrication, his mother had taken Roy, his older sister, and two younger brothers for a walk, with the youngest boy in a pram. When their mother suddenly collapsed and died on the walk, Widdicombe claimed that the children loaded her into the pram and managed to push her home! After his mother's death, Roy went to live with his Widdicombe grandparents in Dartmouth, where Roy chafed under his grandmother's strict discipline. On two occasions, he ran away to his maternal grandparents, the Bowheys, where his younger brother George was living, but each time he was returned to the Widdicombes. Although he was clearly very bright, school held little appeal, and Roy frequently skipped school to mess about in the boats that were plentiful on the River Dart and in the harbor. He often appropriated a rowing or sailing dinghy for his own use without the formality of asking permission.

Just before his eleventh birthday, Roy would later assert, he entered the distinguished maritime training program aboard the training ship *Conway*, moored on the Mersey River in Liverpool. This respected program that had been conceived in 1858 to "train boys to become officers in the merchant service" gave its students a very thorough grounding in maritime skills during their three years of enrollment. With illustrious individuals such as the English poet laureate John Masefield among its former students, it was prestigious to be a "Conway boy." In Roy Widdicombe's case, however, there is serious question as to whether he attended that program. Careful examination of the Conway records at the Merseyside Maritime Museum archive, including the Muster Rolls, the Wages Book, and the Register of All Cadets, reveal no Widdicombe in attendance between 1927 and 1934. Nor does he show up as a student on the *Indefatigable*, another Liverpool training ship that was founded "to train the sons of sailors, destitute and orphaned boys to become merchant seamen." Where he was in school in his early years remains a mystery, but this tendency to embroider upon his background and enhance his standing is one that would continually reappear during Widdicombe's life.

It is known, however, that by the summer of 1933, at age fourteen, Roy Widdicombe began his career at sea as a deck boy in a Union Castle liner on the run to Capetown, South Africa. Within a year, the quick-witted lad obtained his Able-Bodied Seaman's ticket, and moved on to other passenger ships on other routes. In 1937, while serving aboard the *Arandora Star*, he visited Nassau, in the Bahamas, for the first time but thought little of returning since the town had minimal appeal to him. Always seeking creative ways to better his situation, he and a couple of his shipmates developed a plan to increase their status ashore beyond what they had on board. They purchased officers' uniforms, which they could not wear on the ship but were unregulated ashore. In the Navy, there were stiff penalties for impersonating an officer, but in the merchant service, as long as they did not claim officer status, they could use the uniforms to make the impression and let people "judge the book by its cover." Here again the streetwise Widdicombe had found a way to heighten the perception of his status.

He soon shifted from passenger ships to cargo vessels, where he per-ceived it would be easier to save some of his pay. He had a new motiva-tion—a lively, slim young woman. The life of the sailor had taken Roy Widdicombe around the world, and at six feet with his dark complexion, he made a striking impression. There had been other girlfriends, includ-ing Edith, whose name was indelibly emblazoned amid a heart and dagger on his left forearm, one of his many tattoos. But as Roy made his way down a street in Newport, South Wales, exuding self-confidence, he en-countered one girl, in a group of five, who radiated similar confidence and was clearly special. Unlike most girls he had met, Cynthia Pitman stood out because she was not intimidated. She refused Roy's invitation to a movie but offered to show him around Newport in the days ahead. He realized she was something special, but his stay was short and he was soon off on a voyage to South America. On his return, he renewed his ro-mance with Cynthia and, with the prospect of marriage before him, began to look for increased income. He knew the pay was higher for sailors willing to take the risk of carrying cargo to Spain, which was locked in civil war. Not only did Widdicombe see the trips to Spain as a chance to earn high wages because of the 200 percent premium when they were in the war zone, but he saw it as an opportunity to enterprisingly "trade on his own account." He signed on to the *Stanway,* a ship making voyages to Spanish ports like Bilboa and Alicante to supply the Loyalist forces. In these ports, Widdicombe would convert his large supply of American cigarettes, which he purchased inexpensively in Europe, into expensive Spanish products including, no doubt, presents for Cynthia and the styl-ish clothing for which he had a flare. This life was risky, as the harbors were often shelled, and eventually Widdicombe left the *Stanway* for Cyn-thia and the *Anglo-Saxon.*

The near opposite of Widdicombe's personality could be found in another young man, Able Seaman Robert George Tapscott. Two years younger than Widdicombe, Tapscott was born in Bristol and grew up in a simple home in the country village of Usk, 8 miles upstream from New-port, before moving to Cardiff. Growing up in that atmosphere of small village life, centered around Twyn Square with its brick Victorian clock

tower and the rectory in the shadow of Usk castle's ruins, obviously in-
stilled in the boy a sense of decorum and responsibility that would stay
with him throughout his life. His mother faced difficult times after her
husband, a Cardiff ship pilot, died when Bob Tapscott was only two years
old, leaving Florence Tapscott with a pension from the pilots union of a
mere 18 shillings a week. She worked hard as a domestic to earn the extra
funds needed. Bob, the youngest of six, had a stable childhood, and was
looked after by his older sisters, with a brother six years his senior to admire. He was a healthy, strapping lad who would grow to just under six
feet and who enjoyed football and swimming. His schooling was through
the local Council education system and technical schools. He was bright
and did well in school, although he admitted to having difficulty learning
Welsh.

By his mid-teens, it was time for Bob to start making his own way,
and, with his mother's assistance, he managed to get a berth on a tramp
steamer. The wage for this fifteen-year-old apprentice was a minuscule 6
pence half penny per day, but his accommodations and meals were included, although he had trouble looking forward to the meals, which consisted mainly of salt pork or salt beef and always beans and more beans.
The cruel reality of a first voyage to Buenos Aires, and a hard-driving
First Mate, made him question whether this life was for him. After a year
and three passages back and forth to South America, he had completed
his commitment to the ship and promptly left. He had worked hard, been
toughened, and had seen another part of the world. He headed back to
the country, where he sought the "easier" life as a farmhand. He rejected
farmwork faster than he had the sea and returned to sea as a mess boy on
the *Grainton*, where he began to build upon his knowledge and skills to
gain his Able Seaman's ticket. Aboard this Newport tramp steamer, he
made a voyage to Cape Town, where the crew loaded cornmeal for Rotterdam and from there made the passage to Portland, Oregon, and back
to Wales. On that voyage, Bob moved up to deck boy and gained the experience necessary to qualify as an Ordinary Seaman. Like Widdicombe,
he was lured into the more lucrative service supplying the Republicans in
the dangerous Spanish Civil War.

While these men and 33 other mariners were working their way toward the *Anglo-Saxon,* there was another most unlikely shipmate destined to join them. Francis Penny was not a sailor, but a veteran of the Royal Marines, one of the most distinguished branches of the British military, with a rich tradition. While some of his future shipmates aboard the *Anglo-Saxon* had served their country enduring the hazards of merchant marine service in World War I, Francis G. Penny was in the thick of the fighting in France. He was wounded twice and awarded the Military Medal for gallantry in the field.

By the late 1930s, Francis Penny, already in his forties, had seen enough of military service and had retired. However, he possessed artillery skills that were soon going to be in urgent need and scarce supply. In 1937, he could probably not imagine having to leave his wife, Edith, and their home in the naval town of Portsmouth to go to war again.

On the eve of the outbreak of World War II, these men were on their way to the *Anglo-Saxon* with more than thirty others. Some, like Jim Fowler, a greaser; Frederick Tenow, a fireman-trimmer; and Leslie Morgan, the assistant cook, came from Newport, Wales. However, the 41-person crew represented the broadest range of ages and backgrounds, and came from all parts of the British Isles. There were men from Tyneside in the Northeast and Merseyside in the Northwest, and men from Ireland and Stromness, in the Orkney Islands. Some men came from Devon and Cornwall in the Southwest, and others from London and the south coast. In addition, there were men born in Russia, Denmark, and Estonia.

Chapter 4

THE GERMANS

As all these British sailors were advancing from ship to ship and getting the training they needed for their future assignments, Hellmuth von Ruckteschell's naval career had come to what appeared to be a complete halt. To all outward appearances, the brazen Ruckteschell had commandeered a vessel belonging to the German Navy, taken it to another country, and attempted to lure his small crew out of naval service and off to a foreign land. Even amid the chaos of June 1919, which culminated with the signing of the Treaty of Versailles, Ruckteschell's actions were internationally newsworthy. Certainly, his initial statement to the press and explanation to his crew that, with the signing of the treaty, the "honor and fortune" of Germany had been lost had the ring of a disillusioned patriot. A skeptic, however, knowing of the war crimes accusations hanging over him, could easily infer that his patriotic statement was a mere cover for self-preservation. It is likely that Ruckteschell's actions were motivated by both reasons. He was sincere in anguish and disappointment at the plight of his once proud nation, and equally sincere in seeing no reason to sacrifice his life on the altar of the lost cause.

There are two indicators that Ruckteschell's actions during his escape were, if not sanctioned by his superior officers, tolerated and even admired. The first is the fact that he executed his plan with the knowledge of his immediate superior, Oberleutnant Stoas. Unless he and Ruckteschell had foreknowledge that not all the crew would want to stay with him and some would be available to return the vessel, Stoas was taking a serious risk that the vessel would be lost and he would be held responsible. When considered in the context of the scuttling of seventy-two ships of the German High Seas Fleet by their crews, however, the loss of a little 20-ton patrol boat might seem inconsequential. In addition, the escape was made in a manner that would have earned respect from the senior officers. Ruckteschell didn't disguise himself and with false papers slip out of the country into some neutral haven. He demonstrated his self-reliance, exhibited the same dash that had made him a successful U-boat commander, and cleverly utilized the resources he knew well. Certainly, other officers above and below him in rank, on the war crimes list or not, would be sympathetic with his predicament and would admire how he used it to make a public statement against the politicians that many military men felt had betrayed their country.

The official blessing on Ruckteschell's Swedish escapade came five months after the event. The Kaisermarine was no more, but Germany's military was now controlled by the Reichswehrministry. After his escape, the officers in charge of the new military carefully assessed Ruckteschell's actions and came to their conclusions. Rather than a sharp condemnation and stripping of his rank, he received an honorable discharge that was "sweetened" by two additional points. He was allowed to wear his officer's uniform as he sought civilian employment; this would help him in securing an appropriate position. In addition, and undoubtedly more important to Ruckteschell, he was told he could wear the uniform of a Kapitänleutnant, the next promotion in the Navy.

The irony of this act of "commendation" was that the news of it may have taken a long time to reach Ruckteschell in the Swedish wilderness. In July, as his first "permission to sojourn" expired and a new one was granted, he left Gunnebo and headed to the village of Porjus, 30 miles north of the Arctic Circle. For a veteran severely disillusioned by the outcome of the war, having witnessed a huge loss of life and risked his own and those of his men on innumerable occasions, it would not be unusual to seek change. For Ruckteschell, this change was extreme. If he had left the Navy and stayed in Germany, he would have been likely to find work that utilized his training and skills. In Porjus, he cast aside all the trappings and status of his former life and took up the most basic existence. The work available in this part of the world was primarily laboring in the forests. Ruckteschell had never physically labored in his life, except at sea when the constant motion requires bracing to counter the movements of the vessel. This calls for a crew to be in good physical condition, as they often work until exhaustion. We know, however, that by the end of his U-boat command, Ruckteschell was ill. It seems as if this trip into the Arctic may have been a catharsis. Ruckteschell threw himself into his new hard work in the clean, invigorating air, away from the troubles, anxieties, and trials, literal and figurative, that engulfed him in Germany.

Several of those who left the UZ-21 and stayed in Sweden had little difficulty getting jobs in the Gothenburg area. Hermann Baron, one of the machinists, worked in an engineering plant, while another, Willy Moeller, found work in a chocolate factory. With his knowledge and experience, it would seem natural for Ruckteschell to have sought work in that region as well. However, he was in fear of being found and taken to trial. When asked about giving up his plan to go to South America, he told the newspapers that it would have been difficult to get there since his enemies would be looking for him on the Atlantic. It is doubtful that this was indeed the case, but for Ruckteschell it was motivation to disappear. How and exactly why he picked Porjus is not known, but it was an excellent choice; since it was remote, it would be difficult to find him there, and it had ample work. That part of Sweden had three great natural resources that were being increasingly exploited in the early 1920s: timber, iron, and water as a source of hydroelectric power. A power plant was built in Porjus in 1914 to provide electric power for the railway that would carry iron ore and timber to the northern Norwegian port of Narvik, a name and place that would become important to Ruckteschell and his future shipmates. This power plant was the economic engine for the region.

Ruckteschell's first employment was as a lumberjack working in the forests. It is difficult to imagine this slightly built, wiry thirty-year-old wielding an ax in the Arctic forests, so it is not surprising that his skill and intelligence were recognized and he moved into the sawmill. He also apparently worked as a forest warden and then a "Crown Hunter," officially harvesting game from the national forests. With his understanding of mechanical systems, it was a natural progression for Ruckteschell to be employed in the expansion of the power plant at Porjus. He worked in this area from the fall of 1919 through 1921. His final job in Lapland was once again "at sea," as helmsman of a tugboat on Lake Lule, which stretches northwest from Porjus 100 miles, almost to the Norwegian border.

During this time it is unclear how much contact Ruckteschell had with his family or colleagues in Germany, but it would seem that he was getting some information, and this encouraged him to move tentatively from his arctic retreat to the more cosmopolitan south of Sweden. During the spring of 1922, he was employed as a stockroom manager for a car factory in the small city of Malmö, Sweden, a short distance across the Øresund from Copenhagen. Here he weighed whether to risk returning to Germany. It was still a turbulent time in the Weimar Republic. The Friekorps, paramilitary groups usually made up of former military officers, operated as a loose but powerful, erratic, and difficult-to-control organization. In 1921, the Freikorps established a small, violent cell known as the Organizational Consul that used assassination as its tool for change. In that same year, Adolf Hitler became the head of the National Socialist German Workers' Party (Nationalsozialistische Deutsche Arbeiterpartei)—the soon-to-be-dreaded Nazi Party. Despite the turmoil, for a German patriot there was the powerful draw of returning to his homeland and his family. Most importantly, however, he no longer was at risk for being tried as a war criminal.

That huge list of nearly 3,000 names of alleged war criminals, which included those brought forward from all the Allied nations, was reduced to just under 1,600 by the end of 1919. It still seemed a staggering undertaking to consider nearly 1,600 extraditions and trials in international courts. The list was again whittled down, so that by February 1920 the

Allies had agreed on a list of 890. There was tense international debate calling for the trial of those responsible for the war and its atrocities. The debate got particularly sensitive when it involved the potential trial of former national leaders, icons of their age, even the Kaiser himself.

The politics of the war crimes trials became more complicated as the issue of extradition and trial began to threaten the stability of the Weimar Republic itself. The very real fear for the Allied nations was that if they forced the issue of Articles 228 to 231 of the Treaty of Versailles, it would destabilize the government and open the way for a Bolshevik takeover. In a major concession, they determined not to extradite those on the list but to conduct the trials in Germany, under German law, with Allied prosecutors handling the cases. Ultimately, this is what was done. In May of 1921, Germany's Supreme Court, the Reichsgericht, in Leipzig, began hearing the cases. There were no longer 3,000, nor 1,600, nor the 890 names of the previous February, but only 47 cases that were actually tried. In frustration over the lack of prosecutions, France and Belgium began to hold trials in absentia of the people on the February 1920 list. In response, the German court perfunctorily worked its way through the names from the February list, essentially exonerating those who were being tried in other countries without being present to defend themselves. Overall, the entire Allied effort to bring the war criminals to justice would have to be satisfied with those 47 full trials. Among the 12 British cases within the 47, one was brought against a U-boat commander, Oberleutnant Patzig; but since he had fled, it was his two junior lieutenants who were found guilty of, among other offenses, failing to act against their commanding officer when he ordered gunfire on survivors in a lifeboat.

It was just as the Leipzig trials were getting under way that Ruckteschell's accuser in the case of the *En Avant* finally came forward. At the end of the war, Otto Wiedemann had returned to his home in Poland and in 1921 was working as a boatswain on the Polish sail-training ship *Lwow*, which was being refitted in Amsterdam for the Polish government. The work on the *Lwow* was being supervised by a Lieutenant Commander in the British Royal Naval Reserve, T. Burton. Wiedemann knew Burton well and was eager to share with him the details of this terrible story of the drowning of the French sailors. Burton realized the magnitude of this crime and asked Wiedemann if he was prepared to make a written statement and to possibly testify in court. Wiedemann was fully prepared and submitted the statement that was passed through channels to His Majesty's Attorney General. The Attorney General checked with the British Admiralty to see if they had any information on the incident, which they did not since it was a French vessel and there were apparently no survivors. Since it had been such an ordeal and political fiasco to get the few Leipzig trials under way, the authorities in England did not want to create additional complications. The British conclusion was "their Lordships do not consider that any useful purpose would be served in pursuing the matter." Apparently, the allegation was not even transmitted to the French to pursue the case if they wished. So, Hellmuth von Ruckteschell never faced this ominous charge, just as Wilhelm Werner, accused of a similar drowning, escaped prosecution because he was in hiding as Ruckteschell was in 1921.

In addition, the British desire to see the principle of unrestricted submarine warfare condemned and outlawed failed. The charge against the great majority of U-boat commanders was "for atrocities in sinking without warning," followed by a list of specific vessels. None of these "simple" cases ever came to trial. Had Ruckteschell or one of the other officers been tried and found guilty, the British would have won their point and the convicted commander might have had the consolation of knowing that his "sacrifice" might eliminate that practice and make future wars more humane. It is perhaps outlandish to speculate that a convicted U-boat commander would find solace in such a thought, but Ruckteschell would express exactly that feeling a quarter of a century later. However, in 1922 the threat of trial had essentially dissolved and he headed home.

The irony was that had Ruckteschell not fled to Sweden and lived the life of a fugitive in self-imposed exile for three years, but stayed in Germany, he most probably could have been positioned for a significant career in the new German Navy, which although substantially reduced, was about to emerge from the ruins. Instead of being part of the corps of 1,600 officers of this postwar Navy when he returned to Germany in June of 1922, Ruckteschell found himself "lifeless," not literally but in many other ways. His mother was still alive, so he had a home to go to, but he had nothing else. The sense of belonging, the pride in his uniform and country, the camaraderie of fellow officers, and the tangible evidence of achievement through decorations and advancement in rank were all gone. During the summer of his return, he often sailed on the Baltic and pondered his future. The Naval Officers' Relief Society had been established in 1918 to assist demobilized naval officers, but by 1922, Ruckteschell was out of contact and four years behind his former colleagues who had received assistance immediately after the war. It is not known whether he sought the assistance of Kapitan Baron von Büllow, who ran the society. It is possible his flight to Sweden was now viewed by some more negatively, as even a cowardly act, when others had stayed and stolidly awaited their fate. As Ruckteschell's resources ran out by the end of the summer, he settled on a new career that drew on his artistic side, a strong part of his character that had been dormant during his naval career. At age thirty-two, he began the first of several apprenticeships with master woodworkers and craftsmen in the Black Forest, an area that had been known for centuries for its woodcarving. In March of 1923, the apparently lonely, nomadic life of Ruckteschell took on a new dimension when he married Annemarie Loerbroks. He passed his examinations as a journeyman carpenter and cabinetmaker in 1924 and spent several months helping his older brother, Walter, build a house. After he returned to Germany, Walter had resumed his career as an artist, his sculpture inspired by his time in Africa serving in General von Lettow-Vorbek's successful hit-and-run guerrilla-war campaign.

In 1926, Ruckteschell and his wife located in Bremen, not far from his old U-boat base in Bremerhaven and close to the German naval base at Wilhelmshaven, where eight years before, unbeknownst to him, Fräulein Schmidt had borne his child. For a period, Ruckteschell worked at Schafer & Co. on the specialized and complicated ship joinery needed to fit the curved interiors of vessels. The following year, he passed his examinations in front of the Bremen Chamber of Commerce and became a recognized Master Cabinetmaker, eligible to open his own business. With this achievement, it would appear as if his life was finally on an even keel. In the next few years, he designed and built his own workshop and house, a showplace for his designs. These were contemporary in style, influenced by the art community at nearby Worpswede, known for its handmade furniture; these were substantial pieces, with many carvings. His work was sufficiently distinguished to merit exhibition at the Rodelius House in Bremen. He also collaborated with his brother Walter on two church projects: one for the Bismarck Memorial Church, the other for the Osterkirche in Altona where the altar carvings are dramatic, modern, and reflect Walter's African influence.

While outwardly life seemed settled and successful for Hellmuth von Ruckteschell, it was about to change once again. In 1932, his nine-year marriage to Annemarie, which had produced no children, ended in divorce. Either as a cause of the divorce or as a result of it, Ruckteschell left Bremen and went to sea again. A voyage from Hamburg to Rotterdam, across the Atlantic to Newport News, Virginia, and then north to New York, gave him his second contact with the people who would become his enemies less than a decade later. From New York, he steamed back to Bremen and a new chapter in his life, without a wife and with a country responding to a new sense of nationalism.

Nineteen thirty-two had been a transitional year for Ruckteschell, but also one for his country. The collapse of the American stock market in October of 1929 triggered an international economic depression among the industrialized nations. In Germany, economic discontent helped pave the way for Adolf Hitler and his rapid rise to absolute power. In 1932, Hitler had the confidence to run for President against Paul von Hindenburg, and, though he would lose, his 13 million votes served notice that he was a major political force. In the July elections, his party won nearly two hundred seats in the German Parliament and had the largest party representation in that governing body. His power and prestige continued to grow as not only the workers supported him, but as he gained endorsements from major industrialists, and, importantly, the military. As 1933 began,

President Hindenburg appointed Hitler Chancellor of Germany. In February 1933, the Reichstag Building, which housed the Parliament, was burned down in a bold political action that Hitler blamed on the Communists. In order to quell this political crisis, the Parliament and the President gave Hitler precisely the tool he needed to advance his cause, the power to rule by decree. It appeared to the average German that the Nazi Party and its charismatic leader were about to move Germany dramatically forward on the world stage, and there was a sudden rush to join the party in order to avoid being viewed as either opposing it or not sharing its vision. In the elections of March 1933, the Nazi Party won 288 seats in the Parliament and formed a coalition with the Nationalist Party, gaining firm control. Following the election, the coalition passed the "Enabling Act," which gave Hitler the right to rule by decree for four years; people thronged to the Nazi Party. Hellmuth von Ruckteschell was among the "Märzgefallene"—those who "fell in March."

Exactly why Ruckteschell, a man living a simple life as a master craftsman, moved with the political flow and joined the Nazi Party in March of 1933 will never be definitively known. It can be speculated, however, that there were several factors. First may have been his status as a craftsman, his identification with the common man, the worker, the heart and soul of Germany. In the difficult economic times, the Workers' Party's nominal purpose was to help the workingman. Second may have been the increasing military support being expressed for the Nazi Party. With his former military career, it would seem natural for him to ally himself with the party it endorsed. Finally, the core issues of German nationalism and pride obviously meant a great deal to Ruckteschell. After fifteen years of humiliation and perceived abuse from other nations, he could see in this party a force that could renew German pride and stature. For these and no doubt other reasons, Hellmuth Ruckteschell became a Nazi Party member.

A year later, in the summer of 1934, President Hindenburg died. The Army swore an oath of loyalty to Hitler, and he became the supreme leader of Germany, the Führer. That same year, Master Cabinetmaker Ruckteschell was reinstated in the German Navy as a reserve officer and began periodic training. His country was on the road back to promi-nence, and Ruckteschell would be a part of that ascension, not just as a citizen and craftsman, but as a naval officer heading toward command. His career ahead would be illustrious by one measure and notorious by others.

As Ruckteschell took his first steps toward his new commands, there were young men throughout Germany who were also moving along paths that would lead them to service under him. On the *Widder*, he would have nearly 400 in his crew. Some of these would be old experienced hands, but the great majority would be young sailors and officers just coming of age and entering the Navy in the 1930s. Three officers who would serve with Ruckteschell—Malte von Schack, Konrad Hoppe, and Jürgen Herr—illustrate the roots and training of this new Navy.

The oldest of these three, Malte von Schack, born on April 17, 1915, in Windhuk, a town in the German colony of South West Africa, came from a family with military roots in the "old" Germany. Malte's grandfather had been in command of a cavalry division in East Prussia. His father, Siegfried von Schack, was an able young cavalry officer at the court of the Grand Duke of Mecklenburg-Schwerin, who was given the opportunity to establish an Imperial horse-breeding farm in South West Africa. There he met and married a teacher, Lucie Meyer. His work there kept him and his family out of Germany during the rigors of World War I, but with the loss of the war and the German colonies under the Treaty of Versailles, the von Schack family returned to Germany in 1921. It was in this atmosphere of postwar economic difficulty and political turmoil that young Malte von Schack began his formal education in Linz-on-the-Rhine, where the family had settled. After completing his high school ed-ucation, he faced his career decisions just as Hitler was consolidating his power and Germany was beginning to move forward. The family cavalry tradition held little interest for this gregarious young man, since the cav-alry had been mechanized into tanks. There were opportunities for recognition and advancement in the Navy, which held more appeal for him, so in 1934, as Ruckteschell was renewing his naval career, Schack, who would be one of his most able young officers, began his own.

That same year, another young man who would serve with Ruck-teschell throughout his raider commands began his naval training. Konrad Hoppe did not come from a military family, but sought the independence it offered him. His grandfather was a respected master builder and mason who owned a successful company. When he died, his youngest son, Konrad's uncle, took over the company, which struggled during the economic depression. Concerned for his son's welfare, Konrad's father fought for his share of the business. The family strife was intolerable to Konrad, and he looked for a way out. Along with most boys he knew, he had been in the Hitler Youth and was accustomed to the uni-forms and discipline of the military life upon which the youth program was modeled. In 1934, a naval recruiting officer came to his school and Konrad responded to his "sea stories." He saw a way to achieve his inde-pendence and relieve the family stress; he made his decision and entered the Navy. His first training took place at the Stralsund Naval Training School, followed by a training cruise in the outdated 1902 battleship *Schlesian,* where he learned practical seamanship. He then went on to a year of training at the Officer Training School in Flensburg, the same handsome brick school where Ruckteschell had been in the inaugural class. After more training in the small cruiser *Königsberg,* Konrad decided to go into the new area of naval aviation. He received training in naviga-tion, naval gunnery, torpedo operations, and radio work, but Hoppe's specialty was as an aviation observer. In October 1938, he was assigned as a Oberleutnant to the naval air base on Borkum, an island in the North Sea off the northern German city of Emden. Life was good here for the young officer, who enjoyed his administrative work, life on the island, and the people, particularly the young ladies. Although the rumblings of war could be distinctly heard, Konrad Hoppe would look back sixty years later at his time on Borkum and say it was the best time of his life.

While Hoppe and Schack were getting their early naval training, an-other young man who would serve with Ruckteschell was receiving train-ing of a different sort. Jürgen Herr, several years younger than Hoppe and Schack, was an educational pioneer. In 1936, he became the first ex-change student from a non-English-speaking country to attend the Kent

School in Kent, Connecticut. This fine private secondary school, located in the beautiful hills of western Connecticut, had a strong academic reputation and was innovative. They took a risk having a German student attend. Jürgen Herr also took a risk and showed real courage as the first in this new program. In the summer of 1936, Jürgen attended a summer camp in Maine and in the fall semester was a student at Kent, where he made lifelong friends. The sad reality, however, was that in less than a year after he returned to Germany, he was in naval training that would lead him into a war in which his former classmates from Kent would be on the opposite side.

Herr's father was a career Army officer in the tank corps and would rise, during the conflict ahead, to the exalted four-star rank of General der Panzertruppe. With the renewal of the German Navy, it was a logical move for Jürgen Herr to enroll in the officer training class of October 1937. After his initial training at Stralsund, he was fortunate to make his training cruise on the proud new square-rigged training bark *Horst Wessel*, which is today the U.S. Coast Guard bark *Eagle*. The ship went first to the Canary Islands, then across the Atlantic to Trinidad and up to Bermuda before heading home during the summer of 1938. Herr considered this the best of his Navy experiences. Another cruise in the old *Schlesien* took him to Havana, Barbados, Jamaica, and Cork, Ireland. He was completing his naval training in the Marineschule at Flensburg in 1939 when the war began.

With all this thorough, modern training, these three intelligent young men, among others, were prepared to join Hellmuth von Ruckteschell and go to war; but the question would be raised as to how well Ruckteschell himself had been prepared to assume command in this new Navy. The expansion of the Navy after the Anglo-German Naval Agreement of 1935, which relaxed the constraints imposed by the Treaty of Versailles, would both facilitate the rehabilitation of Ruckteschell's naval career and complicate his life.

The five years following his reinstatement in the Navy as a reserve officer were years of contrasts and contradictions for Hellmuth von Ruckteschell. While it might have been logical for him to remain in Bremen near the major naval installations, he sold his house there in 1935. This must have been difficult, since it was his own design and workmanship that he was selling. This was the house he had shared with Annemarie, and it must have held memories, good and bad. With the economy still poor, and lacking real business acumen, he retreated to the famous spa town of Baden-Baden in the Black Forest, where his brothers Walter and Gerhard lived, and set up a workshop with Gerhard.

Apparently at this point, the intellectual Ruckteschell, in his search for spiritualism, became intrigued by the religious sect, the Christian Community, an outgrowth of anthroposophy, the philosophy of Rudolf Steiner. There was a slight family connection with Steiner, since Ruckteschell's older sister, Margarethe, had married Edward F. A. von Sivers in 1879, and in 1914, Rudolf Steiner married Marie von Sivers. In addition, Marie von Sivers was distantly related to the von Ruckteschell family. This connection may have brought Hellmuth under the influence of Steiner at an impressionable age. Since Steiner was a sculptor and building designer himself, as well as an advocate of art and music, Ruckteschell may have emulated him as he designed and built his own home and became an accomplished sculptor in wood. Ruckteschell's spiritualism and religious convictions influenced his life, and in many ways contributed to the enigma that he became.

Immediately upon his return to the Black Forest, the contrasts in his new life were apparent. He was at the same time the typical woodworker, the German "everyman," but also the decorated naval officer, with his discipline and distinction. He took two-week naval training courses while, in the same period, attending the art academy in Karlsruhe. Amid these divergent forces in his life, he found a person who would be his steadfast partner for the rest of his days. In 1938, he married a widow, Amalie Margaret Femerey Reinhardt, who, with a son and two daughters from her Reinhardt marriage, brought an instant family into his life. The extended von Ruckteschell family, including Gerhard and his family and Hellmuth and his new family, moved together to Markenhof, near

Kirchzarten. This remained Hellmuth von Ruckteschell's home for the rest of his life, although as fate would have it, he would spend precious little time there. He was soon to be called to active duty, and his life and the lives of hundreds of others would be transformed by his actions in the war that was about to break out.

Chapter 5

RAIDER!

t would have been difficult for these officers who were completing their training on the threshold of war to imagine the ship on which they would serve. There were many possibilities: pocket battleships, cruisers, destroyers, torpedo boats, and the submarine U-boats. Young officers like Konrad Hoppe envisioned their own heroism in battle and craved the opportunity. If shown a picture of the ship in which they would soon serve, they would have been grossly disappointed. They would have seen an ordinary Hamburg America Line freighter that was making voyages to the Far East. To a naval officer, this was not the ship of which dreams of glory are made.

The Hamburg America Line (HAPAG) was founded on May 12, 1847, and prospered during the second half of the nineteenth century serving the immigrant routes, carrying tens of thousands to the shores of America. A marketing genius named Albert Ballin joined the firm, and under his direction HAPAG built the world's largest passenger ship and originated the concept of the pleasure cruise. In 1900, its new liner, the *Deutschland*, set the transatlantic speed record on her maiden voyage, maintaining nearly 22.5 knots on her trip to New York and winning the coveted Blue Riband. On the eve of the First World War, HAPAG was the world's largest shipping company, with 175 ships. The war was a disaster not only for Germany, but for HAPAG as well, as it lost its entire fleet. Despondent over the ruin of his firm, Albert Ballin committed suicide on November 9, 1918.

HAPAG was not prepared to fold, however, and the first ship in its rebuilding program, appropriately named the *Albert Ballin,* was commissioned in 1923. During the next five years, the company added more ships and reestablished its old routes. Launched on December 12, 1929, the *Neumark,* constructed by Howaldtswerke AG, was the first of six freighters designed for the Far East service to the Dutch East Indies. In 1930, despite the developing economic depression, HAPAG built the five remaining freighters using five different shipyards and put them into service. Within three years, the German government would become the largest shareholder in the Hamburg America Line, and this would put the *Neumark* on a course for government service. In the fall of 1939, only weeks after France and England declared war on Germany following the invasion of Poland, the freighter *Neumark* began her transformation into the formidable raider named *Widder.*

The tradition of the raider goes back to ancient times. Pirates themselves evoke a fascination and romantic admiration that is ill deserved in light of the brutal tactics they employ. Certain acts that are regarded as piracy when practiced by individuals or warlords are, when practiced by nations, judged more ambiguously. Sir Francis Drake, England's great seaman of the sixteenth century, was certainly a raider. He sought retribution from the Spanish for his own losses, and for those of his nation, under the sanction of his queen, Elizabeth I. During the next 250 years, the practice was legitimized under the issuance of "letters of marque," documents issued by governments, including that of the United States, to privately owned vessels, authorizing them to harass and attack ships of an opposing nation. Sailing under a letter of marque transformed a pirate into a potential national hero. By the mid–nineteenth century, the "civilized" nations of the world had come together and theoretically put an end to this practice through an international agreement signed in Paris in 1856.

The respite was short-lived; in less than five years, the United States was torn by civil war and the less industrialized southern states of the Confederacy were desperate. They had an insignificant Navy and few merchant ships with which to face the northern states with their strong United States Navy and a robust fleet of merchant ships and whalers. In addition, the Union had numerous shipyards that could continue to build vessels. The Confederacy initially authorized letters of marque but also developed a longer-term strategy to build and deploy raiders. This Confederate plan involved English shipyards, the recruitment of British sailors, and the collusion of the British government, which saw advantage in a Confederate victory. These ships would be the precise models for the activities of the *Widder* and the other German raiders of World War II.

The CSS *Alabama* was the most successful of the Confederate raiders, and the most dreaded by Union merchant shipping. There are remarkable similarities between aspects of the *Alabama*'s activities under the command of the dashing Raphael Semmes and those of Ruckteschell in his raiders. Both men sailed under false colors and normally sank vessels rather than taking them as prizes. They both took prisoners onto their ships, but were eager to put them off onto other ships or in their own boats if near land. In addition, they both dealt with the ambiguities of neutral ships and, on one occasion, successfully attacked two ships at the same time. Despite these similarities, however, the times and the character of these two raider captains would create marked differences in their tactics.

The result of their raider project did not have the benefits the Southerners and the English envisioned. The Confederacy, of course, lost the war and all that had been invested in the raider campaign. The British sailors in some instances lost their lives, and in virtually all cases never received the total pay and particularly the prize money they had been promised. When its involvement was revealed, the English government suffered loss of prestige, and economic loss when an international tribunal determined that England would have to give the United States the enormous retribution payment of $15,500,000.

For decades after the American Civil War, the issue of commerce raiders and the conversion of merchant vessels into warships was unclear and continued to be debated. Many nations realized that in times of war the large, fast merchant ships would make logical additions to their conventional navies. These countries developed contingency plans to convert ships, usually passenger liners, into well-armed naval vessels. The Second Hague Peace Conference in 1907 issued a declaration detailing the "accepted" protocol for this type of ship. She had to fly the flag of her nation, be under the orders of that nation, and have a captain appointed by that nation. The crew had to function under naval discipline and follow the laws of war. Within these and some other strictures, merchant ships were considered legitimate naval vessels.

There was another distinction, however: Were these ships commerce protectors or commerce destroyers? Was the ship a merchantman that had been armed and converted into a warship with the purpose of escorting other ships or patrolling shipping areas to defend against attacks? Or, was the ship converted into a warship with the intention of preying upon the merchant ships of the enemy? If, as was often the case, these attacks were carried out under disguise and subterfuge, then the ship was definitely a raider.

In World War I, both the British and the Germans used armed merchant ships with varying degrees of success. Converted passenger ships proved inefficient since they consumed enormous amounts of coal and had to refuel often. Freighters, although slower, succeeded where the passenger liners failed because of their ordinary appearance, low fuel consumption, and ability to carry large amounts of fuel. German Korvettenkapitän Count Nikolaus Dohna-Schlodien demonstrated the real potential of such a ship. Assigned to use a converted merchantman, renamed the *Möwe,* to plant a minefield, he then turned to raiding with the innocent-looking *Möwe,* and returned home having sunk fifteen merchant ships. With this success, other raiders put to sea. The most romantic, though not the most successful, was the full-rigged sailing ship *Seeadler.* She was the picture of innocence, commanded by the colorful Count Felix von Luckner, who for decades after the war gave fascinating lectures around the world about his wartime adventures. Another ship, the *Wolf,* entered the record books for her voyage of fifteen months; it lasted so long that the authorities notified the next of kin that the ship had probably been lost. Her commander, the severe Dr. Karl August Neger, was given the Pour le Mérite award, the famous "Blue Max," and his book became the text for the raider captains of World War II.

The use of raiders was a natural option for the ill-prepared German Navy when war with England broke out in 1939. By the terms of the London Naval Treaty of 1935, the German Navy was limited to 35 percent of the Royal Navy in surface ships and 45 percent in submarines. There was a provision that the submarine force could equal that of the British if the Germans gave up tonnage in other categories. To obtain this provision, the Germans agreed that, if war developed, their submarines would abide by the rules of international law, which prohibited the sinking of merchant ships without warning. By insisting on this agreement, the British were reinforcing their long-held position opposing unrestricted submarine warfare. Initially, Hitler was convinced he could carry out his plans for German expansion without being drawn into war with Great Britain, for which he would need a powerful Navy. As a consequence, in the mid-1930s, his emphasis was on Army and Air Force development for his land conquests rather than naval expansion. By 1938, however, Hitler was less sure of his ability to avoid conflict with England. He exercised the option for submarine parity and then abrogated the 1935 agreement altogether. Germany was on a path to war with the world's greatest naval power and, despite a sudden priority on U-boat construction, was underequipped for a major war at sea.

At the outbreak of war with France and Britain on September 3, 1939, Erich Raeder was the Commander in Chief of the German Navy. Grossadmiral Raeder is quoted as saying that, with its lack of ships and preparedness, his Navy "would be able to do little more than show that it could die courageously." The conflict that Hitler had thought would not occur had started, and the German Navy had few resources at its disposal. As in World War I, the Germans put great stock in the U-boats, but it would take significant time to build up that powerful arm of the Navy. Raeder knew from his experience in the earlier war how dependent the British Isles were on their merchant ships and that this was their point of vulnerability. By 1939, over 2,500 British ships kept almost 70 million tons of supplies flowing into the island nation each year. The German strategy was to curtail this flow, and thereby drain the will of the British. A quick way to harass the British merchant ships was with raiders. Existing merchant ships could be taken out of service, quickly converted, and sent to sea to begin the offensive. No one expected the raiders to make a serious contribution to the war effort through the tonnage sunk. It was thought, however, that the psychological impact would be significant, and that the Allies would divert warships from other duties to search for the raiders, straining their naval resources. While the attacks did have a serious impact, they did not produce the debilitating and demoralizing effect the Germans had hoped to create. Once again, as in World War I, the Germans misjudged the strength and grit of the British people and their merchant mariners.

Two days after the declaration of war, the call went out for merchant raiders. The Deschimag Shipyard in Bremen was ordered to begin the conversion of the Hansa Line ship *Goldenfels* into a raider and the Blohm & Voss Shipyard in Hamburg received orders to carry out the conversion of two Hamburg America Line ships, the *Kurmark* and the *Neumark*. The German naval command wanted these ships operational within months. By the end of November, nine more ships were ordered to be converted, with the intention of having twelve raiders on the oceans by early summer of 1940. It was quickly realized that this schedule could not be kept. With the entire German military in accelerated mobilization, every commodity needed for the buildup was precious, and each military program fought to advance its own project. The shipyards struggled to get the steel, aluminum, deck machinery, radios, compasses, and weapons required for the raiders. They were also faced with the daunting task of transforming these freighters into fierce warships without altering their appearance as merchant ships.

The conversion of the *Neumark* posed the typical challenges for the designers and workers at Blohm & Voss. This ship was a medium-sized freighter of 477 feet in length, with a gross tonnage of 7,851. This gave her a carrying capacity of over 600,000 cubic feet of space for bulk cargo like grain, plus an additional 100,000 cubic feet of refrigerated space for perishable cargo. By 1939, the boilers that produced the steam for her four turbines, originally fired by coal, had been converted to fuel oil. A ship of this size in the merchant service carried a crew of 64. Instead, the *Neumark,* after she became the raider *Widder,* would have to accommodate a crew of over 360 officers and men. This meant altering the cargo space into berthing decks where the crew slept, a mess deck for meals, and all the workspaces required to make the *Widder* as independent as possible for a long voyage.

She needed a machine shop with all the equipment to carry out major repairs, which, with her fifteen-year-old engines, would be utilized extensively. In addition to the accommodations for the crew, she needed space to store fuel, food to feed the hundreds on board, spare parts, and other supplies. Storage for the dangerous ammunition for the guns and the mechanisms for getting those munitions to the guns was essential. The *Widder* carried two airplanes that had to be kept out of sight and sheltered from the weather until launched on their reconnaissance flights. A very important aspect of her conversion consumed additional precious space: accommodations for prisoners.

Those who sent these raiders to sea understood that after merchant ships had been captured by the raiders, their crews would be picked up from their lifeboats and housed in special secure accommodations deep in the hull. In the *Widder* and other raiders, there was space for officer prisoners and a separate space for the sailors. In the racial tenor of the times, there was even an effort to provide different prisoner accommodations for whites and prisoners of color. Of course, the accommodation of prisoners included the need for extra food storage, since they had to be fed while they were onboard.

While it was difficult to subdivide the interior space and calculate all the ramifications these alterations would have on the stability of the ship and her handling characteristics, the most vexing job was on the exterior. The *Widder* was going to literally bristle with guns, and yet she had to appear as a merchant ship. This appearance had to deceive observers on other ships viewing from a distance as well as reconnaissance aircraft making repeated inspections from above. One flaw could spell disaster if Allied naval forces were alerted and the hunter became the hunted. The first consideration was the positioning of the biggest guns, six First World War–vintage naval artillery pieces that fired shells 15cm, or 5.9 inches, in diameter. These powerful weapons needed strong, reinforced decks to carry their 5 tons of weight and absorb the recoil. All but one of them were mounted on the main deck, where the obstruction of the solid-steel bulwark around the deck presented a problem. A simple but laborious technique was used: the bulwark was divided into sections and hinged at the bottom. On command, the crew crouching behind the bulwark would release the sections and fold them back onto the deck or down over the sides. Four of these big guns were mounted on the main deck forward of the superstructure, two each on the port and starboard sides, behind the collapsible bulwarks.

The drawback of this configuration was that only two of the four guns on the forward end of the ship could fire at the same time, since they were on opposite sides of the ship. The other two guns were mounted behind the superstructure on the centerline of the ship, so they could be aimed to either port or starboard and the *Widder* could, therefore, bring four of her heavy guns to bear on a target. The next challenge was to make these large guns disappear. On some other ships, guns were concealed inside artificial lifeboats or disguised as deck machinery. On the *Widder*, they were made to look like ordinary deck cargo and deckhouses. Freighters often carried large items such as locomotive fireboxes and other pieces of machinery and equipment that were too large to stow below as cargo on deck, often crated to protect them from the elements. The *Widder*'s "deck cargo" would consist of two large, round reels of cable, one on each side just forward of the superstructure. Of course, these false reels concealed guns. The other four guns were concealed in small "deck houses" forward and aft of the superstructure, designed to be opened quickly, freeing their guns for action. With this armament, the ship had the capability of firing a four-gun salvo of explosive shells every few seconds at a range of 10 miles! She was already a powerful ship.

A long-range 7.5cm cannon was added, right on the bow of the ship. It was a formidable weapon that could fire to both port and starboard and was used primarily as a "stopping gun" to fire the warning shot across the bow of a potential victim to "encourage" her to stop. At the other end of the ship was another lethal weapon, an automatic twin-barreled 3.7cm antiaircraft gun with the innocuous nickname of "pompom." Its name came from the sound emitted as the barrels alternated their fire. While designed as an antiaircraft weapon, this was a terrifying, destructive gun when used in surface combat. On either side of the bridge, and also just aft of the cannon on the bow, were four smaller, but equally deadly, 2cm rapid-fire antiaircraft guns.

Obviously, the *Widder* was well armed and able to subdue and maul any merchantman she encountered, but she also needed to be able to sink her victims. In some instances, once the enemy ship was abandoned, a boarding party was sent to place explosive charges aboard the ship and detonate them from a safe distance. The raiders also had the capability of torpedoing their targets. Hiding these large torpedo tubes, which fired 21-inch-diameter torpedoes, was challenging. On the *Widder,* they were mounted inside the hull, beneath the bridge on either side, with counter-balanced steel doors hinged on the top that simply swung out like awnings. The final armament of the ship was two Heinkel He 114B seaplanes that vastly increased the surveillance range of the raider and carried bombs as well. These aircraft were designed with wings that folded back for compact storage.

In the early stages of the *Widder*'s conversion, the ship's crew was assigned and the critical decision was made as to who would command this vessel. Regular naval officers, the first choice for the assignment, were apparently reluctant to take this command. It is unclear whether this was because they were skeptical of the work of raiders or were shying away from this specific ship. Certainly for regular naval officers, with sufficient seniority to be considered for command, the idea of going to sea in a dowdy freighter, no matter how well armed, and skulking around after virtually defenseless merchantmen, might have little appeal. They probably hoped for command of a ship with more opportunity for glory. Circumstances demonstrated this to be shortsighted, as the conquests of the

Widder would bring ample glory to her crew and commanding officer. The *Widder*'s condition was certainly another consideration. A large, decade-old, and slow ship, she had an even older steam propulsion plant that consumed large quantities of fuel and was not as efficient and reliable as the newer ships powered by large diesel engines. For whatever reasons, no fewer than four naval officers were offered command of this raider and declined the opportunity.

Hellmuth von Ruckteschell's quiet life in the Black Forest with his new family dissolved in 1939. Two days after the declaration of war, and on the same day that the order was issued for the conversion of the *Neumark*, Ruckteschell, a Kapitänleutnant in the reserves, was called to active service. He reported to Bremen for training and three months later, two days after Christmas, was given command of the *Cobra*, a mine-laying ship. This was a very short period of command because, as he was being trained and assigned to the *Cobra*, one officer after another turned down command of the *Widder*. After only twenty days in command of the *Cobra*, he was relieved of that assignment, and on February 18, 1940, assumed command of the *Widder*, with the new rank of Korvettenkapitän. Younger regular Navy officers might have had the luxury of turning down command of the *Widder*, but Ruckteschell, on the eve of his fiftieth birthday and a reserve officer, could not be so selective. He would take what he was given and definitely make the most of it.

The ambitious goal of having the first three raiders, the *Atlantis*, the *Orion*, and the *Widder* at sea by winter had long since been forfeited as the shipyards wrestled with their complicated tasks. Other factors, such as mechanical malfunctions and ice in the Baltic Sea, caused further delay. Among the officers of the *Widder*, most of whom were regular Navy, there was some trepidation about having a reservist in command. Indeed, Ruckteschell was the only reserve officer to have command of a raider. The officers' concern increased when, soon after he assumed command, their Captain became ill with the flu and was unable to assist in getting the ship ready for sea. The officers, including Torpedo Officer Malte von Schack, Aviation Officer Konrad Hoppe, and the Executive Officer,

Ernst-Günther Heinicke, carried out the preparation of the ship and brought the ship through her trials.

While it is difficult to determine precisely what was taken on board in the way of supplies for the voyage, some sense can be gained from the account of what was taken on the raider *Komet*, which made her way to her area of operation in the Pacific Ocean the hard way, through the Northeast Passage. With the help of Russian icebreakers, she crossed through the frozen seas over the top of Russia and entered the Pacific from the north. Her Captain, Robert Eyssen, had been a career officer since the First World War and was well connected in Navy supply circles, so he seemed to be able to get what he wanted. He also had a reputation for the high life and lavish parties, so the quantities of some of the things he carried would exceed those that would be carried on other raiders. This, on the other hand, is somewhat offset by the fact that the small *Komet* carried 100 fewer in crew. In food supplies and other consumables, the *Komet* began her voyage with 35.6 tons of meats, 30 tons of potatoes, 60 tons of flour, 38.1 tons of vegetables, 12.3 tons of fats, 3 tons of coffee, 5 tons of marmalade, 12,000 cans of milk, 10,000 eggs, 1.2 million cigarettes, 46,000 cigars, 100,000 liters of beer, 5,000 bottles of liquor, 25,000 bars of chocolate, and 6,000 packages of cookies. She also had, for her crew's entertainment, 99 movies, 540 phonograph records, and a library of 569 books. While this inventory may seem abundant, these ships had to be self-sufficient for months on end and provisions for a crew of 364 on the *Widder* would require similar quantities. It seems that the *Komet* had everything imaginable, except perhaps a piano, something the *Widder* did have, since Aviation Officer Konrad Hoppe was an avid amateur pianist and made certain he could continue to play his classical music during the voyage.

On the business side of things, the *Widder* was loaded with 4,500 tons of fuel oil, giving her a cruising range that could take her around the world at 10 knots, 1,800 shells for the big 15cm guns, 4,000 rounds for the 3.7cm pompom, 8,000 rounds for the 2cm antiaircraft machine guns, 200 bombs for the airplanes, and additional torpedoes for her four torpedo tubes. Certainly, the *Widder* was prepared for a long and violent cruise.

The other two raiders of the first group had already run the gauntlet of the Royal Navy, which surrounded the German ports, and were at sea. The *Atlantis* left in early March and the *Orion* on March 29. By early May of 1940, the *Widder* was ready for sea.

Chapter 6

THE *WIDDER* AT SEA AND AT WAR

The Captains of raiders were given the unusual privilege of naming their ships. Large warships carried names with national and patriotic significance, such as the *Admiral Graf Spee* or the *Deutschland,* while smaller vessels were designated by letters and numbers, such as the UZ-21. In official communications and records, the raiders went by the simple title of "Ship" followed by a number. For his ship, *Schiff 21,* Ruckteschell chose an appropriately strong and symbolic name, the *Widder,* meaning "ram." It was a powerful image of the male sheep with his bold, curving horns ready to challenge those in his territory, just as the ship would do. A depiction of the ram's head, along with the Nazi eagle and swastika above it, appeared on the banner of the shipboard newspaper, and certainly Ruckteschell and his crew anticipated living up to their forceful symbol. When this name was submitted for approval, it received immediate endorsement. There was, however, another reason why this name was chosen, a very personal reason, which may not have been appreciated by either the naval authorities or even the crew. Born at the end of March, Ruckteschell was an Aries, symbolized by the ram, and this designation for his ship made her, in a way, a personal extension of the Captain himself.

There were questions about Ruckteschell's suitability for this command, including some discussion about his having kicked a sailor in one of his fits of fury. This swing of temperament, which some of his fellow officers described as "choleric," was a constant on the voyage in the *Widder*, where the officers in particular had to be wary of the Captain's moods. Another consideration was Ruckteschell's health. He had developed some problems as a stressed U-boat commander, and it is probable that the difficulties of life as a fugitive and the hardships of the 1920s and '30s exacerbated them. On the *Widder*, he was plagued by stomach problems and wicked migraine headaches. Though never robust, he was tough and pressed on with his duties. The strain carried over into his relationships with his officers and men, adding stress to their lives as well.

On Sunday, May 5, 1940, the crew of the *Widder* expected shore leave after a church service was held on board, which everyone was required to attend. Immediately after the service, to their surprise and dismay, Ruckteschell ordered the crew to prepare to get under way. They steered for the entrance to the Kaiser Wilhelm Canal, today known as the Kiel Canal, which led to the Elbe River and into the danger zone. Since the departure from Kiel had not been announced, there were few family and friends to see them off. One exception was a woman waving from the Holtenau High Bridge over the canal. This was the Captain's wife, who obviously knew in advance of the departure. The *Widder* began a voyage that would last precisely 180 days.

The Seekriegsleitung (SKL), or Sea Warfare Command, determined that the *Widder* would have one of the most important portions of the Atlantic as her exclusive raiding territory. The primary transatlantic shipping lanes for the heavy traffic from North American ports to England were to the north of Ruckteschell's territory in the central North Atlantic and would be the province of the U-boats, but there was ample shipping traversing his area to and from Europe, the Mediterranean, the Caribbean, and South America. His area was vast, consisting of millions of square miles where the *Widder* could hunt for enemy ships without interference. Before he reached that area and came under the command of the SKL, however, he would have to make his escape from the war zone around Germany, with its constant threats from the Royal Navy. During this transit to her area of operation, the *Widder* was under the control of Naval Group West, based in Wilhelmshaven.

At the crack of dawn, less than twenty-four hours after leaving Kiel, Naval Group West ordered the *Widder* out of the Elbe River. With an escort of three fast patrol vessels and protective aircraft overhead, it was probably gratifying to those on the *Widder* that their ship warranted this much protection, but disturbing that they were venturing into an area sufficiently dangerous to require it. It was only a matter of hours before the first ominous sign, a periscope, was spotted, but with her escorts the *Widder* was able to elude this potential attacker. The tension rose as all aboard the raider realized that the threat was real. At 4:29 that afternoon, the wakes of two torpedoes were spotted. Now on the receiving end of a British submarine attack, Ruckteschell, the veteran U-boat skipper of twenty years before, had enough time to maneuver to avoid the torpedoes. To frustrate further attacks, the *Widder* and her consorts accelerated to her top speed of 14.8 knots, altered their courses frequently, and zigzagged their way north, making it extremely difficult for a submarine to get the vessels in her sights. After sunset of their first day, with two escorts ahead and one following, they were able to steer a straight course toward the Norwegian coast.

Since the outbreak of the war, Norway had functioned as a neutral nation with sympathy for the British cause. The Norwegians relied upon this neutrality as protection from German invasion. The Germans, however, were concerned that a minefield could be stretched from the Orkney Islands to the Norwegian coast, as had been done in World War I. This would bottle up the German U-boats and other ships or cut them off from their bases and supplies. Equally as important, it would cut off the flow of Swedish iron ore from the Porjus region that was transported by train to the northern Norwegian port of Narvik and south by sea to Germany. This, of course, was the area in which Ruckteschell had worked as a fugitive. The strategic importance of Norway outweighed its neutrality as far as the Germans were concerned. On April 9, combined German Navy, Army, and Air Force units made simultaneous, devastating assaults on the major cities of Oslo, Kristiansand, Stavanger, Bergen, Trondheim, and Narvik. The Norwegian campaign lasted less than two months, the country's King leaving to live in exile on June 7. The *Widder* entered Norwegian territorial waters on May 6 and was in the midst of an active war zone. The Germans had secured the major ports during the first month of the campaign, but there was the hazard of mines. Twenty-four hours after departing the Elbe and after the two submarine threats, the small flotilla worked its way through the nerve-wracking minefield along the coast, with its own minesweeping gear out and following two small minesweeping escorts. One additional periscope was spotted astern, but no attack was made. With five mines cut and rendered harmless, the *Widder* rested safely in Bergen's outer anchorage.

After a respite of twenty-four hours in Bergen, which, although in German hands was still subject to Allied air attacks, the *Widder*, escorted now by only two minesweepers, got under way in the middle of the night, using darkness and bad weather to mask her travel. One of the minesweepers was lost in an air attack on the morning of May 9 as they left Bergen. Now it was time for the *Widder* to transform herself from a nondescript German freighter with naval escorts into the neutral Swedish freighter *Narvik*. Everyone, from the off-duty boiler tenders to senior petty officers, to the officers themselves, worked feverishly to implement the disguise. The *Widder* now sailed alone and was particularly vulnerable as the weather cleared. She had been promised air reconnaissance to alert her to danger, but the air cover did not materialize. Ruckteschell retreated into Bindness Bay in the Hjeltefjorden north of Bergen to await either air support or foul weather with its poor visibility to mask an escape. Eyes on shore might see the ship, so the majority of the crew were confined below for the three days they remained at anchor in Bindness Bay. Those who were allowed on deck wore civilian clothes. This precaution paid off, as nine British aircraft flew over the ship and no suspicions were raised.

Sailors always feel there is bad luck associated with a ship getting under way on the 13th of the month. With one hour to spare, the *Widder* went back to sea at 11:00 P.M. on the night of May 12, heading farther north. As dawn broke, her protective reconnaissance plane, a Heinkel

He-III, appeared overhead. Rain closed in, however, and the air support was withdrawn. Just before 1:00 in the afternoon, an ominous image emerged from a rain squall in the far distance. Ruckteschell took evasive action, but the other ship followed and drew nearer. It seemed the disguise had not worked as well as they had hoped, since the vessel in pursuit opened fire on the *Widder* at a range of 8 miles. Her first shots fell short, but a battle was under way. The disguised raider continued to attempt to flee, but the attacker, the British submarine HMS *Clyde*, acting on suspicion that a true neutral vessel would have stopped after the first shots and allowed boarding for inspection, pressed the attack. Ruckteschell could not tolerate this, and he unmasked the stern gun of the *Widder*. An artillery duel began that lasted for an hour and a half. Numerous shots were fired with no apparent hits.

At about 3:30 in the afternoon, the submarine broke off the attack after one of the raider's rounds landed precariously close. Ruckteschell's luck had held and his skill had gotten his ship through the battle, but there was further danger. It was highly probable that other British ships were deployed to search for this mysterious freighter with her professional marksmanship. To avoid discovery Ruckteschell once again retreated. He anchored in Sandsfjord, north of Standlandet, and near the island of Rundoy, from where he reported the battle to his commanders and requested further air reconnaissance. The following morning, he was informed that air survey reports indicated no British ships in the area, and the *Widder* once again returned to sea, in stormy conditions that helped protect her. She headed away from the coast, across the sea-lanes used by ships making the passage from Britain to Narvik, and by May 15 crossed the Arctic Circle. After encounters with four submarines that included two attacks, transits of minefields, and the danger of air attacks, the *Widder* had successfully completed the first portion of her breakout. The intense combat area of the North Sea and the Norwegian coast was behind her, but what lay ahead was the hazardous voyage above Iceland and then down through the Denmark Strait, between Iceland and Greenland

The notoriously high fuel consumption of the *Widder* called for resupply before she could make her run to the mid-Atlantic. A rendezvous was arranged with the replenishment ship *Nordmark*, well above the Arctic Circle, near the island of Jan Mayen. When they saw the *Nordmark*, the crew of the raider was sobered by the evidence of the new danger they faced—ice. The *Nordmark* had serious gaping damage at both her bow and her stern from collisions with icebergs, and yet was able to transfer the needed oil to the *Widder*, which then turned to the southwest toward her destination. The run through the ice of the Denmark Strait was uneventful, with the exception of maneuvering to stay out of sight of a steamer making her way from Reykjavik to Jan Mayen. The transit was made easier because of the scouting done by a German trawler that preceded the *Widder*. Despite the fog and ice, they emerged from the strait on May 20 after a harrowing two-week breakout. Now in the Atlantic, just off Cape Farewell on the southern tip of Greenland, the *Widder* ran straight south on the 40-degree west longitude line into her area of operation. During this portion of the voyage, a severe vibration developed when she increased speed and, after sending a diver overboard in calm seas, the crew discovered that the *Widder* had not transited the Arctic seas unscathed. One blade of the single propeller had been bent and could not be repaired at sea; this would limit their speed right from the beginning of their operations.

To get to her mid-Atlantic destination, the *Widder* had to cross the main shipping route between North America and England, the sea-lanes that were frequented by the steady stream of convoys. The *Anglo-Saxon* had passed through these waters a month before on her way from Halifax to London, and she would pass through again in less than a week on her way from London to Hampton Roads; but fate would keep the two ships from meeting for another three months. The *Widder*'s objective was to make her way through these waters undetected so she would arouse no suspicions. With her keen-eyed lookouts aloft, she was able to avoid the few ships spotted and on the 26th, now under control of the SKL, she entered her massive operational area, which was larger than the entire United States. It was a staggering task to work such a large area, but within it there were some traditional sea-lanes that Ruckteschell felt might be the most productive. Refueled by the *Königsberg* on June 7, the *Widder* then positioned herself in a location used by ships making the trip between the Azores and Trinidad.

In less than three days, her first victim came into view and the raider immediately set her course and speed to intercept what the Captain determined was a tanker, carrying only ballast, on her way to Trinidad to pick up a cargo of oil. As the first real test of the *Widder*'s disguise, her tactics worked perfectly but were heavy-handed. The tanker carried a defensive weapon, a single 4-inch gun, and Ruckteschell took no chances. When the *Widder* was about 4 miles away, the Captain opened fire with all the guns that could be brought to bear on his victim. Although the first two salvos missed, the third found its mark, tearing down the ship's antennas so she had no opportunity to get out a distress message. The tanker *British Petrol,* on her way from Glasgow to Trinidad, became a blazing inferno. Most of her crew fled to the far side of the ship and got into lifeboats. Eighteen minutes after the first shots were fired, a torpedo exploded deep in the ship, and a half hour later the ship disappeared from the surface of the sea.

Completely unscathed, the *Widder* maneuvered to pick up the dazed crew from her first conquest. Forty-five officers and men were taken on board, and the prisoner accommodations had their first occupants. The raider's infirmary, or sick bay, was also put to use, since 9 of the sailors were wounded, 5 of them seriously. By the next morning, one of the wounded Englishmen, Courthorpe Carrington, had died, and in a show of decency that also demonstrated his religious orientation to the Rudolf Steiner–inspired Christian Community, Ruckteschell had the sailor's body committed to the deep in a ceremony held before the German crew and the sailor's former shipmates who were now prisoners. His words at the service are fascinating:

> English and German seamen, comrades!
>
> We are standing here this morning before the mortal frame of a man whom death has taken from us.

The fate which today lets men go against each other so that they kill and wound and torture each other, only makes sense by awakening us in order to look for and find the good parts in us.

Around us stretches the wide familiar sea; above us the vault of the eternal heaven with the sun during daytime and the stars during the night. They follow God's rules moving over the water.

Following the same rules, the souls float down from heaven in order to fulfill their fate as human beings.

Pretty much as the phenomenon of a caterpillar which changes in its frame and must pass in order to give life to a pretty, colorful butterfly, our mortal frame must wither.

But then, out of it rises the soul as a sunbird liberated up to the creator in order to get there [in heaven] new forces for another journey to the earth till mankind has learned to live in peace with each other under the sun.

We want to accompany the liberated soul of our comrade with friendliness and affectionate prayers and ask him to send us power out of the sunny empire so that we learn to get along with each other as peace-loving humans.

Yes, so be it.

This speech was held in honor of:

Courthorpe Carrington 2/18/1909 to 6/14/1940
by Korvettenkapitän Hellmuth Ruckteschell
Commander of the German auxiliary cruiser *Widder*

This remarkable document summarizes the enigma that is Hellmuth von Ruckteschell. In the First World War, he had been an aggressive U-boat captain, sending many ships and sailors to their deaths. In this first brutal attack of his World War II career, he violently pounded his victim into submission and then waxed poetic at the sailor's funeral service. His words reflect many of the tenets of Rudolph Steiner's philosophy of anthroposophy, with its images of nature, mysticism, and the "recycling" of souls. It will be increasingly difficult to relate the man behind these words to the warrior who, with increasing vigor while serving in the *Widder,* amassed a record that brought him before a war crimes tribunal at the end of the war. It seems, in simplest terms, that when his enemy was faceless, Ruckteschell was ruthless; when his enemy became his prisoner, he treated him with consideration, if not always respect.

The next ten days produced more frustration than success, especially with the failure of the seaplanes. The engines of both planes failed, so at the beginning of her operations the *Widder* was stripped of her long-range reconnaissance capabilities, with both planes unrepairable. Ruckteschell decided to dump overboard the 23 tons of highly explosive aviation fuel and the 200 aircraft bombs, each weighing 110 pounds, to lessen the danger to the ship if shells were directed at her.

It was not simply the planes' engines that caused problems. The ship herself had to stop for six hours for work on her valves, the first of many engine problems. As soon as the engine repairs were made, the *Widder* responded to the intelligence report that a tanker was heading her way. For two days she searched and finally spotted a Norwegian tanker, the 9,323-ton *Krossfonn.* In one of the *Widder'*s two bloodless conquests, she fired two warning shots across the bow, transmitted a message to the Norwegians not to use their radios, and displayed the German naval ensign, all of which brought the *Krossfonn* to a halt. This was her first and only "prize of war." The crew added the Norwegians to the prisoners on board and a prize crew from the *Widder* took the *Krossfonn* to Lorient, in German-occupied France.

The *Widder* was soon engaged in a delicate game of international politics as she cruised along the extreme southern edge of her territory, which was the boundary of the Pan-American Neutrality Zone, in which merchant ships could travel without fear of attack. With the variables of imprecise navigation, either the raider or her target might be just in or just out of the zone. While seemingly secure within the Neutrality Zone, a victim steamed into the *Widder'*s path. The action that followed would alter the course of Ruckteschell's life, as it resulted in the first of the charges for which he would later be tried. No warning was given before the heavy 15cm guns opened fire on the seventeen-year-old British freighter *Davisian*. The first seven salvos, each with four 100-pound explosive projectiles, destroyed the ship's radio capability and brought the damaged ship to a halt. When the crew was seen lowering the lifeboats, the *Widder* appropriately ceased fire. Some minutes later, several men were seen moving toward the stern of the ship. Even though the ship had clearly surrendered, Ruckteschell determined that they must have been making a courageous, if foolhardy and virtually suicidal, attempt to reach their ship's gun. He opened up with the deadly 3.7cm pompoms and 2cm machine guns. The projectiles cut the three men to ribbons. This act brought the first charge against Ruckteschell.

The surviving 40 crew members from the *Davisian*, of whom 6 were wounded, 4 seriously, were taken aboard, the captured ship was searched, and supplies of potatoes, canned foods, tobacco, and soap were removed. Attempts to sink the ship by scuttling her failed, and the Germans resorted to a torpedo to send the stubborn ship to the bottom. Now Ruckteschell had an escalating problem: over 100 prisoners on board and his sick bay full of wounded. Working the Neutrality Zone line had been productive, however, and he stayed with that strategy as he pondered the issues of crowding and the depletion of provisions. Many navies of the world served higher-quality food to the officers than to the crew. In an unusual display of equitability, the officers, crew, and prisoners of the *Widder*, as on other raiders, all ate the same food, provided in the same quantities. With more than 100 additional people to feed, there was a potential crisis.

On July 13, the well-disguised raider, without creating alarm, approached within a few miles of the 5,228-ton British freighter *King John*, traveling from London to Vancouver. The firepower of all guns that would bear was then unleashed. The damage was immediate and the ship was apparently beaten, when the Radio Officer, Oberleutnant Kindler, reported that the *King John* was sending an SOS signal. Ferocious fire was once again directed at the ship, with the 3.7cm pompom destroying the bridge and the gun on the stern, where the ammunition also exploded.

The attack was quickly over, but Ruckteschell's prisoner problem intensified.

The *King John*'s crew numbered 59 because they had picked up 21 crewmen from a Panamanian steamer that had been sunk by a U-boat. Ruckteschell now faced an intolerable situation. Not only was this a large contingent, but he clearly had distaste for some of them, since he wrote in his war diary that the crew from the Panamanian steamer included "Yugoslavs, Portuguese, Maltese and a Spaniard, a dirty and lousy pack." He only took on the *King John*'s Captain, Chief Engineer, and 7 wounded crewmen, leaving the others in the boats. A key decision was made, with ramifications that would be debated for years.

Knowing that they were only 240 miles from the Lesser Antilles, Ruckteschell had the *King John*'s lifeboats and the largest of his own lifeboats equipped with food, water, life jackets, sails, and compasses. Forty men and the First Mate from the *Davisian* were added to the crew of the *King John* in the three boats, which were left to make their way to land. Attention turned back to the *King John,* and she proved difficult to sink, requiring the planting of explosive charges on board, the use of one valuable torpedo, and no less than forty-two rounds from the powerful 7.5cm guns. Her Captain, George E. Smith, noted, and would later describe, that Ruckteschell, frustrated by this inconvenience, displayed his severe temper. Rid of the released prisoners in the lifeboats, the *Widder* steamed off to the north at top speed. When out of sight of the boats, she turned sharply to the east to escape the area where it was certain a search would begin once the sailors made it to land and filed their report.

In this instance, Ruckteschell's calculations were correct with regard to the ability of the abandoned sailors to find their way to land, but it is uncertain if he calculated the full consequences of their success. They reached the island of Anguilla on July 18 after a five-day voyage and immediately told their story. The Allied naval authorities now knew the reason why a number of ships were overdue. There were raiders in the Atlantic and they knew one of them was disguised as the Swedish freighter *Narvik*.

This was the first eyewitness account the authorities received. The *Davisian* crew told their story of brutality and started Ruckteschell on the way toward a war crimes trial. The *Widder* now had an urgent need to change her disguise. She had blown her cover, and she headed away from the normal shipping lanes to make the conversion.

During the next two weeks, the crew eradicated all evidence that the ship had been the *Narvík* and created her new image, the *El Neptuno*. The reality of knowing that he had announced his presence to the enemy gave Ruckteschell reason to ponder his ship's future, and he developed a deadly new strategy. He called his officers together, and after coffee and some Gordon's gin had been served, he announced his new tactic. It was derived from his U-boat days, and his Executive Officer, Heinicke, who had also been a U-boat Captain in the early days of World War II, quickly recognized the concept. It was the approach that would be used against the *Anglo-Saxon,* of stalking the victim by day and attacking head-on, with total surprise, by night. Concern for his ship and his crew was at the core of this change. They learned that all British ships were instructed that if attacked they were to report the attack by radio, sending their position preceded by "QQQQ" if the attack was by an armed merchant-ship raider, or "RRRR" if the attacker was an enemy warship, and "SSSS" if it was a U-boat. In addition, they were instructed to use their defensive weapons and fight back, which would threaten lives on the raiders. Ruckteschell clearly preferred to smother a victim with gunfire without her fighting back and endangering his crew. Finally, there was purported to be an instruction, which may actually have been a fabrication of the Nazi propagandists, that once in their lifeboats or in the water, the sailors were supposed to fight back with rifles or pistols. Even if this were a legitimate instruction, it seems unlikely that a shipwrecked sailor in a frail boat would take the suicidal step of using a pistol or rifle to fire on the well-armed warship looming over him. Nevertheless, all of this made Ruckteschell nervous and wary. He had never lost a man in combat during his First World War commands and obviously wanted to continue that record no matter what steps he would have to take.

With this new tactic as a concept, it was not long before he had an opportunity to put it to the test, with a particularly cruel twist. During the morning of August 4, a tanker was spotted and the stalking began, with the *Widder* staying about 20 miles away. After darkness fell, the raider closed to just over a mile and a half, and at point-blank range, the 15cm guns ripped into the Norwegian tanker *Beaulieu*. Nine of the thirty rounds fired were direct hits, and the heavily damaged tanker was brought to a halt. Under a hail of shells from the 3.7cm and 2cm guns, her surviving crew members scrambled into their lifeboats and cast off. The predator circled her prey and attempted to sink her with a torpedo, which proved defective, so she finished the job with explosive charges. Fearing that the flare of the flames might attract other ships in the vicinity, particularly warships, Ruckteschell, to the consternation of many of his officers and men, ordered the ship away from the sinking tanker without any effort to search for the tanker's survivors. His men were astonished that he would abandon these souls in mid-ocean without any sense of their physical condition or the condition of their boats. Nor, with the ship's ability to accommodate prisoners, could they understand deserting these men in open boats 1,200 miles from the nearest land. The Executive Officer, Ernst-Günther Heinicke, was particularly outspoken on this abandonment. Ruckteschell felt compelled to justify his actions to his officers and crew and was only marginally successful.

Other raider captains, like Kurt Weyher of the *Orion*, set a very different example. He spent five hours meticulously searching for survivors of the *Turakina*, despite the fact that the ship had gotten off a distress message and he knew warships were getting under way to search for the *Orion*. When some on his crew nervously began to grouse about the delay in escape, they were stiffly reminded what their responsibility was to other seamen. The Captain pointed out that war required the sinkings and the unfortunate loss of life, but once the combat was over "one fought man's common enemy, the seas, to save as many souls as possible." Many men of the *Widder* felt uneasy with the abandonment of the *Beaulieu* sailors. This callousness produced the second charge brought against Ruckteschell.

In the days that followed that first night attack, the ship's Surgeon, Dr. Negenborn, spoke privately to Ruckteschell and apparently convinced him to take a more humane approach with regard to potential survivors. After their next attack, all 34 members of the crew of the Dutch freighter *Oostplein* were taken on board, with no wounded and no one missing. The attack, like the one preceding it, consisted of shadowing during the day, a violent attack after darkness, and a quick victory. Ruckteschell was pleased with the effectiveness of this new tactic, but the raider would not require the dark of night's protection as she sought her next victim.

An image out of the past appeared on the horizon on August 10th, and as simple as this attack would be in one sense, it would be complicated in another. The enthusiastic Malte von Schack accurately reported the improbable sighting, an anachronism in the World War II Atlantic, of a three-masted bark. The majestic Finnish sailing ship *Killoran* was a neutral ship, sailing from one neutral port, Buenos Aires, to another, Las Palmas, with an innocuous cargo of sugar. However, just as Raphael Semmes had done on the *Alabama* in these waters close to eighty years earlier, Ruckteschell sought to untangle the complicated certificates of ownership, and determined to his satisfaction that the cargo was British-owned and, therefore, the ship should be sunk. After taking her 18-member crew and a goodly supply of sugar on board, this beautiful remnant from the age of sail was sent beneath the waves with her sails courses, topsails, t'gallants, royals, skysails, and staysails, still set. The next ship to fall victim to the *Widder* would be the *Anglo-Saxon*.

Chapter 7

PATHS TO WAR

The men and the ship that would become the *Widder*'s next victims followed various paths toward their fate that August night. At the time World War II was declared, the ships and sailors of Britain's Merchant Navy were spread all over the globe, and every ship had a secret packet known as "Envelope Z" stored in the ship's safe to be opened by "the Master" if notified by a special radio message. The *Anglo-Saxon* was in Table Bay at Cape Town, South Africa, on her homeward voyage from Australia when the message of war came. The contents of Envelope Z included the basic points of wartime operations, as well as specific instructions banning radio broadcasts except in emergency situations and the use of new routes to avoid enemy ambush. It also gave the ship a secret call sign to be used in communications.

With the opening of Envelope Z, Captain "Paddy" Flynn, who had become Master of the *Anglo-Saxon* in 1937, was once again a merchant mariner at war and fully understood the stress and danger that lay ahead. His ship was built in the same year as the *Widder*, by the Wear shipyard of Short Bros. Ltd. for £95,000 on the eve of the Great Depression, and had spent her first ten years in the conventional merchant service. The 426-foot ship was powered by a quadruple-expansion steam engine. The largest of the engine's cylinders was a huge 68 inches in diameter, and three boilers generated the steam to move the ship along at 10 knots. Captain Flynn and First Mate Barry Denny had served together on the *Anglo-Canadian* and they made a good team. The crew, few of whom had wartime experience, looked to them for confidence and leadership.

Two days after the declaration of war, the *Anglo-Saxon* left the safety of Table Bay and made her way to Freetown, Sierra Leone, where she arrived two weeks later. Freetown, on the bulge of Africa only a few degrees above the Equator, near the narrowest part of the Atlantic and on the threshold of the North Atlantic, was a logical location to gather convoys for the dangerous run back to Britain. Ships coming from either the Cape of Good Hope, Cape Horn, or South America's east coast ports could rendezvous there. During World War I, the convoy system had proven to be the single-most-effective weapon against the voracious U-boats prowling the waters around England and ranging out into the Atlantic, so the British Admiralty had plans for a convoy system in place when World War II broke out. They knew the rate of loss for ships sailing independently was four times that of ships traveling in convoys. Just as Freetown, Sierra Leone, would be a key location, so would Halifax, Nova Scotia, for the east-west convoys of the North Atlantic. Eventually, a series of interconnecting convoy routes would provide significant global coverage. Experience during the war would continue to show that larger convoys were safer than smaller ones, with one North Atlantic convoy including the astonishing number of 187 ships in 1944. At this early moment in the war, it was reassuring for Captain Flynn to be able to join a convoy of any size for the homeward-bound voyage. The *Anglo-Saxon* nestled into a secure position among twenty-three ships. As the second ship in the second row, there were other vessels ahead, astern, and on both sides of her, all providing insulation from attack. Fortunately for all, attack never came, and three weeks later, on October 18, 1939, Captain Flynn's ship steamed safely into Avonmouth, England.

Despite the prohibition on radio broadcasts, the work of a radio officer like Roy Pilcher serving on the freighter *Beacon Grange* was more arduous and critical than ever. While transmissions were severely restricted, there was an urgent need for passive listening to radio traffic: first for messages and instructions directed to the ship, but also to glean information on what was happening around her and to pick up distress calls that might alert the sailors to danger. Pilcher had a quick mind and good training, so his skills were an important asset for any ship. With the war under way and the threat of German invasion of Great Britain, he had concern not only for his ship, but also for his friends along the south coast of England, where landings by German troops would logically occur if an invasion was attempted. Of particular concern was Marion Blake, his eighteen-year-old sweetheart, who lived in Shoreham-by-the-Sea and worked in Brighton. The two were not engaged, but Marion remembers today that they "were thinking about it." The engagement was to take place when Roy got leave after his second voyage in the *Anglo-Saxon*. Roy Pilcher may have had concerns for himself, but outwardly he expressed a positive attitude. He knew that his skills were essential, and his only complaint was his inability to see Marion. He was envious of his friend Cliff Walder, who, because his work as an aircraft-engine designer kept him out of the service, was able to see his fiancée, Daphne, regularly. For Roy Pilcher, there was a war on, he had a job to do, and he was resigned to the sacrifices.

For Able Seaman Roy Widdicombe, the early months of the war brought real turmoil. He was at sea when the war broke out, and within a short time his ship struck a mine and sank, sending Roy and his shipmates into the lifeboats. They were well equipped with warm clothing, blankets, ample food and water, and, perhaps best of all, rum. He later indicated that this eight-day "ordeal" in the lifeboat was nothing more than an inconvenience. It gave him a lot of time to think, however, and Roy was motivated to return to that special Welsh girl, Cynthia Pitman, and marry her. This was not as simple as he would have liked, since Cynthia's mother was wary of the match and opposed the marriage. Roy and Cynthia overcame the impediment, and after having the banns posted for the appropriate time, Roy, in a stylish Spanish suit bartered for cigarettes, married Cynthia Pitman in Trinity Church in Newport, Wales, in April 1940.

With his savings from his high-risk trips to Spain, Widdicombe was able to acquire a simple, attached brick house on Newport's Lewis Street.

In the thick of the turmoil of the first year of the war, the swaggering, streetwise sailor became both a husband and a man of property. With his pretty, spirited bride and new domestic situation, he was inclined to stay ashore. While on a voyage in the *Quebec City* to the U.S. east coast, he contemplated giving up the sea. He realized how dangerous it was, and he didn't relish the thought of being sunk again. Back in Newport, he seemed to thrive in his new home, new life, and the sense of stature these created. In July of 1940, however, he was torn between the desire to stay with Cynthia and share the ordeal of the German bombing that had reached Newport, and the need for money to sustain their new life. He decided to go to sea again, for one more trip. On July 26, Able Seaman Widdicombe signed on to the *Anglo-Saxon* for what he intended would be his last voyage.

Another resident of Lewis Street had recently completed a stint in the *Robert L. Holt* and was looking for a berth as an assistant cook. Leslie Morgan was a strapping, gregarious young man of twenty who had been born and brought up in Newport. He was cheerful and talkative, but not the brightest of lads, and he found cooking at sea just the right situation. In the first week of August, Lewis Street saw two of its young men about to embark on the *Anglo-Saxon.*

Throughout the Newport maritime community, others were wrestling with the realities that the war had brought upon them. Rationing, used in World War I to conserve food and supplies and ensure equitable distribution of the limited resources, had been reinstated, and the stress of the German air assault was being felt. Jim Fowler, now thirty-seven, had already spent most of his life at sea, working as a "greaser" in the engine rooms of many ships and, like Widdicombe, he was looking for a way to give it up. Also like Widdicombe, he had an economic incentive to go to sea again. Although he was a bachelor, he was the primary source of support for his family, which included his adored niece, Betty. When he had returned to Newport after serving in the *City of Cairo,* he contracted tuberculosis and had to spend significant time in the hospital. In a generous moment, he gave ten-year-old Betty a shilling, which he hoped she would spend on herself in those lean times. Instead, Betty used the money to buy a new rosary for her Uncle Jim to take to sea on the *Anglo-Saxon* after he recovered.

As these men worked their way from ship to ship toward service in the *Anglo-Saxon,* the ship itself had been working hard in support of Britain and her urgent wartime needs, making voyage after voyage carrying precious cargoes such as grain and coal across the Atlantic. At the end of 1939, she departed from Cardiff in outward-bound convoy OB 42 on a voyage that followed the same route as would her fateful voyage later. With a load of coal, she headed for Buenos Aires, where she arrived thirty-two days later. After a short two-day hop farther south to Bahía Blanca, she took on a cargo of grain for the return trip. Trips like this alternated with short home breaks. While docked in London, the gregarious Captain "Paddy" Flynn had an opportunity to spend some time at home with his wife, Monica, a schoolteacher. He also had evenings with his brothers, always marked with laughter and singing, with Paddy in good voice accompanied by Monica on the piano. With a twinkle in his eye, he told his brother's son, Desmond, "When this war is over, I'll take you to sea in my ship the *Anglo-Saxon* as a cadet for a year and 'make a man out of you.' " Desmond created his own path to maturity as an artillery captain in combat in Burma.

As part of another convoy, OA/OGF32, outward bound from London, the *Anglo-Saxon* headed for Philadelphia, where she picked up a cargo of steel and headed for Halifax for two days before joining the homeward-bound convoy. The fiancée of Bill Ellis, one of the officers, lived in Vancouver on the Pacific coast, and with perfect timing she took the train across Canada and was waiting in Halifax for Bill and the *Anglo-Saxon*. Ellis and his girl were married, with several shipmates in attendance, including First Mate Barry Denny and Marine Gunner Francis Penny. The following day, the *Anglo-Saxon* headed back to Newport, where she arrived on July 19 and went into dry dock for maintenance. On the way back from Halifax, one of Bill Ellis's tasks had been to equip the lifeboats with basic supplies. He also had the foresight to put some basic equipment in the two utility jolly boats. This would make the difference between life and death in the months ahead. With the benevolent guiding hand of fate, Bill Ellis signed off of the *Anglo-Saxon* to move to another ship.

After a period of leave, Chief Engineer Eddie Milburn's wife and eight-year-old son, Ted, accompanied him to Cardiff to rejoin the *Anglo-Saxon* in November 1939. Ted was allowed to stay on board the *Anglo-Saxon* under the watchful eye of Gunner Penny, so his parents could have some time for themselves ashore. Thrilled to have the chance to climb all over the ship, Ted absorbed the details of the layout, accommodations, Penny's gun mounted on the stern, and even the small boats on board, including the jolly boat that was about to play a key role in the drama of the future voyage. Before he left the ship, young Ted Milburn ended up with a treasured keepsake—the Royal Marine cap badge from his friend, Francis Penny.

On the eve of World War II, Bob Tapscott was an Ordinary Seaman on an old passenger ship, the Royal Mail Line's SS *Atlantis,* built in 1913. His first cruise in her, during August of 1939, took him to various Baltic ports and then Germany. Tensions were running high during the ship's transit of the Kiel Canal en route to Hamburg, Germany, when Nazi military personnel boarded the *Atlantis* and forcefully confiscated the film from the passengers' cameras. As the ship proceeded through the canal, the *Atlantis* got orders to return to Southampton, England immediately, and arrived on August 25, eight days before war was declared. With astonishing speed, the *Atlantis,* converted to a hospital ship, was at sea again in a matter of days and in the Mediterranean when war was declared. After her safe return to England, Tapscott achieved the rating of Able Seaman, and he signed off of the hospital ship and on to a troopship, the former P&O liner *Orford,* headed for Australia. After a monthlong voyage, she arrived in Fremantle on December 27, then proceeded to Sydney, on the east coast, to embark 1,500 troops, with equipment and supplies, for the African campaign. By spring, she had successfully traveled back to the Mediterranean, in convoy with other troopships, and landed her men and materials. The *Orford* was sent to pick up 2,000 French citizens in Madagascar and transport them to Marseilles, an intense war zone at the time. On her last voyage, the liner was assisting in the evacuation of French troops from southern France when she was attacked by German bombers, badly damaged, and set on fire while between Toulon and Marseilles. The ship was apparently run aground to save lives and the *South Wales Echo* newspaper reported about Tapscott: "A strong swimmer, he saved his life by swimming ashore." While most survived the sinking, 14 were killed and another 25 were wounded. Captain Savage, his officers, and the crew from the *Orford* made their way by train across France to Cherbourg. Despite nearly a thousand vessels being involved in the Dunkirk evacuation to the east, they were able to get a Channel steamer to take them across to England. On June 1, 1940, Bob Tapscott was signed off of the *Orford*. An annotation in his discharge book said, "vessel abandoned." His next discharge entry, for the *Anglo-Saxon,* would read "vessel sunk."

The sinking of the *Orford* and the war that was raging around him had an impact on Tapscott, and he stayed ashore for two months after returning to England. By early August, he was ready to go to sea again, both for his own financial benefit and to serve his country. He and two friends decided to ship out together, but when they started looking for a ship, they couldn't find one with three berths available. Only two days before she was due to sail, the *Anglo-Saxon* was short one man and Captain Flynn urgently needed an Able Seaman. In a move typical of his fundamentally helpful nature, Bob Tapscott signed on, with some reluctance at leaving his friends.

Tapscott had one more day ashore with his friends, as his new shipmates filtered down to the wharf with their gear and went aboard the *Anglo-Saxon.* Jim Fowler was accompanied by his family, including his sister, Liz, and her daughter, Betty. They said their goodbyes, and Jim passed through the barricade at the head of Alexandra Dock on his way to the ship. He heard a voice and turned to see Betty slip past the guard and run toward him. He swept her up in his arms and then, to reassure her, reached into his pocket and brought out the rosary she had purchased for him with her precious shilling. He told her that when he returned there would be a job for him on land and he would be able to stay and provide properly for the family. He gave her the rosary and asked her to keep it for him. The little girl clung to the rosary as she watched her beloved uncle disappear.

After a final evening ashore with his friends, Bob Tapscott made his way down the dock and onto the ship, going aft to the crew's quarters to get some sleep before the *Anglo-Saxon* got under way. On August 6, the ship left Newport for the short trip to Milford Haven, on the western extreme of South Wales, to join two other ships from Bristol Channel ports. After spending the night of the 7th in Milford Haven, the *Anglo-Saxon* left port heading north.

The *Anglo-Saxon* was part of the convoy designated OB 195, which sailed at midday on August 8 from Liverpool. With 27 ships under the command of a Royal Navy Reserve Commodore, F. A. Sommerville, OB 195 consisted of 20 British ships, 3 Greek ships, and 1 each Norwegian, Danish, Swedish, and Dutch. Provided they survived the threats of wartime and the North Atlantic weather, their various destinations would take them to ports in North, Central, and South America, the Caribbean Islands, and as far as India, Australia, and Indonesia. With the intense air battle taking place over the southern part of England, the convoy took the northern route out to the Atlantic. Despite the delicate and demanding task of picking their way through a fishing fleet off the Isle of Man, they reached the open ocean. Protecting them was a small but dedicated escort contingent consisting of an old, World War I—vintage destroyer, HMS *Vanoc,* and two smaller corvettes. These two ships, although not likely to intimidate their enemy with the names of HMS *Periwinkle* and HMS *Geranium,* gave some assurance to those in the convoy that the Royal Navy would protect them for at least the first and most dangerous portion of their voyage. In addition, despite the urgent need for planes and pilots in the Battle of Britain, the convoy was given air coverage from Liverpool that stayed with them until dark on August 11.

Although nothing like the massive transatlantic convoys of the later years of the war, OB 195 was still an impressive sight: twenty-seven ships steaming in close formation, in a line of nine columns. Most probably, they had the destroyer ahead and the two corvettes maneuvering on the flanks, ever watchful for death-dealing periscopes. The Commodore's task of keeping the group in order was shared with a Vice Commodore and a Rear Commodore, so that each had responsibility for three of the columns. The complicated job of station keeping fell to each individual Captain and in turn to his watch officers and crew. They needed to be alert to signals from the Commodore for changes of course or speed and watchful of the ships around them. Those in the engine room had to insure that the propulsion system worked smoothly and that the orders for speed were fulfilled precisely, making such minute adjustments as a few revolutions of the propeller shaft to match the exact speed of the lead ship. With the ships traveling in such close proximity, there was little time and space for maneuvering if a ship in front slowed down or had steering difficulty. In addition, lookouts had to not only watch the other ships, but also continually scan the waters for periscopes or the terrifying wake of torpedoes.

All of this would be complicated enough on a clear day in calm waters, but that was not what OB 195 encountered. In tribute to the skill of these merchant captains and the competence of their crews, the convoy managed this difficult work in severe weather through day and night. Two ships had difficulties in the heavy weather and dropped out during the night of August 10. The SS *Photina*, in the middle of the convoy, managed to withdraw without incident, despite having ships ahead, astern, and on both sides. For the officers and crew on watch on the *Anglo-Saxon*, it must have been sobering to watch the ship on their starboard beam, the Dutch *Bukelo*, drop slowly astern to manage on her own, alone and unprotected. The Dutch ship was able to simply drop back, since she, the *Anglo-Saxon*, and four other ships were in the last row of the convoy. This was a desirable position. Even though the convoy's average speed of 5.7 knots was slower than the speed of a U-boat, attacks seldom came from astern. The U-boats preferred to attack from the front or flank so that the combined speed of the torpedo and the oncoming ships made evasive action more difficult. In the instructions to the convoy, there was one additional note, which read: "In the event of any ship being damaged while in the convoy, the SS *Rabaul* and the *Treworlas* will stand by as Rescue Ships to save lives and then rejoin the convoy." Like the *Anglo-Saxon*, these two ships were in the last row. While this was reassuring, it was also a reminder of the wide-spread, lurking danger.

All but ten of the ships in this outward-bound convoy were traveling in ballast, without cargo. They were headed for ports around the globe to harvest the resources England needed. The few that carried general cargo or coal, as the *Anglo-Saxon* and the *Assyrian* did, would provide critical income from the sale of their cargo, in addition to bringing back the essentials to sustain the war effort. Each of these ships played a vital role and was worth the protection of the convoy, air support, and warship escorts. These protective measures had their limits, however, and a day after the air support was withdrawn, the warships reached their western boundary and departed to escort a homeward-bound convoy. Convoy OB 195 was now on its own, having transited the dangerous home waters with their many perils.

Onboard the *Anglo-Saxon,* the officers and crew made their adjustments to shipboard life. In that tight little community, numerous factors impact peace and tranquillity. There are traditional rivalries, such as those between the deck crew and the engine-room crew. The deck crew, made up of Able and Ordinary Seamen, envision themselves the true sailors, and consider the engine-room crew as little more than seagoing mechanics. It works in reverse, of course, where the engine-room workers see themselves as the modern mariners, masters of the machinery that propels the ship through the seas, while the deck sailors no longer have sails to tend and simply steer the ship. This rivalry is so strong that the two groups are housed separately on most ships.

Aboard the *Anglo-Saxon,* they lived in separate quarters in an area still called the fo'c'sle (forecastle) despite its location aft. The deck crew's quarters were on the port side and the engine-room gang's was on the starboard. The shipboard hierarchy and tradition affected accommodations for everyone. Naturally, Captain Flynn had the best cabin, on the upper boat deck, just below the bridge and just forward of the radio office. This "radio shack" also had accommodations for the First Radio Officer, Michael O'Leary, and the Second Radio Officer, Roy Pilcher. Directly below the Captain's cabin, on the main deck, were the cabins for the First Mate, Barry Denny, and the Second and Third Mates, Alistair Duncan and Walter Pickford. Farther aft, a deckhouse held the cabins for the engineering officers. Chief Engineer Eddie Milburn's cabin was on the port side. After the Captain, Milburn was the highest-paid person on board, even above the First Mate, in recognition of the training and skill required for the job and the responsibility he carried. The other engineering officers—Houston, Hawks, and Rice—were housed in the starboard deckhouse. And so it went: the Bosun and Gunner Penny had separate accommodations a bit farther aft, and the others, like the cooks and stewards, had their own accommodations. This complex plan reflected the traditions of the sea and the roles played by the various members of the crew. They were literally all in the same boat, but there was a distinct structure that governed their lives.

It was not only the rank or rating of the person or where he bunked that influenced shipboard life, however, but also a more subtle and pliable structure that was created in the early days of a voyage. It is natural among animals and humans to create a pecking order. In the schoolyard, someone emerges as the tough bully, someone as a thoughtful facilitator and peacemaker, someone as a leader. This process took place naturally on the *Anglo-Saxon* as well. The fact that 15 of the men on board had made the previous voyage in the *Anglo-Saxon,* and were willing to sign on again, reflected the good management of Captain Flynn and First Mate Denny. Those men already knew one another, but the other 26 were new, and the sorting out had to take place. In the sailors' fo'c'sle, three newcomers began to emerge as strong characters. One was the affable, good-humored James "Paddy" Gormley. The other two, who shared the watch with him, were Roy Widdicombe and Bob Tapscott. The confident, swaggering Widdicombe asserted himself as the tough character he had been since his youth. With an inclination to settle situations with his fists, he was not a person to cross. By stark contrast, Tapscott was the problem solver, always seeking to make things work.

The emerging leadership of this trio revealed itself a few days into the voyage, when the crew began to grouse about the ersatz coffee brewed for them. By this time of the war, real coffee was a rare commodity at sea as well as on land in England, and various "blends" using substitutes like roasted chicory root were common. Despite the sailors' traditional love of coffee, this was so poor that they longed for tea. Tapscott, Widdicombe, and Gormley volunteered to take the complaint to the Captain, who proved to be the fair and reasonable man he was reputed to be, although there was nothing he could do at that point. There wasn't enough tea on board to use as the morning, midday, and night beverage, so the Captain promised that after the *Anglo-Saxon*'s arrival at their next port, he would add to the tea supply. Through this relatively simple promise of success, the three men assumed leadership in the fo'c'sle. From their conversation with the Captain and his estimate of when he could obtain the tea, they were also able to deduce that they were headed for South America, their destination having been a secret up to that time.

This new stature provoked a disturbing display in one of these new leaders. Food played a critical role in relieving the monotony of life at sea, and an argument developed over the abilities of the Cook. Widdicombe, a friend of the Cook, took offense at the remarks made by another sailor, Stan Elliot. At six feet in height, with his ominous looks and numerous tattoos, Widdicombe was the image of a formidable opponent. When Widdicombe challenged him to go out on deck and settle the issue, however, the smaller Elliot accepted. Widdicombe was already standing, and when Elliot started to get up, Widdicombe caught him off guard with a powerful blow to the face. Elliot reeled back, his face cut by Widdicombe's large ring, and the fight was over before it began. To his shipmates, it was clear that Roy Widdicombe was a man to be reckoned with. In maritime terms, they would give him a wide berth.

The convoy steamed on unmolested, and as they increased the distance from the U-boat threat, ships began to disperse toward their individual destinations. It must have been a strange feeling for Third Mate Pickford and Roy Widdicombe to see the ships they had recently served aboard, the *Shivan* and the *Quebec City*, with former shipmates and memories, steam on when the *Anglo-Saxon* broke off on a southerly course, confirming the speculation that they were headed on a voyage like the one the ship had made earlier that year to Argentina.

Now, free of both the security and the confines of the convoy, the crew of the *Anglo-Saxon* settled into their daily activities as their second week at sea came to an end. They left Newport on Tuesday, August 6, and it was now Tuesday, August 20. They anticipated that the next day would be another typical day on their monthlong voyage to Buenos Aires.

Chapter 8

THE RAIDER STRIKES

On the night of August 20, midway through the evening watch, which lasted from 8:00 P.M. to midnight, Korvettenkapitän von Ruckteschell made an unscheduled visit to the bridge, as captains often do. He found the officer of the watch, Leutnant Scharnberg, a former merchant Captain, leaning against the railing, apparently dozing off. Enraged that the man would endanger the ship in this way, he immediately had the officer relieved of his duty and summoned his senior officers to discuss the situation. The incensed Ruckteschell wanted him immediately tried in a court-martial, and instructed the officers of the court that he wanted a death sentence for Scharnberg. It was his intention to make an example of this officer. He wanted Scharnberg shot.

The officers working under Ruckteschell were used to his flares of anger and had learned to cope. An additional difficulty for them was the Captain's disproportionate effort to be liked by the enlisted men of his ship. The officers had received their naval training recently and were dubious of Ruckteschell, whom they perceived to be an anachronism from the Kaiser's Navy of World War I. On a number of occasions, he tried to win favor by ridiculing the officers in front of the enlisted men, calling some of them stupid bunglers. This was risky for Ruckteschell, since it further alienated him from his officers; but he counted on the professionalism of those he ridiculed to carry on with their work without protest. For a number of them, such as Konrad Hoppe, this called for the utmost in self-control.

The officers on the court-martial were in a particularly difficult position. The Captain was obviously interested in summary "justice" and had directed what the outcome of the trial should be. It took courage on the part of the court-martial officers to reject the urging of the Captain, who seemed rabid on this point, and to conduct a proper trial and deliver an appropriate sentence. During the morning of August 21, the court brought back its verdict, finding Scharnberg guilty. Rather than awarding a death sentence, however, he was given three years in prison, a reduction from Leutnant zur See to the junior rating of Matrose (Seaman), and the loss of his Merchant Captain's Certificate. In wartime, sleeping on duty is a serious offense; but the *Widder* was far from land, steaming independently, and had numerous other people on watch and apparently alert to their surroundings. To the officers of the court, the punishment they awarded was appropriate for the offense. To Ruckteschell, it was another frustrating example of the incompetence of his officers and their resistance to his directions. This confrontation certainly started August 21 off on a note of near crisis on the *Widder*. Ruckteschell was furious, and the officers wanted to make sure they did nothing else to further incur the Captain's wrath. It was at that point that the mast tops of the *Anglo-Saxon* came into view of the *Widder*.

Once the British ship was spotted and the *Widder* reversed course to shadow her and get in a position to strike, one of the lookouts was relieved by an officer. Skilled at monitoring the enemy ship's movements, the officer directed the *Widder* to sustain contact while remaining undetected. With the news of the court-martial a prime topic of shipboard discussion, the men of the *Widder* went about their daily activities with the full knowledge that they were stalking their prey, and also talked proudly of adding another victim that night to their growing list of conquests. They methodically prepared for their evening's "work." The Gunnery Officer, Oberleutnant zur See Damschen, and his men checked all their weapons, ensuring they were in perfect firing condition and their sights were in proper adjustment. He also made certain that the three range finders they had on board were well calibrated. His men got the ammunition they needed from the storage magazines deep in the ship, and laid out the 100-pound projectiles and the charges of gunpowder in their casings so they were ready for rapid, overwhelming fire. The experienced and well-trained gun crews on the six heavy guns could load and fire every 25 seconds, remarkable for the World War I–vintage weapons, which required hand loading and ramming.

Kapitänleutnant Rödel, the Navigation Officer, was busy all through the day keeping a meticulous plot of the tracks of the *Widder* and her prey. He also worked with the Captain and the Executive Officer to determine the optimum time for the attack and the ideal position from which to strike. In the radio room, Oberleutnant zur See Kindler and his crew were scanning the radio waves in search of any clue that there were other ships, particularly enemy warships, in the territory. They were also preparing for their important role in the attack, which was to listen for possible broadcasts from the target during the attack, and to "jam" that transmission by broadcasting interference on the same frequency.

Both planes were out of action, so there was no flying for Konrad Hoppe. He was the logical officer to spend long hours aloft in the lookout position observing the masts of the victim, hull down over the horizon, and conning the ship by shouting directions down a simple voice tube to the bridge. This freed Oberleutnant zur See von Schack to work with his torpedomen in readying their tubes, on both the port and starboard sides, for the action to come. Each of the tubes was loaded with a massive torpedo and all the concealment, aiming, and firing mechanisms would be checked and double-checked, since they wanted no mistakes to trigger the anger of the Captain.

In the engine room, there was strain as Kapitänleutnant Penzel and his crew constantly nursed their recalcitrant engine along. For the engineering crew, it had been a particularly arduous voyage, with constant problems. It had been so stressful and exhausting for the engineers that ten days earlier Ruckteschell noted in his ship's log, or war diary, that "these men have been working almost without any break since April, 2½ months of this in the tropics." To ease their workload, he took the extraordinary step of having a dozen sailors from other divisions trained to stand watch in the engineering areas to give the engine-room crew some relief. The traditional rivalry between sailors and engineers would be set aside on the *Widder* for the good of the ship.

The sick bay and the ship's surgery were not exempt from the preparations under way around the ship. The ship's Surgeon, Dr. Negenborn, and his assistant, Dr. Schröder, prepared for the worst. Although it had not happened in past attacks, this quarry might become aware of the presence of the raider and fight back, or the ships could collide. The surgeons had to be ready to tend the wounded and injured men of either ship. Throughout the day, every conceivable preparation was made, so that as the *Widder*'s crew went to their evening meal, they were confident that their Captain would bring them another triumph, adding further distinction to their growing record of successes.

On board the *Anglo-Saxon*, the day was routine. The warm weather made the deck work comfortable. There were important things to attend to, but they were part of everyday life in mid-ocean, with more than two weeks to go until arrival in Buenos Aires. The ship's small boats were subject to regular inspection. In peacetime, the boats would have been resting in chocks on deck, but rigged with "boat falls" to the davits, which would enable them to be lifted and maneuvered out over the side and lowered into the water. The lifeboats were only used in times of emergency, but the ship's utility boats, the jolly boats, were launched for chores and work while in harbor. Swinging a boat out is a laborious and time-consuming process, taking as long as fifteen minutes of coordinated effort by many men. In a crisis, there wouldn't be the time or manpower available, so during the war the boats were carried in a "swung out" position. This was done upon leaving port, so the *Anglo-Saxon*'s two lifeboats and the two jolly boats were out over the side, ready to launch.

One of the regular tasks at sea for the deck crew was to check the boat falls, the pulleys, or blocks, and the line that runs through them, used to lower the boats to the sea. They would check to be sure the line was in good shape, that the sheaves in the block were lubricated and able to roll freely, and that the gripes—straps that would keep the boats from swinging back and forth with the rolling of the ship—were secure and in good condition. With everything in good shape, the boats were poised for use, and it only took the severing of the gripe with a sailor's razor-sharp knife or one swing with an ax to get the boat ready to be lowered. The two jolly boats were swung out on either side of the superstructure, one deck below the bridge. The two 30-man lifeboats were on the port and starboard sides, above the engineers' quarters, toward the stern.

The deck crew would also examine the lashings that held the four life rafts, which were another wartime addition. They had minimal equipment, only a self-righting, automatic light, but would provide flotation for a number of men if necessary. These were lashed to the shrouds, the cables that ran from the tops of the cargo masts to the ship's rail. In an emergency, they could be released and pushed overboard, or the rafts could break free from a sinking ship and bob to the surface to serve any possible survivors. The crew knew how important these boats and rafts were and made careful inspections, despite the fact that the threat of a U-boat attack had diminished enormously.

This reduced threat also made the gun mounted on the stern seem less vital, but it is certain that the dedicated Francis Penny was as thorough as ever. He removed the canvas cover, inspected the gun, and made sure that several cases of ammunition were in place around the gun, ready for the use of the gun crew, which included Roy Widdicombe. Some would argue that the presence of this single gun was more of a danger to the ship than a help, since without the gun an attacker would have little excuse to fire on the merchant ship. The attacker could simply fire a shot across the bow and order the vessel to stop and the crew to abandon ship before sinking her or taking her as a prize. However, without the gun, a ship could be captured by even a small, well-armed enemy craft. The gun certainly was a deterrent to U-boats attacking on the surface using their deck guns, but a merchant ship with one antiquated 4-inch gun was no match for a heavily armed enemy warship. It was just that kind of ship that had been secretly stalking the *Anglo-Saxon* all day and was about to make her presence known.

The crew of the *Anglo-Saxon* had completed their day of work and watches and had finished their evening meal. The sausages and meatballs that made up the bulk of the meal appealed to many, but left others, like Widdicombe, without much interest. He passed up the meal and took the time to roll six cigarettes to smoke during his evening watch, from 8:00 P.M. to midnight. The rest of the crew, people like Jim Fowler, were either on watch, getting some sleep if they had the mid-watch, starting at midnight, or relaxing in some other way. Some wrote letters to friends or loved ones to be mailed when they got into port. Others read, played cards, or just talked. In the crew's messroom just forward of the port-side crew quarters, there was a game of cribbage. This was one of the traditional pastimes on ships and engrossed four men—three sailors and one fireman from the engine-room gang.

At eight bells, marking the end of a four-hour watch, the new watch standers headed for their assigned places. Firemen and engineers went into the heat below to tend the boilers and the huge steam engine that quietly hissed as its pistons turned the shaft and propelled the ship toward Argentina. The new deck watch consisted of Gormley, Widdicombe, and Tapscott. Gormley headed forward to take over as lookout on the bow, straining as his eyes adjusted to the darkness. Widdicombe took over the wheel for his trick as the helmsman on the bridge. Since he was "stand by" for the first part of the watch, Tapscott held back, staying to finish his hand in the lively cribbage game.

On the *Widder*, the crew had been making their "blind" run-in since 7:10 P.M. Because of the darkness and the fact that their target was proceeding with only her dimmed navigational lights showing, they could not see the *Anglo-Saxon*. Had the British ship been aware of the presence of the raider and made a sharp turn to port or starboard as darkness fell, she could very possibly have slipped away into the night. The lack of radar would have made it difficult for the Germans to locate their victim. The British had no idea they were being stalked, however, and held their course. The blind run-in placed the *Widder* directly in the path of the on-coming freighter. Ruckteschell, still seething from the morning's court-martial outcome, was on the bridge and in control of his ship. The Navigation Officer, Kapitänleutnant Rödel, was with him as were the Executive Officer, Heinicke, and Oberleutnant Hoppe, the aviation observer. It was Hoppe's job to watch the side of the ship away from the attack, to ensure that another vessel wasn't approaching while all eyes were on the action.

As it neared 8:00 P.M., all hands were at their battle stations. A faint light was seen dead ahead and it was clear that they had their quarry. By approaching from the victim's bow, Ruckteschell made it impossible for the *Anglo-Saxon*'s gun to be trained around and fired at them. Their timing was flawless, since the bright moon that had been full only four days earlier had not yet risen. Just before the first shots were fired, Ruckteschell's war diary states, "They must have seen us, but instead of turning to starboard they turned to port." He ordered a turn to starboard and with the distance between them less than 1.5 miles, Ruckteschell gave the order to open fire.

On the bridge, Roy Widdicombe relaxed at the helm since the *Anglo-Saxon* was easy to steer. There may have been an alert from Gormley on the bow or the officer of the watch, Third Mate Walter Pickford; or Widdicombe may have caught a glimpse of a shadowy form looming off the starboard bow. Following instinct, Widdicombe, inside the pilothouse with its cement-block "armor," put the helm over to port and the *Anglo-Saxon* began to turn away. In seconds, with no time to sound an alarm, the ship was slammed by the first, accurate, deadly salvo. Widdicombe dashed out to the wing of the bridge, saw the stern ablaze and instantly realized the shadow was a raider.

The ships were now parallel to each other. Within the first minute, three salvos of heavy explosive shells were fired at point-blank range, and the attacker then opened up with her particularly deadly smaller weapons. Ruckteschell would assert that the freighter attempted to get out the message signifying a warship attack, "RRRR" and her position, and that is possible; but in a matter of moments the destructive fire from the pompoms and the 2cm automatic guns tore the radio room to pieces and destroyed any chance of calling for help. Captain Paddy Flynn was in his cabin below the bridge. Realizing the *Anglo-Saxon* was under attack, Flynn gathered the codes and other secret materials to send them to the bottom in a weighted sack. He never got the opportunity to complete his task. When the First Mate dashed into the Captain's cabin within minutes of the first shells, he found that projectiles from the raider had cut Paddy Flynn down.

In the crew's quarters aft, the first round hit and exploded, bringing instant death to those in the engineers' area on the starboard side. The cribbage game that was taking place on the other side of the ship dissolved as the sailors grabbed their life jackets and leaped out onto the deck. Just as Bob Tapscott reached the deck, there was a blinding flash and an enormous explosion behind him, as further enemy rounds set off the *Anglo-Saxon*'s munitions around the disabled ship's gun. The force of the blast picked him up, hurled him along the deck, and slammed him into a deckhouse on the starboard side. He lay there bleeding from shrapnel wounds on his back, unconscious amid the pandemonium of the attack.

For the crew on the *Anglo-Saxon*, there was nothing they could do to fight back. Their only hope was to get into the lifeboats and away from their ship, which was being dissected by the precision fire of their enemy. The guns swept the decks, back and forth, bow to stern, chewing up everything in their sights, and in the words of Ruckteschell, "hastening the crew into the boats." Ruckteschell's plan had an obvious and literally fatal flaw. Those guns shattered the British sailors who crowded the deck seeking escape, as well as the boats they were trying to reach.

In minutes, Bob Tapscott regained consciousness but lay there stunned by the carnage around him. During a lull in the firing, he struggled to get to the port side of the ship, out of the line of fire. The gunfire picked up again, with a dazzling display of pyrotechnics from the red, yellow, white, and blue tracer rounds fired from the 2cm guns. They streamed through the night from their source, sitting at a safe distance. On impact, they shredded the steel, wood, or flesh they hit, and when they exploded, they disintegrated, sending their incendiary fragments in all directions to set fire to whatever would burn.

The decorated hero of World War I, Gunner Francis Penny, never had a chance to even consider firing back. His cherished gun and its munitions disintegrated in the first moments of attack. Like all the others on board, he was in a fight for survival. He came out of his accommodations and attempted to make his way to the shelter of the port side. Wounded twice in the previous war, on this night he would feel that searing pain again.

On the bridge, Widdicombe was briefly abandoned, as the Third Mate, in a decision that cost him his life, decided to leave the modest protection the fortified pilothouse offered and go for instruction. He never reappeared, but within minutes the First Mate, Barry Denny, came bounding up the port ladder, past the jolly boat to the bridge. He assessed the grim situation. The attack was raging furiously, the Captain was dead, and First Radio Officer Michael O'Leary reported the radios were destroyed. Denny ordered Widdicombe to hold the ship steady on her course and headed outside to take stock. O'Leary, a fatalist who had declared that if attacked he would go down with the ship, headed off for the liquor locker in the Steward's Pantry two decks below and to his death. Widdicombe, twenty-one years of age, once again stood alone on the bridge of his stricken ship.

On the foredeck, the lookout, Paddy Gormley, quickly abandoned his exposed position and crawled aft toward his assigned lifeboat, but it was a futile effort. Those near the boats were struck with horror as they saw the lifeboats disintegrate under the fusillade of shells and bullets. Making their way, first to one boat and then the next, driven senseless by the cacophony, and disoriented by the fire and explosions, they faced one devastating scene of carnage after another. In the midst of this turmoil, Leslie Morgan searched for escape. He had been relaxing in his bunk, listening to his radio, when a projectile from the initial salvo tore through the starboard bulkhead, carried off the radio, and left him in stunned disbelief. He found the Chief Steward, Harry Willis, a Newporter like himself, and together they headed aft to the lifeboats. A burst of machine-gun fire from the 2cm's raked the deck and killed Willis. Morgan moved on alone to the starboard lifeboat where he witnessed its destruction under the full blast of the renewed gunfire, which also maimed or killed a number of men heading for the boat.

The Bosun, Thomas Maher, an old salt of thirty-four, survived that assault, and together he and Morgan set off, scrabbling crablike on hands and knees across the bullet-riddled deck toward the port lifeboat. Once again, Morgan was left on his own as a bullet instantly killed Maher. The risky trip seemed useless, as Morgan joined a small group staring at the shattered hulk of the lifeboat. Among these men was Lionel Hawks, the Third Engineer, who had initially scrambled up to the boat deck from his cabin below, only to realize that the boat was a wreck and he was in a very exposed position. He quickly retreated to the relative shelter of the port side, partially protected from the bullets by the engineers' deck-houses.

When Tapscott reached the interior alleyway between the same deck-houses, he saw his chance and wormed his way across the hatch cover seeking the safety of the port side of the superstructure. There he found Gunner Penny, and as they gathered their wits, Penny was shot through the wrist. They dove for the steel deck and flinched as bullet after bullet screamed past or thudded into their ship or shipmates. Groping forward, Tapscott found the lifeless body of his watchmate, Gormley. He was im-mediately drawn back to Penny, however, as a piece of shrapnel slashed the gunner's thigh open. The two dumbfounded men were struggling to find escape when they heard activity on the deck directly above them.

The First Mate made a quick assessment tour of the aft portion of the ship, ordered those who were still able to abandon ship, and raced back to the bridge. The port jolly boat was intact, and he called Widdicombe to assist in getting the boat in the water. It was a formidable task for the two men, who worked feverishly to cut away the gripes and control the boat's descent to the water. Any mistake at this time and the vehicle of their sal-vation could crash into the sea and drift uselessly away. That mistake nearly happened when the gripes were cut and the weight of the heavy boat tore at the rope in Widdicombe's hand. The runaway line literally stripped the pants off Widdicombe and wrapped around his hand, yanking it to the block where it jammed, causing excruciating pain. They fought to free the hand and clear the jam, and then began to lower the boat.

To Tapscott and Penny on the deck below, the boat appeared as a gift from above. In a split second, they hurled themselves in as she passed. Always the competent sailor, Tapscott grabbed the boat hook and began to fend off, keeping the boat a safe distance from the rolling side of the dying ship. Moments after the boat hit the water, First Mate Denny and Widdicombe slid rapidly down the boat falls into the boat, burning their hands on the ropes. As the attack began, Second Radio Officer Roy Pilcher had grabbed the attaché case containing his emergency kit and made his way perilously from one demolished lifeboat to the other. Dragging a wounded foot, he appeared above the jolly boat and slid down into her, just as she was released and began to drift aft as the ship continued forward. The five men in the boat looked up at the shattered port lifeboat and saw a knot of men peering over the side at them. With a raw instinct for survival, two of them, Hawks and Morgan, flung themselves over the side and crashed into the boat. Other faces, possibly Eddie Milburn, whose cabin was right there, or Jim Fowler, if he hadn't been killed in the first instant in the crew's quarters, stared stunned as the boat drifted away from under them.

For those seven in the boat, a new danger loomed: the huge slashing propeller. Partly out of the water since the ship was down by the bow, it threatened to suck them in and devour the boat and the men. Grabbing large oars to fend off, Tapscott and Widdicombe fought against the suction of the vortex the propeller created. At one instant they seemed doomed, but suddenly they were clear and their crippled blazing ship, with 34 of their friends and shipmates, limped slowly on without them. Incredibly, despite the fact that the *Anglo-Saxon* was clearly a floating wreck, the gunfire from the *Widder* continued. It was, in fact, so intense that Ruckteschell would record in his war diary that "they [the 2cm and 3.7cm guns] are hardly to be stopped and make so much noise that the 'Cease Firing' gets through very late." It seems odd that with seven previous successful attacks they would still have had difficulty with critical commands such as cease fire, but the end result was devastating for the *Anglo-Saxon* and her crew. Over 400 rounds from the 2cm and 3.7cm guns, ten rounds for each man on the British ship, had shrieked through the night inflicting destruction and death.

The jolly boat drifted astern. The men lay low, trying not to attract the attention of the expert German gunners, who were still firing. Heroically, some desperate and courageous British sailors clambered up onto the rail at great risk, freed two of the life rafts from their lashings, and pushed them over the side. Although Ruckteschell stated that the smaller guns on his ship simply swept the decks back and forth without firing at specific targets, an American, George Duffy, who later faced Ruckteschell's fury, would contest that statement. On his ship, the *American Leader,* Third Officer Duffy leapt into the rigging during Ruckteschell's attack to free a life raft and says he immediately came under direct fire. That may have been the case on the *Anglo-Saxon* that August night as well. The glimpse of lights bobbing in the water alongside the ship gave the seven men in the jolly boat hope that some of their shipmates had escaped the careening inferno and were on the rafts. Their optimism was abruptly snuffed out as they watched the rafts come under fire from the *Widder* and then saw no more of the lights. This act became the one charge that could bring a certain death sentence for Ruckteschell, and there were seven British witnesses.

With the attention of the crew of the *Widder* riveted on the mutilated freighter, the men in the jolly boat got out their oars and tried to quietly put some distance between themselves and the decimation they were witnessing. They were absolutely convinced, by the ruthlessness of the attack, that this Captain wanted no one from the *Anglo-Saxon* to survive to testify as to what occurred that night. As the stunned sailors slipped away into the dark ocean, they watched the predator circle its prey before the kill. A searchlight beamed from the raider and sought out the *Anglo-Saxon*'s name on her burning stern so the kill could be properly reported. Then at 9:01 P.M., less than an hour after the attack began, a torpedo burst out of one of the *Widder*'s tubes, and a few seconds later triggered an enormous explosion deep in the hull of the *Anglo-Saxon*. The tramp settled by the stern, lifted her bow out of the water, and slid backward toward the ocean floor. She carried with her the pride of England, the best there was, true heroes, 34 courageous merchant seamen. Their wives and sweethearts, parents and children, friends and relatives at home that night had no way of knowing what a loss they had just incurred.

Part II

FORTITUDE

Chapter 9

SPECK IN THE OCEAN

Astounded by the ferocity of the attack they had endured, the men in the jolly boat felt that the raider's intention must have been the annihilation of all from the *Anglo-Saxon*. They did everything possible, therefore, to avoid being seen, and did not attempt to send a distress signal to the Germans with the Mate's flashlight, since they were certain that would be suicidal.

The First Mate instantly took charge at the tiller, and the others in the boat labored at the oars to distance themselves from the raider, despite their wounds and injuries, some of which were grievous. The rowing became increasingly difficult, and they realized that the water level was rising in the jolly boat. They appeared to be in a damaged vessel that would soon have them awash and swimming in the Atlantic waters, still cold even in the tropic summer. Tapscott and Widdicombe started to bail, while Hawks and the wounded—Penny, Pilcher, and Morgan—pulled on the oars. The sailors could not gain on the rising water. Had the boat been somehow hit? Did she have shattered planks? The leak and the extent of their danger had to be found. Tapscott was the first to proffer a reassuring thought: perhaps it was as simple as the boat's drain plug. The Mate groped around in the dark, increasingly deep water and, indeed, the drain plug had been left partially open. With a few deft strokes with the blunt end of his ax, the Mate set the plug in place, the flow of water was staunched, and the bailers began to gain on the water.

Once the raider disappeared, Denny made the decision that the group should stay where they were for the night, perhaps in the hope that if anyone else had survived, they might hear him in the night or find him in the morning. Aboard the jolly boat, there was a sea anchor, a conical canvas device that did not sink to the bottom, but rather hovered below the surface and acted as a drogue, holding a boat in place. The two Able-Bodied Seamen, Tapscott and Widdicombe, rigged the sea anchor with a long line, and it helped to keep the boat headed into the ocean swells. The Mate, Barry Denny, felt the men still needed to keep the oars manned since the water continued to spray over the bow. They established "watches," using the men with only minor injuries—the Mate and Third Engineer Hawks in one watch and Tapscott and Widdicombe in the other. As they shifted position that first night in an attempt to get some sleep in the crowded boat, it was clear that Second Radio Officer Roy Pilcher was in agony. He thought his foot had been blown off. Denny, confident that it couldn't be that bad if Pilcher had been able to row, took a look at the foot with his flashlight. Although the water in the bottom of the boat was cloudy with blood, he reassured Pilcher that his foot was there and that he would attend to everyone's wounds in the morning. Despite the reassuring words, Pilcher must have known the truth. In excruciating pain, he tried to rest with the others. Understandably, no one slept that night. They talked quietly, tried to voice optimism, but did not talk about their lost ship.

The jolly boat was the merest speck in the ocean. She occupied 75 square feet of ocean surface. Each square mile consists of over 27 million square feet, and there are more than 33 million square miles in the Atlantic Ocean! Yet, this infinitesimally small floating hull was the salvation for seven souls. She was a very sturdy, lapstrake workboat 18 feet in length. From her full bow, she widened to 6 feet at her broadest point and then narrowed to the transom with a wineglass stern. She not only had oars, but also a mast and a trapezoidal sail bent onto a small wooden spar. This single sail was part of the "dipping lug" rig, which had been used as a reliable workboat rig for centuries. It was easy to set and easy to handle, with its only drawback being the need to lower, or "dip," the sail and set it again on the other side of the mast when changing tacks. The jolly boat was steered with a tiller set into the rudder that functioned despite missing the lower of its three pintles. Within the boat, there was a broad stern seat that flowed into seats which ran up both sides of the boat and met in the bow. Three thwarts ran from one side of the boat to the other, forming three additional benches. All of these seats and thwarts were secured firmly to the hull with eight heavy, galvanized angle braces, or knees, that were bolted through the seats, four on each side. It was on these seats and thwarts with the protruding knees and bolts, in a boat only 18 feet in length, that the seven men—battered, wounded, injured, shocked but alive—tried to rest on that first bewildering, wet, cold night.

At first light, still held in the vicinity of the *Anglo-Saxon*'s sinking by the sea anchor, the men in the jolly boat scoured the ocean around them for any glimmer of life, any trace of their ship or shipmates. Absolutely nothing of the *Anglo-Saxon* was evident. There was only the lone jolly boat and those whom happenstance had thrown together. There were three officers, two sailors, the Assistant Cook, and the Marine Gunner. Barry Denny was a mature thirty-one years of age; the Gunner, Penny, was forty-four; and all the rest—Pilcher, Hawks, Tapscott, Widdicombe, and Morgan—were young men, ranging in age from nineteen to twenty-three. In a sense, it was a cross section of the ship's officers and crew that was going to be tested to the absolute limits during the voyage that lay before them.

As First Mate on the *Anglo-Saxon,* Barry Collingwood Denny was positioned for his ascension to "master" of his own ship. Certainly, the little jolly boat was not the command he sought, but in the tradition of his family, he would apply himself to his utmost to make a success of the responsibility that had been thrust upon him. The first task was to look after his men, and in this case that meant assessing their physical condition. As the sun rose and eased the chill of the night, Denny examined each man and contemplated what treatment he might administer once they got the boat under sail and steady on course.

The first and most urgently in need was Pilcher. In the cold light of day, the extent of his wound was apparent to all. The men were astonished that he had stoically managed to row and suffer quietly through the night with such an appalling wound. Pilcher's left foot was shredded. It hung loosely as a mangled mass at the end of his leg. The others eased him forward into the bow, where he would be least disturbed, and rigged a sling for his leg, to reduce the impact as the little boat wallowed in the ocean swells. The courageous Penny was the next-most-seriously wounded, shot through the wrist and suffering a gaping shrapnel wound in his thigh. He too was positioned in the bow. Another jagged wound was found on Assistant Cook Morgan's right leg, above his badly battered ankle. While obviously painful, the injury was not as serious as those of the first two. This was also the case for Tapscott. He had had an upper right front tooth knocked out and had absorbed several small pieces of shrapnel when he was hurled across the deck by an explosion, but was able to function. The other injuries, Denny's badly rope-burned hands and Widdicombe's jammed hand, were comparatively minor.

As he wrestled with how to care for the most serious wounds, Denny knew he had to establish a positive tone and give the men a sense of hope and purpose. In the long hours of the night, he had obviously weighed the possibilities and options and was ready with a decisive plan early that morning. First there was the hope that despite her small size the jolly boat would be seen by a passing ship and quickly rescued. This was conceivable, since the men were in a part of the ocean through which ships traveled on voyages similar to their own. This was, of course, everyone's hope, and a quick rescue would be of great help, particularly to Pilcher and Penny. Such a rescue was not something that could be depended upon, however, so the sailors clearly had to look to their own abilities and fend for themselves.

Barry Denny was a competent seaman and navigator, but he was faced with an enormous challenge. He knew the *Anglo-Saxon*'s location at the time of her sinking, but he had no navigational tables or instruments other than the most fundamental, the boat's compass. The nearest land lay about 800 miles away, with the Azores to the northeast, the Canary Islands east of them, and the Cape Verde Islands to the southeast. Their little boat with her lug rig and minimal keel was not able to sail well to windward. This made an attempt to reach the Azores or the Canaries extremely difficult, since the boat would have to beat into the prevailing winds, with both the winds and currents pushing them away from their goal. It was perhaps more feasible to consider heading for the Cape Verdes, since they could sail in that direction on a "reach," with the wind on their beam or quarter, but there was a serious risk in that option. With only the compass to steer by and with the jolly boat being imperceptibly shifted by the winds and unseen currents, it would have taken a miracle to find the little grouping of islands. If they missed the Cape Verdes, the gargantuan, desolate South Atlantic would lie before them.

The other option was counterintuitive. It called for turning away from the nearest land and setting a course in the opposite direction, toward islands that were more than twice as far away. The advantage was that the prevailing winds would favor the men, as would the ocean currents that would carry them along toward their objective even when the winds died. The course would be toward the the chain of islands known as the Windward and Leeward Islands that stretch almost 500 miles, north to south, forming the eastern edge of the Caribbean Sea. In those long first hours of the boat voyage, Denny reasoned that the chances of finding one of the islands in this vast chain were far superior to those of finding the smaller clusters to the east. If the group went west, there was always the possibility of sailing through the chain, between islands without sighting them, but then they would be within the Caribbean with its significant boat traffic and the American continents ahead of them. None of these options was a simple one, but the responsibility for the decision was Denny's and he did not shrink from it. Once the wounded had been made as comfortable as possible, he explained his decision and then rallied his crew to step the mast, hoist the sail, and set their course toward the Leeward Islands.

They were fortunate to have the compass, but it added to the challenges they faced. They discovered a note on the compass indicating it was off by several points. This imprecise bit of information was critical, but frustrating since it was so vague. An error of several points in a long voyage could translate into being hundreds of miles from the expected destination; and the Leeward Islands lay some 1,600 miles away toward the southwest. Denny ordered that the crew steer west on the compass, which according to his calculations, would produce an actual course of west-southwest directly toward their goal. While the Leeward Islands were their intended objective, there was the fervent hope among everyone on board that a passing ship would spot them in a matter of days and carry them safely to port.

With the wind blowing gently from the northeast and the seas in a slight swell, the men were now organized and on their way, on a broad reach with the sail well out over the port side. This point of sailing was reasonably comfortable, and the sail would not interfere with the next difficult task, administering to the wounded. Denny's assessment the night before of Pilcher's condition had obviously been far from accurate, and now he was faced with aiding a very seriously wounded man. The boat had been equipped with a first-aid kit, but it was intended to give just that, first aid, to a minor injury someone might incur while using the boat in harbor, before he received professional medical help. There was no such help for Roy Pilcher. Denny knew from the condition of what had once been a foot, with pieces of bone protruding from the torn tendons, muscles, and flesh, that Pilcher, who had bled extensively, was fighting for his life. Bob Tapscott and Third Engineer Hawks helped shift Pilcher to the middle of the boat and assisted in bathing his wound with seawater. It was hoped that the healing power of the Atlantic's salt water would cleanse the wound. Denny then bandaged the mass of tissue, and the men, as gently as possible, eased the brave, unprotesting Pilcher back to his position in the bow.

Denny then turned to Gunner Francis Penny, who, with a stoicism matching Pilcher's, underwent the primitive treatment of his wounds. The piercing of his wrist had been relatively clean and left a neat hole. This was washed, treated with iodine, and bandaged. The jagged shrapnel wound in his thigh presented a greater challenge. Using his meager resources, Denny attempted to sterilize the wound with the iodine and bind it closed with bandages. Penny rejoined Pilcher in the makeshift sick bay in the bow while Denny applied the same treatment to the Assistant Cook's nasty leg wound. The shrapnel wounds in Tapscott's back, left buttock, and hand had stopped bleeding and, because of the limited resources, remained unbandaged. The exposed nerve of his broken tooth was extremely painful, but he realized it was nothing compared to the ordeal Pilcher was experiencing. Tapscott's respect and that of everyone on board had increased for Pilcher, the fine, gentle man whom they all liked.

The next order of business was to assess the resources the men possessed and determine how to allocate them. Cigarettes were of prime interest to virtually everyone on board and were one of the rarest commodities. The men pooled their supply and before setting about to inventory the rest of their assets, indulged in what seemed the sublime pleasure of a smoke. In addition to the oars, sailing rig, rudder, boat hook, sea anchor, two bailers, ax, and compass that had already been used, a search of the locker under the stern seat produced several useful and some useless items. There were some precious flares and a few matches in waterproof containers, as well as a few lengths of line that could prove useful. An oil lamp and a bucket used to make the lamp a signaling device proved to be frustrating when the lamp wouldn't light. The binnacle lamp on the compass also refused to light and made steering by compass impossible at night. One item that had been ignored in the months before the voyage would prove to be inordinately important.

When the jolly boat hung in the davits aboard the *Anglo-Saxon*, she was protected by a boat cover that was in a state of deterioration. It was probably because of the holes in the cover that let water into the boat that the jolly boat's drain plug had been loosened to allow the water to flow out. Now this mundane piece of tattered canvas proved valuable beyond measure. The boat was completely open from bow to stern, so there was no shelter from the blistering sun during the day or the icy spray during the cold nights. The modest shelter that the boat cover provided was a godsend.

Provisions were the next category to be assessed, despite the fact that at this early stage of the ordeal no one had an appetite. There was a copper storage compartment with a round, watertight access port located under the middle thwart. In this was stored what had been the traditional staple of shipboard eating for centuries: 32 pounds of ship's biscuits. As appetizing as these may sound, in reality they were rock-hard squares, made of a simple flour-and-water dough that had been baked without salt. If they were kept dry, they would remain edible for many years. They were all encouraged to discover eleven cans of condensed milk, sewn into a protective canvas by Bill Ellis a couple months before. Perhaps most appreciated were the three 6-pound cans of cooked mutton that would surely produce several feasts for the men. Although they were relieved to have what seemed like an adequate, if basic, amount of food, they were about to become aware of their most serious problem. In the middle of the boat was a small wooden cask, the water breaker, with a capacity of about eight gallons. The only person who had asked for and been given a small drink was Pilcher, who was now beset with fever. It was during his delivery of this drink that Denny discovered a most discouraging fact: the cask was only half full. As everyone inventoried their meager provisions, they became aware of this deficit and its dire ramifications.

In his calculations, Denny had determined how long he anticipated the voyage to the Leeward Islands would take. At an optimistic 100 miles a day, the sailors would need sixteen days. This was indeed optimistic, since a modern yacht does very well to cover 200 miles in a day and the jolly boat with her simple rig was far from an oceangoing yacht. They were, of course, anticipating that rain would supplement their tiny reserve of water, but Denny knew that this was no more guaranteed than the possibility of another ship finding them. He made the determination that the daily ration for each man would be a minuscule 4 ounces of water and an equal amount of ship's biscuit, a spartan diet. When the voyage began, all of the men were well nourished and physically strong sailors and four were not seriously wounded. It seemed difficult yet feasible to survive for a little over two weeks on this regimen, and with their incredible strength and optimism, there was a positive air in the jolly boat as they settled into the routine of their first day on the sea.

The scant equipment and supplies of the jolly boat had few supplements. On board ship the men carried few things in their pockets. The cigarettes had already been produced and shared and there was little else. Denny bemoaned the fact that he had changed into his tropical uniform only the day before and had not shifted useful items from his pockets. He did have a knife, but nothing else. Although each man had been encouraged to prepare an emergency kit with personal items to take with him in the event the crew had to take to the boats, only one had had the time and the wit to grab his and keep it with him during the chaos of the attack.

Roy Pilcher, always a quick mind, had grabbed the attaché case that served as his emergency kit, and miraculously had it with him as he hobbled to the edge and slid down into the boat. Under these circumstances, there was no claim of personal possessions. Just as with the cigarettes and everything else on board, Pilcher's case belonged to all the men. For most, the greatest treasure in it was a full pound of pipe tobacco. There was also a pipe and a razor. This was not an antiquated straight razor, but a very fine modern device known as a Rolls Razor. It came in a handsome stainless-steel case that contained not only the razor but also a honing device to sharpen the heavy, fine-quality reusable blade. This was the state of the art in shaving at the time. Other items in the case included Pilcher's wallet, his discharge book, an unmailed letter to his friend Cliff Walder, his radio operator's log, and some time sheets. A final item was appreciated doubly by all. It was a small volume with a Bible quotation for every day of the year. The men in the boat realized that they would not only have inspiration from the quotations, but the pages would then make perfect cigarette papers for the tobacco.

They passed their first day in their new environment in good spirits, telling tales, joking, feeling positive about their future, and not dwelling on what had happened less than twenty-four hours before. Denny, with his sense of order, began a log of the voyage, using the backs of the blank time sheets from Pilcher's case. The log began with two paragraphs of description of the attack by a raider they thought was the *Weser,* since the ever confident Widdicombe asserted he knew the ship from earlier contact when she was a simple merchantman. Denny also recorded witnessing the firing upon the rafts and went on to list who was in the boat and the wounds of the men. His entry for the first day at sea was short, noting the weather, the boat's course, that medical treatment had been given, and then "All's well." He also used his knife to carve a notch into the inside of the boat's rail on the port side at the stern. This primitive calendar would indelibly mark the days he spent in the boat.

That first evening, each man dined on a single ship's biscuit, but there was no request for or distribution of the precious water. With the original watch list still in place, Denny and Hawks alternated with Tapscott and Widdicombe through the second night, which was warmer and drier now since the jolly boat was running with the wind. Because the binnacle lamp would not light, the sailors reverted to the ancient maritime tradition of steering by the stars.

As the sun rose on Friday, August 23rd, their second full day at sea, Denny reached for the "thief" and prepared to issue each man his allotment of water and ship's biscuit. The thief was a small narrow dipper, especially designed to "steal" into a cask through the small bunghole and retrieve the precious liquid. This thief would hold about 4 ounces, but at 6:00 that morning, each man got only half a dipper, a mere 2 ounces of water, half a ship's biscuit, and a tiny amount of condensed milk. Twelve hours later, every man would be issued the same ration as his evening "meal." For grown men who had not had anything to drink for at least thirty-four hours, the 2 ounces of water didn't begin to lessen their thirst; yet none complained since they acknowledged the limits of their supply and knew that the wounded, feverish men were suffering far more.

Standing "watch and watch"—four hours on, four hours off—the quartet of fit men monitored the passing of the day as the conversation dwindled. As the day ended, Denny carved another notch and the crew settled in for another long night. However, before midnight, Denny, who was on watch, excitedly awakened his shipmates. Salvation was at hand! Their short voyage could soon be over. A ship was passing, heading on a north-northeast course nearly opposite to their own. Denny worked quickly to extract a flare from its waterproof canister and soon had it lit and held high. The night vision of those in the boat was ruined by the brilliant red light, and they fought to regain their perception after the flare had burned itself out. They peered into the darkness searching for the ship that was showing no lights. Then they saw her and realized that she was turning in a large sweep back toward them. Their spirits soared. But then the professional Barry Denny grew wary. He was suddenly suspicious of this ominous dark shape that seemed so like the group's adversary of two nights earlier. With incredible discipline the men ceased their celebration at the Mate's order and watched.

Was this the raider, continuing her search for survivors from the *Anglo-Saxon*, intent on silencing them forever? This apprehension reinforces the understanding of how convinced these men were of the raider's objective. The darkened ship obviously searched for further signs of distress but could not locate the silent, inconspicuous jolly boat and resumed her course. The men in the boat coped with their conflicting emotions of initial elation at the presence of the ship and then their relief that the raider had not appeared above them with guns blazing. What they didn't know was that the *Widder*, after departing the scene two nights earlier, had steamed north and was now over 150 miles away. Further, since this was the *Widder's* exclusive operating area, there would be no other German warship in the vicinity. In a crucial decision, motivated by their urge to survive, they resisted the temptation to light a second flare, and thus let an opportunity for survival steam away.

By Sunday morning, a new reality began to set in. When the men tried to chew their ship's biscuits, also appropriately called hardtack, they found that the small amount of saliva they were producing was insufficient to soften the biscuit and make it possible to swallow. With only 2 ounces of water to wet their parched mouths and throats, they would not waste it on softening the hardtack. Water had become the most precious commodity and this was clear to everyone. The urgent need for rain was on all their minds and yet they were coping with the opposite. The sun shone clear and scorched the men as they sat or lay exposed. The wind had died off and the boat drifted in the current. Other physiological effects had already been felt. The minimal amount of food they took in was totally absorbed by their bodies and they ceased to produce any waste to eliminate. Their bodies were fighting to retain and use anything that could bring the men through this time of deprivation.

As the day dragged on, the men sought refuge from the beating sun under the boat cover, but found it was oppressively hot and there was a strange, putrid odor beginning to develop. While in the process of making a cigarette from Pilcher's volume of inspirational messages, Widdicombe read aloud a somber quote: "Call ye on the Lord all who are in peril of the sea." Realizing the need to help raise his men's spirits, Denny declared there would be a Sunday meal of mutton. This plan worked superbly, not only lifting the men mentally but physically as well, as they each savored every minute morsel of the nearly half pound of cold boiled mutton they had been issued. Denny knew that in their current state the crew could easily overeat, so he had issued only half of the meat from the first of the three 6-pound cans. He would preserve the rest to continue the feast the next day. The meaty meal energized all the men and a long animated conversation about food and drink ensued. Each spoke rhapsodically about his preferred food and its individual merits: roast beef and Yorkshire pudding, fish and chips, pickled herring, on and on. The lively debate continued on to beverages and the best way to drink them. It was the most natural conversation for a group deprived of not only their favorites, but of nearly all food and drink. Their minds were consumed with their thoughts and their fantasies.

In testament to the courage and spirit of these men, Denny noted in his log entry for that day that their morale was "splendid." He also noted, in understatement, that they were "hoping for rain showers but none around yet." His estimate of the distance traveled from the site of the attack was 225 miles on a course of west-southwest. This is possible but probably optimistic, since they had been becalmed all of Sunday, which would mean that they had achieved the 225 miles during the first three days in the boat. Seventy-five miles a day would be very good progress, since that exceeded the best day's travel of the sail-powered raft *Kon Tiki* that later sailed with the currents in the Pacific. However, even though it would be good progress, their average would be only about 56 miles a day for the first four days, and this was a substantial difference from the 100 miles a day needed to get them to land in the sixteen-day time frame they anticipated.

The feast that was envisioned for the next morning was less successful despite the menu being the same. Although the remaining mutton had kept well through the night, the continued deprivation of water made it difficult for the men to digest. The digestion of the protein the night before had consumed most of their gastric juices. Their saliva had completely ceased, and with a totally dry mouth and a stomach with no fluid the men struggled to take advantage of their special meal. The joviality of the night before was also gone. The situation was worsening.

It was more extreme for the wounded men. When Denny set about that morning to change the dressings on their wounds, he confirmed for all what he had suspected since he had loosened the dressings on the swollen feet of Pilcher and Morgan the day before—gangrene. As he unwound the bandage from Pilcher's foot, Denny unleashed an overwhelming, repugnant stench that had been perceived in whiffs the day before. The tangled rotting mass at the end of Pilcher's leg was hued in green and black and reeked with the indisputable odor of gangrene. When blood is no longer able to flow through tissue providing nourishment, there often follows a bacterial invasion that leads to the mortification of the flesh and its putrefaction. There was no doubt that the Radio Officer had a flourishing gangrenous infection and Denny had nothing with which to fight it.

Demonstrating once again his sterling character, Pilcher apologized to his shipmates for the difficulties he was creating and for the stench his deteriorating body was producing. This only elevated him once again in the eyes of those in the boat. Desperate to help in some way, Denny, assisted by the Engineer, Hawks, and Tapscott, turned once again to their only abundant resource, the salt water around them. With Pilcher in obvious excruciating pain, they positioned him, without protest, so that his leg was over the side. Tapscott then spent an hour continuously bathing the grotesque wound with buckets of seawater. When they felt that all the cleansing that was possible had been accomplished, Denny wrapped the foot in fresh bandages and Pilcher was helped back to his niche in the bow.

Treatment was then given to Morgan, whose right foot was severely swollen and whose raw wound just above the ankle was showing no signs of healing. His wound was also bathed and then rebandaged. For the Gunner, Penny, the wrist wound seemed to be doing well and was covered with iodine and bandaged. His other wound posed greater problems. The ripped thigh was not responding and worried Denny considerably. With the last of the bandages from the first-aid kit, he covered the wound and hoped for the best. He had consumed all the medical supplies at hand. In his log that day, he noted, "Hoping to sight vessel soon but praying for squalls and a decent wind."

The decent wind remained elusive throughout the day, with the little boat bobbing on the swell, totally becalmed. In an attempt to ease the sweltering heat, buckets of water were poured over the wounded men, giving them some relief. Since the boat was hardly moving in the still air, Denny, Hawks, Tapscott, and Widdicombe took turns going over the side and immersing themselves in the sea. The boat was rigged with lifelines that hung like sweeping garlands from the rail along both sides. Some of the men clung to these lifelines and soaked calmly, but Tapscott, the accomplished swimmer, demonstrated his prowess by swimming under the boat several times to the entertainment of the others. All who had been in the water emerged feeling reinvigorated. However, the reality of their situation was always with the men, and they settled in for their evening ration, enhanced with a little fat from the mutton can. By this time in the voyage, they were nibbling only a half a biscuit each day, their bodies calling for no more because of the lack of fluids.

After two sweltering days becalmed, the wind rose that night and their journey continued at a steady 5 knots, the pace that would give the crew those hoped-for 100-mile days. The breeze continued through the night and the following day, so they had the encouragement of real progress toward their goal. They also had their hopes raised by clouds that brought the promise of rain. The raised hopes slipped slowly back into disappointment, as none of the clouds materialized into even a faint drizzle. Denny, always concerned for his men, worked hard that day to distract their thoughts and boost their morale. During the afternoon, he produced a cigarette for each man from Pilcher's tobacco and the inspirational message papers. After they lighted up, he cautioned that they had only eight matches remaining, so "this luxury will soon be stopped."

That evening, encouraged by the sailing progress, Denny enlivened the atmosphere by conducting a lottery. Contests such as arrival and anchor pools and similar lotteries are staple pastimes on ships whether they are merchant, naval, or even passenger steamers. These lotteries give all on board an opportunity to look to the future with anticipation. The objective was to pick the date closest to the day upon which they were either rescued by a passing vessel or reached land. The seven dates selected began with September 9, thirteen days in the future, and ran until the 15th. They were reasonable dates, perhaps a touch optimistic, but possible; and of course the objective was to encourage the men.

Names were drawn to match up with the dates and the effect of it all was precisely what Denny sought. A spirited debate developed among all on board as to why each date was the most likely to be correct. The discussion had a strange element, however, since the sunburned lips of the increasingly gaunt men and their dry mouths and tongues altered their speech if not their enthusiasm. To everyone's pleasure, the tortured Pilcher was among the most eloquent in defense of his date for arrival and they all would have been delighted if he was the winner, with the prize being all the drinks he wanted, purchased by the others.

As they settled down for their seventh night in the boat, it was remarkable that they remained in such good spirits. Their fortitude was reflected in a portion of Denny's log entry for the previous day: "Trusting to make a landfall in the vicinity of the Leeward Islands, with God's will and British determination."

Chapter 10

DRASTIC CHOICES

The morning of the seventh day began with an increased awareness of a nauseating smell. Gangrene was now progressing unchecked up Pilcher's leg. It was apparent, too, that Gunner Penny's jagged thigh wound had the same infection, and that Morgan's leg wound was also turning gangrenous. There was no way to escape the stench. Pilcher continued to apologize and others attempted to reassure him. They could see that the disease was coursing through the Radio Officer's system and taking its heavy toll. The spark in young Pilcher's eye was disappearing. During the morning, his condition took an ominous turn: he lost feeling in his leg. The blessing of this was that he was no longer in anguish, but it also meant his body could not sustain its interaction with the rotting limb and had essentially amputated it. Of course, this was not a true amputation and the rampant infection was making its way into other organs of his body. There was great frustration in the inability of the others to help Pilcher, Penny, and Morgan.

The four fit men again went over the side and immersed themselves. Primarily done to obtain some relief from the oppressive tropical sun and stench, this seemed to provide an additional benefit as they took some fluid into their systems through their skin. They had not been able to salivate for several days, but after their time in the water they found that saliva had returned. Various studies show that only a superficial amount of water is absorbed during immersion and it cannot penetrate deep into the tissues of the body. Those problems that developed from the lack of water would have the most devastating impact on those in the jolly boat. Modern scientists assert that the second most fundamental requirement of the human body, after oxygen, is water. It is the presence of adequate water in the system that facilitates virtually all other bodily functions, from digestion to blood circulation. Without adequate water, basic human functions begin to shut down and fail. The daily minimum fluid required from food and liquid sources by an adult is nearly 2 quarts. The men in the jolly boat got a mere fraction of that.

Thirst had long replaced hunger as the sailors' primary consideration. As the day wore on, it was not food they fantasized about, but beverages. They discussed not only favorite drinks, but also wistfully thought about moisture-laden sweet fruits such as peaches, pears, and oranges. Denny remarked on this in his log, which still carried an optimistic tone despite the crew's declining condition. Part of that optimism was due to the fact that strong winds were enabling them to make good progress. The following morning, their eighth, brought disappointment as the breeze diminished and continued to do so during that uneventful day. Penny and Morgan seemed to be somewhat better, but that encouragement was countered by Pilcher's deterioration. The men also observed physiological changes in themselves, such as the total lack of sweat, even in the stifling midday heat. With the lack of fluids, they refused the quarter of a ship's biscuit offered morning and night. Their desiccated throats and mouths were choked by their swollen tongues. The physical impact of their lack of fluids and nutrition was obvious. Their weight loss was apparent and their clothing, which only a week before had fit them, now was too large.

In this sad state, they settled down for what became a sleepless night. They had learned to tolerate the uncomfortable seats as makeshift beds, but the discomfort of the various protrusions interrupted what rest they could achieve. They were suddenly roused from this uneasy state by an unearthly, plaintive cry. Its source was Pilcher. Up to this point, the brilliant young officer had borne his suffering with a courage admired and respected by all. Now a voice they did not recognize was among them.

Denny made his way to Pilcher to see what he could do to help. The Radio Officer stared blankly into the distance. The Mate tried to get him to respond, to focus, or to react, but Pilcher was mentally in another world. This was the beginning of a long night, during which the delirious Pilcher took on a persona none would have associated with him. Gone was the refined, thoughtful, concerned man, and in his place was a ranting body, wracked by the poison of gangrene. There was no way to curb the flow of sound that came from Pilcher. He used language the others had never heard from him and most thought he didn't even know. There was no doubt his fine mind was in the clutches of his disease. He cursed, broke into an hysterical cackle, sang, and then cursed or laughed again. This went on for a long time, and then a calm came over Pilcher. He quietly coped with his agony, groaning and softly talking nonsensically to himself. Gratefully, the others eased back into their rest, sobered and saddened, but glad for the relative quiet. This was not to last, however, as the night was once again pierced by Pilcher's tortured cry, and he began the cycle of cursing, singing, and inane laughing again. No one could rest, but Denny struggled to find something he could do to ease the deteriorating situation for Pilcher and the rest. The Radio Officer was in a desperate way, the condition of Penny and Morgan was of great concern, and they were all visibly declining. Barry Denny carried an enormous burden. As the night came to an end, so did Pilcher's ranting as he slipped into near unconsciousness.

The entry in Denny's log for the day following Pilcher's delirious night began to show discouragement. He had done a remarkable job keeping their spirits up, setting a positive tone, reminding them that rescue by a ship was possible at any time, and that they were making progress toward their island objective. But it was increasingly difficult to rally the men. The wind had died off, which added to the disappointment. The first two lines of the Mate's entry for August 31 read: "Becalmed, partly cloudy, nothing sighted whatsoever. Have not had one speck of rain but living in hopes." Those last, powerful three words were the only positive strain in this subtle roster of woes—becalmed, cloudy, nothing seen, no rain. Added to all of this was the condition of the Radio Officer.

Pilcher swung back and forth between sleep and ranting during the morning. Try as they might, the others could not tune it out, and Pilcher's ravings added significantly to their miseries. With many sleepless hours during which to think, the Mate reluctantly had made a drastic decision.

After the morning ration of water, he spoke quietly with the other fit men—Hawks, Widdicombe, and Tapscott. He had decided something had to be done about Pilcher; the crew couldn't continue this way. The others agreed, but what? They were astonished to hear what the Mate planned. It was barbaric. It was unthinkable. They had to amputate! The concept was staggering. This was major surgery they were talking about, the kind that required sterile operating rooms, teams of surgeons, blood transfusions, effective anesthetic, and an array of fine, sterile, razor-sharp surgical tools. They had none of that and in fact had almost nothing. None of them had any medical training. Denny had done the normal patching up of an injured sailor, but nothing in this realm. The operation, if you could even consider calling it that, would not take place in a proper environment, but exposed in a rocking, dirty, germ-laden, fetid boat. Of course, there was no blood for transfusion and worse, no anesthetic. Finally, what did they have to substitute for those fine instruments? When questioned on this point, Denny gave an appalling answer to his stunned listeners: the ax. The ax was dirty and rusty and undoubtedly had lost its edge, but what else was available? They had no saw, and neither the Mate's knife nor the sturdy little blade from Pilcher's Rolls Razor could carry out this plan.

It was hard to argue with the fundamental point in Denny's reasoning: Pilcher's leg was literally killing him and something had to be done. Amputation was the only choice. Even in the most professional hospital ashore, amputation would have been the only course; even then its effectiveness would be questionable, since the use of the first antibiotic, penicillin, didn't begin until 1941.

Widdicombe and Hawks, despite the incomprehensible gravity of the decision, went along with their leader. They all respected and cared for

Pilcher. If there was any way to help, they were for it. Tapscott had equal regard and concern for Pilcher, but he couldn't accept this approach. In his mind, the entire idea was ludicrous. There would be the brutal, crude butchery, with the ax causing incredible pain for Pilcher, since the amputation would have to be in untainted living flesh to be effective. In addition, how could the others control the bleeding, dress the stump, or inhibit infection? If they managed to get the leg off, perhaps they could cauterize the stump with the flares, but the thought of the entire horrific process was alien to Tapscott. Instinct told him that the disease had gone systemic and infection was raging throughout Pilcher's body. He simply could not endorse the procedure, which seemed too primitive and too late.

Without unanimous agreement, the Mate opted to bring Pilcher himself, who at that moment seemed lucid, into the decision-making process; but his capacity to make a rational decision was questionable. The stellar Roy Pilcher was a desperate man. When the Mate posed the question and gave him the option of having the leg off, he readily agreed and the decision was made. The ax was cleaned as thoroughly as possible, and every effort was made to restore its edge. Pilcher was positioned, and Hawks and Widdicombe prepared to hold him down. Penny and Morgan looked on, undoubtedly thinking of their own wounds and growing infections. Barry Denny grasped the ax, hesitated, searched for the strength to perform the task, and could not find it. When it came to that final act, there was no willpower in Denny to carry out the deed. None of the others was sufficiently convinced of the benefit to step forward and take over the terrible task. With both relief and a sense of failure, the Mate put the ax away. He told Pilcher that with the probability of being picked up by a ship soon, the foot should wait for the proper medical care.

These stalwart men were dealing with incredible physical deprivations and enormous mental stress. Their fortitude had been remarkable, but they would have to dig deep into their reserves. In this forlorn moment, Denny resorted to his most powerful morale booster; for the second time he offered the boiled mutton. They had been in the boat for nine days and had consumed a quarter of their ship's biscuits, half of their condensed milk, and, most significantly, half their water. With Denny's firm leadership and the discipline of the crew, they were on the schedule they had set for the consumption of their provisions for the sixteen-day voyage they had anticipated. With the days becalmed, they now knew it would take longer. The logic of giving everyone an equal amount each day until expected arrival was flawless. After nine days of experience with this minuscule daily ration, however, the question that had to be in their minds was, Could they survive on this scant supply for nine more days? Surely they would reach the Leeward Islands by then.

The crew had two cans of mutton left, and since it had lifted everyone's spirits the first time, Denny decided to indulge in this luxury once again. They had a feast of mutton that Saturday night, but unfortunately it had the opposite effect. The meat had moisture, which enabled them to chew and swallow it, but their shrunken stomachs had virtually shut down from lack of food. A minimum of 2 pints of fluid in the body's system is needed to generate the gastric juices necessary to process meat and dispose of the waste. The salt in the mutton just increased the men's thirst; they were all suffering, their bodies screaming for water. With his usual decisiveness, Barry Denny broke with his strict regimen and doubled the water ration that night. It was the only option he had to reduce the suffering the treat had induced. This luxury of water was only marginally successful, and some of the men spent an agonizing night, twisted with abdominal pain and nausea. The Mate himself was among those who were crippled with cramps and vomiting that night.

The following day, Sunday, September 1, was a pivotal day for the men on this voyage. After an uncomfortable night, they roused themselves for another routine day. When they looked at their leader, Denny, they were taken aback by his altered condition. His only problem had seemed to be his rope-burned hands, which hadn't healed and were oozing pus; but now there was an unmistakable change in the man. The wracking sickness of the night before had drained him of vigor. His skin was pallid and he was clearly still coping with wrenching internal pain. This shocking transformation was difficult for the others to consider. Barry Denny was their leader and everyone respected him in that capacity.

Suddenly, the others felt enormously threatened by this change and fervently hoped that as the day wore on the malady would wear off and their leader would again be himself. Drawing on nearly exhausted reserves of willpower, Denny first made a decision of enormous import. He had mentally reckoned the boat's position, since he had no charts. Having calculated the compass error, he had been steering essentially southwest. He had estimated the boat's speed and the currents and knew the time elapsed, so he could estimate the distance traveled. He must have felt that the jolly boat was far enough south to be on the latitude of the Leeward Islands, and ordered that the crew steer west. If Denny had had a chart, he would have seen that the boat was well north of the desired latitude, and steering due west would cause her to miss the Leeward Islands completely. Without instruments, charts, or navigational tables, and with the exhaustion of the ordeal, a fateful decision had been made.

Denny's next task was to issue the 6:15 A.M. 2-ounce water ration. As usual, each man was eager for this taste of liquid. Back to his old gentle self, but weaker than ever, Pilcher turned away from his ration and said that others needed it more than he. This generous act of sacrifice was typical of what they might have expected from Pilcher in his prime; but now it saddened everyone, since it indicated that he could not envision recovery, even if they were rescued soon. In these moments when his mind was clear, Pilcher was able to assess his condition.

Less than two hours later, Morgan, who was convalescing in the bow, made the lamentable discovery: twenty-one-year-old Roy Hamilton Pilcher, exemplary shipmate and admired friend, was dead. Despite being among a small group, all of whom truly cared for him, Pilcher had slipped away silently and alone, without anyone to comfort him, without anyone to whisper his endearing family nickname, Bun, and without anyone to assure him that all would be well. His life and his loss was so typical of the tragic waste of war. Those in the boat had seen death before, had witnessed it on board the flaming *Anglo-Saxon,* and knew now that death was truly stalking them in their little boat. All of this added to the gravity and demoralization of what had just occurred. Perhaps if he were not dealing with his own physical deterioration, the Mate might have organized a more appropriate service for Pilcher, or perhaps he was thinking the men shouldn't dwell on this morbid situation. The result was a swift, abrupt disposal of Pilcher's body, with no ceremony.

The Mate ordered Tapscott and Hawks to simply lift the body over the side and let it go. There were no words, no prayer, no eulogy, no simple Godspeed. The awestruck men could do nothing but watch the body drift away. Undoubtedly, there were individual thoughts and silent prayers and good wishes lingering with the body as the boat sailed slowly on, but the weight of this moment bore heavily on each of them. They knew Pilcher was very sick, but no one had wanted to admit that death was so near, or that it could claim one of them at all. The hope that a ship would find them before it was too late and everything would be solved proved to have been a dream, and one of their number had been taken from them.

There was nothing that could be said to ease the mourning that saturated the boat that day. Each man dealt with his grief for Pilcher and his fears for the future privately. This had to be particularly terrifying for Gunner Penny and Leslie Morgan, whose own wounds were already infected. They had witnessed the agonizing decline of the Radio Officer in excruciating detail. They had seen his pain and were coping with their own. They had seen the fever and the delirium. They had witnessed the alteration of his character. For Penny this was a grim prelude to what he knew would be his own trip down the same twisting, tortuous trail. It had to be unnerving for the other officers, Barry Denny and Lionel Hawks, who observed the loss of dignity of their fellow officer as the disease reached his mind. Everyone knew the true Roy Pilcher and that it was the gangrene distorting his personality, but they were forced to contemplate their own uncertain futures. Tapscott and Widdicombe must have had their own misgivings, despite their comparative health. Pilcher's death drained the optimism from the boat and demonstrated that everyone was vulnerable. Things would not be the same.

The day following Pilcher's death brought no relief. In fact, numerous factors contributed to an even more somber mood, if that was possible. Denny fought to rally himself and attend to his morning water distribution, but struggled to get to the water breaker and carry out the task. The others were shocked by his continued decline, and each must have pondered how to manage if Denny were unable to exert his steady leadership. The other wounded men created additional cause for concern. The veteran Penny demonstrated extraordinary control and restraint despite his gangrenous thigh. There were no outbursts or signs of the ordeal he must have been experiencing, except that he grew visibly weaker each day.

By contrast, young Morgan had begun to act very strangely. His previous good humor and lighthearted chatter disappeared, and he now sang incessantly, repeating the same tired song over and over, driving the others to distraction. This was not only the result of his infection, but the fact that he was taking the very risky course of drinking seawater. The others knew that, despite their warnings, he had used one of the empty condensed-milk cans to ladle up water from over the side to try to quench his growing thirst. They suspected that at night he surreptitiously continued to consume more seawater. It was known that drinking seawater was a futile method of relieving thirst and had grave consequences. Although it is difficult to create a laboratory experiment to assess this impact, observations by medical personnel who were themselves in survival situations during World War II documented the fatal results of drinking seawater. In 1965, the Marine Division of the British Board of Trade issued Merchant Shipping Notice No. M.500, which in bold letters asserts NEVER UNDER ANY CIRCUMSTANCES DRINK SEAWATER. Morgan was not alone in consuming the seawater. Tapscott on several occasions attempted to relieve his raging thirst with a can straight from the ocean, but found the relief short-lived. He also knew that this was a very dangerous path to follow, and with his wits still keen, avoided the trap of continuous consumption that would certainly lead to his death.

The lack of water had a psychological impact in addition to the physiological effects. Studies show that coherent behavior can be sustained for as long as seven days on a ration of 5 to 6 ounces of water per day, but that much more water is needed to sustain life. After a week on the 4 ounces a day consumed in the jolly boat, dehydration would have begun to impair the crew's judgment and, by this time, they had been on the minimal rations for twelve days. Widdicombe seemed particularly unnerved by the events around him. He tried to be hopeful and optimistic but then plunged into despondency. He claimed to have experienced heat stroke in the past and, just as frostbite creates a hypersensitivity to cold, he had trouble tolerating the unforgiving rays of the sun. He frequently requested relief on the tiller by his watchmate, Tapscott.

The weeks on the *Anglo-Saxon,* followed by the days in the jolly boat, had given Tapscott ample time to size up Widdicombe, and he didn't trust him. Tapscott strongly suspected that Widdicombe's complaints of feeling faint and needing him to take over the tiller were an act. He felt that Widdicombe was malingering and manipulating him to his personal advantage. On the afternoon of their twelfth day in the boat, Tapscott refused to respond to Widdicombe's request. In typical fashion, Widdicombe, who was used to getting what he wanted, ranted and berated Tapscott. A lesser man might have given in to this verbal assault and threatening gestures, but Tapscott was not a man to be intimidated and rose to the challenge. Quickly, Hawks threw himself between the two men before the violence began. This was fortunate, because instinctively Tapscott had grabbed the ax, and in the heat of the moment the result could have been disastrous. Most importantly, for their future days in the boat, Bob Tapscott had demonstrated to Widdicombe that he would not be bullied.

The role of intermediary in the Tapscott-Widdicombe dispute had been assumed by Hawks, when it would normally have fallen to the Mate. Denny was by then unable to play the active role he had assumed for the last eleven days. He was crumpled in the bottom of the boat, suffering from the undetermined illness that gripped him, and wracked with cramps and nausea most of the day. Nevertheless, he sought and found the energy to mark the end of the discouraging day with another notch on the rail and another log entry. There was not a glimmer of optimism as he laboriously wrote with typical understatement: "Crew now feeling rather low. Unable to masticate hard biscuit owing to low ration of water." As if sensing that this would be his last opportunity to make some recommendations that might help future shipwrecked sailors, he struggled to add his suggestions to the log. These included two breakers of water, various canned fruits and fruit juices, and, curiously, baked beans. These were not suggestions reflecting a consensus of those on board, but the poignant personal desires of a sick man.

The night brought no rest for the weakening Denny and little for the others, who had to listen to him heaving and retching. At dawn, the depth of their crisis was obvious: the Mate was unable to rise from his cramped position in the bottom of the boat. The others did the best they could to rig a more comfortable berth for him, but it was clear that he no longer had the ability to lead the other five sad souls in the little boat. It would seem appropriate that Hawks, the only other officer on board, would assume command. This was challenged by Roy Widdicombe. Hawks was a relatively new officer and an engineer. To Widdicombe, Hawks might do fine in an engine room, but they were sailing and that was the province of real sailors, like himself, with far greater sea time than the Third Engineer. She was a small boat in extreme circumstances and no place for a mutiny. Hawks found a compromise, a distribution of responsibilities. The Engineer would be responsible for keeping the log and the allocation of the provisions. Widdicombe would be responsible for the seamanship: the sailing and navigating.

The efficiency and order that the compromise promised never materialized. As soon as Hawks prepared for the morning distribution of water, he was challenged again by Widdicombe. The sailor argued that the crew should have double the ration that had been so strictly allocated by the Mate, who was now incapable of resolving the dispute. Hawks felt the men should continue to conserve and stay with Denny's plan. Once again, confrontation loomed and Widdicombe exhibited his belligerence. Resisting Widdicombe would surely end in violence, so once again the Third Engineer retreated from his position. Widdicombe won his point and the full double ration of water was issued.

As the men began their fourteenth night in the boat, they were an image of despair. The water supply was nearly gone. Three men were in serious condition: two suffering silently and the other raving mindlessly. The other three reasonably healthy young men were distraught about their future and confused about who would make the critical decisions that lay ahead. It was hard to imagine what further hardships could befall them.

Chapter 11

DESPERATE DECISIONS

As their thirteenth day in the boat ended, Third Engineer Hawks wrote in the log, "Things going from bad to worse, 1st Mate who wrote this diary up to this point going fast." Unfortunately, Hawks was correct in his assessment. The crew spent another difficult night, with Morgan ranting incessantly and Denny continually wracked with heaves, as his stomach twisted and churned. Everything seemed to conspire against them: illness, disease, starvation, and thirst, all compounded by exhaustion, since no one was able to sleep. The men had now completed two full weeks in the boat and hoped they were nearing the Leeward Islands. Even in their fatigued state, however, they knew they had not made the daily distance required to put them close to land. It was a sobering and depressing prospect.

When Hawks went to the water breaker to issue the morning double ration of 4 ounces, it became apparent that once that allotment had been made, there would be only one more meager portion left for each person on board. The crew had consumed all their condensed milk, so this smidgen of water was the last liquid they had. This was the dreaded moment everyone knew was approaching but hadn't wanted to face. They took their morning drink and began another interminable day of oppressive heat. With their minds preoccupied with the ominous thought of having no water at all, they broke their routine once again. Rather than discipline themselves to wait all day for the last of the water to be distributed that evening, the suggestion was made to share the water at midday. With raging thirst, it was torture to sit there, staring at the cask that held the last of the precious fluid. Hawks did not assert himself as the officer in charge of the provisions, but rather held a vote. Those who favored finishing the water then and being rid of the temptation won the vote, and the last of the water was carefully and equally distributed.

While the other men's focus was on the doling out of this final taste of water, the courageous Gunner Penny, as badly wounded and gangrenous as he was, volunteered for another trick at the helm. Penny had kept to himself since the death of Pilcher and silently endured his trial. With difficulty, he positioned himself in the stern and kept the boat steady. When the boat suddenly veered off course, all eyes whipped to the stern to find a problem of greater magnitude than they could have imagined: Gunner Francis Penny had disappeared. The stunned men scanned the sea astern and caught sight of Penny, floating facedown, disciplined, motionless, waiting for the sea to take him. The boat was moving farther and farther away, but no one attempted to rally the others for a rescue. It was clear that the Gunner had considered his plight, made his decision, and chosen his time and opportunity. He had consulted with no one and, like Pilcher, would die alone, but by his own choice. His incredulous shipmates stared in awe, feeling a sense of loss and respect for the valiant veteran of two wars who was passing from their midst.

One can only speculate at what went on in the recesses of Penny's mind in the days leading up to his decision. There had been no evidence that his mind was any more disturbed than the others'. He had remained rational, reserved, controlled, and stoic. The end of the water seemed to be the catalyst that brought about his action. By going over the side, this man who had endured wounds time and again accomplished three important objectives. He put an end to his extreme suffering. He chose death on his terms rather than having death choose him after days of uncontrollable delirium. And, finally, he removed a burden from his fellow voyagers. Certainly, none of his shipmates would have desired or encouraged his act, and they would have cared for the respected Royal Marine as his condition worsened. But it can be understood that Penny didn't want that, and by choosing that very moment to go, he turned his back on his final water ration, just as Pilcher had done, and made that minuscule portion, his token gift, available to the others.

Hawks took the helm, not to bring the boat about and retrieve Penny, but to steady the jolly boat once again on her course. A somber change came over the five mariners. They had shown honor, self-restraint, and fortitude during the first two weeks of their ordeal. Their spirits had remained outwardly strong, even if they privately anguished over their fate. Death had snatched Pilcher from them, and in retrospect it seemed inevitable, but a new and stunning reality was present among them. Perhaps the thought had simmered in the depths of each of their minds, but when it pushed forward they made no room for it and forced it back. Penny had changed all that. He had demonstrated how easily it could be done, how simply an end could be put to the suffering. This concept was now front and center in everyone's minds and the focal point of discussion that afternoon. They debated what had been, until then, unspeakable. There was no effort to rally the morale and raise hopes. The men were collectively and individually confronting their mortality. The discussion revolved around the alternatives of making a quick end of it, or struggling on until dehydration took its final toll. Some expressed fear of the water, while others simply wanted to cling to life. For whatever reasons, the discussion waned. No one took action, and each was left with his own thoughts: of miseries, home, life, loved ones, and shipmates lost.

The lethargy that permeated the boat is reflected in Hawks's log entry for that day. He simply recorded, "Penny very much weaker slipped overboard." He went on with a ragged entry he hoped others would read when everyone was all gone: "From 10:00 pm tonight 14 days out, tried to make Leeward Islands or Porto Rica [*sic*], Hayti [*sic*], but the German raider given none the right to take a sextant, chronometer, extrer [*sic*] water, tin fruit or bottled fruit, no rum or brandy for the wounded crew. Evidently intended to smash all life boat gear to kill all inquiry, but we got the small gig, seven of us by wind somewhere in the vicinity of Leeward Islands."

Men can live for thirty days or more without food, but only about ten days without water. The men in this boat had consumed so little water over the preceding two weeks that they were near the end of their resources. They dragged through their tasks, while those off watch tossed in fitful attempts to sleep.

Although he had been relatively quiet most of the night, Morgan was the herald of the dawn, with a plaintive cry for his mother, not an unusual occurrence for people in crisis. Their situation was desperate. The crew was in the mid-Atlantic, about 700 miles from the site of their sinking, and over 900 miles from the island of Barbuda, the nearest land. In two weeks, they had covered only half the distance to the Leeward Islands, and Morgan's cry for his mother reminded them that they could expect succor from no one.

With no water to distribute, the crew no longer had the moment that "officially" began the day. They sluggishly shifted around the boat, and Denny, rallying somewhat, heroically took a trick at the tiller, positioning the rudder to head them to the west. Not long into the watch, he felt no response when he shifted the tiller. He looked aft and watched the rudder, which had been an extension of the men's will and intent, guiding the little boat in the direction of salvation, floating away. The steady back-and-forth movement of the rudder had worn the pintles loose. Disgusted, Denny left the stern seat and made his way back to his makeshift sickbed in the middle of the boat. Despite their own debilities, the two Able Seamen, Tapscott and Widdicombe, found the steering oar and slid it through the deep notch on the centerline of the transom and secured it in place. Although not as efficient and easy to handle as the rudder with its tiller, it was an adequate substitute. The boat made her way west, with the favorable current pushing her along at about half a knot, and with the prevailing wind on her starboard quarter or occasionally directly over the stern.

Widdicombe and Tapscott took shifts on the steering oar under the increasingly intense, withering sun. Morgan was slumped in the bow and Denny and Hawks were sprawled amidships. The tedium of previous days had increased, since there was no distribution of food or water to break the monotony. Hour after hour passed. The sailors reflected on their dire situation and the loss of Gunner Penny the previous day. They had no clue whether they were near their goal of the Leeward Islands. No bird activity had been seen, and there had been no change in the color of the water to reflect the shoaling of a continental shelf. They were all aware of the days spent becalmed or with light winds limiting the distance they sailed. They might still have hoped they were near land, but certainly these experienced mariners sensed this was not the case.

Out of this lassitude rose Denny, decisive as always. He announced that he was going over the side. Once again, the unspeakable was spoken. His decision signified that for him, and probably all of them, there was no hope and only slow, agonizing death lay before them. He would take the affirmative step of controlling the time and manner of his death. He then raised the grave question: did any of the others want to go at the same time? They all must have been thinking similar thoughts, but now it was real, and there in front of them. The first response came from the sick, weakened, and fearful Morgan. In a desperate plea, he implored the others, including the Mate, not to leave him, implicitly indicating his unwillingness to go.

Surprisingly, one of the most fit, Lionel Hawks, was the next to respond, asserting his willingness to go. He had earlier expressed his fear of the water, and he asked the Mate, for whom he had utmost respect, if he would help him, and Denny agreed. All eyes then fell on Tapscott, the youngest of the lot, still in his teens, but a strong lad with four years of seagoing maturity. He had demonstrated his optimism in the past and now declined the invitation. There was still a chance of rescue. Widdicombe was clearly unnerved by this turn of events, but he, too, was not prepared to take this drastic step. The decisions had been made. Hawks seemed to have a huge sense of relief, and tranquillity settled over him. He said he would like to get some sleep before carrying out the plan, and promptly did so.

There was speculation among the others as to whether the two officers would indeed consummate their agreement. Denny was extremely frail and he knew he was dying. The days and nights of retching and heaving had deprived him of the last scintilla of bodily fluid. Hawks had suffered the same deprivation as the others, but was the only one who had no wound or injury at the beginning of the voyage. It is only speculation as to why he chose to go; but the competent, evenhanded, professional First Mate was his role model. Hawks felt comfortable and reassured in Denny's presence, and now he would place his fate in the hands of the man he most admired. It is possible that Lionel Hawks dreaded the thought of the days ahead as the situation worsened further, with Widdicombe's challenges to the authority he had been trained to employ and was unable to achieve. He certainly felt death was inevitable and chose to share that ultimate experience with his admired leader rather than stay and endure the unimaginable ordeal, inevitable confrontation, and certain struggle that lay ahead.

After an hour of rest, Hawks rose, followed by the enfeebled Denny. The others were amazed at the stamina the Mate rallied as the two set about their awful task. With the calm of a man who was at peace, Hawks decided to have a final supper. His feast consisted of several cans of seawater and a ship's biscuit that had been softened in the water of the Atlantic. He had no qualms about ingesting the seawater now. The departing shipmates took off their jackets and gave them to those who remained behind. Poignantly revealing that First Mate Denny had some hope the others would survive, he took off his signet ring and gave it to Widdicombe, with the request that it be returned to Denny's mother. Through his parched, cracked, and swollen lips, the Mate gave his last fateful order: sail west and go no farther south.

The men shook hands in a formal farewell. As the Mate grasped the hand of Robert Tapscott, a man with virtually no fluid left in his system, tears miraculously developed in Tapscott's eyes. Barry Collingwood Denny and Lionel Henry Hawks, who was afraid of the water, stood precariously on the seat, silently shook hands and then went over the side. As the others looked on, they saw that, unlike the first two to perish in the boat, these two would not die alone; they were locked in a deathly embrace, comrades sharing their last moments.

As the boat moved on, Hawks's hair, bleached white by the sun, shone as a beacon on the sea. Those left in the boat fumbled awkwardly for some solemn observance of this devastating event. They mumbled their way through the Lord's Prayer as their minds struggled with the deep emotions of the moment, and the reality that there were now only three of them. Later that day, Widdicombe made the perfunctory log entry: "Sept. 5th Chief Mate and 3rd Engineer go over the side no water."

There is little doubt that Roy Widdicombe had leadership potential. He had always been one to speak his mind, expect a response, and most often get his way, even if that required force. With the two sailors and the terrified Cook remaining in the boat, it was natural for Widdicombe to take the lead. Morgan was cowering in the bow, trying to wrap his disturbed mind around the most recent grim turn of events. Tapscott, the facilitator, had stood up to Widdicombe's threats in the past, but saw no need to challenge Widdicombe's authority now. The oldest of the three young men, Widdicombe had the edge on experience at sea, and had already been responsible for the sailing of the boat for a few days, so the transition went smoothly.

Despite the loss of the two officers, or perhaps due to it, Widdicombe was infused with new vigor and spirit. His attempts to inspire his companions, however, were less than successful. Both Morgan and Tapscott were depressed and listless as Widdicombe got the boat on course toward the west again. They were all at the limits of their strength and ability to cope with the elements. Every movement required exhausting effort, but Tapscott somehow found the fortitude to resume the simple duties that needed to be fulfilled. Morgan seemed to slip deeper into his nonsensical rambling and loud raving. With the sun reaching its zenith, its heat and blinding rays beat the men mercilessly.

With only Widdicombe and Tapscott reliable on the steering oar, they determined to stand only one-hour watches. In their exhausted state, that hour interval was all they could endure and was periodically modified when the man on the helm had to have earlier relief. Morgan slipped in and out of his deranged babble. On rare occasions, when the steering was simple, with no following sea to cope with, he was put on the steering oar. His mistakes, however, often caused seawater to surge over the side, and the others had to bail out the boat, draining physical resources they could not spare. The steering had to be done almost exclusively by the two ABs. Widdicombe's earlier sunstroke continued to affect his ability to deal with the glare and the scorching rays, while Tapscott's stomach continued to knot and wrench, causing intense pain that sent him into a writhing heap in the bottom of the boat. It is astonishing that these three men could manage to press on under blistering heat with absolutely no water.

The remaining shipmates simply did not have the strength to steer and trim the sail through the night, and the only option was to use the sea anchor to keep the bow pointed into the swells and reduce the possibility of getting broadside to a wave. This anchoring was necessary, but it took miles off their daily progress, and that meant more days of torture before they could find land, if they lived that long. The following morning, the wind diminished, and they bobbed on the broad ocean swells with no hint of relief. They noted that gross, raw boils covered their skin, a common but extremely debilitating condition known as saltwater burns, which develops on those in constant contact with salt water. The boils can be particularly difficult if there is persistent pressure from hard seats or railings on one part of the body. Fortunately, the jolly boat sailors could change positions frequently to lessen the severity of this painful situation. The condition was caused by the frequent spray of waves over them and the buckets of water they poured over themselves, unaware that they were exacerbating the problem.

Saltwater was also a part of Morgan's increasing dementia. While the others had long before realized the terrible ramification of drinking seawater, Morgan had no will or ability to resist. Tapscott and Widdicombe saw him drinking during the day and knew he continued at night while they tried to sleep. By the morning of September 8 Morgan was beyond reason and ranting incessantly. The others were driven to distraction. They tried to humor Morgan one minute and shout him into silence the next, but nothing quieted the tormentor. Sea survival manuals urge physical restraint of a deranged shipmate to prevent damage he might do to himself, others, or the boat. A token effort to blockade Morgan in the bow was ineffective, and the two ABs didn't have the heart to gag him and lash him down.

Tapscott's equanimity gave him a greater tolerance for Morgan's cacophony, while Widdicombe was increasingly infuriated by it. Gone was the calm boat commander of three days earlier. The incensed Widdicombe added to the mayhem with his own frequent outbursts of damnation and frustration over Morgan's never-ending monologue of incomprehensible singing, swearing, chanting, and one-sided conversation. Woven through his ramblings was Morgan's earlier theme of wanting his mother. The hardened, self-reliant Widdicombe shot back the rhetorical question, "Do you think you're the only one who wants his mother?" It was a stunning human response from the tough guy who had lost his own mother as a child, and revealed the desperate yearning each of these men had for relief from their tragic state.

In a fit of depression, Widdicombe grabbed the empty water breaker and hurled it over the side. Tapscott was appalled, since this was the container for storing water when rain came. For the bitter Widdicombe, the possibility of rain was a joke. The men had been sweltering on the unforgiving sea for seventeen days without even a hint of rain, and he couldn't imagine that changing. Widdicombe's temper flared again later that day. Morgan had been in a lucid state, and to give themselves some relief and perhaps some precious sleep, Tapscott and Widdicombe put him on the steering oar. Within minutes Morgan's erratic steering brought gallons of water over the side onto the startled Widdicombe. In a fury, he leapt at Morgan and thrust him over the side. Tapscott moved with a speed and strength he no longer knew he possessed, grabbed Morgan before he was out of reach, and dragged the bewildered Cook back into the boat. Each man was at the breaking point. Despite Widdicombe's pleas, Morgan continued with his unceasing and unnerving meaningless chatter. Pressed beyond his limit, Widdicombe grabbed the ax and sent it whirling end over end toward Morgan. His aim was wide and it swept past his target and sank into the sea. Another of their precious possessions was gone and the tormentor remained.

The sun-baked boat continued listlessly under light air. As darkness came on, the drained men rigged the sea anchor again and attempted to rest. Deeply in the grips of his insanity, Morgan kept up his babble through the night, and it was only toward dawn that the others realized he had slipped into a deep stupor. The morning brought an increase in the wind, and with dogged determination the two sailors hoisted their sail and began to put yards and then miles of ocean behind them. It would have been yet another unremarkable day except that Widdicombe was able to add a cryptic entry in the log: "Sept 9th 2nd cook goes mad dies. Two of us left."

Their relief was palpable. They had lost another shipmate, but he had contributed nothing to the voyage except adding to their misery with his tireless rantings. Because of his infected wound and consumption of seawater, Morgan had been on a course toward death for many days, and the two men found it impossible to mourn his demise. They no longer had to expend coveted energy coping with the infuriating babble; their bodies were depleted and they, too, were close to death. Once again, they considered ending their own lives. When Denny had posed the question only four days earlier, Tapscott and Widdicombe had been firm. The Mate and the others were gone now, and those four days had been completely without water. That fragment of spirit that had shown itself a few days earlier had eroded as they faced the vast sea around them and discussed ending their lives.

This was the beginning of a strange "brotherhood" between these two sailors who were so different in character. It had been clear from the earliest days on the *Anglo-Saxon* that they did not like each other and merely tolerated one another based on their mutual respect for their skills as mariners. Tapscott had shown himself man enough to stand up to Widdicombe's bullying attitude, and this put the men on the same level. Now, of the seven who began the voyage nineteen days earlier, they were the last alive. They would not have chosen each other as companions to share the intimate discussion of ending their lives, but there was no choosing. They were now bound together with a certainty that only death would dissolve. Widdicombe argued that they should not give in and Tapscott accommodated himself to that thought. They would press on.

As other shipwrecked sailors had done over centuries before, the two men looked to the minute amount of fluid waste they themselves could produce, and drank their dark, acrid urine. While the desperation of the moment forced the decision and the act, it is generally abhorred, and myths such as urine being poisonous added to the reluctance and fear that accompanied the consumption. The taboo against this was so great that in some historical instances the act contributed to long-term depression in the surviving sailors. Whether it was an attempt to purge the urine from his system, or a response to his still raging thirst, Tapscott again dipped a can of water into the sea. That temptation for shipwrecked sailors over millennia, and as immortalized by Coleridge, drove them nearly mad. All around the sailors, for as far as they could see, was cool water. The small amount of seawater Tapscott drank had an immediate effect: not the desired relief from his thirst, but an involuntary revulsion that brought all the fluid he had consumed back up. Widdicombe was also plagued with stomach pains, and the two men writhed in their misery. Day and night passed, and when morning came, the boat bobbed on a flat, calm sea. The boat was dead in the water, being moved only imperceivably by unseen currents.

The futility of the situation was clear to Tapscott, but it was the drained and exhausted Widdicombe who acquiesced: they would end their ordeal. To record a last message, Tapscott awkwardly wrote a brief note to his mother. He placed it in the attaché case with the other records of the crew's tragic experience, which he hoped would be recovered and document their fate. The two were now prepared, and without ceremony or a dramatic plunge, they lowered themselves over the side. Tapscott was the first in the water, followed immediately by Widdicombe. Widdicombe, however, instantly scrambled back into the boat; he couldn't go through with it. The water had awakened the instinct to live, and Tapscott, now bound in the brotherhood, would not go alone. He, too, with great effort, clambered back into the boat. Completely drained, they lay dazed in the listless boat, absorbing more and more of the sun's burning rays.

As the sun reached the meridian, it was Widdicombe who signaled he was ready again for the final act. There was nothing to attend to, and

Widdicombe simply lowered himself over the side. Tapscott toppled in after him and began to float away from the boat. When he realized that Widdicombe, although fully in the water, had not let go of the lifeline, Tapscott urged him to let go, but Widdicombe held fast. Tapscott, the swimmer, managed the few strokes required to get back to the motionless boat. The two men clung to the line and argued the case. Yes, they had decided to end it, but in the water they felt refreshed and renewed. Life glimmered faintly within them, and it was still too soon to give up; they laboriously helped each other out of the sea and back into the frail craft that was their home.

Twice in that day, Tapscott and Widdicombe had courted death and twice found the will to struggle on. As the afternoon wore on, they conceived a remarkable idea. Their guide through the preceding twenty days, and arguably the most precious of all their meager treasures, was the compass. Through it, they could keep their little craft headed west toward land. The compass contained an even richer treasure: liquid, and not just any liquid. The compass card, which carried the compass rose with its markings of direction in both degrees and compass points, floated in a reservoir of alcohol. It would be the act of madmen to misuse this most necessary instrument. These were indeed madmen, with one urgent need. There was no future for them, there was only the moment; and at that moment they stared at a bounty of fluid. The decision made itself and Tapscott carefully unscrewed the plug. He drained every drop of alcohol from the compass, dividing it fairly, filling two of the empty condensed milk cans. With remarkable discipline and a spark of optimism, Tapscott replaced the alcohol with seawater and screwed the plug back into place. To all appearances, the compass still functioned. Although it seemed hard to imagine, they might have a need for it. That was in the future, however, and at that instant the two shipwrecked sailors enjoyed a drink, a real drink.

That first trickle of alcohol down their raw throats cauterized its way into their desiccated bodies. The effect of the drink was immediate and within moments they were feeling no pain. With nothing in their systems to absorb the pure alcohol, the power of the spirits had its full effect. Sitting facing each other, the men imbibed, laughed, told sea stories and tales of shoreside escapades, and for a brief time the burden of their dire predicament was lifted. Careful as they were to prolong their enjoyment, the drink was soon gone. There was no doubt that they were drunk, but wonderfully drunk. With all their cares dissipated in the alcoholic haze, the two exhausted sailors slipped quietly and for once happily into a long, deep sleep.

Chapter 12

WATER!

For hours after their binge, Tapscott and Widdicombe lay sprawled in the jolly boat, deep in sleep. Waking in the middle of the night, they paid the price for their delicious indulgence. Just as the alcohol had acted quickly and powerfully on them, so did the hangover, with the aching head, rebellious stomach, and thirst, the symptoms accentuated by their terrible condition. There was nothing to ease their headaches, nothing to soothe their twisting stomachs, and nothing whatsoever to diminish their thirst, which now raged more than ever. If the two sailors regretted their raid on the compass alcohol, suspicion dictates they would have done it again.

It was the earliest hours of the morning of the beginning of the men's fourth week in the boat. In their merriment the night before, they had failed to set the sea anchor; they fumbled to get the device over the side and then collapsed. Deep sleep was a thing of the past, and they tossed restlessly under the shelter of the boat cover as the hours wore on. Both sleeping at the same time was risky, but the exhausted men had no choice. Abruptly, their rest was ended by brilliant, startling lightning, followed by the low rumble of thunder. In twenty-one days in the boat, they had been tantalized only occasionally by the appearance of clouds in the far distance. Soon they were in the midst of a dazzling display of lightning and ear-splitting thunder, which boomed and cracked on and on. They could not muster optimism. They had been disappointed too many times. This storm, also, might pass them by, leaving their situation unchanged. Then, raindrops fell.

The men scrambled out from beneath their shelter, since this was the one thing from which they wanted no protection, and tilted their heads back to catch the precious drops. The boat cover became a catch basin, and a small reservoir of rainwater gathered in its hollow. The sailors grabbed their cans and scooped up the fluid, eager to feel its relief slide down their throats. One taste, however, brought bitter disappointment. The water was tainted: pure salt, causing instant disgust. The boat cover had protected them from so much salt spray that it was completely coated with the evaporated residue, and the desperate men had to wait for the rain to rinse the salt from the canvas. They had enjoyed only the slightest taste of fresh water when the rain ceased. The brief shower passed on, and they sat stunned and transfixed by their plight.

As daylight emerged, not a shower, but real prolonged rain began to fall, a true tropical downpour that saturated the men and everything they possessed. Their catch basin now functioned as hoped and they were able to ladle sweet fresh water from the pool in the canvas and let it caress its way down their throats and into their bodies. With the water, life flowed back into their desiccated tissues. Despite all their earlier discussions and fantasies about favorite beverages, nothing could have been more satisfying and more appreciated than this simple, cool, clear water. In his headlong rush for satiation, Tapscott guzzled too much, too quickly. Unaccustomed to this amount of liquid, his system rejected it and sent it all up. The rain continued to fall, however, and the teenaged sailor simply began again, letting measured amounts cascade luxuriantly down his throat.

The men's thirst was slaked for the first time since leaving the *Anglo-Saxon*. As they sought a way to collect and save some of this life-giving water, Widdicombe's impetuous acts of the previous week came to haunt them. The perfect receptacle, their water breaker, had been hurled over the side, as had the ax, which now could have been used to puncture one of the watertight copper flotation tanks that Tapscott wrestled from under the seat in the bow. Fortunately, the soft copper yielded to the point of Denny's sharp knife, and Tapscott cut a rough bunghole in the tank and directed the flow of water from the boat cover into the reservoir. A bung was carved from an oar handle and the precious reserve of approximately six gallons of water was secure. This was incredible wealth! The two of them had half again as much water as all seven had had at the beginning of the voyage. Only hours before, they were in a completely hopeless situation. With this urgently needed commodity, they felt life coming back to them.

Over the previous weeks, the two men's bodies had called for less and less food as the fluid in their systems diminished, time and again rejecting what could not be tolerated. Since their agony after eating the boiled mutton, the sailors had eaten absolutely nothing. Now, their need for water had been met, and for the first time in many days, they felt hunger and craved something to eat. The ship's biscuit was perfect: bland, somewhat nutritious, and palatable, now that they had ample water for soaking and softening the hardtack. Each savored his one-biscuit banquet and felt that their fortunes had turned. They had endured unfathomable hardships and horrid experiences. They had witnessed suffering and agony beyond measure. They had watched their ship sink, taking many shipmates with her. They had watched all their other boat voyagers succumb. Now they were alive in their sturdy little boat, with a small supply of food, on their way toward land of some sort, and, most importantly, they had a reserve of water. The flame of optimism that had been all but extinguished began to flicker again.

When the wind picked up the following day, it was with real confidence that Tapscott and Widdicombe set their sail and began to make significant progress to the west. They drank all the water they wanted from their seemingly abundant supply, and enjoyed another meal of softened ship's biscuits. A few days earlier, they had tried the last can of mutton and, unable to eat it, dumped the precious six pounds over the side.

With water, the dream of the mutton was on their minds, as was the nightmare of having dumped it into the sea. They would have to subsist on their supply of hardtack.

The water coursing through the men's tissues brought physical changes. For weeks, they had not generated a drop of sweat, despite the oppressive heat. Charged with fluid, they began once again to sweat. Their pores had closed to conserve water, and now, as perspiration tried to vent through the skin's surface, it could not. Blisters developed all over their bodies, and at the merest touch they opened and spilled forth the fluid. Their legs, which had begun to wither, now were noticeably swollen. The impact of the water in their systems fascinated them.

The breeze held and day followed day, with good distance made during the daylight hours and reasonably good rest at night. There was little to occupy the men's attention, but in checking their supplies they realized they still had several matches. There was also Pilcher's pipe, but no tobacco. With all the time in the world, they scoured Pilcher's case, extracting fragments of tobacco from corners and creases. It was hardly a full pipe's worth, but it provided the two men with a moment of pure enjoyment after so many tortured days. These were good days, if such can be imagined under the circumstances. They had noticed changes in the color of the sea and clumps of floating seaweed, which they interpreted as signs that they were nearing land. Any day they were sure they would see land loom in the distance. With this rationalization, they continued to enjoy the luxury of free access to water.

While Tapscott and Widdicombe had ceased making daily log entries because of the uniformity of the days, they had made an entry on the day of the deluge, which said, "A cloud burst gave us water for six days." Either they were exceptionally farsighted in predicting that they would each consume two quarts of water per day, or the entry was actually made six days later. The deluge had been on September 12. On the 18th the wind died off and their water tank was dry.

Fortunately, relief was not long in coming, and on the morning of September 20th, the rain fell again. The two shipmates once again drank their fill and replenished their storage tank. Eager to eat, they indulged in an extravagant feast of five ship's biscuits softened in the rainwater. Although their supply of biscuits was dwindling, they rationalized that they had to be near land and would not need the food much longer. This consumption of hardtack, combined with those they had eaten since the 12th, produced an unexpected effect. Their bowels, which had ceased to function almost a month earlier, resumed the elimination of waste. A wonder of the human body is that essential functions such as that can remain idle for long periods, and then, given the right conditions, simply begin to function normally again. Documented cases show bowel activity suspended for as long as forty-six days, two weeks longer than Tapscott and Widdicombe had experienced.

The sailors still had a full roster of miseries, including the saltwater boils, which were now painfully chronic where their bones were no longer cushioned by healthy flesh. At least, however, they had water. This rain warranted another log entry, one with a degree of finality, as it was signed by the two men. It reads, "Sept. 20th. Rain again for four days. Getting very weak put [sic] trusting in God to pull us through. R. Widdicombe. R. Tapscott." Whether they thought they were so near land that this would be their last log entry or whether they were signing their names for posterity will never be known, but the next four days, blessed with copious water, slipped past. The breeze was light, and they sailed during the day toward the distant islands.

Peering at the horizon, the men would distinctly see land under cloud formations. Their spirits would soar, as they could all but feel the sand under their feet. Excruciating disappointment answered, as each of these "islands" evaporated into the clouds and dispersed. Each island hallucination sent them deeper into despair. Following the Mate's instructions, they had made their way west, and were nearing the longitude of the Leeward Islands, not knowing they were hundreds of miles north in latitude. Still they pressed on toward the west.

All these disappointments were about to pale in comparison to the sobering reality of September 24. Widdicombe and Tapscott had consumed their store of water and the tank was once again dry. They knew the suffering of dehydration and had already experienced eight days without any water. That prospect lay before them again, compounded by the fact that they had eaten the last of their ship's biscuits; they had no food left on board.

There are numerous accounts of shipwrecked sailors reverting to cannibalism, either feeding on the flesh of fellow castaways who have died, or killing one of their number to provide sustenance for the others. The question naturally arises whether there was cannibalism in the *Anglo-Saxon* jolly boat. The simple answer is no. As the crew was diminished from seven, to six, to five, to three, and finally to two, there had been so little water that they could not eat the food they had on board, the mutton and the hardtack. It was after all the other five were gone that the rains came for Tapscott and Widdicombe and their ability to eat returned. By then, the two men were bound together by their shared ordeal. Companionship, even of someone they did not particularly like, was the highest priority. They needed each other to face the ordeal ahead. Widdicombe made the final log entry: "September 24th All water and biscuits gone but still hoping to make land." This was their thirty-fourth day in the boat, and they would not have been able to imagine that they were less than halfway through their incredible voyage. At that moment, with no food and no water, they had an additional thirty-six days to endure.

Two days later, a nighttime deluge filled the water tank and flooded the boat so that the sailors had to bail the excess fresh water over the side, a task that seemed criminal after their parched desperation. The abundance of water accentuated their hunger. During the month they had been in the boat, they had precious little of either food or, until recently, water. At the beginning of the voyage, each man had been fit, weighing about 170 pounds. Now, as they looked at each other, they were morbidly fascinated by their transformation. Their hollow cheeks and prominent chins were covered with scraggly beards. They were gaunt, with the bone of their skulls prominent under the veil of sun-darkened skin, marred by blisters and sores. Their bodies were shriveled to nothing but bone and muscle. When they had had their fill of rainwater, they were amused at the protrusion of their shrunken bellies. They were acutely aware of how vulnerable they were. Without food, their bodies would slowly devour themselves, eating up muscle until they perished.

The two remaining crew members had being voyaging for twice as long as the sixteen days Denny had originally projected to landfall, and despite being periodically becalmed, by now they should have sighted land. In actuality, they were approximately 400 miles northeast of the Leeward Islands chain. Had they known this, they could have changed course, and, with the wind on their port beam, sailed on a close reach for Barbuda. Deprived of that knowledge, they continued to sail west. In order to put more distance behind them, they began to sail again at night. They had more stamina because of the renewed fluid in their systems, but the task of sailing the boat with her awkward steering oar was taxing, and easily sapped their energy. Standing the night watch alone, there was no one to converse with to stay awake, but they had no choice. Something was fundamentally wrong in their navigation, and they had to proceed with the one fact they knew: land lay to the west; any other direction was a risk. By sailing west they knew they were decreasing the distance to land of some kind.

The morning following the rainfall, the sailors began to ration their water consumption. Gone was the optimism that they could drink all they wanted because they were surely near land. With legitimate hope that they would get more rain, their ration was three dippers per man per day. This still amounted to only 12 ounces, less than a pint per day, but they felt they could manage on that and periodically slake their thirst when it rained. Their minds dwelled on food. They made good progress through that day, with a fresh breeze that held into the night. Sailing through the lengthening tropical nights was difficult and exhausting. The man on watch sat in the stern sheets, clutched the steering oar, and fought to stay awake. They kept on course by the stars. By keeping the North Star, the polestar, on the starboard beam, they made their way west.

For some time, they had seen floating masses of seaweed, which Tapscott thought they should try to eat, as seaweed was part of the Welsh diet. The two species of floating seaweed the two could gather, *Sargassum natans* and *Sargassum fluitans,* were far from the tasty and nutritious seaweed

they knew from home. While they appeared appealing, with golden tendrils festooned with pneumatocysts, or little floats, clusters of what
seemed like berries, the "berries" contributed little if any nutritional
value. The sailors collected some of the sargassum, and after using precious fresh water to rinse it, began to chew. And chew they must, since the
salty mass in their mouths was tough and elastic, resisting all attempts at
mastication, but giving them the sense that they were eating. Not only
did the sargassum lack appetizing or nutritional properties, the tannins
and other natural chemical compounds it possessed made it distasteful.
Desperate as they were, however, they continued to periodically chew,
and sometimes manage to ingest, small amounts of the seaweed.

After giving up keeping the log, one day melded into another, with
significant events standing out only in a vague sense of time. In the sleepy
hours just after midnight, a few days after they renewed their night sailing, Tapscott had the watch on the steering oar while Widdicombe was
deep asleep forward. In fact, Tapscott was also slipping in and out of sleep
at the helm when the jolly boat came to a sudden halt. It was astonishing!
Suddenly, keenly awake, with adrenaline pumping, Tapscott searched for
the land they had stumbled upon. Neither he nor Widdicombe had detected any hint of land, no waves breaking in the distance, no birds, no
smell of land. Indeed, there was no land, nothing to be seen; and yet, the
boat had hit something. As Tapscott moved forward to investigate, the
boat heaved and glided backward off a huge creature. The tranquillity of
the whale's night had been disturbed by the boat, and it returned the
favor with a resounding smack of its broad tail as it headed for the deep.
The jostling disturbed Widdicombe's sleep and he emerged from the
canvas shelter. On hearing Tapscott's story, he arrogantly declared there
were no whales in that part of the ocean. Widdicombe took over the helm
and Tapscott, disgusted that his shipmate doubted his word, retreated
under the boat cover for his own opportunity to sleep.

Sleep did not come easily, as he thought he heard the flapping of a fish
on the boat cover. Hope soon faded as a search of the boat failed to produce a fish. He pressed his search the following morning and this time
was well rewarded. Wedged in the bottom of the boat was his prize, a

fresh flying fish, only a few hours from the sea! Widdicombe and Tapscott had a meal before them, having eaten nothing for a week except the rubbery sargassum seaweed. The heavens had delivered fresh water and the sea, fresh food. Tapscott cut the fish in half with the blade from Pilcher's razor, and choosing head or tail, they savored the sweet meat of the small fish and crunched down every morsel, including head, fins, and tail. Twelve to fourteen inches in length and a couple of inches in diameter, the fish was delicious, but meager. They craved more.

Although conscious of fish swimming near the boat, the sailors had a surprisingly difficult and futile time catching any. As is typical, their boat attracted some large predators. The tropical waters in which the jolly boat now sailed had ample sharks, which usually could be seen menacing the boat from afar. When they approached, Widdicombe defended their vessel with an oar, which seemed to discourage their closer inspections. While he wanted to keep these fearsome predators away, Widdicombe dearly wanted to attract and catch smaller fish. He would frequently flail over the side with the knife at fish swimming nearby, his efforts always ending in bitter frustration. The men were remarkable in their fortitude, but the subtle dullness of mind they suffered from the effects of starvation and dehydration may have made them less creative at catching fish than they would have been early in the voyage. With their knife, they might have fashioned one of the oars into a harpoon with a barbed tip, but they may not have been able to muster the energy to manage such a heavy implement and spear a fish. Adding to their inventory of disappointments, they could see fish but not catch them.

Some days after the "grounding" on the whale, they spotted a pod of whales, forcing Widdicombe to reluctantly admit there actually were whales in the vicinity. These sea mammals were an impressive and somewhat threatening sight. While they were able to discourage sharks by splashing the oar, these whales were larger than their boat, and the two sailors felt quite vulnerable. They now encountered large floating mats of the sargassum seaweed and dragged a hefty amount into the boat. To their joy they found a species of small swimming crabs, *Portunus sayi*, enmeshed in the seaweed. Though only the size of a thumbnail, they were food, life-giving food. With patches of the seaweed all around them, it seemed as if there could be a steady, if small, supply. In addition, they also found tiny snails clinging to the tendrils of the seaweed. Known as *Litiopa melanostoma,* the snails have shells only ¹⁄₁₆ to ¹⁄₈ of an inch in size and, therefore, produce only an infinitesimal amount of meat. The desperate men had time in abundance, the time to pick out the snail meat with a pin.

In Pilcher's attaché case, the sailors found a safety pin, which they fashioned into a hook, baited with a piece of a crab, and dangled over the side. Their hopes soared when a fish took the bait. The excited men worked together, with Tapscott maneuvering the line carefully to draw the fish within reach of Widdicombe with the knife. Success seemed theirs, until the fish forcefully twisted himself free, straightening the soft metal of the pin. Ravenous with hunger and seeing their chance for food so close, they tried again and again, but to no avail. Their pliable little barbless hook could secure no fish. In utter frustration they resigned themselves to the meager picking of crabs, snails, and newly found tiny shrimp from the floating platforms of sargassum. Even with extensive searching and picking, these little creatures, which they ate alive and raw, provided only the barest minimum of food. One day, they found an old, small fish in the bilges of the boat and, despite the fact that the fish was clearly rotten, desperately devoured it. They waited with trepidation for some violent physical reaction to the rotten fish, but none came.

As the second week of October began, Tapscott and Widdicombe experienced a weather shift. Dark clouds formed and squalls battered the little boat. This meant they could replenish their water supply, but it also meant that sailing the boat would be more difficult, particularly since they had to steer with the oar. The unpredictability of squalls made them truly dangerous for the men and their boat. A mistake under those fierce conditions could put the boat on her beam ends, swamp her, and end both the voyage and the sailors' lives. The risk of sailing in the squalls was too high. Their decision was to heave to, take down the sail, set the sea anchor, and let the heavy, erratic weather pass by. To provide better shelter, they used both the tattered boat cover and the canvas sail, and crawled underneath to ride out the storm. They weathered the night, but conditions were little better in the morning, so they kept to their makeshift cabin. The decision to both sleep at the same time was a serious gamble, but one they had taken before. When Tapscott awoke and realized that the deluge continued, he raised the canvas cover and looked out to see if the sea anchor was still set properly. He then looked toward the horizon and there, less than a thousand yards away, a ship was steaming her way south. He frantically roused Widdicombe from his sleep and fought to get the sea anchor in.

Rising and falling in the broad ocean swells, in the midst of the pelting rain, without even her sail hoisted, the tiny boat was virtually invisible. The two men madly wrestled oars into place and began rowing. Despite their best effort, they could not gain on the fast-moving steamer. They shifted to a frenzied effort to attract attention, flailing their oars and shrieking at the top of their voices. But those voices could not be heard on the steamer, with all the engine noise and the wind and weather dampening sounds. Desperately, Tapscott blew First Mate Denny's whistle until he could blow no more, and still the ship proceeded south, and then turned east and steamed away. Their frustration was intolerable. Why hadn't they been seen? What were the people on watch on the ship doing?

It is not hard to imagine that on the steamer on a nasty October morning, steaming hundreds of miles from land, with sheets of rain blasting the ship, those on the bridge were staying dry inside the wheelhouse. Lookouts were most likely huddled, scanning the distant horizon for other ships, muffled in foul-weather clothing, and perhaps seeking shelter in the lee of some piece of deck equipment. This was another crushing disappointment for the disheartened sailors. They had endured so much. Once again, they had seen salvation, had their hopes and spirits raised, and watched impotently as salvation sailed on. Surely, this was more than they could bear.

Chapter 13

FORTITUDE

The postman delivered letters to Tapscott's mother, Widdicombe's bride, and the other families of those lost on the *Anglo-Saxon* on the day the two remaining sailors watched the steamer pass by without seeing them in the squalls of the open ocean. The letters were from the Shipping Federation, identical except for the names and ranks of the men. Cynthia Widdicombe's began, "It is with considerable regret that I have heard from Messrs. Lawther, Latta & Co. Ltd., that the S.S. 'Anglo-Saxon' upon which your husband was serving as Able Seaman is gravely overdue and must be presumed lost." The dreaded words that these family members had prayed they would not confront were now there before them, in bold letters, on official stationery. The ship was a month overdue on a voyage that should have taken only a month. The letter was carefully worded so as not to preclude the survival of the men, but, for the recipients, the letter was a staggering blow.

Other than the "considerable regret" mentioned in the first line, the only compassion in the letter was the offer of temporary financial assistance. The wording was cold and bureaucratic, with the letter continuing: "With a view to avoiding any undue hardship until it is known what has happened to the crew or a decision reached as to the cause of the vessel's loss, I have been asked to investigate the circumstances of your dependency upon the earnings of your husband for your support, so that a provisional allowance may be paid." It included a request to fill out forms and attach documents, such as marriage and birth certificates. The letter then concluded with a stern warning: "It must be understood, however, that anything which I pay you will be on account of whatever may eventually be found to be due to you when it is known what has happened to the crew and the cause of the vessel's loss has been established."

This letter with its terrible news came during the depths of Britain's ordeal. The first horrendous year of the war, with its numerous defeats on the Continent, was over, and there was little to encourage the people of the island nation except the stirring words of their pugnacious Prime Minister, Winston Churchill. The Battle of Britain still raged, and for over a month the country had been experiencing the "blitz" following Hitler's directive of September 5 "for disruptive attacks on the population and the air defenses of major British cities, including London, by day and night." The valiant airmen of the RAF withstood the massive air assault and, at least for the time, discouraged any land invasion of the British Isles; but the devastating toll would grow increasingly costly. The blitz took more than 3,000 civilian lives each month during this early period of the war, with a total of over 43,000. All over the country families received grim news of military and civilian deaths, many from the merchant marine community. These numbers did little to console those on the receiving end of the letters; this was their intensely personal loss.

Despite the deliberate ambiguity about the fate of the crew of the *Anglo-Saxon,* some would resign themselves to the reality. For the majority, however, these letters were the beginning of a period of emotional torture. There were the words "must be presumed lost," but they left room for hope. Could their loved ones be alive? The ship had lifeboats. Were their husbands or sons at that moment in boats nearing land, or about to be picked up by a passing ship? There were numerous stories of such occurrences. Were they castaways on some deserted island? Was it possible that they had been taken prisoner? Their relatives had no way of knowing. With the necessity of wartime secrecy regarding maritime operations, they had not known where the *Anglo-Saxon* was bound, or in what part of the world she was overdue. Had the ship disappeared in the frigid North Atlantic on a trip to the United States, in the tropics, or in the Indian Ocean? Each family member wrestled with their own hellish images of the ordeal their loved one faced. Most grasped at the possibility their loved one was alive and would return.

The burden of the letter had particular weight for Ethel Milburn, whose husband, the ship's Chief Engineer, was missing. She had to bear the burden stoically to protect her two sons, nine-year-old Ted and six-year-old Derek, from the devastating thought that their dad would not return. This was for Ethel Milburn, as well as the others, a period of painful suspense and with each passing day, diminished hope.

Although prompted by the "business" of providing assistance to the dependents of those on ships that were long overdue, this correspondence also protected the shipping industry from having to continue payments to crew members or allotments to their families when ships were missing and there was no revenue from cargo that failed to reach its destination. The Shipping Federation represented the shipping industry as a whole and, through an arrangement with the government, provided assistance to the families of those missing. The second element of the process followed immediately on the first.

In a letter Ethel Milburn received from Lawther, Latta & Co., managers for the *Anglo-Saxon*'s owners, the Nitrate Producers Steam Ship Co., dated the day after the federation's letter, she was informed that the allotment note her husband had set up was being recalled. Eddie Milburn's pay was £31 5s per month, second only to that of the *Anglo-Saxon*'s Captain, Paddy Flynn. He had devoted almost 80 percent of his pay to his family, by setting up a monthly allotment of £24 for Ethel and the boys. This second letter informed her that the Borough of Tynemouth Savings Bank was being asked to return the allotment note. At that moment, Ethel Milburn had no way of knowing that her husband had been lost fifty days earlier. The reality she faced was that it would not be his earnings that would provide for his family until his fate was certain, and possibly forever. She was now among those who suffered the torment of waiting for news of the 41 on board the *Anglo-Saxon*, and the untold thousands who had waited, were waiting, or would wait for news of their missing merchant mariners.

None of those who waited, with their hope dwindling, had any idea whether the *Anglo-Saxon* had been the victim of an accident or of enemy action. They had no idea that there were two *Anglo-Saxon* survivors clinging to life on the Atlantic.

Fifty days in the boat had passed for those survivors, when, on October 10, the two dazed sailors watched the steamer pass by. The sailors had themselves and no one else to depend on if they were to survive. Somehow they had outlasted their five companions and endured for seven weeks. Fortitude would not allow them to give up, and they would no longer consider going over the side. With their water tank full, the promise of some meager nourishment from the minute crabs, snails, and shrimp they could find in the seaweed, and knowing they must by now be nearing land, they mustered the strength to once again hoist the sail and set their course to the west.

By plotting their voyage on a chart, it can be estimated that Tapscott and Widdicombe were about 250 miles north of the Virgin Islands, which lie to the east of Puerto Rico. First Mate Barry Denny's decision to turn away from the nearest land and sail southwest and then west took the men with the current and prevailing winds, and what wind there was usually came from the starboard quarter or the stern. This direction should also have carried them into an area of increased rainfall. Denny's decision had been made without the benefit of charts or manuals, but is in accordance with the advice the manuals of today prescribe. Through no fault of his own, the vitally important rainfall did not come in time to give the succor and encouragement some of them required to press on.

With no navigational instruments except the compass, Denny had had to reckon the jolly boat's location as accurately as he could. He made notations in his log of her estimated course and speed, and made a mental compensation for the set and drift of the current. If there was any cause for his premature decision to turn west, it was wishful thinking. Denny's estimates of the distance the vessel had achieved were undoubtedly overly optimistic, but they were the estimates of a man who was willing his craft along with all the mental power he could generate. That willpower was not enough to alter reality. Ten days into the voyage, Denny estimated that they had gone far enough south and should turn west. This put them on a course that would make the voyage much longer for anyone who survived to make landfall. If Denny had held on the west-southwest course for another week, they would have been in the latitude of the northern islands of the Leeward chain. Turning west then would likely have brought them to one of those islands, probably Antigua or Barbuda, by about October 1. Of course, hindsight does not reveal what difficulties might have befallen them or if they would have encountered rain as early as they did on the course they did steer. The heavy ocean rollers off Antigua might have sent the boat crashing onto a rugged stretch of coast. There is no way to know if the voyage would have been easier or if anyone would have survived. It is only certain that the distance would have been shorter. The basic tenets of Denny's decision were sound: the rain did come, albeit too late for most, the wind favored them, and the currents assisted in carrying them westward.

There is a clockwise sweep of ocean currents around the perimeter of the North Atlantic basin. The strong Gulf Stream current surges from the Gulf of Mexico, around the tip of Florida, and up the east coast of the United States. As this current glides out toward the open Atlantic south of Nova Scotia, it encounters a current coming down from the Labrador Straits. This forces the Gulf Stream waters straight across the Atlantic where they split, with some of the water heading north toward Britain, Ireland, and Norway. The bulk of it turns south off the Spanish coast, continuing southwest through the area of the Azores, the Canary Islands, and the Cape Verde Islands. It then curves around to head west and runs back across the Atlantic toward the West Indies and the Gulf Stream, where the cycle begins again.

In this broad, sweeping current, Denny's decision to head west practically assured that if the boat remained afloat she would eventually strike land. The log would tell the tale if the boat was found abandoned. When the voyage began in late August, the current flowing down from the Azores pushed them west at half a knot, despite their aiming the boat west-southwest. While half a knot of "drift" from the current does not sound substantial, if it affects a boat hour after hour, day after day, and week after week, it can have a significant impact. A float drifting with a current of half a knot can traverse 12 miles of ocean in a day, and nearly 100 miles in a week. This can be of great assistance if travel is being favored by the current. If required to go against the current, however, it will work against progress to that degree.

The current throughout September continued to push Tapscott and Widdicombe west. They were aimed on a course that would take them to the Turks and Caicos Islands, at the southern end of the Bahamas, if the currents continued to flow west. As this transoceanic current reaches the West Indies, however, instead of continuing west, it begins to sweep northwest and flow into the Gulf Stream to start the round-trip again. In mid-October, the jolly boat was heading west, with the drift moving them slightly northwest each day. They were making progress toward the west and the unseen islands that lay ahead, but also being swept northwest. It was a question as to what force would prevail: sailing west or the currents. Would they be swept past the islands?

The monotony of the men's existence—watch on, watch off, around the clock, with some sleep in between—was broken only by their scavenging for marine life among the mats of seaweed. They were now emaciated images of their former selves. From their original weights, they had each lost approximately 75 pounds. The clothes they had were rags, providing little protection from the sun or sea. After two months in the boat, their hair was a disheveled tangle covered with salt. Their eyes peered out listlessly from the two deep cavities of their skulls. Only in moments of crisis did life return to those eyes. Their skin was stretched over skeletal forms. Shoulders, elbows, hips, and knees protruded from the remaining bulk of their bodies and pressed against their skin, which, though burned dark brown by the unceasing tropical sun, had a claylike pallor. The most remarkable achievement of these men was the retention of their mental faculties despite the dehydration and ongoing malnourishment they had endured for so long. Approaching the sixty-day mark, their condition was deplorable yet astonishing.

The average person can survive starvation for sixty to seventy days. The body goes through three stages during this process. The body looks to its stored resources and begins to consume them. In the first phase, long past for Tapscott and Widdicombe, their bodies produced the glucose needed to maintain their blood-sugar levels by raiding the liver for its store of glycogen. This is only enough for a matter of hours, so the body then begins to draw on fat and then protein. In the second stage, it is the fat of the body that is consumed. Fat is broken down into fatty acids to supply energy for the muscles, and glycerol to support the brain. For Tapscott and Widdicombe, this phase probably ended soon after the last of their food was consumed. By early October, they were in the final stage of starvation, in which the body, with no more fat to convert, starts to to consume the protein it has remaining, largely found in muscles. Throughout this process, the body has been consuming itself in an amazing sequence, moving methodically through its reserves in a way that begins with the least damage, while always supplying energy to the most essential systems, such as the brain, before meeting other needs.

Tapscott and Widdicombe exhibited the symptoms of starvation in textbook fashion. A landmark study was conducted later in the war years by Dr. Ancel Keys and others at the University of Minnesota. A group of conscientious objectors volunteered to participate in a study to provide information to relief workers going to help starved people in war-torn Europe, preparing them for what they would find physically and psychologically among this battered population. These volunteers endured a semistarvation diet for six months, with results parallel to what was experienced by Tapscott and Widdicombe. There was preoccupation with food and lengthy discussions and fantasies about food. "Hunger pangs" manifested themselves with staggering power. For the sailors, these pains were at times crippling. In the scientific study, there were also emotional and personality changes similar to those of the sailors. Extreme emotional deterioration was common, with the volunteers slipping into depression. This was sometimes offset by moments of elation, but the mood swing back was often into deeper depression. This was, of course, the case when the sailors, for example, spotted a ship promising rescue,

The *Anglo-Saxon* in the Mersey River, Liverpool, with the crew's quarters at the stern, the lifeboats on the boat deck over the engineering officers' quarters, and the port jolly boat just aft of and below the ship's bridge.

The port jolly boat onboard the *Anglo-Saxon* in the mid 1930s. Denny and Widdicombe came from the bridge above the boat while Tapscott and Penny scrambled in as the boat was lowered past the main deck below.

The *Anglo-Saxon*'s Captain Philip "Paddy" Flynn shown while he was 1st Mate in the *Anglo-Canadian* just prior to joining the *Anglo-Saxon*.

The *Widder* in the disguise of the neutral Spanish vessel *El Neptuno* of Bilbao, which was used during the time of the attack on the *Anglo-Saxon*.

Hellmuth von Ruckteschell shown with his Knight's Cross around his neck, his Iron Cross on his chest, the oval World War I submarine badge, and his idiosyncratic, and nonuniform, white handkerchief in his breast pocket.

6

The starboard side, foredeck of the *Widder* with the gun crews manning two 15cm guns. The gun in the foreground is disguised as a reel of cable, common freighter deck cargo, while the gun in the background is disguised as a deckhouse or large crate. On the right in the photograph, the sections of the collapsible bulwark can be seen folded in onto the deck or out over the side.

7

The only known photograph of the sturdy but weathered jolly boat at its landing spot on the east coast of Eleuthera near Alabaster Bay.

Betty McAteer's favorite uncle,
Greaser Jim Fowler, who went
down with the *Anglo-Saxon*.

The *Anglo-Saxon*'s Chief Engineer,
E. E. (Eddie) Milburn, who left
behind his wife, Ethel, and two
young sons, Ted and Derek.

Third Engineer Lionel Henry
Hawks, one of the three officers in
the jolly boat. This, the only known
photograph of Hawks, appeared in
the Newcastle *Evening Chronicle*.

Ten-year-old Ted Milburn, a year
after the sinking of the *Anglo-Saxon*,
training for his own merchant marine
career in his uniform of the Royal
Navy Merchant School.

The *Anglo-Saxon*'s 1st Mate, Barry
Denny, shown while he was 2nd
Mate in the *Anglo-Canadian*, just
prior to joining the *Anglo-Saxon*.

13

2nd Radio Officer Roy Pilcher, who was particularly respected by his shipmates, entered the jolly boat severely wounded.

14

The retired Royal Marine, Francis Penny, was called to service in his second World War to serve as gunner in the *Anglo-Saxon*. He was among the seven in the jolly boat.

15

Able Seaman Roy Widdicombe, posing at the steering oar of the jolly boat, in early December 1940, after more than a month of recuperation.

16

Able Seaman Bob Tapscott, shown with his hand on the jolly boat mast under its tattered sail, after five weeks of recovery in Nassau.

17

Elijah Mackey (*left*), the James Cistern Constable involved in the rescue of the sailors from the beach, as shown at age eighty-nine with Garnett Thompson (*right*), the nephew of the dreamer, Florence Johnson, in Eleuthera in 2002.

✝

Memorial Tribute and Funeral Services

FOR THE LATE

FLORENCE v PINDER
THOMPSON JOHNSON

18

Florence Johnson, of James Cistern, Eleuthera, whose dream brought about the trek to the isolated beach of Eleuthera and the rescue of Tapscott and Widdicombe.

19

The morning after their rescue from the beach, Tapscott, too weak to walk, is carried while Widdicombe, in the background, is assisted by two men to the plane that will take them from Eleuthera to Nassau. The sailors have been bathed, shorn of their long hair, shaved, and outfitted with new clothes, which hang loosely on their emaciated forms. There is no known photograph of them in their condition upon arrival.

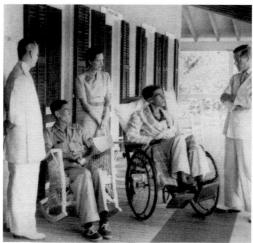

20

The recuperating sailors, Widdicombe and Tapscott, in the wheelchair, are visited by the Governor of the Bahamas, H.R.H. the Duke of Windsor and the Duchess. The Chief Medical Officer of the Bahamas, Dr. John M. Cruikshank (*left*) monitors his patients, still frail after only six days of recovery.

21

The memorial plaque at the Merchant Marine Memorial on Tower Hill in London, honoring the seamen of the *Anglo-Saxon* who perished during the attack and the jolly boat voyage. The plaque lacks the names of the survivors, Widdicombe and Tapscott, and also Francis Penny, who is memorialized among fellow Marines.

22

Relatives and friends of the men of the *Anglo-Saxon* gathered for the opening of the Imperial War Museum's Survival at Sea exhibition, featuring the *Anglo-Saxon* jolly boat, on May 12, 1998. Pictured from left to right are: Brenda Harrison, friend of Ted Milburn; Neil McAteer; Ted Milburn; Pat Phillips; Anthony Smith; Norma Tapscott; Diane Tapscott; Kevin Penny; Emily Penny; Sue Irvine; Desmond Flynn. Present that evening but absent from the photograph are Betty McAteer and Desmond Denny, who was instrumental in the return of the jolly boat.

only to realize that it had failed to see them and was steaming on, oblivious. The frayed emotions of the volunteers in the starvation experiment, like those of the two mariners, produced irritability, anger, anxiety, and apathy.

The two sailors' voyage was coming to an end, either through starvation or rescue. But there was no sign of rescue, and it was pure fortitude that enabled these brave sailors to continue. For the most part they had been spared the ordeal of storms and heavy weather. Their path across the ocean was just south of the Tropic of Cancer, where the water temperature was warm in comparison with that in the northern North Atlantic, where Nazi U-boats continued to sink ships and send other dazed survivors into boats, rafts, or the frigid water. But the warm water that was of benefit to those in the jolly boat also concealed a serious threat. It is across the warm waters of this part of the Atlantic that tropical disturbances roll off the African continent and often gain strength. Some of the disturbances mature into tropical depressions in which the barometric pressure drops and winds increase and circulate in a counterclockwise direction. Reaching the even warmer waters near the Caribbean, they draw more energy and may develop into deadly tropical storms or hurricanes. The season for these storms in the Atlantic begins in June and continues into the fall, with the most intense activity normally in late August and throughout September. The month of October is near the end of the season, but lethal storms are still able to materialize, sometimes very quickly, and bring devastation to whatever lies in their path.

Because of their timing and track about 200 miles north of the normal storm path, the sailors had not had to contend with any of the fierce storms that had developed during the summer of 1940. Prior to October, there had been six identified storms. The first had been a tropical storm with winds ranging from 39 to 72 miles per hour. Storms with winds above 72 miles per hour are officially hurricanes. This first storm of the 1940 season became a tropical storm north of the Dominican Republic, a month before the *Anglo-Saxon*'s final voyage began. It went north until turning northeast off Cape Hatteras, North Carolina, and out into the Atlantic. In August, there were three hurricanes, two of which hit the

United States. The third brushed Cape Hatteras before moving swiftly north, heading to sea off the New England coast. Although Tapscott and Widdicombe would have wished themselves farther along on their track, they were fortunate to be ten days "behind." On the 10th, the first tropical storm of September was 300 miles east of Barbuda, in the waters directly ahead of the jolly boat. It churned destructively along the path they would soon follow before it curved north, with enough energy to cross Nova Scotia and Newfoundland, and then create problems for the North Atlantic convoys bound for Britain. The other September storm and the first storm of October were of no consequence to mariners on the Atlantic, since they originated near Panama and moved through the Gulf of Mexico, with one going ashore in Louisiana and the other petering out in the Gulf. However, the elements did not let the sailors from the *Anglo-Saxon* proceed without another daunting test.

The last tropical storm of 1940 achieved that designation off the north shore of the Dominican Republic, and at that moment the two beleaguered sailors were directly in the path it would take. For days, they were tangled amid a series of squalls that confronted them with strong, erratic winds and pelting rain. These squalls were just a preview of what was to come, the outer bands of the large tropical storm system developing to their south. After several days of rough weather, Tapscott and Widdicombe were relieved to see things settle down and have the sun appear, although the quality of light was like nothing they had ever seen before. Through the thick hazy atmosphere they watched the sun set in the west, while behind them to the southeast they could make out the ponderous leading edge of an oncoming storm.

Physically depleted as they were, these two men were still good seamen and had dealt with storms and squalls before. Prudently, they decided not to fight the storm by trying to sail through the night, but to heave to, lower their sail, and ride the night out in the relative security of the sea anchor and the protection of the canvas cover. They lashed two of their oars together and secured them to the sea anchor line as an added drogue. With everything as secure as they could make it, the wet and hungry men, who hadn't been able to forage in the seaweed for days, settled in for the night. This would be a night unlike any they had experienced.

As the tropical storm moved north from the Dominican Republic, it nicked the eastern edge of Great Inagua Island and then made a gradual turn toward the northeast. For the two sailors hunkered down in their 18-foot boat, this was a stroke of good fortune. Had the storm tracked to the northwest, it would have placed them in the "dangerous semicircle" of the storm, and they would have faced its full fury. With southerly winds of up to 70 miles per hour, it would have driven them away from the direction they desired and farther out into the Atlantic. As it was, they were on the other side of the storm and because of its counterclockwise winds, in the euphemistically named "navigable semicircle" of the storm. It might be navigable for a powerful ship, but the killer storm that was now stalking the jolly boat would do its best to end her odyssey.

Well into the night, Tapscott was jolted awake by a burst of wind in the fierce gale. The seas had been mounting, and the boat was twisting and turning on the sea anchor, the way a fish on a barbed hook writhes to free itself. Tapscott realized the jolly boat was responding sluggishly. Widdicombe was roused from his sleep, and they realized they had been taking heavy water over the sides. The boat was filled almost to the seats on which moments before they had been asleep. With this water in the boat sloshing back and forth, she slewed dangerously from side to side, threatening to capsize. Seizing the bucket and cans, they bailed water over the sides in a frantic fight for their lives. With the boat so low in the water, more and more of the sea came aboard, and for some time it was impossible for the two men to get the upper hand. They filled their containers and poured them over the side time and time again, their strength sapped. Finally, they saw the level in the boat receding; once again they had cheated death. The pace of their bailing slowed, as they now could work methodically to get as much water as possible out of the boat and restore her buoyancy.

They knew they faced an even more deadly threat. The sea anchor, with its drogue of the two oars, had kept them with the bow into the

J. REVELL CARR

winds and mounting seas; but those seas were too large now, and the bow
sank deeply into the oncoming waves. To stay on the sea anchor would be
suicidal, yet the only other option was fraught with incredible danger: to
run before the storm, with the wind and waves coming from astern. Tapscott and Widdicombe fully understood the risk of this choice. Somehow
they had to release the sea anchor, which was holding them into the
weather, spin the boat around, quickly get it under control, and move
with the wind and waves. They were riding up huge seas, splashing
through their crests and seeming to glide down the other side of the
mountain of water passing under them. With their sail reefed, reducing
its size, they hauled in the sea anchor and retrieved the drogue oars. With
the anchor aboard and the steering oar back in place, the reefed sail was
hoisted. A few strokes on the steering oar headed the bow in the desired
direction, and instantly the wind on the bow forced her farther around.
The full force of the wind filled the sail to its limits, the boat completed
her pirouette, gained speed, and began racing before the wind. The
sailors fought to keep the wind coming over the starboard quarter, which
gave them the best chance to control the boat on the downhill slide of the
towering waves that the storm generated.

Tapscott and Widdicombe knew full well that this was not a simple
storm, and understood the fury of the tropical storms and hurricanes of
the Atlantic. They knew it was hurricane season and that they were in the
clutches of a true tropical cyclone. The boat was now speeding forward,
propelled by the blasting wind and huge following seas. Both men
clutched the steering oar, since neither had the strength to wrestle it
alone, as the boat gyrated under the forces of nature. Behind them, fearful waves built and built until they hovered precariously over the boat. To
look back was an awesome, horrifying experience. And yet, when they
managed to tear down the front side of a wave, their skills and instincts as
master helmsmen enabled them to anticipate the boat's response to the
swirling water and battering winds, and deftly adjust the steering oar to
compensate before the boat twisted out of control. Wave after wave
chased them across the Atlantic waters for hours on end. When daylight

came, weakly filtered through the thick storm clouds, it revealed the magnitude of their peril.

As the day wore on, the intensity of the storm and the height of the seas continued to increase. The ceaseless torrents of tropical rain and the stinging wind-driven spray kept the men soaked. Time and again, they managed to control the careening boat and settle into the momentary lull in the trough between waves, prior to being lifted again to start the process all over. Periodically, one of the sailors would bail out the water that was raining down from above or splashing over the side. As soon as possible, he would crawl back to his partner at the oar and continue their fight for survival. Throughout the day, without respite, they coped with the storm. Their only consolation was that their seawater-filled compass indicated they were being propelled in the right direction. Any momentary lapse of concentration could cause the boat to slew off course and bring them broadside to the waves. If that were to happen, a wave would certainly churn them under, tumble the boat, rip the sail to shreds, and snap off the mast. The boat, which still had two watertight buoyancy tanks, might remain afloat if she stayed intact. If the men went overboard, there would be no chance at all.

Where Tapscott and Widdicombe found the strength to sustain this fight for life is bewildering. By all rights, they should have been shivering and cowering in the boat until the storm took them, but that was not the case. These brave sailors used their talents, wits, and remaining strength to stay just ahead of disaster. After eighteen hours, they sensed the winds moderating slightly, but still could not relax their guard for a moment. All that night the two clung to the oar, acting as one in response to the still shrieking winds and immense seas. In their exhaustion, the shroud of sleep would engulf one or the other of them for brief moments, as their bodies continued to instinctively carry on with their task, but they would wake with a start to the nightmare they were living.

Night melded into the first light of the second day and the men were still alive. The winds continued to roar but were more stable in direction. The seas, though even higher than the preceding day, were more widely spaced, more predictable, and manageable. Mercifully, the deluge ceased. Toward evening, they were rewarded with a glimpse of the sun. Encouraging as it was, they stayed at their post and fought their way through the third night, sensing a continued diminution of the storm, and hopeful for what the next day held for them. This last storm of the 1940 hurricane season moved gradually to the northeast and lost strength as it hit the colder water of the central North Atlantic. As dawn came on the third day, the mariners knew they had met the consummate test of their skills, endurance, and tenacity, and had managed to absorb all the abuse that nature had thrust upon them. With the sun rising, they decided it was safe to set the sea anchor and heave to. Their battered and torn sail was lowered, and after more than fifty continuous hours of hellish torment, Tapscott and Widdicombe drifted into deep sleep.

When the midday sun woke them, the bond between the two seemed stronger than ever, and it was with shared pride that they quenched their thirst with water somewhat tainted with salt from the storm. To quell the ravenous hunger they were now feeling, they chewed on bits of sargassum, and Widdicombe gnawed on a leather shoe, breaking a tooth. Grateful for the sun's warmth, which would dry their saturated clothes and everything else they possessed, they once more hauled in their sea anchor and set sail toward the west. They were hopeful that the wicked storm had at least driven them much closer to land.

The next day, the day after that, and the one after that not only failed to produce a landfall, but added to the sailors' misery. They were famished. The turbulence of the storm had scattered the seaweed, and when some was found it was almost devoid of the tiny creatures that had given them a bit of protein in the weeks past. After extensive foraging, Tapscott managed to glean only three tiny crabs. He forced the wriggling creatures into his mouth all at once, and despite their vigorous attempts to escape, munched them to bits and swallowed them down. This was the extent of the sea's bounty. Desperate, they stripped the rubber from Pilcher's tobacco pouch and chewed it for hours. They gained nothing from the rubber, but there was some degree of satisfaction found in the mere act of mastication. Their physical condition continued to deteriorate, with nothing to inhibit the decline. With the lack of water first, then food, their bodies had been systematically devouring themselves, but now, in a more active form of self-consumption, they began to peel their own skin from their burned and blistered bodies and eat it.

Mirages now occurred to Tapscott and Widdicombe with great frequency. A low cloud formation on the horizon would give every appearance of land and their spirits would rise, but time and time again the "land" blew away with the disintegration of the clouds. Through all of this disappointment, they pressed on as best they could. They hardly had the strength to drag themselves around the boat, and gave up any semblance of standing watch. When the wind died away, they would drift with the current. Doing so brought them good fortune, although they were unaware of it. In October, an unusual current develops that splits off from the dominant northeasterly flow, sweeping west toward the middle of the Bahama Islands. The storm had pushed them into the influence of that current. As they dozed in the still air, they were in fact making very slow progress toward the islands. When the wind blew, they forced themselves to man the oar and head the boat west. This, too, was bringing them nearer to land.

While throughout the voyage the mariners had talked and goaded each other into whatever needed to be done, they were unable to do so any longer. They had nothing to say to each other and could not find any encouragement to share. In the midst of this torpor, Widdicombe would break into a ranting diatribe against his circumstances and then just as quickly sink back into silence. He seemed to be fading, and his abhorrence of long exposure to the sun was more acute than ever. The two sat sullen and self-absorbed, with their minds slowing as their bodies already had. Surely, death could not be long in coming. Deeply sunken in their heads, their eyes had nearly lost the flicker of life.

When the breeze blew, Tapscott crawled to the helm and served his time, but when it was Widdicombe's turn, he would steer for only a short period. Then, as he had often done before, he would call for Tapscott to relieve him. This was exasperating for Tapscott, but that was the pattern they had settled into in their third month in the boat. Around October 28,

Tapscott had had enough. Widdicombe had been on the steering oar and called for his shipmate to take over. Tapscott was reluctant, but once again gave in to Widdicombe's entreaties, to keep the peace. After changing places, Widdicombe promptly sank into sleep. After hours on the helm, Tapscott roused the sleeping sailor and called for him to take his turn; his call was ignored. Frustrated, Tapscott simply left the helm, allowing the boat to veer off course. Sitting in the middle of the boat, Tapscott warily watched Widdicombe, who had risen from his sleeping position. Life had come back into Widdicombe's eyes, but with an ominous glint. It was a look that Tapscott had seen once before and had not forgotten.

Months before, in the messroom of the *Anglo-Saxon*, Widdicombe had challenged their shipmate Stanley Elliot, decking him with a preemptive and decisive blow before Elliot was prepared. The expression on Widdicombe's gaunt face was unmistakably the same one he wore during his attack on Elliot. Tapscott, not one to pick a fight, but also not one to shrink from doing what needed to be done, this time struck first. These two antagonists, who had been confined in the 18-foot boat for over two months, had witnessed horrors and tragedies, had endured famine and thirst, had conquered all that nature had thrown at them, were now engaged in combat. The two men, who could not rally enough strength to do more than crawl around in the boat, were now locked in a tangle of withered arms and legs, flailing at each other. They did not have the strength to hurt one another, and the fight was short-lived. Spent, they pulled warily apart. The point, however, had been made, and without a word, Widdicombe dragged himself aft to the steering oar.

Tapscott apologized later that day but received no verbal response from Widdicombe. After all this time, the same animosity that they had felt at their first meeting still flourished. The strain persisted throughout the day, that night, and all the next day. This was truly the lowest point of the voyage. They had been through so much and had no idea what future tribulations lay ahead, and yet there was a barrier between them. To stay alive, they would each need the support of the other, but that had evaporated in the absurd fight. How could they go on?

On the second night after the fight, the wind faded and again they simply let the boat flow with the current. In the dead of night, Tapscott thought he heard another fish land, twisting and gyrating in the boat. Famished as he was, Tapscott could not find the strength to crawl around to look for it until daybreak, when, revitalized somewhat by the night of sleep, he rolled off the seat and began his search in the bottom of the boat, where he joyfully discovered a small fish. At that moment, Widdicombe proclaimed a far greater discovery: land. After so many crushing disappointments, in disbelief Tapscott hauled himself up from the bottom of the boat and stared. Could it be? This time there was no doubt. What lay arrayed before them was an interminable strand of beach, with low scrubland behind it. Finally, they thought, they had reached the long-sought Leeward Islands.

One more deadly obstacle was in their way, however. The beach was on the far side of a treacherous reef. In addition, there was no hint that anyone lived in this forsaken spot. If the men took the risk of crossing the reef, they could find themselves exhausted, on a barren, inhospitable island from which they would be unable to scratch out their survival. In their condition, there was no real option. They were near death and had to cross the reef or die trying.

Just as Third Engineer Hawks had prepared a last meal before his life ended, Tapscott took the blade from Pilcher's razor, cut the fish in two, and shared a last meal in the boat with his companion. Before them lay the breaking surf on the jagged coral outcroppings that could easily rip the bottom out of the jolly boat, sending the men tumbling into the swirling waters amid the sharp lacerating spines of coral and the voracious barracudas that inhabited those reefs. It was now time for the fateful business of navigating through the reef that confronted them. They had the wind behind them, which made handling the boat relatively easy, but made it extremely difficult to retreat if they got into trouble. They were on what every sailor dreads: a lee shore, with the wind forcing them toward the reef. This would be an all-or-nothing gamble, and the beleaguered mariners had to once again reach into the deepest recesses of their beings for the energy and mental acuity to make the split-second decisions and execute them.

They spotted a break in the turbulence of the reef and, using the sail and steering oar, Widdicombe maneuvered the boat as Tapscott positioned himself in the bow to call out directions. Tapscott looked down into the crystal-clear water at the magnificent but murderous coral, reaching up as if to snatch them and draw them down. Heading first one direction, then instantly the other, they evaded the watery talons beneath them. The coral diminished, and clean white sand, accented by dazzling exotic fish, appeared below the boat. They had survived the final challenge of the reef, and the jolly boat slid silently onto the soft sand.

Chapter 14

WARRIOR *WIDDER*

A s the two emaciated sailors crawled over the gunwale of the jolly boat and onto the beach, almost 4,000 miles to the east, Ruckteschell and the crew of the *Widder* arrived off the French coast, getting their first glimpse of land since they had left the Norwegian coast six months before. The German ship had been hard at her destructive work since the night of August 21, when she sent the *Anglo-Saxon* to the bottom. Tapscott, Widdicombe, and the others had seen the raider circle her victim and then, after the *Anglo-Saxon* sank, steam off to the east without searching for survivors. Cruelly, as he had done with the *Beaulieu* after his first night attack seventeen days before, Ruckteschell left any survivors to fend for themselves. In the *Widder*'s war diary, he rationalized his decision to steam away, saying: "Only for a short period of time two lights were being observed near the steamer—obviously from 2 boats having brief Morse contact; this, however, was illegible for us. Then, no further lights were seen. As no S.O.S.-calls were made, I did not start any further search."

Ruckteschell's record was self-serving. Looking for excuses to leave the site, he made assumptions that people had escaped into boats and would be fine. In fact, he saw no boats, not the jolly boat or any others. Lights were briefly seen but quickly extinguished. It is unlikely he gave an order to fire on those lights himself, but possibly an overenthusiastic sailor, charged with adrenaline, had swung his automatic weapon on the lights for a moment and extinguished them, as those in the jolly boat saw. If Ruckteschell thought there might be men in boats, why would he assume they were in fine shape, prepared to sail off to the nearest land? Well over 400 rounds had been fired at the *Anglo-Saxon,* and Ruckteschell had full knowledge of the efficiency of his gunnery and the destructive impact of this kind of fusillade. He had no way of knowing how many people might be crammed into boats, how badly wounded they were, what provisions were on board, or what propulsion or navigational equipment was in the boats.

Coldly, Ruckteschell continued to rationalize in the war diary: "The distance to the Canaries is about 800 sea miles with a moderate wind so they can be reached by the boats." He assumed that any survivors could make the 800-mile voyage, against the prevailing winds and currents, and navigate with sufficient accuracy to find the little islands of the Canaries. Leaving the scene, the *Widder* ran north at 12 knots, to put distance between the ship and the location of the *Anglo-Saxon*'s sinking. By noon of the following day, she began to cruise the territory 125 miles to the north. The *Widder*'s log precisely records her location at noon that day, guaranteeing that she was not the ship the jolly boat encountered on the crew's second night in the boat. During the afternoon, Ruckteschell assembled all hands to hear the outcome of the court-martial of the sleeping officer. While he had wished for a death sentence, the severe punishment that was awarded served as a warning for all on the *Widder* that the watchful eye of their Captain was on them. Their day was brightened by receipt of a message that their Assistant Medical Officer had become the father of a baby girl, and the child and mother were well.

It was now time to begin anew the search-and-destroy mission. Ruckteschell continued to move his ship north and several degrees east, so potential victims would appear to his west. From this position, the late moonrise would enable him to attack out of the dark eastern sector, rather than from the west, where the *Widder* might be silhouetted against the twilight. At midday on August 26, the raider simultaneously encountered two victims going in opposite directions. One, a tanker, was bound for Trinidad; the other, a freighter, was on her way to the Canaries or Cape Verdes. Ruckteschell wished he could attack both at the same time, but chose to go after the freighter. This proved a mistake, since it became apparent that the *Widder* could not keep up with the fast, modern ship. His commitment to attack the freighter put too much distance between him and the tanker, so there was no option to turn around and pursue her.

Ruckteschell comments on this annoying event in his war diary entry for September 2, which reads, "For nearly four weeks I have been in these waters, have sunk three ships, decided not to attack one at night due to the moonlight, and have seen two ships which sailed away, seven days ago, on 26 August 1940." He then adds, almost as an offhanded postscript, "The men from the *Anglo-Saxon* could have reached land by now." At the time he made this entry, the men from the *Anglo-Saxon* were farther from land than they had been at the beginning of their voyage; it was written the day before the heroic Roy Pilcher died. It is impossible to understand Ruckteschell's reason for this entry. It could have been a simple after-thought, but that does not seem to be his disciplined style. Was it a guilty conscience that he was trying to placate with wishful thinking? Or, was he concerned about his superiors or others who might someday read this official war diary and judge him as callous or possibly criminal if he showed no concern for possible survivors? Whatever the reason, with this entry, Ruckteschell completed his written record regarding the attack on August 21 and turned to the business at hand.

That "business" appeared at 9:32 on the morning of September 2 in the form of a distant tanker. Just prior to spotting the tanker, the *Widder* had generated excessive black smoke while accelerating to 12 knots. This smoke was seen by the tanker, which took an evasive course. The raider sought to regain the element of surprise by steaming out of sight and then doubling back to get into a position to attack, without, as Ruckteschell says, "disturbing the 'game' again." Clearly, he saw himself as a hunter pursuing "game." His efforts were successful. At twenty minutes before nine that evening, after almost twelve hours of "cat and mouse," the attack began. It took only twelve minutes to overwhelm the ship, destroy her boilers, and have her bridge in flames. The *Widder* circled the vessel and determined that she was the *Cymbeline,* a 6,300-ton tanker out of Liverpool. One hour and three minutes after the attack began, a torpedo sent the ship to the bottom. Whether the crew or the Medical Officer objected to the abandonment of possible survivors, as they had after the sinking of the *Beaulieu,* is not known, but Ruckteschell spent four hours that night searching. They picked up 26 men, but 10, including the Captain of the *Cymbeline,* were missing. Unknown to Ruckteschell, the *Cymbeline*'s Captain, J. A. Chadwick, had not only changed course upon spotting the raider's smoke that morning, but had also reported the suspicious vessel to British naval authorities. Alerted to the *Cymbeline*'s potential fate, they would be searching for the enemy in that part of the ocean. Although he lost the *Cymbeline,* the tanker's Captain managed to survive. He and two others were picked up in their lifeboat fourteen days later and taken to Venezuela.

The *Widder* now carried an astonishing 142 prisoners. Ruckteschell learned from the *Cymbeline*'s survivors that on a previous voyage they had found the 28 Norwegians of the *Beaulieu*'s crew on August 9, five days after the *Widder*'s attack, and delivered them to Gibraltar. He also learned that Captain Chadwick had signaled that a raider was attacking in this part of the ocean. Now facing a very serious threat, Ruckteschell's first step was to change his ship's disguise. He felt that by painting the ship's superstructure gray she would appear "as an Englishman." This would also cover any white paint on the ship, which was conspicuous in the moonlight. With acetylene torches, the crew cut away some of the distinctive heavy lifting equipment and dumped it over the side to change their profile. Another concern was refueling, scheduled in two weeks near the site of the sinking of the *Cymbeline.* He decided to attract the British to another location by revealing his presence there and steamed straight south toward the southeastern corner of the ship's area of operation.

During this passage south, the Germans received a radio message alerting them that a German tanker, the *Eurofeld,* would transit their area on her way to "West France," the French Caribbean possessions. This message was essential because of Ruckteschell's deadly methods of night attack, operating as if any ship was fair game. Stalking at great distance during the day, his tactic was to close with his target and pounce with murderous force after dark, without knowing who it was he was attacking. It was vital that the *Widder* be informed when friendly vessels would be in her territory, to prevent a deadly disaster. This disregard for whom she attacked makes the *Widder*'s operations seem that much more detached and ruthless.

Reaching her southern ocean boundary, the *Widder* encountered weather that a few days later and a few hundred miles west would become that year's Tropical Storm No. 5. While contending with that nasty but not threatening weather, the engine began "spitting." The following morning, September 8, the problem grew more serious, and the ship's speed was limited to 8 knots while Chief Engineer Penzel and his crew made repairs during the day. By evening, Penzel had the engine functioning, able to make 12 knots again, and as evening came on, the crew spotted the lights of a vessel in the far distance. Determining her course and speed, they realized that the distance was diminishing while the bearing remained unchanged. This meant the two ships were on a virtual collision course. All the *Widder* had to do was maintain her course and speed and the prey would steam right to them.

At the appropriate moment, the *Widder* turned on her lights. The target responded by illuminating her national ensign, the flag of Greece. Ruckteschell countered with a star shell, which brilliantly lit the area, followed by a signal-light message to halt. The defenseless Greek ship, the *Antonio Chandris,* had no option, and the Greek Captain put his crew at the mercy of their captors. The freighter's voyage duplicated that of the *Anglo-Saxon,* carrying coal from South Wales to Buenos Aires, and was doomed by this encounter. This had been one of the few "bloodless" conquests of the *Widder,* and not a shot had been fired. There was little mercy shown that night, however. With 142 prisoners already onboard the raider, Ruckteschell was not about to take on more. He decided that these men would have to strike out on their own, and allowed Captain George Gafos to provision his lifeboats for a long voyage. Equidistant between the bulge of South America and the bulge of Africa, land was 1,000 miles away in either direction.

As the 22 sailors from the Greek ship began their own nightmarish boat voyage, Ruckteschell again penned his rationalization for abandoning this crew into his war diary: "It is ideal sailing weather and I was interested in being reported in these waters. Water will be no problem for them, because it is raining often." If it is true that Ruckteschell's motivation for this cruel act was his plan to be reported in that location, he chose a most ineffective way to accomplish that. He had no idea how long it would be before the men in the lifeboat might be picked up or could reach land, or if they would survive at all. It was doubtful they would make a report in time to attract attention away from his scheduled resupply rendezvous. His objective could have been accomplished by simply letting the freighter get off a warning message that she was being attacked by a raider. He could then have taken the crew onto his ship and saved them from the terrible ordeal they were about to face. With her crew adrift, the *Antonio Chandris* was scuttled in the first hour of September 9. That same day in the jolly boat, Leslie Morgan died and Tapscott and Widdicombe became the last two alive. Back in England, the Lawther, Latta line offices began anxiously to await news of the *Anglo-Saxon*'s safe arrival in Buenos Aires.

Ruckteschell counted on being far from the sinking of the Greek ship by the time the British searchers arrived. He headed on a northwesterly course of 320 degrees, but limped along at a speed of only 8 knots. The crew enjoyed the fresh meat taken off the *Antonio Chandris* before she was scuttled. Engine problems continued to develop, and the 8-knot top speed diminished to 5 knots, and then to nothing, as the ship was stopped completely to make repairs. The *Widder* was no longer an effective hunter, but a sitting duck for any Allied naval vessel. For a full day, she wallowed helplessly within 120 miles of the scene of the *Antonio Chandris* attack. The engineering crew, who knew that their lives, and those of their shipmates, depended on getting the engine repaired, worked feverishly.

Not only was the ship and her German crew vulnerable as she lay disabled, but so too were the 142 prisoners in their locked quarters deep in the ship. The prisoners were constantly conscious of their peril and aware of the heightened danger when the ship went to battle stations. At any moment, the *Widder* could come under fire and they might be trapped. This horrid fate did befall prisoners in other raiders. When the cruiser HMS *Cornwall* attacked the raider *Pinguin,* her British crew did not know that huddled deep in the bowels of the raider were 225 Allied merchant seamen. As the pitched battle raged and the German Captain, Ernst Felix Kruder, realized his ship was lost, he ordered the prisoners released from their confinement. Moments later a huge explosion tore the raider apart. Of the 225 prisoners, only 22 survived to be rescued.

The *Widder* was dead in the water, her engines disabled, until the engineers got the ship under way again. The rendezvous with the tanker *Eurofeld* was a meeting Ruckteschell urgently wanted to make, since it might give him the opportunity to transfer some of his prisoners. On September 16, after a week of limping toward the rendezvous, the lookouts on the *Widder* spotted the *Eurofeld* and maneuvered to close with her. The tanker was wary of the approaching raider and fled, having sent out a message earlier that had not been heard or answered by the *Widder.* The tanker's Captain Blessin was taking no chances in this life or death game. The struggling *Widder* chased the tanker, until after an incredibly frustrating four-and-a-half-hour pursuit, the tanker acknowledged the raider and the rendezvous took place. There was no opportunity to transfer prisoners to the *Eurofeld,* however, as she was not heading back to Europe, but staying in the Atlantic to replace the *Rekum,* the ship that had been supporting the *Widder.* There was, however, the possibility of transfer to the *Rekum,* since she was bound for occupied France.

Together, the raider and the *Eurofeld* steamed southward to a rendezvous with the *Rekum.* The three ships remained in close company for two days while the *Widder* took on the last 1,600 tons of fuel oil from the *Rekum*'s tanks, leaving her with only the fuel she needed to make her way back to France. Then, to Ruckteschell's great relief, he transferred almost half his prisoners. On the last night the three ships were together, 65 of the prisoners from the *Widder* were shifted under guard to the empty tanker bound for Saint-Nazaire, at the mouth of the Loire. Ruckteschell retained all 77 of his English prisoners.

It is difficult to explain this decision. One possibility is his expressed distaste for the "dirty and lousy pack" from the *Santa Marguerita,* which included "Yugoslavs, Portuguese, Maltese and a Spaniard," so in this decision he was "ethnically cleansing" the *Widder* of the prisoners he felt were less desirable. Another more sinister possibility was that, since he had such enmity for the British, he was keeping them as hostages. With his ship's engines faltering, he might be set upon by the Royal Navy. If the ship was discovered, with no chance of fighting because of her damaged machinery, Ruckteschell might prevent the sinking of the *Widder* by revealing that a large number of English prisoners were on board.

Whatever the reason, the non-English were transferred. In addition, Ruckteschell entrusted to the supply ship various reports, letters from his crew to their families and loved ones, and, most significantly, a copy of his war diary. Ruckteschell was very proud of what he and his crew had accomplished, and while brief reports had been made over the radio by special, encoded "short messages," he wanted the authorities to have the full, "glorious" story in his own words. The war diary told that story in detail, including the various attacks, and the abandoning of the sailors from the *King John,* the *Beaulieu,* the *Anglo-Saxon,* and the *Antonio Chandris.* The raider Captain was acutely aware of how vulnerable he and his crew were, and sensed they might not get safely home. By sending off a copy of his war diary, he doubled the chances of its reaching the SKL, so that their full success could be recorded in the annals of the Kriegsmarine, and people would celebrate the accomplishments of the *Widder* and Hellmuth von Ruckteschell. Just after midnight on September 21, the ships parted company. The *Rekum* headed for Europe, the *Eurofeld* steamed to service another raider, the *Thor,* in the South Atlantic, and the *Widder* hoped to resume her stealthy attacks on unsuspecting victims.

During the resupply, Ruckteschell received news that the ship's area of operation was being expanded to the east below 30 degrees north latitude. This meant he could operate as far as the Canaries and the Cape Verde Islands, opening the active shipping routes of the eastern Atlantic to his attacks. Ruckteschell and his senior officers were aware of just how frail their engine was, however, and doubted that they could take advantage of this broadened area. Everyone on board knew how hard the engineers were working to keep the engine and its various pumps, valves, and bearings functioning. They also knew that there was very little chance that a German ship could come and take them under tow, or that two ships, proceeding slowly with the burden of the towed raider, could make it safely to France. It was also doubtful that a rescue ship could reach them and take the entire crew and prisoner population of almost 500 off the stricken raider. Because of the weakened engine, Ruckteschell did not steam to the east into his new hunting ground.

After days of endless work requiring the frequent stopping of the ship, the raider was once again able to muster 8 knots of speed. Yet, when a slow-moving coal freighter came into view at midday on September 26, the frustrated Germans realized that they did not even have sufficient speed to stalk and attack this tempting target. The powerful raider was forced to hide from this "lowly" merchantman. It was a wise decision, since that evening the middle pressure turbine's main bearing burned out and the ship was once again crippled. The following morning, the event they most dreaded occurred. As they lay immobile and impotent, a ship was spotted heading directly for the raider. There was nothing to do but bluff her out. The *Widder* hoisted a Norwegian flag and two large canvas black balls, the international signal of being "not under command," meaning "not under control." The raider went to battle stations, with the guns and the gun crews concealed. A "simulation" crew, appearing to be the normal crew of a freighter, showed themselves busy about the deck. The *Widder* was ready to fight, but could only await her fate, as the ship drew closer and closer. As the ship passed at a distance of two and a half miles, the raider recognized the freighter as the French steamer *Capitaine Paul Lemerle*, which they had been informed by the SKL was in this vicinity. The French ship was on her way from Martinique to Casablanca with a cargo of sugar, and to the great relief of the disabled raider, simply passed her by.

Frantic repairs went on all through the day of the 27th and into the night. The following morning, the engine was back on line again and the ship could make 8 knots at 1,000 rpms. Gradually during the day, they increased speed to 12 knots and were able to begin hunting again. However, by 7:00 P.M. the turbine bearing had failed for a second time, and the raider glided to a halt. In such tremendously stressful circumstances, some captains would lose their patience and blame the Chief Engineer and his crew, but Ruckteschell exhibited the utmost confidence in Kapitänleutnant Penzel and the men working with him. The Captain had been aware of his ship's shortcomings from the moment he took command and knew that the engineers were doing everything possible to keep the ship operational. This time, the ship lay exposed and adrift for almost a week, since the exhausted engineers, who had worked around the clock, needed to rest and new bearings had to be cast.

Ruckteschell realized that it was doubtful the *Widder* could continue her mission. His compassion for his crew, as well as his frustration, was revealed in his diary when he recorded, "My great Chief Engineer and his wonderful team make me feel sad, and then my crew so eager for action! I know almost certainly that we have to return home, but I cannot pass that word around yet." On October 4, they again got under way, able to make only 7 knots. The bearings began to heat up, accompanied by strange noises and vibrations. Ruckteschell lamented in his war diary, "Now we will be happy if we can reach home."

The *Widder* was forced to stop for two more days, during which the Captain finally made the decision to end offensive operations and head for home. On the night of October 6th, Ruckteschell sent his commanders at SKL his message of regret, "Envisage breaking off the operation due to engine trouble. My position is Square 'DR.' Envisage heading for a port in West France. ETA: early November." Initially, Ruckteschell received no response to his message, and sent it again the next day. As he was waiting for his reply, the victims of his last attack, the 22 men from the *Antonio Chandris,* were found by a Portuguese ship, the *Serpa Pinto.* They had traveled 1,400 miles during their month of suffering, exposure, and deprivation.

On October 9, Ruckteschell received acknowledgment and permission to head for France, and the gratifying news that the *Rekum* had safely reached Saint-Nazaire. The Captain happily shared this message with all on board, since it meant that everyone's personal mail had made it to the mainland. For Ruckteschell, fearful that his ship would not make it to France, the message meant that his war diary covering their activities up to September 20, 1940, had gotten through, and the extent of his exploits would be known. In his continuing war diary, he wrote, "Finally the SKL knows for certain what we did, in case we are lost."

On October 10, the day that Tapscott and Widdicombe watched the steamer pass them by in the squall, 1,200 miles to the east of them Hellmuth von Ruckteschell turned his limping ship for home. No longer a hunter, the *Widder* made her way slowly northward, passing the sites of her attacks on the *Anglo-Saxon,* the *Cymbeline,* the *Oostplein,* and the *Killoran.* On October 18, she was transferred from the SKL back to Naval Group West, which had controlled her dramatic outward-bound voyage almost six months earlier. As they made their way homeward, several ships were passed at a distance. On the 25th, 550 miles west of Cape Finisterre, on the northwest coast of Spain, they sighted a ship of England's famous Blue Funnel Line, managed by Alfred Holt & Co., which would always be on the lookout for suspicious vessels. If detected, the *Widder* would certainly attract interest. One message of alert broadcast by the Blue Funnel ship this close to England would bring the Royal Navy in hot pursuit. Despite extreme weather, with winds of force 7 on the Beaufort scale, the tired raider took evasive action.

The *Widder* struggled to manage 6 knots of speed and was successful in avoiding detection. The storm helped conceal the raider, and on the 27th she turned directly east to close with the French coast. Later that day, a submarine appeared that, the crew was relieved to discover, belonged to their ally, Italy. The submarine reported the raider's position to Naval Group West, which assured Ruckteschell that he would have the protection of air reconnaissance the following day as he neared France. The storm continued the following day, and no planes were seen. The next day, October 29, at a little after nine in the morning, a German aircraft was seen overhead. The raider made smoke and fired off recognition flares in order to attract attention but was unobserved. Supposed to protect the ship from potential dangers, the plane couldn't even see her. Disgusted, the crew of the *Widder* pressed on.

Later that night, with no ship in sight, the Morse code letter *L* blinked out of the blackness, as if from nowhere. The challenged raider, realizing there was a submarine off her starboard bow, flashed back the correct response, the letter *X*, with her signal lamp. After tense moments, the *Widder* received the unambiguous welcome "Heil Hitler," flashed back from the submarine *U-29,* which had been sent to escort her the final miles. The next day, October 30, the coast of France appeared out of the mist, and the raider, with her escort, passed between Pointe du Raz and the Isle de Sein on their approach to the port of Brest and sanctuary.

Part III

DESTINIES

Chapter 15

RESCUE

Their boat resting firmly on the sand, which was tinged pink by minute fragments of red coral, Tapscott and Widdicombe tumbled over the side. They staggered and lurched on sea legs up the beach toward the scrub at the verge, heading for the shade cast by small bushes, where they collapsed. They had not been on solid ground for eighty-five days. Used to the quick movements of the little boat, their inner ears could not compensate for the sudden solidity of the beach. Their minds raced with the fact that they had finally found land, but their bodies would do nothing more than seek the relief of shade.

For over two months, the survivors had been obsessed with reaching the Leeward Islands. Now they were on an island, but it was not one of the Leewards. They had missed the Leeward chain and the islands that form the northern border of the Caribbean, but the benevolent October currents had carried them to a magnificent strand. The island was Eleuthera, a thin stretch of coral and sand 90 miles long from north to south and often only a mile or two wide. The eastern shore of the island presents itself to the broad Atlantic, the sea constantly pounding on the coral reefs that range all along the coast. The coral, pulverized by the sea, combines with the superfine sand to form a mixture with the consistency of dry brown sugar. The western shore of the island is lapped by the tranquil waters of Exuma Sound, sheltered from the steady ocean winds and waves by the island itself. Eleuthera is the epitome of a tropic isle, a lush paradise of abundant vegetation, endless beaches, beaming sun, and tranquil solitude.

For most people, these attributes would be supremely appealing, but the two cadaverous sailors feared they had landed on an uninhabited island and would not find help. They could do little to help themselves. The sun, which so many vacationers sought, had become their enemy, and they could not tolerate its debilitating rays. The magnificent beach, stretching as far as could be seen in both directions, was not paradise, but presented an impossible trek in search of help, water, or food. They could not walk. Even if they could find the strength to rise and stagger along, in which direction would they go? They saw no sign of human life. The lush growth of trees, bushes, and plants that edged the beach and extended inland as far as they could see did not provide reassurance but appeared the most formidable of barriers. The brush grew in a tangled, impenetrable thicket waist-high or higher. There was no possible way they could make their way through this mass of branches and vines that would halt an amphibious assault force. After they had come so far and endured such torture, the cruelest of fates would be to die on the beach, which would be inevitable without the miracle of rescue.

The previous night, a Bahamian woman, "Baby" Florence Thompson Johnson, and her husband, Lewis, were sleeping in their little house, high on Gidd's Hill, toward the southern end of James Cistern, a village on the Exuma Sound side of the island, about 12 miles north of the main settlement of Governor's Harbour. Like the majority of the islanders, the Johnsons were hardworking members of the community and active in the Methodist Church, where Lewis was choirmaster.

Lewis Johnson had been working in Hatchet Bay, 5 miles away, and had returned home the day before. He slept soundly that night. Florence slept fitfully, wrestling with a vivid dream, so strong that it seemed a vision. When she awoke before dawn, she had to follow through on the bidding of that dream, which called for her to go to the beach where she would "find something." She was convinced that there was importance to the message, which could not be ignored; there was a logic to it that promised potential benefit to the Johnsons.

Since the beaches of the eastern side of the island confronted the Atlantic, with the prevailing wind and currents pushing any floating items toward those beaches, it was a local pastime to comb the beach for treasures. Florence Johnson roused her somewhat reluctant husband, and, with the power of her dream motivating them, the two set out before the sun was fully up. They made their way down the steep road of Gidd's Hill, turned left at the bottom, and started southward on the main road past the fields they and others farmed. The beach they sought was located about 4 miles south of James Cistern. With Alabaster Bay on their right, they turned off the road and began to make their way east to the ocean and its beach. Lewis went first with his razor-sharp cutlass, the local term for a machete, slashing from side to side to make a way through the dense brush. With the sun gaining height in the morning sky, they made slow but steady progress.

Throughout the voyage, Widdicombe had complained of dizziness and been unable to carry on in the blaze of the sun, but he was in better shape than his companion now. Tapscott had often done the extra duty when Widdicombe seemed unable, and now was spent. After a while, Widdicombe suggested they make their way along the beach, but Tapscott was unable to walk. They were sprawled out on the beach in a near comatose state. Widdicombe rolled onto his back and let the lids of his dark sunken eyes close. His long black hair and beard were matted and caked with the fine talc-like sand. The rags that clung to his frail body had been a uniform coat and khaki shorts. Tapscott had given the shorts to Widdicombe when his tattered pants could no longer be held together. His withered arms and legs protruded from this pile of rags, hardly recognizable as human appendages. Close by, Tapscott was also sprawled on his back, with his head twisted back awkwardly, his sun-bleached blond hair and shaggy beard the color of the sand. Having lost nearly half his weight, he was no more than sun-parched flesh and protruding bone. His rags had been a shirt and a pair of underpants.

With his wife a safe distance behind, to stay clear of the backswing of the cutlass, Johnson knew they were nearing the beach, as the brush began to thin out. Soon their search for that "something" from the dream would begin. They knew the beach extended interminably and they had no idea how long they would prowl its length before they came upon their mysterious treasure. As they pressed through the last few yards to the beach, Lewis stopped in astonishment. Through the remaining brush, he could see, directly in front of them, a well-built boat.

As he cut through the last of the brush, Lewis stopped in his tracks. Florence crowded in behind him. There before them lay the skeletal castaways. The dream had led them to two bodies on the beach. How long had these remains been lying on the deserted beach? When had they crawled from their boat, only to meet their end a few yards away? Then the eyes of one of the bodies snapped open. Lewis reeled back, urging Florence to retreat along the path. The men on the beach were not yet dead. They ran to notify the Constable in James Cistern.

Widdicombe had heard the voices speaking English. He insisted that Tapscott go back with him to the boat, so they would be found when the people returned, as he was certain the rescuers would. With great effort, they made their way to the edge of the beach near the boat, which lay stranded by the receding tide.

Once back on the road, the Johnsons came to the farm fields and rallied several friends to come with them and to bring the food they had brought for their midday meals. One went to tell the Constable in James Cistern, twenty-eight-year-old Elijah Mackey. When Widdicombe and Tapscott heard the urgent voices of their rescuers in their lilting English, they knew their ordeal was over. The group stared at the incredible sight. Who were these men? Where had they come from? Widdicombe, who thought the date was October 25, told them that their ship had been destroyed sixty-five days earlier, on August 21. The Bahamians told him it was October 30. After seeing the documents from Pilcher's case and Denny's primitive log, the rescuers were convinced that these were not enemy infiltrators. The farmers got the men to their feet, but Tapscott could not stand, and Widdicombe was only slightly better off. Two of the strongest farmers hoisted the two sailors onto their backs to carry them out. One of the rescue group brought coconuts. Tapscott clawed at the sweet meat within the shell as others arrived with more food. Any doctor, aware of the deprivations and stresses the survivors' digestive systems had experienced, would have winced at the assortment of food and drink. So long deprived, Tapscott and Widdicombe were overwhelmed with choices. Widdicombe paced his consumption, but Tapscott overdid it. His favorite drink was there before him, a tall bottle of beer. Tapscott savored this beer as he had never savored a drink in his life. There were also some carbonated soft drinks, canned corned beef, and sweet cakes. Widdicombe carefully picked, but Tapscott was ravenous. Realizing that Tapscott's gorging would make him sick, the Bahamians withdrew the food, and they all rested until the sailors seemed able to continue.

Constable Elijah Mackey, now in his nineties, still clearly remembers that day over sixty years ago. As the resident Constable in James Cistern, he was the government representative and took immediate action. As the rescue party reached the road, a truck that the Constable had commandeered was waiting for them, and the two young men were eased onto the truck bed. Mackey says they didn't speak, but communicated with feeble gestures as the truck made the rough trip to the seat of government.

Governor's Harbour is the main settlement on the island of Eleuthera and in October 1940 was the location of the residence of the island Commissioner, a career civil servant, Michael Gerassimos. Word of the remarkable discovery had already reached Governor's Harbour and the Commissioner, so there was considerable commotion as the truck bearing the sailors jounced into town and onto Cupid's Cay at two o'clock in the afternoon. Gerassimos was prepared to extend a formal welcome to the visiting seafarers but was unprepared for the sight of the men.

With no hospital or clinic, the only government accommodation was the jail, and it was no place for these heroes who had suddenly brought the reality of war to the Bahamas. They took the men to the home of Mr. and Mrs. Claude Moss. Their low, crisp white bungalow accepted paying guests and could provide the most comfortable accommodations available.

Their rags were removed, the sailors were bathed and placed in a large, soft bed and allowed measured amounts of liquids. There was no possibility of sleep for either man. Tapscott's nerves were raw, and it was impossible for him to let go of the reality around him and drift into sleep. When he tried to relax and close his eyes, his mind raced. Only hours before they had been in the boat, in the final days before inevitable death. Was it all a dream? If he faded into sleep, would it all be gone when he awoke? Tapscott was content just to rest in the comfortable bed. Widdicombe was keenly alert, but agitated and in constant movement, eager after so many weeks to talk. The afternoon passed into evening, and the men were given a simple, bland meal of bread and butter and a treasured beverage, cocoa, loaded with sugar.

The first hint of media frenzy was being felt in Nassau. The editor of the *Nassau Guardian* newspaper, Mary Mosely, was putting the evening edition of the paper "to bed" when she received some scant information. She shouted to her staff to hold the front page and pounded out the first of many stories. She managed to slip three short paragraphs onto the upper right corner of the front page, beside a photo of a belligerent, eggsplattered Wendell Willkie, the Republican Party candidate in the last days of his presidential campaign. The headline read, "Late News. Torpedoed Seamen Arrive in Governor's Harbour." The brief article, giving no names or details, announced that they had been adrift for two months and that the government was providing medical assistance. The final paragraph promised readers further details of this "remarkable battle with the sea." As the editor of the paper went home that evening, she reveled in the fact that with a reporter already on Eleuthera, she had a scoop on a story of international importance. It is impossible to know if she fully envisioned that this story would create a sensation in the newspapers, international radio broadcasts, and magazines such as *Time* and *Cosmopolitan.*

Commissioner Gerassimos arrived at the Moss residence at 10:00 P.M., eight hours after the sailors' arrival in Governor's Harbour, to take down their first official statements. While these statements cannot be found in the official files of the Colonial Office, the Commissioner's son, Dr. Michael Gerassimos, now living in Nassau, has signed copies of them.

The statements are one-page accounts of the ordeal and are very similar. They each record the fundamental details of the *Anglo-Saxon's* voyage, the attack, and the list of who was with them in the boat and their deaths. They include no information on the voyage of the two survivors after the others perished. Each ends with the name and address of the next of kin. While there are slight differences, the accounts are so alike it is almost as if they were composed by one person. This may be accounted for by Commissioner Gerassimos asking the same questions of both men. It is also probable that, considering their frail condition, the sailors were not moved to separate rooms to give their statements, so that whoever gave the first account, most probably the talkative Widdicombe, set the precedent for the other to follow. The Commissioner was pleased to tell them that they had attracted the full attention of the Governor of the Bahamas, who had ordered that they be moved to Nassau, where they could be given the best medical care. This was to take place the following morning by special plane. The Governor had also made provisions to secure the boat they had used to make their historic voyage. To these two solid British seamen, this attention from the Governor was a particular honor, since he was their former King, Edward VIII, now the Duke of Windsor.

At midnight, the only doctor on the island, Dr. Francis Kline, arrived to examine the mariners. Dr. Kline shared a strange kinship with the two sailors, since he too was a victim of Hitler. As a German Jew, he had witnessed the rise of the Nazi Party and felt the deadly threat of persecution. He had been fortunate to escape from Germany to England. The influx of refugees with medical skills seemed a windfall for England, as civilian casualties required more doctors and nurses. However, with the number of foreign doctors available, some of these refugee medical professionals were placed in the Bahama Islands, in order to deliver better medical services to remote areas. It was a distinct benefit for the island of Eleuthera to have Dr. Kline in residence as Medical Officer.

Dr. Kline, referred to as "the saltwater doctor," is remembered for his standard cure, which almost always included curative salt water. In the case of the two sailors, however, it was abundantly clear that they had already had more than their share of salt water, and the doctor withheld his normal prescription. Beyond the obvious state of starvation and dehydration, Kline observed that the classic symptoms of pellagra were evident in his patients. Their skin had the typical dark scaling, particularly where exposed to the sun, as most of their bodies had been. Their sore and swollen mouths and tongues were typical of the inflamed mucous membranes found in patients with pellagra. Diarrhea is usually associated with the disease, but they had had so little to eat it had not been a factor, except that very morning. When they first sighted the reef and the beach beyond, Tapscott had been suddenly gripped by the urgent need to evacuate and used the boat's bucket. Pellagra also affects the nervous system, indicated by their sleeplessness, agitation, and Widdicombe's unceasing nervous energy.

The final symptom of pellagra is broadly defined as dementia, but consists of such manifestations as depression, irritability, anxiety, confusion, disorientation, delusions, and hallucinations. Certainly, some of these symptoms were evident to Dr. Kline that night, and as time went on, many would appear in varying degrees of severity. Knowing that the recovery process was going to be very long for the men, and that they were going to be taken from his "jurisdiction" within hours, Dr. Kline could do nothing more than see that his assessment was delivered to the Chief Medical Officer of the Colony and monitor the men for the remaining time they spent on Eleuthera.

The remaining twelve hours on the island were no easier than the first for the sailors. The reality of their safety was finally sinking in but was so overwhelming that their minds continued to race, and the night passed with little or no sleep. After a light breakfast in which they devoured more sugar with their corn flakes, they were visited by the English Methodist missionary, Reverend William Hyslop. He was there to transform the men, not spiritually but physically. He cut their hair back to what would be considered a full but conventional appearance, and after trimming their beards, shaved them clean. They were given new underwear, white duck trousers, white shirts, and sleeveless V-necked sweaters. Gone was the image of the castaway, but despite their new appearance, the physical toll was evident. Their eyes remained sunken deeply within their skulls, Tapscott's listless and blank, Widdicombe's occasionally flashing. Their new clothes bagged on them.

At midday, a gleaming Bellanca seaplane circled Governor's Harbour and made its landing in the calm, crystal-clear water of the harbor. The first person to get off the plane was the Colony's Medical Officer, Dr. John M. Cruikshank. Determining that the sailors were fit to fly to Nassau, the party made its way toward the plane. Either at this moment or at the other end of the flight, the American photographer Arthur Blood was poised with his camera. His pictures reveal that, while both men attempted to walk with support from others on either side, Tapscott had to clutch onto his trousers to keep them from falling off. Another image shows that Tapscott, in fact, could not walk and had to be carried.

As the plane made its short trip to Nassau, the first flight for both sailors, the news of their arrival made its way around the world. At 12:14 P.M. on October 31, the Governor of the Bahamas sent the official telegram to the Secretary of State for the Colonies, stating that two sailors had arrived in the Bahamas and that they were from the *Anglo-Saxon*, which had been torpedoed and sunk in August. The telegram gave their names and the names and addresses of their next of kin, but misinterpreted "Tapscott" as "Tapsavin." Government telegrams were also sent to the next of kin. On Lewis Street in Newport, however, it was not by telegram, but over the radio early on Friday morning, November 1, that young Cynthia Widdicombe, who for a month had mourned the loss of her husband, caught the name Widdicombe in a news broadcast about sailors washing up in the Bahamas. The report was confirmed a half hour later when the government's telegram arrived. It said, "Governor of the Bahamas reports that Wilbert Roy Widdicombe has arrived safely in the Bahamas and is receiving all possible attention and medical assistance. Will report progress later. Under Secretary, Colonial Office."

A similar telegram arrived for "Mrs. Florence Louise Tapsavin," Bob Tapscott's mother. She told reporters that she had been ill since receiving the news that her younger son's ship was missing but had never given up hope. She also told how he had cheated death once before, when his ship was bombed off Marseilles, and that she had had faith that he would somehow survive this ordeal. "He is a big strong strapping lad with an iron constitution, otherwise he would not be alive today," Mrs. Tapscott said. She had no idea how much of that iron constitution had been corroded away during the previous seventy days.

As the details of the survival of Widdicombe and Tapscott emerged in papers around the country, thirty-nine families had the grim confirmation that there would be no joyful news for them. It was confirmed that Denny, Pilcher, Hawks, Penny, and Morgan had survived the sinking but not the boat voyage. There was no definitive proof that the other 34 who had been on the *Anglo-Saxon* had died, but as the description of the attack, the wrecked lifeboats, and the machine-gunning of rafts in the water came out, reality settled on the families and friends of the others. Betty McAteer, the ten-year-old who still kept the rosary for her adored Uncle Jim's return, visited Cynthia Widdicombe with her mother and watched as the women shared each other's joy and grief.

As the news radiated out from Nassau, the Bellanca taxied up to the Pan Am seaplane terminal and the two men were assisted to the waiting ambulance. Treated as VIPs, they were taken to the private wing of Nassau General Hospital. It quickly became clear that Tapscott was far the worse off. His condition deteriorated, and the medical staff feared for his life during his first week in the hospital, whereas Widdicombe seemed to make a remarkable recovery. His volubility presents one of the real quandaries of this story.

All the fundamental details of the attack and the ordeal of the survivors that followed seem solid, logical, and are often verifiable through the log that was kept, first by Denny, then Hawks, and finally Widdicombe. That log had been turned over to the authorities by Tapscott and was being transcribed by Captain R. M. Millar, the Superintendent of His Majesty's Prison in Nassau. The elements of the story are consistent, with one exception: the death of Leslie Morgan. No less than five different versions of his death emerge. One of them is vague, three of them are variations on the same theme of his going over the side, and the fifth is startlingly different.

In his entries in the log of the jolly-boat voyage, the Mate is brief but explicit in recording the deaths of Pilcher and Penny. Widdicombe's entry for the suicide of the Mate and Third Engineer Hawks is similar: "Chief Mate and 3rd Engineer go over the side no water." His entry for Morgan's death says nothing as to how he died, it simply chronicles, "2nd Cook goes mad dies. Two of us left."

The two sailors' statements to Commissioner Gerassimos offer similar accounts but with slight differences. Tapscott's signed statement says, "Two days later the Cook went mad and he jumped overboard." The same event related by Widdicombe has a slightly different twist. His signed statement says, "Two days later the cook went the same way. It was rough and he fell overboard into the sea." Tapscott relates a deliberate act, while Widdicombe says it was accidental.

Some months later, a more elaborate version developed while the sailors were working with the writer Guy Jones, who published their story. In this telling, Morgan, who had been slipping in and out of lucidity and driving Widdicombe to the point of throwing him overboard once, and throwing the ax at him on another occasion, says, "I'll go down the street for a drink." He then stands up in the rocking boat, walks toward the stern, and topples over the side before the others can react. Since Morgan had a serious, gangrenous leg and ankle wound, it is hard to imagine how he would have managed the stroll toward the back of the boat bobbing on the ocean, but perhaps this is the difference between falling in and jumping in.

The tale also varies with each of Widdicombe's initial press interviews. The talkative Widdicombe, always fond of being the center of attention, was quick to give interviews. In his first, with Edwin Brownrigg of the *Nassau Guardian* just after the plane landed at 1:00 P.M. in Nassau, he recounts that Denny, Hawks, and Morgan steadily lost their mental faculties, and he and Tapscott were, according to the paper, "alone in the small boat with three mentally deranged shipmates" and that hunger was largely responsible "for the decision of these three men to take their lives by their own hands."

That same day, October 31, Widdicombe told a reporter from the *Nassau Daily Tribune* that two of the men in the boat died of their wounds,

"Two others became so crazed that they jumped overboard" and then, in relation to Morgan, the astonishing statement "Another slashed his throat with a razor."

This sensational part of the story appeared in numerous papers in England, Canada, and the United States, including the *New York Times*. The Nassau reporter for the *New York Sun* recounts how, "propped up in bed here, the cheerful Widdicombe" told the story including the assertion that "another slashed his throat." The following day, the *Nassau Guardian* carried a story with the bold headline "Widdicombe Says: 'Then My Next Door Neighbor Threw Himself Overboard.' " Widdicombe had changed the story back to his earlier account and is quoted in the paper as saying, "Two days later, L. Morgan the assistant cook, who lived next door to me in South Wales, went completely mad and threw himself overboard in a fit of frenzy."

There is no definitive accounting for these variations in the story. A strong possibility is that with his propensity for exaggeration and creating a sensation, Widdicombe let his imagination run wild and put out the story of Morgan slashing his throat. It does not seem likely that Morgan in his state could have done this, since killing oneself by slashing the throat is extremely difficult. It is one thing for a person to slash another person's throat; but with all the thick muscles, tendons, and other organs in the throat, the cutting is difficult and must go very deep to be effective. This is a nearly impossible wound for a person to inflict upon himself. In addition, the razor they had on board was not a traditional straight razor of the sort associated with throat slashing, but the latest innovation, the deluxe Rolls Razor, looking much like the safety razor of the mid-twentieth century, which had a relatively small, removable blade that could be honed to sharpness within the special stainless-steel case. The sailors might have been able to bisect a fish with this blade, but it would have been a clumsy device for throat slashing. Nevertheless, Roy Widdicombe floated this story out to the public and created a mystery in the jolly-boat story.

During the first week of their recovery, Tapscott clung to life, while Widdicombe continued to chatter with whoever would listen. Some people internalize their feelings after a traumatic experience and seldom talk about the event, while others constantly discuss it. These two men manifested those two extremes, and it would continue that way for the rest of their lives.

It had been a strange course of events that placed the Duke of Windsor in the governorship of the Bahamas during the wartime years and made Tapscott and Widdicombe his "charges." After his abdication of the English throne, the Duke and his American-born wife drifted around fashionable European centers, with a particular liking for France. The Duke's trips to Nazi Germany during the thirties worried many that his leanings were too pro-German, and he may have encouraged Hitler to think that Germany would not provoke a war with Britain when he began his aggression. As the blitzkrieg rolled over the Low Countries and France, there was fear that if there was a German invasion of the British Isles, the Duke might be "restored" to his rightful throne as a pawn of the Nazis. Expressing his interest in assisting his country in its time of need, the Duke lobbied for some significant military or diplomatic post. What he got was the Bahamas. He was placed where he could do little, if any, harm.

It is doubtful that any of these political subtleties were in the minds of Tapscott and Widdicombe when, after only six days in the hospital, they were honored by a visit by their former King and his wife. With Tapscott still so frail he had to be moved in a wheelchair, the two sailors received the Duke and Duchess on the covered porch of the Masonic Ward. In clear recognition of the condition of the two mariners, the patients were allowed to sit while the distinguished visitors stood and conversed with them. Dr. Cruikshank was also there to keep an eye on his patients. The Governor and his wife asked questions and listened earnestly to their story, showing deep compassion for these two heroes of England. The Duchess concluded the visit with a personal contribution to the sailors' well-being. She had prepared a caramel pudding for them as a treat, liberally laced with rum. Widdicombe later said, "There was so much rum that two teaspoons of pudding made us tight." For the two sailors, it was a memorable visit, and an equally memorable pudding.

Chapter 16

RETURN, REDEMPTION, AND REWARD

As Tapscott and Widdicombe devoured their sugar-laden cornflakes at the Moss house on Eleuthera, Hellmuth von Ruckteschell enjoyed a moment of supreme satisfaction and relief as he dropped anchor in Brest, on the Atlantic coast of France. For 180 days, he had ranged over the North Atlantic, brought his ship safely back to German-controlled territory, and lost none of his 364 crewmen in combat. The only loss was that of one man who was washed overboard in a fierce storm and could not be found despite a lengthy search. Ruckteschell was proud of this record, and now that they were safely in port, many on the crew who had initially harbored doubts about their Captain had to acknowledge this achievement and were grateful for it. In addition, Ruckteschell and indeed everyone on board were proud of their roster of ships sunk or captured and sent home as a prize. It totaled ten ships, constituting 58,644 tons, a tally that surpassed the nine ships and less tonnage sunk by the famous pocket battleship *Graf Spee*. Furthermore, they had accomplished this with a slow steam-powered vessel plagued with mechanical problems and a wardroom full of officers skeptical of the Captain's ability to command the ship.

Ruckteschell hoped for a hero's welcome for himself, his ship, and his crew. Almost immediately, however, a controversy arose that threatened their achievement and put Ruckteschell's career at risk. Soon after they dropped anchor, an officer from shore hand-delivered a message to him from the command group, the SKL, in Germany. The message ordered Ruckteschell and his crew to take the ship back to sea, through the English Channel to Hamburg for the complete mechanical overhaul the *Widder* required. The Captain was incredulous and incensed. He had just nursed his crippled ship through the hazards of the wartime Atlantic to reach safety, and now was ordered to place his sailors in jeopardy on a suicidal mission, running the gauntlet of the narrow, heavily patrolled Channel. The *Widder* would be easy prey for British warships or aircraft, as she would be traveling within 20 miles of the British coast.

Ruckteschell had a reputation as a renegade who made his own decisions, and raider command was appropriate for him since it normally allowed him to operate independently. To defy this order would be an extremely risky and serious matter. That, however, is what he did, to the astonishment of the officer who had delivered the message and who had to relay the response. The officer tried to reason with the Captain, beneath whose seemingly calm exterior seethed a furious man. Emphatically, Ruckteschell made the point that the skilled men of his crew would not be risked for a piece of hardware, a dubious piece at that. He declared he would go to Berlin personally and make his case if necessary, but he was not taking the *Widder* back to sea.

This act of defiance put the *Widder* into a sort of purgatory. After six months at sea, the sailors were eager to go ashore in France and enjoy the pleasures that were available in the conquered country; but they remained at anchor, the shore temptingly close. One of the crew drowned trying to swim ashore. The sagging morale of the crew was boosted a few days later when twenty large bags of mail arrived. The following day, bus tours of the countryside were arranged and the crew got their first taste of Brittany, if not liberty ashore. Shore leave was not allowed, but a full-blown "homecoming" celebration was held on board the ship, with ample beer, wine, and schnapps available to all. None of this satisfied the frustrated crew, however, and worry over the defiance of the order dominated the thoughts of many.

For two weeks, the ship lay at anchor, until finally, on November 14, she was moved to the shipyard in Brest. The crew was given their long-awaited shore leave, and Ruckteschell was summoned to Berlin by train to account for his actions. The officials in Berlin, while giving significant consideration to his stubborn defiance, clearly measured it against all that he had accomplished. In three days, the Captain was back with his ship and the entire crew was summoned. Wearing their best dark blue uniforms, the officers and men were reviewed by the Chief of Staff to the Naval Commander, Brittany, Kapitän zur See Bauer. To everyone's relief, this was an occasion for congratulations, as Bauer moved down the line presenting the important award of the Iron Cross 2nd Class to the crew and the Iron Cross 1st Class to the officers. The Captain was singled out and awarded the extremely high honor of the Knight's Cross of the Iron Cross. This was the award for the "stars" in the German armed forces, the aviation aces, the tank commander aces who achieved 100 "kills," and for the naval aces. The ceremonies were often shown in newsreels in theaters preceding movies, and there were postcards circulated that depicted these heroes and their deeds.

Despite his defiance, Ruckteschell's achievements had convinced his Nazi superiors that he was a hero. They also went on record endorsing the brutal tactics he had used. This was a key moment of redemption for Hellmuth von Ruckteschell.

As a fiercely proud and nationalistic German, he had followed the traditional path into service in the Kaiser's Navy, had aggressively prosecuted the war against the British and their allies as a U-boat commander in World War I, and then had fled in ignominy.

As a fugitive, he had hidden in the extreme north of Sweden and then returned to Germany when he thought he wouldn't be put on trial. Then for years he led the life of a craftsman, having lost his prestige as a naval officer. Hitler's rise and the outbreak of World War II had given him a chance to regain his past stature, and yet there were many doubters of the ability of this reserve officer. With the bestowing of the Knight's Cross, which was awarded to only 318 people in the entire German Navy during World War II, Korvettenkapitän der Reserve Hellmuth von Ruckteschell was redeemed. He was recognized as a true German hero, and that stature in the eyes of his fellow officers and countrymen could not be taken from him. A new phase in life could begin for this man who had renewed confidence and no longer carried the burden of having to prove himself.

In addition to the Knight's Cross, Ruckteschell also received what he most desired, a new raider command, a new ship built as a cargo vessel, and he would have control over her conversion into a deadly raider. When the war erupted, the ship was in the Schichau Shipyard in Gdansk, Poland, being built for the Gdynia America Shipping Lines as the motor vessel *Bielsko*. She was designed to be fast, since her role would be to carry perishable fruit to market. After the lightning-fast conquest of Poland, several German entities vied for this valuable prize. The North German Lloyd Lines sought her but so did the Navy, and they had priority.

Ruckteschell was given wide authority with regard to the conversion of the ship, as well as the opportunity to handpick the officers and crew to assist him with the conversion and then take the ship to sea. The Captain held a series of personal interviews with the officers who had been with him in the *Widder*. Many of the officers in his wardroom had been antagonistic toward him, and it was logical that he would be happy to be rid of them. The Executive Officer, Ernst-Günther Heinicke, was let go, as were the Radio Officer, Kindler, and the Gunnery Officer, Damschen. Dr. Negenborn, who had urged Ruckteschell to be more humane after sinking the *Beaulieu* and abandoning her crew, was not invited to stay. The rejection of the Chief Engineering Officer, Penzel, who had been praised by Ruckteschell for his tireless work to keep the engines operating, may have been because the Captain realized, as some of the other officers felt, that some of the problems experienced were due to Penzel's incompetence. The *Widder*'s identical sister ship, the raider *Orion*, stayed at sea for eighteen months, compared to the *Widder*'s six.

Ruckteschell retained the trusted Navigation Officer, Ludwig Rödel, the high-spirited and competent Torpedo Officer, Malte von Schack, Dr. Schröder, and two of the prize officers, Carl Cords and Adolf Wimmel. While Aviation Officer Konrad Hoppe was among those with doubts about Ruckteschell, the Captain knew he was a professional, experienced, and reliable officer. The "known commodity" of Hoppe was a more desirable option than bringing someone new aboard, even if Hoppe brought his skepticism with him. It is understandable why the Captain wished to keep Hoppe, but not as immediately clear why Hoppe would decide to stay with Ruckteschell. But just as the Captain's choice of Hoppe was for him the lesser of two evils, so was Hoppe's choice to stay with the Captain. Hermann Göring, with the full confidence of Hitler, held the supreme rank of Reichsmarschall and asserted his authority over everything that flew in the German military, including naval aviation. Although a pilot and Aviation Observation Officer, Konrad Hoppe was at his core a professional naval officer. He had no desire to shift to the gray uniform of the Luftwaffe under the command of the self-aggrandizing Göring. If he were to leave Ruckteschell, there would be no certainty about his future. With a degree of reluctance, he agreed to move on to Ruckteschell's next raider. The Captain also selected half of the *Widder*'s crew to move on with him.

Officers and crew alike appreciated the fact that their Captain had worked hard to ensure the safety of all onboard, and there was the sense that Ruckteschell made good decisions that not only kept them safe, but also achieved victory after victory for the raider. They thought if they stayed with him, there would be more success in their future, at minimum risk. Since the *Widder*'s success had earned the Knight's Cross for the Captain and handsome decorations for the officers and crew, they could all hope for even greater glory.

With the decisions about the crew determined, those selected boarded a train on December 1st for the forty-eight-hour trip, via Paris, to Gdansk and their new ship, designated simply *Schiff 28*. In early December, meetings were held with the shipyard management to lay out the plans to alter the vessel into Ruckteschell's ideal raider. Christmas leaves were given, since the shipyard would not begin work on the ship until after the holidays. While the relatives and friends of those lost on the *Anglo-Saxon* and the other ships Ruckteschell sank spent their first Christmas without their loved ones, their enemy enjoyed dream holidays. Most of the crew of *Schiff 28* were able to spend time with their families. Konrad

Hoppe, who had found a girlfriend in Gdansk, was able to go off with her to enjoy Munich's raucous beer halls and famous glockenspiel on the New City Hall. They went on to Vienna and enjoyed its famous architecture and tasty desserts in establishments like the Hotel Sacher and the Café Demel.

The advent of the year 1941 saw work begin in earnest on the transformation of *Schiff 28*. Gdansk was a city out of context; it was as if there were no war on and life went on as usual. Since Allied bombing was concentrated on German targets, there were no blackouts at night. The officers and crew of *Schiff 28* wore civilian clothes and were housed in private quarters rather than in military accommodations. The work on the ship progressed well. Some of the crew earned extra money working in the shipyard, while others were sent off for training.

Aware of the difficulty of sustaining the morale of a crew of 407 men at sea and envisioning a cruise far longer in duration than the *Widder*'s, Ruckteschell applied himself to the challenge of maintaining his crew's spirits while deployed away from home. Some of the crew were sent to conventional naval training classes to improve and refine their skills. Reflecting his personal artistic interests, he sent some of the men to study drawing and painting, sculpture and carving, and even puppetry and puppet theater. This effort to provide an "arts" atmosphere on board his ship even extended to the selection of the crew. He recruited a painter and sculptor, so that instruction in those arts could continue at sea. He also made a special effort to procure a music specialist, Oskar Erhardt, the former director of a music school in Heidelberg, who would be the ship's choirmaster as well as the conductor of the ship's orchestra! Konrad Hoppe's piano was part of the wardroom furnishings, as it had been on the *Widder*. Ruckteschell shaped his new ship to reflect himself and his tastes, and he was convinced this would be of benefit to his crew.

The Captain applied the same thoroughness in completing his selection of officers. A bright young man came under his scrutiny, Oberleutnant zur See Jürgen Herr, who five years before had studied in the United States, at the Kent School in Connecticut. Herr had served as a young officer aboard a German destroyer, *D51*, the *Diether von Roeder*. In the thick of the Norwegian campaign, the ship had been part of the carefully orchestrated attacks of April 9 on all the major Norwegian ports, which had caught the Allied forces by surprise. In the early hours of the following day, Jürgen Herr's birthday, the British launched a counterattack with a flotilla of destroyers. Two German destroyers were destroyed and Herr's ship, the *Diether von Roeder,* was hit by five shells, one in a gun turret, another in the superstructure, and three below the waterline. The crippled ship was afire and out of action. In the days that followed, with nine destroyers and the battleship HMS *Warspite,* the British finished off the remaining German ships. On shore, the survivors of the sunken destroyers, including Herr, joined the German troops who had landed and captured Narvik, and the destroyermen assessed their options. Two and a half months later, these survivors, in mismatched uniforms, managed to get back to Germany by traveling through neutral Sweden under guard and as "shipwrecked persons." In Luleå, a German passenger ship waited to take them home.

His first destroyer shot out from under him, young Herr returned to the destroyer base where he received orders to report to Dunkirk, on the French coast, where his task was to command a group of barges to be used in Operation Sealion, the invasion of England. All the ports along that section of the French coast saw boats being requisitioned, and it appeared as if the Germans, who had observed the heroic evacuation of the huge British and Allied force from the beaches of Dunkirk by every imaginable type of boat only a few months before, were now attempting to use the same strategy for invasion.

Initially, Hitler had not expected to be at war with England, so preparations for an invasion by sea had not been made. The Dunkirk evacuation demonstrated what could be done, and Herr was one of those sent to make preparations. In addition to gathering vessels, he was to recruit crews. In order to fill this need, Herr recalls, Berlin told him to recruit people with boat experience, including "anyone who has rowed a boat on a lake!" In the process of this work, for an invasion that would not take place, Herr was wounded when a bomb from a lone British plane hit his pier. After his initial recovery, he was sent to Italy for a more comfortable recuperation. It was on his return from Italy, while checking in at the naval personnel office in Kiel, that he first encountered a formidable Korvettenkapitän with the Knight's Cross who was seeking fine officers for his crew. Herr's competent demeanor obviously impressed the Captain, who investigated his record and realized that this was the type of officer he wanted with him. After some further convalescence at home, Herr received orders, not to the destroyer force, but to Gdansk. There he once again encountered Korvettenkapitän von Ruckteschell and joined the crew of his raider.

The conversion continued for eight months, during which the ship's crew and the shipyard workers attended to innumerable details. In the midst of this work, Hellmuth von Ruckteschell was confronted with a serious personal challenge. In April 1941, the Nazi intolerance for "deviant religions" focused on the Christian Community, the spiritual congregation based on Rudolf Steiner's philosophy of anthroposophy, of which Ruckteschell was a member. His church was closed and his pastor sent to a concentration camp. While Ruckteschell might have turned a blind eye to other Nazi initiatives, feeling the restoration of Germany's pride and stature were worth the sacrifices, this impacted him personally.

The Nazi Party, which he had joined in March of 1933, had taken a stand against his faith, and he faced a crisis of conscience. On one hand, he was a highly decorated hero who eagerly wanted to take his new ship to sea and, with nationalist zeal, win more victories for his beloved Germany. On the other hand, the government of his country was persecuting his faith and his pastor. He considered resigning, but consulted the Navy's Commander in Chief, Grossadmiral Raeder, with whom he had established a good rapport. In a somewhat similar situation in 1937, Raeder had intervened directly with Hitler on behalf of a former World War I U-boat commander who had become a Lutheran minister and worked against Hitler's totalitarian control of the church. Raeder understood the pressure Ruckteschell was experiencing. When the Captain explained his problem, Raeder urged him, "Command your ship." With this guidance, Ruckteschell let his nationalism outweigh his religious convictions and returned to his ship.

Other challenges developed. With his desire to fashion the perfect raider out of the cargo vessel, Ruckteschell sought the latest in shipboard artillery. Although he succeeded with many requests, this was turned down flatly. The modern 15cm guns were in great demand for vessels with higher priority, and the German military was desperately searching for even antiquated weapons wherever they could be found. They were being salvaged from World War I battleships, and even from the gun emplacements of the Westwall, a 400-mile-long chain of fortifications intended to make Germany impregnable from attack from the west. Ruckteschell was offered the old 15cm guns from the *Widder*. After his refusal to take the old ship from Brest to Hamburg, others had managed to do so, and the *Widder*'s guns were taken off and shipped from Hamburg to Gdansk.

Ruckteschell also wanted improved reconnaissance aircraft to ensure the safety of his future voyages and fully use the talents of Aviation Officer Hoppe. The old Heinkel He 114Bs that he had on the *Widder* had failed on their first flights and were useless. Now he sought the latest-model seaplanes, but was told that with Reichsmarschall Göring's tight grip on all aviation allocations and low regard for the Navy, this was not possible. He settled for two Arado Ar 196 seaplanes, which were something of an improvement over the Heinkels.

Remembering the constant frustration from the slow speed of the *Widder,* Ruckteschell introduced the concept of the ship carrying not just surveillance aircraft, but also a high-speed torpedo boat to enhance both his reconnaissance and his destructive power. Other raiders had carried small, fast boats, but they were equipped only as minelayers. No one had ever suggested this new tactic before. After some discussion, Admiral Otto Schniewind, the Chief of Staff of the SKL, agreed to Ruckteschell's plan. A small boat that would meet these needs was being developed at the Dornier works in Friedrichshafen, on the German side of Lake Constance, the Bodensee, which forms part of the border between Germany and neutral Switzerland. The design was for a light, fast boat powered by two Jumo diesels, enabling speeds in excess of 40 miles an hour. With twin torpedo tubes in the transom at the stern, the boat would make her run in to the target, turn her stern toward her victim, fire her torpedoes, and be on her way out of danger. For her own defense, the boat carried a 20mm machine gun mounted in a glass dome behind the control station. Ruckteschell made a trip to negotiate with the manufacturers and, satisfied that he had been successful, returned to Gdansk and the conversion of the raider.

The work progressed well, but some strained relations developed when the traditional rivalry between soldiers and sailors periodically erupted in town, and Ruckteschell had to make a number of trips to the Army authorities to retrieve some of his men from the military prison. Other than this intramural rivalry, life was deceptively peaceful in Gdansk and the crew established many comfortable relationships that would be painful to end. The tranquillity of Gdansk made this an attractive place for families of the officers to visit. With his father, a tank corps general, away, Jürgen Herr's mother and sister Ingrid were among those who visited, as were the parents of Malte von Schack. That summer, Ingrid Herr and Malte von Schack met and, to their parents' pleasure, became engaged.

Toward the end of August, Hellmuth von Ruckteschell's chosen *Leichtschnellboot* commander, Torpedo Officer von Schack, went to Lake Constance to test and take delivery of the new torpedo boat. Being a party-loving individual, he hosted a gala dinner for the shipyard people and then presented the staggering bill to the bewildered paymaster of *Schiff 28*. A few days later, Flight Officer Hoppe and his pilot went to Kiel to claim their new Arado seaplanes and flew them to Gdansk. Everything seemed to be coming together nicely, with the commissioning ceremony only a few days away.

However, Captain Ruckteschell was about to have a very dangerous contretemps with none other than the Navy's most senior officer, Grossadmiral Erich Raeder. The controversy developed over what many would have thought was the most minor of points, but it reveals much about Ruckteschell's tenacity. It was the tradition among the raiders to allow the Captain to select the name for his ship. As was seen with the *Widder,* Ruckteschell selected a name that was forceful (the ram), but also a reflection of the Captain himself, whose Zodiac sign was Aries.

As the time for *Schiff 28*'s commissioning approached, Admiral Raeder sent a message to Ruckteschell inquiring as to what the ship's name would be. Ruckteschell's well-considered response was *"Michel."* The Admiral immediately rejected this name as totally unsuitable and requested another. His objection came from the fact that this name was the commonly known moniker for a short, rotund character with a pointed hat who symbolized the German common man and was often the brunt of jokes. Ruckteschell was fully committed to the name and did not wish to relinquish it. His reasons are not fully understood and may have had several dimensions, as his character did. It was certainly a reference to Saint Michael, the warrior saint who many felt was the patron saint of Germany. It may also be the case that Ruckteschell was subtly interjecting his Rudolf Steiner sympathies into the issue, since Steiner had written at least fifteen lectures on the subject of Saint Michael. Another reason may have been that Ruckteschell identified himself with the German common man. For many years between the wars, he had led the simple life of the craftsman. On the *Widder,* he seemed to relate more to the enlisted men in his crew than to the elitist officers. Once again selecting a name that would be an embodiment of himself, making him and his ship one, he chose *Michel.*

Rather than disobey his Admiral, who fortunately seemed friendly toward him, Ruckteschell offered an outrageous alternative, the *Götz von Berlichingen.* When he instructed his Radio Officer, Götz-Friedrich von Rabenau, to send the alternative proposal, the Radio Officer was stunned and said he could not send it. Götz von Berlichingen was a sixteenth-century Swabian knight who had an iron prosthesis in place of his right hand and who in the eighteenth century became the central character in a famous play by Goethe. In what is possibly the most quoted sentence in German literature, Götz says something similar to "Lick my butt," and consequently, when someone says "Götz" or "Götz von Berlichingen," they are expressing that specific meaning. Rabenau could not imagine sending that thinly veiled insult to the Supreme Naval Commander, but the Captain insisted. Ruckteschell could, of course, fain innocence and suggest that he was naming the ship for the iron-fisted knight, but it was doubtful that this excuse would have been accepted. In response to his message, there was stony silence from the Admiral.

The day of the commissioning, September 7, 1941, came, and the ship was honored as Admiral Raeder arrived by special train to officiate. The tension on the ship was palpable, since most knew of the friction over the intended name, and there was serious concern that before they began the crew would lose their Captain, whom most now respected. As he was about to leave the ship at the end of the inspection and the commissioning ceremony, Admiral Raeder, impressed with all he saw, apparently said, "I am very content with everything I've seen. You've got a good ship. So, set sail in your . . . *Michel*, Rucki."

With great relief, the *Michel* began her sea trials and combat exercises in the Baltic under the command of newly promoted Fregattenkapitän von Ruckteschell. For the next six months, in the midst of the Baltic winter, this training took place. There were a few mishaps, such as running aground, but no serious damage was done. There seemed to be a flaw in the ship, however, as the sewage system regularly became obstructed, requiring a return to the shipyard to have it cleared. It was not long before Ruckteschell realized that these sojourns to the shipyard to solve this chronic problem also permitted sojourns for the crew under the cozy featherbeds of Gdansk. As soon as he insisted that the clogged pipes be cleaned out by the crew at sea, the fault was miraculously cured. The crew's skills grew and were refined through the rigorous training, and at the end of January 1942, the ship left Gdansk and the comfortable life there for Kiel, which had been under air attacks since September 4, 1939, and the reality of the war.

On February 4, the *Michel* left Kiel and transited the Kiel Canal as the *Widder* had done almost two years earlier, heading for final training off Cuxhaven, in the North Sea. The ship made several more trips back and forth through the 60-mile-long canal for minor repairs and supplies. The Commanding Officer went to Berlin for his final instructions, and other officers went to France to complete the thorough preparations for the dreaded, hazardous duty that lay ahead. Although Ruckteschell had refused to bring the *Widder* eastward through the English Channel, his only option in the case for getting his handsome new ship out into the Atlantic was to run the gauntlet from east to west. This would be a true test of ship, crew, and Captain.

Chapter 17

CELEBRITY

Other than the beneficial effect of the Duchess's well-laced pudding, the visit of the Duke and Duchess of Windsor had no medical advantage, but it marked the beginning of the survivors' recovery. Up until that time, the sailors had been kept in near isolation, under constant care, with fear for Tapscott's survival. After the initial flurry of newspaper interviews in which Widdicombe expounded on the attack and ordeal that followed, Dr. Cruikshank restricted access to his two important patients. Their hydration and nutrition were monitored carefully and, gradually, balance was brought back. Incredibly, their seventy days of privation did not seem to have caused permanent physical damage. They were still weak and frail when the Duke and Duchess paid their visit but had begun to put on weight.

The greatest concern was for the men's emotional and mental well-being. They had been through a trauma that few could fathom, fighting to maintain their mental grasp during the interminable boat voyage. The impact on their minds was enormous, and just as the men were different in many ways, those differences were reflected in their responses after finally reaching safety. Always the cocky, streetwise extrovert, Widdicombe seemed to rebound quickly. Eager to talk about his experience, he loved to be the center of attention and reveled in his newfound fame. With a renewed lust for life, he was eager to immerse himself in the exotic social scene of the resort community.

Bob Tapscott had a very different response. Almost from the moment he tumbled onto the beach, he seemed to shut down. While Widdicombe wanted to live life to the fullest, it was a question whether Tapscott wanted to live at all. He endured long periods of depression during which he expressed his desire to die. Dr. Cruikshank and his dedicated staff gave the very best care they could to the two young men, but there was no care that could revive the love of life that Tapscott had had until his death-defying voyage. It may have been the very fact that he had cheated death while so many of his friends and shipmates had succumbed that contributed to his condition. At that time, there was little understanding of the devastating effects that traumatic experiences and "survivor guilt" have on many people. The medical staff in the Bahamas realized Tapscott was coping with serious complications from his ordeal, and worked hard to help him.

Another group was caring for the other survivor of the sinking of the *Anglo-Saxon,* the jolly boat. From the first realization that these two young men had made a heroic voyage, there was concern that the boat be protected and preserved. According to the retired Constable Elijah Mackey, people helped themselves to some of the items in the abandoned boat before her importance was realized. Since it appeared in those early hours that the boat was being left behind, some locals felt it would be a shame to just leave usable items like the Mate's knife, the binnacle with its saltwater-filled compass, and the malfunctioning oil lamp to deteriorate or be taken by others.

Within days, Mackey says, at the Governor's command, the Commissioner of Police came from Nassau, with two detectives and two policemen, to search for items taken from the boat. While some things were recovered, others, such as its nameboard, had simply disappeared. A combination of government and private efforts accomplished the task of getting the boat to Nassau. The boat was moved down the coast, where a truck belonging to a wealthy American, Austin T. Levy, who was developing pineapple plantations on the northern portion of the island, transported her to his construction vessel, which delivered her to Prince George's Dock in Nassau.

Mid-November was early for the beginning of "the season" in socially conscious Nassau. The news reports that had circulated in American newspapers may have increased interest in Nassau, and some seasonal residents and vacationers advanced their timetables for arrival in the Bahamian capital. One of those who did so was Cora Mallory Munson, widow of Frank C. Munson of the Munson steamship lines, who owned one of the best hotels in Nassau, the Royal Victoria. Cora Munson was the personification of the American shipping industry. She was born into the Mallory family, which had been in the American maritime industry for almost 130 years by that time as sailmakers, shipbuilders, and shipping-line owners, and she married ship owner Frank C. Munson. Mrs. Munson wanted people to see the boat that had made this historic voyage, and by December 5th the boat was on display on the veranda of the Royal Victoria Hotel.

Interest in the boat was rivaled only by interest in the two sailors. They had become celebrities. As they gained strength, they gave more interviews. Newspapers in North America and Britain that had originally reported the scant information available in the first few days ran follow-up stories sparking the imaginations of their readers. The presence of the two sailors not only brought the reality, the face, of the war to the Bahamas, but it put the Bahamas on the front page of innumerable newspapers. This was an important, almost unbelievable story. Until now, the Bahamas had been a backwater during the war, with only newspaper accounts of the Battle of Britain and other war news to remind the tranquil holiday destination that there was a war on. The United States wouldn't enter the war for another year, and Munson Line ships, which traveled safely within the protected waters of the Pan-American Neutrality Zone, continued to bring vacationers to Nassau, along with provisions and supplies.

It was only natural for Robert Ripley, the explorer and adventurer who had an international reputation through his "Believe It or Not" cartoons, to respond to the story. Ripley had sold his first drawings to *Life* magazine at age fourteen. Eleven years later, in 1918, he was a sports cartoonist with the *New York Globe,* and compiled a list of strange sports facts. When he put these into cartoon form, they evolved into "Believe It or Not." The tale that Tapscott and Widdicombe had to tell was tailor-made for Ripley, who by this time had an extremely popular radio program heard across the United States over the ninety stations of the Columbia Broadcasting System. He was determined to share their heroic story with his listeners, and the only way to do that was through a direct broadcast from Nassau, where the young men could be interviewed live. The rumors that Ripley was coming to Nassau became the center of interest and speculation in late November. On December 2, 1940, Ripley and his staff arrived to see if they could get permission to interview the two men on radio and to determine whether the complex technical details could be arranged for an international broadcast.

The evening edition of the *Nassau Guardian* for Monday, December 2nd, gave the public their first look at the two survivors since the early images of the emaciated patients at the hospital. Their physical appearance was remarkably changed. Photographs were taken of them with Ripley at the Royal Victoria Hotel, where he was staying. The jolly boat was launched into the shallows of Nassau Harbor for the purpose of taking staged photos. Widdicombe was seen talking or gesturing, while Tapscott looked on with a calm air. Both men looked thin but fit in sport shirts and slacks. While not back to their normal weight, they had lost their gaunt look. They were still patients at the hospital but were well enough to participate in the historic broadcast.

The intention was to conduct the live radio program from the dining room of the Royal Victoria Hotel from 10:00 to 10:30 on Friday night, December 6, 1940. This was one year and a day before the American entry into the war, and Americans were insulated from the toll the war had taken. This broadcast brought them personal contact, albeit over radio waves, with two heroic survivors of the war. Many hoped that this personal exposure to the war would foster greater American sympathy for the British and their Allies.

With a potential audience of 50 million listeners, this was a media blockbuster for its day. The task of making the broadcast was technologically daunting and reported by the program's announcer in New York as "the most difficult broadcast ever attempted by Mr. Ripley." The original plan to send the program to Miami via overseas telephone, and then by landline to New York where CBS would broadcast it on their nationwide network, seemed fraught with the potential for failure. The decision was made to eliminate the use of phones and broadcast it directly from Nassau to CBS in New York, and in Miami, as a backup, and then to the nation. During tests in the days preceding the actual broadcast, they confronted interference on their wavelength from a station in Colombia, South America, but were able to convince the station to go off the air during the broadcast.

The *Nassau Daily Tribune* reported some of the extreme measures used to ensure that the program would succeed. "In order to guard against almost any contingency, Nassau decided to put four transmitters on the broadcast of this event. Actually the station [ZNS] had only one transmitter for broadcasting purposes. That meant they had to convert three of their telegraph transmitters to broadcasting use. One of these transmitters was tied in with New York, a second with Miami, a third with both Miami and New York, and the forth with ZNS in Nassau. In addition, the American Telegraph and Telephone Co. closed one of its transatlantic telephone receivers and turned it over to Nassau for the purpose of relaying the broadcast through Miami." This was obviously an all-out effort to be certain the broadcast reached its audience.

Although atmospheric conditions played havoc with the broadcasting tests prior to the 6th and on the days following, on the night of the actual program the atmosphere cooperated and everything went perfectly, thanks to the careful planning and the priority that CBS gave to this event. Part of that priority came from the fact that Ripley was not only going to interview Tapscott and Widdicombe, but the Duke of Windsor was also going to speak as part of the broadcast. This was of particular interest to the American audience because of their fascination with the former King and his American wife.

Prior to the broadcast, the dining room of the Royal Victoria Hotel was a lively scene, with the invited guests holding a number of dinner parties. Present that evening were several people who would have an ongoing interest in and commitment to the story. Seventeen people, including Ripley, were entertained at Cora Mallory Munson's table. This group included her brother Clifford D. Mallory, then the President of the Board of the Marine Historical Association in Mystic, Connecticut, which would evolve into Mystic Seaport, the famous maritime museum. His daughter, Margaret, a trustee of the museum, was there with him. Sir Harry Oakes, the rough-cut baronet, reputed to be the richest in the realm, and Lady Oakes were also in attendance. In another part of the dining room, a dinner party was being hosted by the writers Guy Pearce Jones and his wife, Constance Bridges Jones. Each of these people formed significant connections with the saga of the sinking of the *Anglo-Saxon.*

As the broadcast time of 10:00 P.M. neared, the remnants of the dinner had been cleared away and there was a sense of anticipation as the technicians made last-minute equipment checks. Off to the side of the stage was a large radio with several of Ripley's aides anxiously crowded around it. The interviews were to be conducted in Nassau, but the program's announcer was in New York. B. A. Rulfe's forty-eight-piece Believe It or Not Orchestra, also in New York, provided music during the breaks. The only way the technicians in Nassau could be sure things were going smoothly was to tune in to the radio and listen to the program as it was broadcast in Nassau as part of regular CBS service.

After the New York announcer opened the program, Robert Ripley, standing between the flags of Great Britain and the United States, was given his cue to begin. First acknowledging His Royal Highness, the Governor, and other distinguished guests, he gave a rhapsodic description of the Bahamas before introducing the central subject of his program. He commented on the miraculous journey of the two British seamen in an open boat, which, he said, "topped the fabulous voyage of Captain Bligh." He pointed out that Bligh had a significantly larger boat, which was well provisioned, including full navigational equipment. In addition, Bligh was able to land on several islands for provisions. Regarding Tapscott and

Widdicombe's voyage, he said, "They had covered 3,000 miles of the Atlantic, lost five of their crew members, but dauntlessly, in this small boat, brought honour and distinction to the flag they love by iron will and British determination . . . Believe It or Not."

After this introduction, Ripley drew the story from the two sailors, which many already knew from the papers; but hearing it from the two survivors in their own words added power and reality to the event. At the conclusion of the interview with Tapscott and Widdicombe, he introduced His Royal Highness, the Duke of Windsor. In an opening statement that must have thrilled the program's host, the Duke said: "You have just heard Widdicombe and Tapscott tell you their amazing story. I had a long talk with these two British merchant seamen soon after they had fetched up on the beach of one of the islands of the Bahamas in an open boat seventy days after their ship was torpedoed and I thought at the time that here indeed was an extraordinary adventure up to the standard of Mr. Ripley's famous feature, 'Believe It or Not.'"

The Duke continued, saying, "This epic of the sea prompts me to pay tribute to the men of the Merchant Navy and the Fishing Fleet. Normally employed in the great industry of the sea in times of peace, in war they are mobilized for the most arduous, exacting and hazardous duties. Not only do they man the ships that supply Great Britain with her many vital requirements, but to them is also entrusted the task of sweeping the channels clear of mines in order that the merchant vessels may reach their destinations."

He went on to add, in regard to the merchant mariners, "They wear no prescribed uniform—no glamour surrounds them—but without their devotion to their job and their complete disregard of the dangers to which they are vulnerable as soon as they put to sea, Great Britain's plight would indeed be a serious one today." The Governor concluded with remarks aimed at his American audience, encouraging their support of the war effort. Ripley thanked his guests and announced that after the program the jolly boat would be auctioned off for the benefit of the two sailors and several war relief causes, including the Red Cross.

As the program concluded, the aides hovering near the radio were ecstatic—the complicated feat had been accomplished. The Duke had his second private conversation with Tapscott and Widdicombe, and then departed for his residence. The festive atmosphere at the Royal Victoria was ideal for the fundraising that followed. The jolly boat was on display on the hotel's veranda, and all in attendance had seen her.

Among the eager bidders was Clifford D. Mallory, who knew that it was important that this little boat be preserved. The maritime museum in Mystic, Connecticut, with which he was affiliated, was a place where she could be preserved and exhibited. He raised his voice in the genteel, enthusiastic bidding, but soon dropped out, not because of an inability to purchase the boat, but because a unique bidding duel developed that was likely to escalate, benefiting the recipients of the event and causing a sensation in itself. One of the formidable bidders was Sir Harry Oakes, whose fortune knew no limits. The other was Lady Oakes, who also seemed to have unlimited resources at her disposal, probably the same resources Sir Harry would have drawn upon. The amusing but vigorous rivalry between the two bidders finally peaked. Sir Harry realized he had met his match and relinquished the prize to his wife, with the winning bid from Lady Oakes of £300. This might not seem a princely sum, but was equal to 10 percent of the annual salary for the Governor of the Bahamas. When asked what she was going to do with the boat, Lady Oakes said she had no idea. Her goal had been to help the two sailors and the war relief efforts. With the heroes present, a spontaneous outpouring of generosity followed, which produced another £50 for the sailors.

At the evening's end, the two young men, who had lost all their personal property in the sinking of their ship, came into a small fortune as a reward for their heroism and hardships. They received half of the money from the sale of the boat—£150, or $600—plus the £50, or $200, and a check from Robert Ripley for $500. The young men, who the day before had nothing, suddenly had $1,300 to share. Their monthly pay was £10.12.6, so this was the equivalent of over one year's pay for each sailor. Some other comparisons put this into perspective. A night in a double room with bath in the Royal Victoria Hotel cost £4/10, or $18, *Time* magazine sold on the newsstands for 15 cents, a pound of Barricini chocolates was 68 cents, a saddle horse could be purchased in Nassau for $40, and a used Buick automobile in good condition cost $150. Well on his way to full recovery, Widdicombe was ready to move into the fascinating life of this resort community and now had money to support his new celebrity lifestyle. Tapscott was still recuperating and needed more time in the hospital.

One more benefit came of that evening. The drama of the sailors' tale captured the interest of one of the writers in the audience, Guy Pearce Jones, who was quick to realize that the story of the remarkable boat voyage would interest significant numbers of people and that the brief newspaper accounts had told only a fraction of their story. He was confident that he could coax the details of the story from the two lads and convinced them to work with him toward that end. Over several months, he met regularly with the sailors and pieced together their story. On December 10, three days after the radio broadcast and the day after the announcement of the book project, with the encouragement of Guy Jones, Roy Widdicombe returned to Eleuthera on the vessel *Content* to gather information for the book from those who had assisted in the rescue. Tapscott was still under strict hospital care and not ready for such a trip.

Widdicombe's return to Governor's Harbour, where he apparently made a number of visits, created great interest. He met with Constable Mackey of James Cistern and it is likely that he obtained the details of her dream from Florence Johnson. A disturbing trait of Widdicombe's, which had been evident since his youth, when he appropriated other people's property (in that case sailing dinghies) for his own use, may have also surfaced during this trip. He visited and had tea with the Commissioner, Michael Gerassimos. After Widdicombe left, Gerassimos reached for his silver cigarette case, which had been there at the beginning of their meeting, and found it missing.

The silver cigarette case fit perfectly into the new lifestyle Widdicombe envisioned. Since the sailors had arrived with nothing, the community responded generously. Mrs. Percy Lightbourne gave them a radio for their hospital room, while others supplied stamped postcards for them to write home, among other things. After they regained their body weight, the shops along Bay Street were happy to assist with clothing. Widdicombe took full advantage of the offer and selected the best and most expensive clothing from The Men's Shop, Nassau's finest clothier. In keeping with his earlier habit of using clothes to achieve stature, his suits had style. While in the past he had often "dressed up," or in one instance bought an officer's uniform he was not qualified to wear, in order to create an image of importance, now there was no longer the need to masquerade. He was a legitimate celebrity, sought after in this vacation paradise. Three days after the radio broadcast, Mrs. John Brinkley from Texas entertained the two mariners at a luncheon at the British Colonial Hotel. After hearing their story on the radio, a lady in California offered to adopt both young men. They had the opportunity to become part of a social world unlike any they had experienced in the past. To be fully prepared, Widdicombe acquired a white dinner jacket: he would be properly turned out for the nightlife. Widdicombe's new life was in full swing by mid-December, despite still technically being a patient in Bahamas General Hospital.

For Tapscott, the story was different. Rather than take up the fast life that attracted Widdicombe, Tapscott looked for diversions that were slower paced. Nassau's Imperial Order of Daughters of the Empire had set up a canteen in the Masonic Building on Bay Street, not far from the hospital, which they staffed and operated for the duration of the war. This was a retreat where visiting sailors and servicemen could find a welcome and friendly greeting and conversation with the IODE ladies who volunteered to staff the facility, as well as enjoy the company of others from the merchant marine or military service. While the canteen atmosphere was too tame for Widdicombe, it seemed right for Tapscott, who began to spend long hours there, enjoying the refreshments and playing cards with the hostesses and other visitors.

To serve his need to move about the island, Widdicombe acquired an automobile, probably the first he had ever had, and possibly the first he had driven. How he made this acquisition is not known, but he had enough money to purchase a used car, or to lease a U-Drive-It car for as

little as $15 per week. By the end of December, the high-living Widdi-
combe was mobile, with his car, license number 733, able to transport him
wherever he wanted to roam. There was an indication that perhaps Widdicombe was not an experienced driver when on December 23 the car,
with Widdicombe at the wheel and Tapscott as passenger, "came out of
the hospital gate and, in order to avoid colliding with a car traveling west
on Shirley Street, he ran it into the wall on the opposite side of the street.
The fender was damaged." This was the first of Widdicombe's vehicular
mishaps that punctuated his time "in the fast lane" in Nassau.

Both men were still hospital patients, and the newspapers reported
that, while they had made significant physical recovery, their "nerves were
still a little unsettled." A controversy raged about them within several
government offices regarding their status and return to England. During
the earlier weeks of their recovery, there had been a steady flow of information from the Governor's Office to the Colonial Office and directly
on to Cynthia Widdicombe and Tapscott's mother. News of the Ripley
radio interviews reached the Ministry of Shipping in Berkeley Square,
London, and three days later, on December 9, a coarsely worded message
was sent to the Under Secretary of State in the Colonial Office. The message read: "I suggest that it would be well to request the Governor of Bahamas definitely to repatriate Widdicombe via New York. At New York
he should report to the Ministry of Shipping Representative, 25 Broad-
way, in case they are able to use him in one of the ships requiring crew to
come back to this side." After only five weeks of recovery, the Ministry of
Shipping was not only asking that Widdicombe be sent home, but that he
work his way back across the winter North Atlantic with its U-boat peril.
The strong response from the Colonial Office pointed out that the request "betrays a lack of imagination and of sympathy and understanding
to which Widdicombe is entitled in view of his ordeal" and went on to say
that under the circumstances the request would not be forwarded to the
Governor. The Minister of Shipping, Ronald Cross, backed off and suggested that the ministry take advantage of the public relations potential,
saying, "Not only ought we to make a fuss over them, but it would be fool-
ish to miss this opportunity of doing so." The British Merchant Navy was

in need of all the experienced mariners it could muster, but whether Tap-scott and Widdicombe could return to their old careers was difficult to determine.

While the Colonial Office and the Ministry of Shipping were dealing with the issues of the two survivors, the Admiralty was in communication with the Nitrate Producers Steam Ship Co., the owners of the *Anglo-Saxon*. On November 14, 1940, the company posted letters to the next of kin of the crew and officers of the ship. The letter to Ethel Milburn read: "We deeply regret to advise you that we are this morning in receipt of official confirmation from the Admiralty of the calamitous loss of the above ves-sel [the *Anglo-Saxon*] through enemy action. According to this informa-tion, only two survivors landed at the Bahamas, and as the Admiralty state that their boat is believed to be the only one that got away from the vessel, we greatly fear little hope can now be entertained of any other members of the crew being saved. In conveying this tragic news, may we again ask you to accept our deepest sympathy." The newspaper accounts and the informal network among the families of the *Anglo-Saxon* sailors had carried the grim news to most of them before the receipt of the letter, but now it was in hand, with the imprimatur of the shipping company and the authority of the Admiralty.

Ethel Milburn had to deal not only with her own grief, but help her young sons, Ted and Derek, cope with the loss of their father and make plans for the family's future. Her in-laws lived nearby and gave occasional advice. Their relationship in the past had not been the most helpful. However, for the sake of her sons, Ethel Milburn worked to sustain a re-lationship with the senior Milburns, who had difficulty dealing with their own grief. Eddie Milburn's father refused to accept the fact that his son was lost. Throughout the war, he combed through lists of prisoners of war in newspapers and regularly listened to the broadcasts from the German propagandist "Lord Haw Haw," who lured British listeners to his pro-German propaganda by including the names of some prisoners of war in his broadcasts. Without her husband, Eddie, to share in the decision-making, as the year 1940 came to a close, Ethel Milburn applied herself to the task of determining an appropriate course for her sons' futures.

The "celebrations" ringing in the year 1941 in Nassau were muted. Virtually everyone wished for an end to the war. The Americans were hoping that their country would not be drawn into this war, and President Roosevelt was carefully balancing his desire to help Britain with that of keeping the United States neutral. For the British in Nassau, the situation "at home" in England was grim indeed, and the only quick end to the war that they could imagine was through their defeat. Yet, the overall air in Nassau was one of anxious detachment. With the war so far away, the hotels were filled with American holidaymakers, the dance bands played at the Yacht Club and the Prince George Hotel, and lights shone brightly while England was blacked out. As 1941 began, Tapscott was still in need of hospitalization. That was not the case for Widdicombe, but he remained a resident of the hospital for as long as Tapscott did. Tapscott would require extended outpatient treatment, but on January 9 they were released from Bahamas General Hospital.

Chapter 18

HOMEWARD BOUND

In Nassau, the two main newspapers offered periodic reminders of the sailors' adventure and their presence on the island to their readers. On December 30, 1940, the *Nassau Guardian* published a special photo page under the banner "It Happened in 1940." Photographs of the sailors shared space with those of King George VI, the Duke of Windsor, Prime Minister Winston Churchill, and the Marquis of Lothian, who, until his death, had been the British Ambassador to the United States. The photo of the two sailors was larger than any of the others, including Churchill's. With hospitalization no longer necessary, on January 9, 1941, the government moved them to the Lucerne Hotel, where they would have more social latitude while continuing their recuperation. The Lucerne was not in the top tier of hotels, which included the Royal Victoria, the British Colonial, and the Fort Montagu Beach, but it was a comfortable establishment. Those who knew it say its owner, R. M. Lightbourne, insisted that its visitors be well served. It was a three-story wooden structure of the traditional Bahamian style, with balconies on three sides of the building, offering a cool retreat from the tropical climate. An advantage for the government, which was footing the bill, was that the Lucerne was one of only two hotels that offered a discounted weekly rate, even at the height of the tourist season.

For the sailors, it had two distinct advantages: a light breakfast was included for the guests, and it had a popular bar, known at one point as the Bucket of Blood, in reference to the islands' earlier pirate days. Just liberated from the confines and constraints of the hospital, the hotel and its bar seemed the perfect spot for them. Members of the Lightbourne family, who remember the young men while they were at the hotel, say they took full advantage of the bar and created a real presence in the hotel.

From its central location on Frederick Street, between the two main streets, Bay and Shirley, the two men could move about central Nassau on foot with ease. Tapscott could walk to Bay Street and then on a few blocks to the IODE Canteen, or head up to Shirley Street to return to the hospital for continued treatment. During this period, they spent hours with Guy Jones as he extracted details of their story for his book. They also had the chance for relaxation, including several opportunities to go sailing. It is hard to imagine that after all the "enforced" sailing they had done that they would ever want to set foot in a small sailboat again, but they did. Widdicombe admitted that he always "felt a little nervous" when out of sight of land.

While both seemed to be enjoying their improved health, liberty, financial stability, and life in the secure holiday resort, Widdicombe was the more flamboyant, with his stylish clothes and the mobility his car afforded him. Gwen French, an IODE member who served as a hostess almost every day at the Canteen, recalls Widdicombe as a very cocky and self-confident person who loved to dress up in fancy clothes and gave the impression of having money. "You would have thought he was a member of the Royal Family." She remembers Tapscott spending considerable time at the Canteen, dressed simply in shirt and slacks, playing bridge or cribbage. On occasion, French joined their card games and came away feeling that Widdicombe and Tapscott didn't like each other.

A few days after they left the hospital, on January 11, the *Nassau Guardian* reported that the two sailors would leave the Bahamas soon, Widdicombe intending to enlist in the Royal Canadian Air Force, and Tapscott planning to join the Canadian Navy. That first airplane trip the dazed sailors made from Eleuthera to Nassau had inspired Widdicombe.

He had no interest in returning to the Merchant Navy but would seek his future in the glamorous Air Force. Although Tapscott had not yet completed his medical treatment, Widdicombe had been released, and the pressure was mounting for a decision regarding his departure. In mid-January, Widdicombe had his third automobile accident in as many weeks, this time crashing his car into the fence of the Botanical Station on Shirley Street. He was obviously having some difficulties with life in the fast lane.

Plans were being made through the authorities in the Bahamas for Widdicombe's "repatriation as a passenger in the first suitable ship." The Minister of Shipping asked to be informed what ship Widdicombe would be sailing on, so that an appropriate hero's welcome could be arranged for his arrival. Widdicombe gave up his thoughts of joining the Canadian Air Force, and plans moved forward for his return to England, where his bride, Cynthia, had been waiting since his departure almost six months earlier. A message was sent to Tapscott's mother by the Colonial Office reporting on his status. It indicated that as of January 21, 1941, the Governor of the Bahamas reported that Tapscott "is not yet well enough to travel" and that "he is reported to be unwilling to return to this country [Great Britain] and an endeavour is being made to arrange for his enlistment in the Forces of Canada."

After the six stressful months together, the two sailors were about to be separated. They had shared an intimacy of terror and triumph and were bound together as few people are. On January 26, Widdicombe sailed for New York, while Tapscott remained behind, more alone than he had ever been.

Widdicombe was finally back at sea, but this time it was in the safety of an American flag vessel, one of the Munson Line ships, making the sixty-five-hour voyage to New York within the protected waters of the Pan-American Neutrality Zone, where the feared Nazi U-boats and raiders could not ply their deadly trade. It nevertheless was the first step back to reality for the castaway turned celebrity. He was leaving the good life of the tropic resort behind and sailing to an unknown reception in the great American port of New York. For the last three months, Roy Widdicombe had been a big fish in a little pond in Nassau, but now he was about to enter a very big pond and he had no way of knowing what kind of attention would be paid him. By then, his story was old news in a world where startling new stories were generated every day.

In New York, he made his way to the great seamen's benevolent organization, the Seamen's Church Institute. Established in the mid–nineteenth century, it was a Christian organization dedicated to providing seafarers with wholesome options other than the crimps, prostitutes, and unsavory characters who preyed on the sailor ashore. The Institute wanted to pray with, rather than prey upon, the sailors, and endeavored as part of its mission to "protect the unprotected and to empower the weak." They provided help and a sense of safe haven for the sailors who, as the Institutes' early motto said, were "Anchored Within the Vail." By the time of Widdicombe's arrival, almost a hundred years after its founding, the Institute was a prominent fixture on New York's East River, at 25 South Street. It was an impressive sixteen-story structure that filled an entire city block. It served thousands of merchant seamen every day and had accommodations for over 500. Widdicombe registered at this seamen's hotel and had a room with running water on the island of Manhattan for the sum of 75 cents per day.

If he feared that he would pass through this city in anonymity, that fear was quickly dispelled. His story might have been old news, but there was still a fascination with his adventure. For three months, he had been in the relative seclusion of the Bahamas, but now he was easily accessible to the news media and journalists who had their first opportunity to interview him personally. His celebrity status alive and well, numerous newspapers and magazines ran stories, and he was interviewed on the radio several times. Just as he had in Nassau, Widdicombe basked in the attention he received. Long-lost relatives, anyone with the Devonshire name "Widdicombe," got in touch with him. The volume of telephone calls at all hours to the Seamen's Church Institute increased severalfold during his stay.

While his family history derived from Devonshire on both his father's Widdicombe side, as well as that of his mother's Bowhey ancestry, Roy was able to adapt to whatever opportunity was presented, and suddenly the Devonshire lad was a Scot. There was to be a gala ball at one of the city's most elegant hotels, the famous Waldorf-Astoria, to celebrate those with Scottish heritage. Not only was Widdicombe the celebrity invited, but Widdicombe the Scot was to be among the honored guests. His ease and ability to move in all levels of society was once again displayed. He had a problem, however. He had been properly dressed for the formal nightlife of Nassau with his white tropical dinner jacket, but the Scottish ball called for full-dress evening clothes. In this time of need, Widdicombe looked for his salvation to the Seamen's Church Institute. The Institute maintained a supply of used clothing in what was known as the Sloppe Chest, derived from the word "sloppe," an Elizabethan term for pantaloons. The Sloppe Chest was frequently the source of a warm coat or a stout pair of work pants for a needy sailor, but its contents were generally utilitarian. With his usual luck, Widdicombe found a full tuxedo in the Sloppe Chest that fit him as if it were tailor-made. He celebrated with his "fellow" Scots, to the benefit of Scottish war relief efforts. It was a stirring occasion, with forty bagpipers leading the Colour Guard of the British War Veterans, after which singer Ray Middleton sang the American national anthem and Muriel Dickson followed with "God Save the King."

Not all his time was spent socializing on the town. The British Merchant Navy Club was located at the Seamen's Church Institute, and he spent time there in the company of fellow sailors. The Institute also provided a dental clinic. Widdicombe had cracked his front teeth while trying to chew shoe leather during the voyage, and the free dental service offered the opportunity to have the damage repaired in preparation for his homecoming. By this time, his plans after his return to England had become clearer, and he told a reporter for the *New York Herald Tribune* that he hoped to be commissioned in the Royal Air Force. Apparently, that first plane flight and the glamour of the Air Force still influenced him.

In that interview, he painted a somewhat different story of his role in the jolly boat than he conveyed to Guy Jones in the presence of Tapscott. Probably feeling that it was unlikely that Jones or Tapscott would read the

Herald Tribune article, he talked about his strained relationship with Tapscott and described himself as Tapscott's savior. He said, "Sometimes we looked at each other and would stare with a sort of hate. One day Tapscott asked me what did I think I was looking at. We quarreled and he went out of his head and tried to jump into the sea. I had to sit on him for two hours." He went on to assert that he used up much of his strength in preventing Tapscott from ending his life. The story as written and published by Jones, the product of his interviews with the two men, tells of Tapscott frequently helping Widdicombe because he was debilitated by the sun. It is difficult to know which version is accurate, particularly in light of future events.

Widdicombe's life of leisure and celebrity in New York would last only a matter of days, as plans were made for the last leg of his trip back to England. As had been promised by the Minister of Shipping, there was no question of forcing Widdicombe to work his passage home in the crew. Befitting his hero's stature, he was to be a passenger on the Furness-Prince Line's *Siamese Prince*. The ship departed New York on February 2, 1941, to go first to Halifax and then on to Liverpool and Widdicombe's reunion with his wife of ten months. The constraints of wartime security prevented direct communication with dates of arrival, but by February 10, the Colonial Office informed Cynthia that Roy had left New York and was on his way home. She was assured that she would be informed in sufficient time of his arrival date. With the news that he was indeed on his way home, his wife and neighbors began to plan for his triumphant return to Lewis Street in Newport. For the official welcome, the Colonial Office communicated with the Ministry of Shipping to ensure a proper reception for Widdicombe when the *Siamese Prince* docked in Liverpool. The wheels were put in motion and quickly gained momentum.

As Roy Widdicombe relaxed, to the extent that he was able, as a passenger on his homeward-bound voyage, Tapscott's situation in Nassau became more strained. A message sent from the Governor's Office to the Colonial Office on February 18 raised a number of very complex issues that reflected the conflict with regard to Bob Tapscott's future. The first point was that he was unwilling to return to the merchant service. This is certainly understandable after his ordeal. There was no question that Tapscott was a brave sailor, but it would take extraordinary courage to once again place himself among the hazards of life in the Merchant Navy in wartime. Tapscott's decision was reinforced, since the Governor's message said, "Medical authorities advise me that he is psychologically unfitted for further work at sea." The numerous references to Tapscott's slow recovery and need for further treatment obviously referred to the huge emotional toll his ordeal had taken on him.

The authorities in England and the Bahamas were challenged by the extremely delicate issue of the fate and future of their young hero. The Governor went on to say that he had investigated the option of Tapscott joining the Canadian Navy instead of returning to the merchant service, but that while it seemed possible on the part of the Canadian authorities, Tapscott indicated his unwillingness to go. The Governor opposed Tapscott's desire to go to the United States and become a lecturer. Apparently, someone had assured Tapscott that, with the interest shown in his story, he could make a living traveling around the United States and lecturing about his experiences. It is not known who instigated this thinking, but it's not hard to imagine Robert Ripley casually planting this seed in Tapscott's mind, or Guy Pearce Jones might have envisioned the lectures in conjunction with his pending book. It would seem that this kind of endeavor would have been more appropriate for the talkative Widdicombe, who always seemed to be telling the tale, rather than for the introverted Tapscott, who seemed reticent to talk about the events. Nevertheless, considering his harsh alternatives, this might have appealed to Tapscott.

The most fascinating and sobering part of this message from the Governor was the question "Do you recommend that he should be returned under compulsion to England as a 'distressed British seaman'?" Here was a fine young man who had been lauded as a hero and who was piecing himself back together after a shattering experience. He was struggling to find his path in the maze that lay before him, while at the same time the government was considering draconian measures to decide his future. Prolonged assessment of the legal, political, and public relations merits or demerits of utilizing the Distressed Seamen Regulations to force Tapscott out of the Bahamas and back to England ensued. Fortunately, Tapscott was unaware that this debate was going on at the time.

While Tapscott continued his recuperation and wrestled with his future in the warmth of the Bahamas, Widdicombe faced the realities of February in the frigid North Atlantic, although as a passenger he was not required to work the ship and stand watches in the bitter cold. The first few days were routine, as the ship was within the Neutrality Zone as far as Halifax. On February 7, 1941, five days after leaving New York, the *Siamese Prince* eased herself out of the protective harbor of Halifax and set off for the final leg of her trip back to England. The 441-foot ship carried a large crew of 58, a gunner, 7 other passengers, and Roy Widdicombe. Built in 1929 in Glasgow by the firm of Blythswood Shipbuilding Co. for the Prince Line, the ship was the same age as the *Anglo-Saxon* and the *Widder*, which were both steam-powered. She had the advantage of being a motor ship, propelled by two eight-cylinder diesel engines that generated 1,350 horsepower, and was able to make a speed of 15 knots, so she was a difficult target for any U-boats that crossed her path. Captain E. Litchfield wanted to make a fast trip because he carried a precious cargo of frozen sides of beef that were especially desired in war-torn Britain. Like the other mariners throughout the Merchant Navy, Litchfield was doing his duty to deliver valued cargo and passengers.

In winter, the North Atlantic can be gray, bitterly cold, and stormy. Those were the conditions the *Siamese Prince* encountered as she plowed her way toward Liverpool. For her crew and Roy Widdicombe, this weather was no surprise, but some of the passengers may have retreated to their staterooms for most of the rough passage. Celebrity that he was, Widdicombe likely entertained whoever would listen with the story of his jolly-boat voyage. It is certain he spent time in the fo'c'sle, regaling the crew members with his stories, listening to some of theirs, and then topping them with another of his own.

As the days passed at sea, the final arrangements were made for the hero's welcome Widdicombe deserved on his arrival in England. The

Minister of Shipping, Ronald Cross, would not be able to travel from London for the occasion, but the ministry had both its Principal Officer from Liverpool, Captain Hunter, and the Ministry's Representative, Mr. Torrey, prepared to welcome Widdicombe back to England on behalf of the Minister. The Nitrate Producers Steam Ship Co., owners of the *Anglo-Saxon,* also would be represented and had made arrangements for a celebratory meal for Widdicombe and the welcoming party. Adding more prestige to the occasion, the Lord Mayor of Liverpool would also attend. In a generous but appropriate gesture, the ship owners provided Cynthia Widdicombe with her ticket from Newport, Wales, to Liverpool, so she could be among the first to greet her heroic husband as he set foot on British soil. The government alerted the press regarding the event, in order to share this proud and joyful moment with a nation that had coped with so much bad news.

Out on the Atlantic, onboard the *Siamese Prince,* there must have been a feeling of anticipation on February 17, since the rough voyage was nearly over. Despite the howling winds and high seas, those onboard had only one more day before their arrival in Liverpool. While uncomfortable for some, the weather added protection for the ship, since it would be difficult for an enemy U-boat to get into position and launch a successful attack in the huge seas. For added security, the *Siamese Prince* was zigzagging, altering her course at random intervals to random courses, making the ship even more elusive. Throughout the day, she slogged her way homeward.

The *Siamese Prince* was not alone on that storm-ravaged stretch of the Atlantic southwest of the Faroe Islands, however. For several days, a sinister black form, *U-69,* had been working her way from her German home port, around the northern extreme of the British Isles into the Atlantic, where she would wait to pounce upon just the kind of target the *Siamese Prince* presented as she trudged toward home. Since the foul weather had precluded any star sights for celestial navigation, the Captain of the *U-69,* Jost Metzler, had to rely on his Navigation Officer, Marienfeld, and his skill and precision in dead reckoning to be sure of the ship's position. By meticulously recording each change of course and speed, and compensating for the impact of currents, the crew was confident that they had passed the islands to the north of Scotland and were in the Atlantic. The change in the sea, with huge ocean rollers causing their boat to leap and gyrate, signaled their arrival in their hunting ground.

This was the first combat cruise for this submarine and her crew, and while there were a number of experienced hands on board, there were also many who had never experienced a real attack on an enemy ship. For many months, Metzler and his officers had drilled the crew until he felt they were ready, but they were untested. The performance of the crew was not the only questionable element for the *U-69* as she began her quest on February 17. The U-boat had been supplied with two types of torpedoes and each had serious drawbacks. The older torpedoes, designated G.VII.a, were more reliable but produced a visible wake that could be spotted and provide a chance for the target to turn out of the way. While the new electric torpedoes, the G.VII.e's, left no wake, they had temperamental firing mechanisms that often failed. Added to these challenges were the rough weather and poor visibility.

However, balanced against these difficulties was the enthusiasm of the untried crew. After all their training, they were eager for their first attack and the anticipated annihilation of the enemy's shipping capability. The Captain and other experienced crew knew they could spend many days in fruitless searching under rough conditions and murky skies. All day long, watch after watch, the men on the conning tower peered into the thick atmosphere, constantly drenched by spray and sometimes waves that knocked them to the deck. The U-boat rolled and twisted as she motored on the surface, seeking her prey. It was late afternoon and it seemed that their first day would end in frustration as they rode up and down on the heaving seas, when the helmsman, Bade, caught a glimpse of a masthead.

The big freighter was approaching from the west and zigzagging as she came on. Captain Metzler went to action stations and sought to intercept his victim. His crew, on edge as they went into an attack for the first time, wanted to achieve a success. The zigzagging posed little problem, since the U-boat was well ahead of the freighter and could monitor her and determine the actual course she was trying to make. With the heavy seas, the Captain took the risk of using the older, compressor-driven torpedo. The submarine closed with her target: to 3,000 yards, then 1,000 yards, and then 800 yards, at which point the command was given and a deadly torpedo hissed out of Tube No. 1.

Onboard the freighter, in the pitching seas and growing darkness, no one had any sense that a U-boat was near. The ship's defensive weapon sat idle and unattended on the bow, and those onboard went about their business in anticipation of arrival in Liverpool. Suddenly, the evening was shattered by a deafening explosion and enormous shock as the *Siamese Prince* took a mortal wound. The freighter continued on briefly, but then the engines stopped and the listing ship lay crippled, dead in the water. Those onboard who had not been killed by the blast began lowering the lifeboats. If Widdicombe was among them, it would have been his third evacuation into the boats. As the boats were lowered, the ship wallowed helplessly. Somewhere onboard a courageous Radio Operator remained at his post and began to send out an SOS with the ship's position.

Captain Metzler feared that if that message got out, it would bring British destroyers in pursuit. Someone reported the possibility of a searchlight on the horizon, which might mean British warships. These were Metzler's excuses for firing a second torpedo while the lifeboats were still close to the *Siamese Prince*. The second explosion was devastating to the ship and those in the boats nearby. Within seconds, the glare of the blast faded, and the *Siamese Prince* was vertical, with her stern in the air. She sank into the sea, and with her were lost her crew of 58, the gunner, the other 7 passengers, and heroic Roy Widdicombe.

On Lewis Street in Newport, the neighbors had been decking the street in patriotic bunting in preparation for the return of their hometown hero. That street had lost others, including Leslie Morgan, and the anticipation of Roy's arrival had given everyone a sense of elation. Cynthia Widdicombe had her bags packed and ticket ready for her trip to Liverpool the instant she got the final word on Roy's arrival time. Instead, the word she received was final indeed. His ship had been sunk. Rescue vessels that raced to the scene in response to the SOS found no survivors. Now, instead of going to Cynthia to celebrate, as they had done only three months before, people like Betty McAteer's mother went to console the grieving widow, even as they still mourned the loved ones they had lost.

This cruel twist of fate was unfathomable to almost everyone who knew Roy Widdicombe or had heard his story. Of course, there was that fine thread of hope that somehow this man, who had cheated death in two other sinkings, had managed it again and would struggle ashore. That news never came, however, and throughout Britain and across the United States, in subdued articles the newspapers spread the sad news to their incredulous readers. How could this have happened to a man who had endured so much? For a nation that was experiencing such pain and devastation from Hitler's assaults, the loss of Roy Widdicombe became another ironic, tragic footnote in a war that was testing the mettle of even the most stoic of British men and women.

At the Seamen's Church Institute, where people had been dazzled by the gregarious Widdicombe, the news was the center of all discussion. On hearing the news, one of Widdicombe's former shipmates went to the Apprentices' Room, where the men register their names and addresses. After Widdicombe's registration of several weeks earlier, he solemnly crossed out the Lewis Street address and inserted "Davy Jones Locker." These were the merchant seamen of the Allied nations, who continuously risked the same fate that had not once, not twice, but three times reached out and taken the ships from under Roy Widdicombe. For all of them, even if they did not know Roy Widdicombe, the loss was personal.

Wartime security slowed the news of Widdicombe's death to the Bahamas. The first report came as an Associated Press dispatch on the morning of February 27, 1941, a full ten days after the U-69 sent the *Siamese Prince* to the bottom. The Associated Press report was vague. It did not include the ship's name, and gave an incorrect date for the sinking, but it correctly indicated that she was the ship on which Widdicombe was returning to England. The only glimmer of hope was that the ship's agents "were unable to reveal the details of her sinking or the fate of her crew or

Widdicombe." Since there was nothing definitive, those who wanted to grasp at the hope that somehow he had managed to survive in the frigid waters of the wintry North Atlantic could do so.

Bob Tapscott was one of those who grasped at that hope. When the message came into the *Nassau Guardian*'s newsroom over the wire, the paper's editor, Mary Mosely, knew how devastating this news would be to the only other *Anglo-Saxon* survivor. In order to prevent his hearing about it inadvertently or reading it in the paper later that day, she sought Tapscott out at the Lucerne and in private passed on the grim news. She reported in that evening's paper that the considerably distressed and stunned Tapscott said, "This is terrible. I only hope that it was a submarine which did the sinking—Widdicombe would stand a much better chance of getting away from the ship than if it had been an armed raider." Tapscott was obviously thinking back to the attack on the *Anglo-Saxon,* and the sense he and everyone else in the jolly boat had had that the rafts from the ship were brutally machine-gunned. He must have thought that this was the standard procedure for raiders. He would have had no way of knowing that the *U-69* had sent a second torpedo into the *Siamese Prince* while the lifeboats were still close aboard and vulnerable to the destructive force of the blast.

For Bob Tapscott, a troubled man struggling to establish equilibrium in his tangled life, this was a staggering blow. He and Roy Widdicombe had been polar opposites in nearly every way, but they were brothers, bound together by an excruciating ordeal. Only the two of them would know how strong those strange bonds were, but now one of them was gone. Tapscott had become the sole survivor. He alone, of all his shipmates, was alive. At age nineteen, he had experienced horrors and hardships that would devastate even the strongest soul. Now he was in a hotel, in the surreal atmosphere of a resort community in wartime, grappling with his past and his future, truly alone.

Chapter 19

WOUNDED WARRIOR

By mid-February 1941, Bob Tapscott appeared to have made a complete recovery. He had gained back his lost weight and the shrapnel wounds had healed, leaving only small scars. Physically he was in good shape, but this brave sailor carried a gaping wound, a mortal wound that would not heal and festered for decades, until tragically it killed him.

In 1980 a new term, "post-traumatic stress disorder," was formally accepted in the medical lexicon and added to the third edition of the *Diagnostic and Statistical Manual of Mental Disorders* by the American Psychiatric Association. The aftereffects of trauma are not something new. Throughout civilization, this severe problem has been treated in a variety of ways, ranging from pure neglect to hospitalization. There are descriptions of similar disorders among combat veterans of the American Civil War, both World Wars, and among Holocaust survivors. The tragedy is that this complex disorder was not clearly recognized and defined until after the Vietnam War. Previously, the difficulties of those exposed to traumatic experiences were attributed to other related disorders, such as depression and anxiety. Treatment options were limited, especially for doctors without specialized training in mental disorders. The difficulty in making an accurate diagnosis was compounded by the lack of physical symptoms, for those afflicted often appeared to be in fine shape.

A passage from the National Center for Post-Traumatic Stress Disorder Fact Sheet describes the problem:

> Post-Traumatic Stress Disorder, or PTSD, is a psychiatric disorder that can occur following the experience or witnessing of life-threatening events such as military combat, natural disasters, terrorist incidents, serious accidents, or violent personal assaults like rape. People who suffer from PTSD often relive the experience through nightmares and flashbacks, have difficulty sleeping, and feel detached or estranged, and these symptoms can be severe enough and last long enough to significantly impair the person's daily life.
>
> PTSD is marked by clear biological changes as well as psychological symptoms. PTSD is complicated by the fact that it frequently occurs in conjunction with related disorders such as depression, substance abuse, problems of memory and cognition, and other problems of physical and mental health. The disorder is also associated with impairment of the person's ability to function in social or family life, including occupational instability, marital problems and divorces, family discord, and difficulties in parenting.

The seventh edition of the *Psychiatric Dictionary*, published by Oxford University Press in 1996, provides a similar definition, with the addition of another symptom: "in many of those exposed to mass disasters, feelings of guilt about having survived (survivor guilt)."

Today the National Center for Post-Traumatic Stress Disorder, within the United States Department of Veterans Affairs, is doing extensive research and developing treatments and therapies to help those around the world who are dealing with this devastating disorder. It cannot be definitively stated that Tapscott suffered this problem, but as his life progressed and he tried valiantly to move forward with all the normal elements of life, there can be no doubt that he wrestled with serious difficulties. The medical community could do little to help this courageous, wounded sailor. He was left to cope and make his own way.

The Medical Officer of the Bahamas, Dr. Cruickshank, was attentive and sympathetic to Tapscott's plight, but because of the lack of understanding of the disorder, he ran out of treatment options and excuses to give government officials who increased the pressure for Tapscott's repatriation. The Governor's Office had raised the subject of forcing Tapscott back to England under the Distressed Seamen Regulations in its telegram to the Colonial Office, which concluded with the reminder that Tapscott was being maintained at government expense in Nassau. The Colonial Office replied with the words, "I should be reluctant to agree to any resort to compulsion so soon after the ordeal through which he has passed." In an effort to remove him as a burden on the government, the question was asked, "Would it not be possible for him to secure temporary employment in Nassau for the present, subject to his case being reviewed in six months time?" This exchange took place at the time Tapscott was dealing with the blow of Widdicombe's loss.

Cynthia Widdicombe was also reeling from that blow. In mid-March, when the last hope for Widdicombe's survival was relinquished, the Governor of the Bahamas sent her the following message: "Having known your gallant husband in the Bahamas after his amazing deliverance from the perils of the sea, the Duchess and I were deeply shocked to learn of his tragic death due to enemy action on his voyage home and our hearts go out to you in your sorrow. (Signed) Edward." Thousands unknown to her around the world sympathized with the young widow as she faced her loss and moved on with her life, alone.

Tapscott found it extremely difficult to move on with his life. In a later medical report, Major J. C. Richardson of the Royal Canadian Army Medical Corps stated: "When he was discharged from hospital in Nassau [he] says he felt changed, that he did not want to meet anyone, that he wished to be alone. He started drinking heavily, partly to forget his past experiences and partly to make himself more sociable." Some tried to help by creating diversions for the likable young man. An American from

Long Island, New York, Franklin Remington, who wintered in Nassau, invited Tapscott out for a sail after he left the hospital, and somewhat to his surprise, Tapscott accepted the invitation. They sailed in the harbor on Remington's sloop, *Peg Leg,* and anchored near a small island for a picnic and swim. Remington said of Tapscott, "I found him a delightful companion, modest, well mannered and mentally and socially equipped to go anywhere." This was Tapscott at his best, as he had been and often would be in the future, likable and admirable; but as Tapscott had explained to Dr. Richardson, this took control and effort. Nassau attorney Andrew McKinney took Tapscott for a sight-seeing drive around New Providence Island. McKinney remembers that he was extremely quiet and didn't want to talk about his terrible experience. This was a tendency that grew within him as time went on.

As March of 1941 progressed, so did the official discussion about Tapscott's future. A Colonial Office message refers to him being destitute. The government was "maintaining" him, covering his hotel costs, paying him 5 shillings per week, and sending his mother in England 11 shillings and 8 pence per week for her support. The question is, of course, what happened to the $1,300 that Tapscott and Widdicombe had after the Ripley broadcast in early December? Did they divide it equally? Did Tapscott bank his funds or send some home? Did Widdicombe's high lifestyle, which included the car, consume Tapscott's share of the money in addition to his own? There are no sure answers to these questions, but in mid-March, Tapscott was subsisting on the 5-shilling allowance, his accommodations provided by the government.

The medical staff had done all they could for Bob Tapscott, and on March 20, Dr. Cruickshank officially declared him "medically fit." With that declaration, the urgency for the sailor to resolve the question of his future increased. With his release from medical care came the end of the government allowances to him and his mother. However, a bit of good news also developed. Because of his special circumstances, the owners of the *Anglo-Saxon* and the Ministry of Shipping agreed to an exceptional payment to Tapscott. This amounted to his full wages from the time of the ship's sinking to the time he was declared medically fit, less the allowances already paid to him and his mother. This seven months' pay, less a third for allowances, was enough to give him a new start.

The officials gave up their attempt to compel Tapscott to return to England and service in the Merchant Navy under the Distressed Seamen Regulations. Their apparent strategy was to wash their hands of him and let him determine his future for himself. The suggestion that he get temporary employment in the Bahamas had no appeal to him. Influenced by his ordeal and the recent grim news of Widdicombe's loss, Tapscott was not prepared to return to the service that had been his life up to that point. After the boat voyage, he was afraid of being alone in the dark, was shaken by loud noises like thunderstorms, was very depressed, and fearful of going to sea again. All of these responses are completely understandable.

Dr. Cruickshank had genuine concern for his patient. He had observed Tapscott's increasing "seclusiveness" following Widdicombe's loss and felt that he would benefit from being in the company of others. Cruickshank himself, feeling that the wartime backwater of Nassau was not the best place to use his skills, was considering joining the Canadian forces, and urged Tapscott to consider this as well. The Army would provide accommodations, food, some pay, and another chance for Tapscott to serve King and Country in the time of crisis. His other options and resources were limited, and he decided to follow the recommendation, but his plans were delayed by a somewhat long wait for his pay.

Also that spring, plans for the jolly boat were made. These were affected by the death of Clifford D. Mallory in Miami on April 7. The brother of Mrs. Cora Mallory Munson, he had been one of the bidders for the jolly boat during the December auction, with the thought that she could be preserved at the Marine Historical Association in Mystic, Connecticut, the birthplace of the Mallory maritime enterprises. Ten days after the report of C. D. Mallory's death, the Nassau papers announced that Lady Oakes had decided to place the jolly boat on loan to the museum in Mystic, and Cora Munson arranged for the boat to be shipped to New York on the SS *Evangeline,* which departed on April 22nd. Within weeks, the boat was on exhibit in the museum that would become Mystic Seaport, where she remained for almost sixty years.

Just over a month later, Bob Tapscott's pay came through and he was at last prepared to depart the Bahamas. On May 29, page 2 of the *Nassau Guardian* contained two slightly related articles. One, entitled "Chief Medical Officer Going on War Service," contained three full paragraphs about the departure of Dr. Cruickshank and his wife and son for Canada, where he would join the Royal Canadian Air Force as a Medical Officer. Farther down the page, the other article was entitled "Tapscott to Leave for Canada," and contained only one short paragraph stating that he planned to leave four days later, on June 2, "to join the Canadian Army and later to go overseas."

Upon departing Nassau, Tapscott followed a nearly identical route to that of Widdicombe. His first stop was New York City, where, like Widdicombe, he found a haven at the Seamen's Church Institute and was pursued by the press. His photograph appeared in the *New York Times,* and the June 9, 1941, issue of *Time* magazine had a full-column article about the ordeal of Tapscott and Widdicombe, with a large photograph of the men in the jolly boat taken after five weeks of recuperation.

Like Widdicombe, Tapscott enjoyed the hospitality of the British Merchant Navy Club located at the Institute, and Dr. S. B. Norton at the Institute's Dental Clinic replaced the tooth he had lost when he was hurled across the *Anglo-Saxon*'s deck during the attack. Unlike Widdicombe, however, Tapscott confined his socializing to the Institute and placed no demands on the Sloppe Chest for evening clothes. He seemed to be back in his element, back among fellow British merchant seamen, with whom he could discuss his jolly-boat voyage and know that they fully understood the ordeal. Some of those he talked with had spent time in lifeboats, but none had experienced the duration or grim horror of Tapscott's voyage. Photographs taken at the Institute show him looking fit, handsome, and apparently at ease in this maritime atmosphere. After a few days of relaxation there, he set off, just as Widdicombe had five months earlier, for Halifax and his new career.

The trip from New York to Halifax was uneventful. Tapscott settled in at the YMCA Hostel, and a few days later, on June 23, 1941, he enlisted in the Royal Canadian Army Service Corps (Active Force) as a Private with the classification of "A," indicating he was "fit for general service." Probably the only Private to enlist in the Canadian forces within two weeks of being featured in *Time* magazine, he became a member of the 3rd Division, Petrol Company, which had the critical task of supplying the vehicles of the division with fuel to keep the advance going. It was a dangerous job under any circumstances, since they were constantly dealing with explosive gasoline, but in combat it would be even more dangerous.

It not only took courage for Tapscott to enter the military, but what lay immediately ahead for him would require a level of bravery few would have been able to muster. Within six weeks of his enlistment, he boarded a ship to begin a journey that would duplicate the last leg of Roy Widdicombe's voyage from Halifax to Liverpool. The same lethal U-boats that had destroyed so many ships lurked unseen around him. He was now among strangers with whom he had little in common. Most were Canadians who had grown up in an environment totally different from his childhood in Usk and Cardiff, Wales. He was an experienced merchant mariner with five years of sea duty behind him, as well as a combat veteran who had survived the destruction of two of his ships. As he fought to control his fears and phobias, he had no one in whom to confide; he had to press on and live up to the expectations others had of him as a soldier. Week followed week as the ship made her way across the Atlantic, as Widdicombe had done in February. Near Liverpool, she eased past the spot where the *Siamese Prince* had been torpedoed, no doubt with heightened apprehension. On August 19, 1941, Bob Tapscott set foot on English soil for the first time in over a year.

Just prior to Tapscott's shipping out from Halifax, in mid-July, Guy Pearce Jones's book, *Two Survived*, was published in the United States. The public was already interested in the story due to the numerous newspaper reports, the Ripley broadcast, and the *Time* magazine article, so there was a ready audience. The information from the two sailors and the jolly-boat log were Jones's primary sources, since he researched under the constraints of wartime security. The book was featured on the front page of the *New York Times Book Review*, strongly praised by Clifton Fadiman in the *New Yorker*, and received excellent reviews in the *New York Herald Tribune*, the *Christian Science Monitor,* and the *Saturday Review of Literature.* The book was on the *Herald Tribune*'s bestseller list for at least three weeks, and by late August was in a third printing, with a total of 12,000 books in print. The story appeared in abbreviated form in *Cosmopolitan* that August and was a feature in the September 1941 issue of *Reader's Digest.* The gripping story of the two young sailors was an instant success in the United States. The initial publication and related attention took place while Tapscott and his unit were making their way across the Atlantic, so he and those around him were unaware of the sensation it created.

Once in Liverpool, the 3rd Division, Petrol Company was transferred south to Tweedsmuir Camp, near Godalming, in Surrey, where most Canadian troops went on their arrival, prior to going to their regular English bases. Tapscott had not seen his family in over a year. He requested and received four days of "Landing Leave." On August 25, he went home to Cardiff, a visit that must have triggered painful emotions, because a month later he made the first of several unauthorized trips home, which made his Army service very difficult. He went "absent without leave" for 4 days, 17 hours, and 55 minutes, and when he returned to his unit was fined 14 days' pay. This absence was a surprise to Tapscott's officers, as he had gotten off to a fine start while in Canada; he seemed satisfied with his situation, and his conduct sheet was good. In later explaining his absence, Tapscott said he knew it was wrong, but felt that after his ordeal he needed the time to visit with his family.

Ironically, Tapscott was not aware that there were several people with close links to the *Anglo-Saxon* near the Tweedsmuir Camp. The parents of the highly respected Roy Pilcher, whom Tapscott had watched die, were living in Godalming. In addition, Ted Milburn, the ten-year-old son of the ship's Chief Engineer, Eddie Milburn, was attending the Royal Merchant Navy School in Wokingham, less than 20 miles from Godalming. The war had displaced Ted, as it had so many other children. At his young age, Ted was enrolled in a school 300 miles from his home, his mother, and his brother Derek, who joined him at the school two years later, both boys on their way toward careers in the Merchant Navy. American sympathy was growing for the British war efforts, and Ted Milburn was "adopted" by an organization known as Young America Wants to Help. The Shore Country Day School in Beverly, Massachusetts, wanted to assist a boy who had lost his father in the war, and for the remainder of the war sent £80 per year toward Ted's welfare. As he made his way around the Royal Merchant Navy School's handsome campus, Ted did not know that a short distance away was a man who had shared the terrible ordeal of the attack on the *Anglo-Saxon* with his father. Some months after the time of her husband's death, Ethel Milburn received a card from Buckingham Palace, saying: "The Queen and I offer you our heartfelt sympathy in your great sorrow. We pray that your country's gratitude for a life so nobly given in its service may bring you some measure of consolation." It was signed: "George R.I."

Several months passed during which, outwardly, life seemed to be going smoothly for Tapscott. In November 1941, the English edition of *Two Survived* was published; with all the wartime suffering and other tales of heroism that appeared daily in the papers, it did not seem to create the response it had in the United States. Within his company, there seems to have been little or no notice of Tapscott's celebrity. He was considered a good soldier and a likable young man who got along well with the other men in his unit. The officers and noncommissioned officers also liked Tapscott and felt he was a good soldier.

The only unusual behavior his compatriots observed was his nervousness and fear of the dark. This created a problem in February 1942, when he was assigned to night guard duty. With his deep phobia of being alone in the dark, this was intolerable, yet few could understand how significant his aversion was. Once again, he went absent without leave, this time for less than two days, for which he was fined nine days' pay. This relatively minor offense was a prelude to a more serious situation, which proved to be a pivotal moment in his Army career. On the night of March 16, Tapscott and another soldier took a large Army truck from their unit and drove it to Cardiff. Tapscott later insisted that the other soldier actually took the truck, and that the following morning, while at his mother's home, he realized the seriousness of this offense and attempted to locate the truck and return it. When he couldn't find the truck, he simply stayed at home. A week later, the military police apprehended Tapscott and the other soldier and they stood trial before a court-martial. In the course of the trial, Tapscott's earlier ordeals at sea, his long hospitalization, and his undoubted courage and heroism emerged. While his "accomplice" was found guilty and sentenced to six months' detention in a military prison, the court, which also found Tapscott guilty, recognized the special circumstances of his situation and ordered that he enter the 1st Canadian Neurological Hospital in Basingstoke, England, for full medical assessment. This was, at last, an opportunity for Tapscott to be seen by medical officers with the specialized training to recognize his symptoms and possibly help him.

Admitted to the hospital on May 6, 1942, Tapscott found doctors with whom he could speak about his ordeal, his anxieties, and his hatred for his situation in the Army. These were things he could not share with his fellow soldiers, and it must have been a great relief to be able to unburden himself. In doing so, he revealed the depth of his despair and response to military life. The medical staff observed that he was "quiet and seclusive," spent time "staring vacantly in front of him," "never speaks spontaneously," and was "usually mildly depressed." At last, he could explain that he had never liked the Army. He told them he sought a discharge so he could return to the merchant service, where he could more effectively serve his country rather than waste his time doing the routine Army tasks of guard duty and kitchen work. For Tapscott, what seemed the impossibility of getting out of the Army had made him even more depressed and introspective.

The doctors also drew from him the full horror of his experiences aboard the *Anglo-Saxon* and in the jolly boat. These easily meet the requirement for a diagnosis of post-traumatic stress disorder today, "a catastrophic stressor that was outside the range of usual human experience." Tapscott told of the anxieties that plagued him and then, indicating the depth of his misery, revealed that he had been so depressed for the last two months that he would kill himself if he had the nerve.

Fortunately, Dr. J. K. Richardson and the others on the medical staff at Basingstoke, including Drs. H. H. Hyland, C. R. G. Gould, A. E.

McKercher, and L. Boxer, recognized the magnitude of the problems confronting Bob Tapscott and sought to help him. Dr. Richardson wrote, "I would feel that this is one of the few examples of true 'war neurosis' seen here—in that his psychoneurotic state was caused almost entirely by the mental stress of his experiences at sea through enemy action, and there is apparently little factor for predisposition." The doctor recognized that Tapscott was a normal, intelligent, kind, gentle person who had lead a perfectly normal life until his sea experience opened this wound in him and that, as a result of that experience, he was having to cope with enormous anxieties. The doctor went on to state that "his condition then, would appear to be one of a subsiding anxiety state, and an increasing (reactive) depression. Would feel that he is totally unfit for army service and that if kept in the army might well develop a dangerous degree of depression—as well as possibly getting into more behavious [sic] difficulties. Would think that for the present he is best suited for a quiet civilian occupation. After a few months at such work, living at home, he may be fit to return to the merchant marine."

The doctor's diagnosis, which became officially "anxiety neurosis," was correct, and the recommendations were in line with what Tapscott felt would help solve his problems. It seemed as if, finally, the service was being responsive to his needs. The Commanding Officer of the 1st Canadian Neurological Hospital released him on May 27, after three weeks of examination, with three recommendations. The first was that he be categorized as "E," meaning "unfit for any service, full or limited." The second was that he be returned to his unit for disposal of the court-martial charges. And the final recommendation was that Tapscott "should be discharged in England." The first two recommendations were acted on quickly, as he was reclassified as "E" two days after leaving the hospital, and the punishment of six months' detention and a fine were remitted. The court showed its understanding and compassion with the statement "The contribution which this boy has already made in the war is undoubtedly a factor which takes his out of the ordinary run of cases." Captain R. A. Ritchie, in closing the case, reinforced the recommendation that Tapscott be discharged in England.

It was on this point that the Canadian Army failed Bob Tapscott. While this may have been under consideration for a period, it never happened. One of the conditions raised in considering his discharge in England was whether Tapscott could get employment there. It seems as if this was investigated, since there is a letter to that point from an employer in Godalming, dated July 24, 1942. Why they did not follow this course, which would have benefited Tapscott, is not known; but he was transferred back to Tweedsmuir Camp to wait for further action. The frustration was enormous, and Tapscott went absent without leave again. Finally, on October 2, over four months after leaving the hospital, instead of being discharged in England, Tapscott boarded a ship to once again venture out onto the dangerous Atlantic, making the return voyage to Halifax, where he arrived safely on October 12.

Back in Canada, the bureaucratic process of the Army ground onward at an exasperatingly slow pace. During the month of November, the desperate Tapscott went absent without leave two more times and concluded another short hospital stay before the moment he had been waiting for arrived. On December 7, 1942, a year after the attack on Pearl Harbor, and two years after the Ripley broadcast, Robert George Tapscott received a medical discharge from the Canadian Army. He had served for 1 year and 174 days in a situation that, for him, was intolerable. There is no explanation why it took over six months for the Army to carry out the recommendations of the Medical Corps, but this obviously added to the anguish and anxiety of Tapscott, who, the court recognized, had already made a significant contribution to the war.

A lesser man than Bob Tapscott might have felt that by his merchant service at the beginning of the war and his year and a half in the Army he had done enough. But he was not one to shrink from what he perceived as his duty. He made his way from Halifax to the Merchant Seamen's Manning Pool on Craig Street in Montreal. There, with incredible bravery, he offered his services, willing to return to the danger of wartime merchant service. With the urgent need for mariners, it did not take long for him to get a ship. On March 5, 1943, he signed on to the *Fort Bedford*. This was a new ship, under construction in Vancouver, on the west coast of Canada, requiring him to make the long train trip across the vast North American continent. Over two and a half years had passed since he had been attacked in the *Anglo-Saxon,* but the oceans were still extremely dangerous with the war raging around the world. He would be setting off in the Pacific this time, but the enemy that lurked under the surface there was just as lethal as the wolf packs of U-boats preying on Atlantic convoys. His voyage in the *Fort Bedford* would take him into the Atlantic again, and hopefully home to England.

As he proceeded down the American west coast in the Pacific ocean swells, Tapscott had no way of knowing that not only were enemy submarines lurking in that ocean, but that Hellmuth von Ruckteschell's second raider, the *Michel,* was also in the Pacific. Ruckteschell had completed his command of the ship two weeks after Tapscott signed on to the *Fort Bedford,* and the *Michel* was in Japan being prepared by her new Captain for her second cruise. Although they were in the same ocean, the *Michel* posed no threat to the *Fort Bedford.*

Like other British merchant ships of the time, the *Fort Bedford* carried a defensive weapon, and gunners from the DEMS (Defensively Equipped Merchant Ships) organization formed the nucleus of the gun crew. Harry Griffin, who now lives in Bristol, England, served as the Gunner on this voyage and remembers Bob Tapscott well. Griffin had been in the Royal Naval Reserves and was called into active service in 1942. After DEMS training in Scotland, he made several trips across the Atlantic, to and from Halifax. In January of 1943, he made the trans-Canadian train trip to Vancouver to join the *Fort Bedford,* which was just being completed. As so many people did, he liked and respected Tapscott, recollecting that Tapscott was very quiet and never smiled. Remembering him as a thorough professional who had little tolerance for the poor performance of others in the crew, he recalls that Tapscott had trouble sleeping and he would go up on deck during the middle of the night to have a smoke. On one evening, he saw the wake of the ship curving back and forth and took it upon himself to call the bridge on the ship's telephone and tell them to "steer a straight course!"

The *Fort Bedford* made her way safely down the U.S. and Mexican west coasts and passed through the Panama Canal. Along the way, the crew naturally got to know one another, but Harry Griffin recalls that Tapscott kept to himself. While others talked of their adventures, he said nothing about his ordeal. Only the Captain and the Second Mate were aware of his history. When the ship docked at Pier 83 on the Hudson River, in New York, the word somehow got out to the press that the hero Robert Tapscott, about whom they had written almost two years earlier, was back. He wouldn't talk about his experience, however, either to his shipmates or to the press. In New York, and later in Boston and Halifax, Tapscott went ashore with his shipmates, but remained quiet.

They reached England safely, and on the last day of May 1943, Bob Tapscott signed off of the *Fort Bedford,* home again. He had proven to himself that, despite the severe anxieties that gripped him, he could perform his duties as an Able Seaman.

During the remainder of the war, Tapscott made six more voyages serving his country, although two of them were not completed, in one case for medical reasons and in the other for a reason unknown. This was part of an erratic pattern of occupational instability, going back to his absences without leave, which persisted into the future. At the end of the war, there was no doubt that Bob Tapscott had served his country well, and he received the medals to prove it. From the British government, he received the War Medal 1939—45, the Merchant Navy 1939—45 Star, the Merchant Navy Atlantic Star, the Merchant Navy Pacific Star, and the Merchant Navy Italy Star. And from a grateful Canadian government, he was awarded the Defence Medal, the Canadian Volunteer Service Medal with Clasp, and another War Medal 1939—45. In addition, he was authorized to wear, with honor, the War Service Badge.

Bob Tapscott was a war hero, with service from the opening day to V-J Day. Like so many, he was wounded. The wounds to his flesh had healed, but he still carried the open wound of depression and anxiety, which affected him the rest of his life.

Chapter 20

MICHEL—THE SHIP AND THE MAN

As Bob Tapscott struggled with his dissatisfaction with Army life and the lingering stresses inflicted by Hellmuth von Ruckteschell, in mid-March of 1942 the German Captain was poised to take his new, fully equipped, and well-manned raider, the *Michel*, on the extremely dangerous run down the English Channel from Cuxhaven, Germany. Only a month before, in Operation Cerberus, the German battle cruisers *Scharnhorst* and *Gneisenau* and the heavy cruiser *Prinz Eugen* had made a successful Channel dash past surprised and frustrated British forces. This meant that the British would be keenly alert to further attempts to run the Channel. The raider was, however, of critical importance to the Germans, and they made a full commitment to her safety during the breakout. Numerous meetings were held to plan the details of the escape and arrange for appropriate support. A special team of radio operators was supplied by B-Dienst, the radio intelligence gathering service. This team was expert in monitoring the British military radio waves and deciphering and interpreting their messages to give the *Michel* and her escorts advance warning of what was arrayed against them.

On the morning of March 10, 1942, Ruckteschell called all hands together and prepared his untried crew for the test ahead. When they got under way, they were escorted by five large minesweepers, which carried the burden of clearing the path for the raider. The following day, the remainder of the escort flotilla, twelve small minesweepers and five 1,320-ton torpedo boats, joined them, and the small but formidable armada ventured westward. If the British had any question about the importance of this seemingly legitimate fruit carrier exiting the Channel, the fact that she had twenty-two escorts telegraphed her significance.

Late in the day of March 12, just as the breakout was beginning, the *Michel* ran aground, not once but twice, amid the shifting sands of the Dutch coast, and was forced to retreat; in the process, the ship was spotted by a British reconnaissance plane. The decision was made to press on before a heavy force of British planes could return. In the darkness, the *Michel* and her swarm of protectors headed out again. Just after midnight on the 13th, a British force of six torpedo boats and three gunboats from Dover were on the attack, but the B-Dienst team had done its job. Not only was the flotilla around the *Michel* expecting them, but German artillery on the French coast joined the fight with accurate fire. The British vessels were forced to retreat without inflicting any serious damage on the German contingent. If the *Michel*'s crew were relieved, the feeling was short-lived. A far more formidable force was heading to meet them, five destroyers that had been patrolling off England's south coast near Eastbourne. What followed at 4:30 in the morning was a wild, pitched battle in which the *Michel,* the fruit carrier, could not simply rely on her escorts. Against orders, the raider revealed her true nature and employed her guns. The ships careened around one another with all guns firing. On several occasions, the raider was able to avoid British torpedoes by the merest of margins. Using his uncanny ability to avoid danger, Ruckteschell ordered a sudden turn and piloted his ship through the minefield guarding the port of Le Havre. By this time, the Luftwaffe had put planes into the air to prevent attacks on the *Michel* from British torpedo planes.

Aboard the German vessels, only one man was killed, and this Leutnant zur See was given a military burial in Le Havre. Among the British forces, there were a number of hits on the destroyers, but none was sunk, as the Germans would later claim. In Le Havre for a little over twelve hours, the *Michel* was able to replace the precious ammunition consumed in the naval battle. That night, Ruckteschell and his crew stole out of Le Havre and made their way undetected to the medieval walled city of Saint-Malo, where they were able to conceal the *Michel* behind the small islands off the harbor. In an attempt to locate and destroy the raider, British planes attacked both Le Havre and Vlissingen, on the Dutch-Belgian border, but the *Michel* was far to the west. After spending the daylight hours of Sunday, March 15, at anchor in Saint-Malo, during which Ruckteschell alone went sight-seeing ashore, the *Michel* slipped out into the darkness. Escorted only by torpedo boats now, she made her way around the western headlands of Brittany, past the familiar approach to Brest, and the naval base at Lorient, where impenetrable submarine pens with concrete ceilings and 3-foot-thick steel doors were being built to protect the German U-boats, and on to Bordeaux. Once anchored in the Gironde River, the departure of the B-Dienst team was confirmation that they had successfully broken out.

The *Michel* was about to start her mission in earnest and took the opportunity to stock up on as much fresh produce as possible. In what was regarded as a good omen, the ship was refueled by the tanker *Spichern*, formerly named the *Krossfonn*, which Hellmuth von Ruckteschell had captured and sent home as a prize during his cruise in the *Widder*. Fully supplied, on the morning of March 20, 1942, the *Michel* set off for her hunting grounds in the South Atlantic and the western Indian Ocean. As she made her way toward her "territory," she sidestepped several Allied ships and convoys to remain undetected. During this part of the voyage, the "cultural life" that would be a unique part of this raider's operations started to take form. The ship's orchestra began rehearsals, and several motion pictures were shown. At Ruckteschell's direction, the crew lived in quarters specially decorated with murals of flowers. Flowers and warships are not usually associated with each other, but the Captain felt this would create a pleasant environment for his crew. Ruckteschell had also created another special environment, a holiday space, a portion of the ship prepared as a place of recreation. He realized on the *Widder*'s six-month voyage that it was difficult for the crew to stay constantly alert without any break. The concept was that during the voyage, which the

Captain hoped would be substantially longer than the *Widder*'s, groups of men would be relieved of their duties and allowed to go "on vacation" for several days in this special space. It had a festive atmosphere, with murals and a deck inlaid with a raider motif.

On Easter Sunday, after a sermon from the Captain, the crew gathered for the first concert by the ship's orchestra. The following day, the full curriculum of voluntary adult education courses began, with subjects from mathematics to painting and sculpture, all an effort to keep the crew's morale and effectiveness high. Ruckteschell had a very ambitious goal: to add to the *Widder*'s tally of 58,644 tons of ships sunk or captured, and to reach a total of 200,000 tons. This Captain, who had just celebrated his fifty-second birthday, had his sights set on glory.

The ship arrived in her area of operation in mid-April and immediately sank her first target and brought on board the 23 survivors of her 26-man crew. A few nights later, the next victim was attacked by Malte von Schack in the torpedo boat, which he had named the *Esau*. This was the nickname the radiomen in the *Widder* had used for their ship, taken from the biblical story of Isaac, whose son Esau was a great hunter. The name was appropriate for the torpedo boat as well, since Schack hoped she, too, would be a great hunter. Her first attack was on the 8,684-ton American tanker *Connecticut*, and she proved lethal to the tanker's crew. The first of *Esau*'s torpedoes set her ablaze. The second, before the lifeboats could pull clear, exploded the cargo of gasoline, which rose in an enormous fireball and incinerated the boats in the water. Only 19 of the 50 men on board were picked up by the raider.

The next encounter for the proud new *Michel* was a fiasco. On Sunday, May 1, a large, fast merchant ship was spotted. Ruckteschell launched his special weapon, Schack's *Esau*, to attack the *Menelaus*, whose Captain, J. H. Blyth, had transmitted the alert "QQQQ" and his ship's position, indicating that she was being chased by an armed merchant raider. The *Michel* opened fire with her 15cm guns, but the range was too great and the shots fell short. On the *Menelaus*, the crew had tied down the safety valves on their engines to achieve maximum speed for escape, but their speed was a fraction of that of the *Esau*, which charged in to attack. Both of *Esau*'s 18-

inch-diameter torpedoes were evaded by the clever Captain Blyth. Schack, aware of the fury he would face from his enraged Captain when he returned from the failed attack, raced toward the fleeing *Menelaus* and opened fire on her bridge with his only remaining weapon, the 2cm defensive machine gun. After only a few rounds, the gun jammed, leaving the *Esau* impotent. As the *Menelaus* steamed away at a speed the *Michel* could not equal, Captain Blyth broadcast a detailed description of the raider and her torpedo boat, as well as the location of the attack. In the ultimate humiliation for Ruckteschell, Captain Blyth broadcast aspersions on the incompetence of the attack for anyone monitoring the radio to hear. The *Menelaus* achieved the distinction of being the only merchantman to escape from a raider once an attack had begun.

Ruckteschell, who continued to suffer from severe migraine headaches and other internal problems, was incensed by this debacle. He knew full well that the broadcasts from the *Menelaus* were heard widely by friend and foe alike and, in addition to the humiliation, would bring British warships in pursuit. He assembled his crew and threatened to cancel their mission because of this incompetence, exposing those responsible to public reprimand. He made an ominous decision to revert to his ruthless tactic, developed on the *Widder,* of stalking by day, attacking in the dark of night and smothering the surprised victims with overwhelming force.

Three weeks later, Ruckteschell used this approach to subdue his next target and, after the first barrage of shells smashed into the ship, ceased firing when the hapless Norwegians on the *Kattegat* waved a white lantern in surrender. The next victims never knew who or what hit them. They were on the crippled American Liberty ship *George Clymer,* which had called for assistance. Instead of help, at 8:00 P.M. on June 6, she was struck by first one torpedo and then another. The mortally wounded ship was scuttled the following day, her crew believing that they had been the victim of a submarine. They were, in fact, victims of *Esau,* the hunter they had not seen or heard.

After a vicious night attack that destroyed the *Lylepark,* Ruckteschell's next kill was the small, old liner *Gloucester Castle,* bound for South Africa with 154 passengers and crew on board. Out of the darkness came Ruckteschell's fusillade, which decimated the ship. Those on board, including women and children, were in panic as the ship astonishingly sank in a matter of a few minutes. Only one lifeboat got away, and the raider sent her boat to assist in the rescue. In all, 61 were saved, including 2 women and 2 children, while 93 perished, including 6 women and 2 children.

The day after the sinking of the liner, Ruckteschell had an opportunity he had dreamed of since the frustrating time when the Widder had two Allied ships nearby and because of her slow speed was unable to attack either. On June 16, two prime targets were steaming on parallel courses. All day, the Michel worked into the ideal position, and after dark the Esau was launched. In a synchronized attack at 9:00 P.M., the Esau launched her torpedoes into the Norwegian tanker Aramis, while the Michel devastated the American tanker William F. Humphrey. Ruckteschell had all his guns tearing up the Humphrey, which valiantly got off a few rounds of return fire. Struck by three of the Michel's large 21-inch torpedoes, the tanker quickly sank. The Michel picked up 29 survivors, while 11 others eluded capture and, after five days in a lifeboat, were rescued and transported to Freetown. Schack's light torpedoes had wounded his quarry but not stopped her, so the Michel pursued the Aramis and finished her off the following night, at the cost of 20 members of the tanker's crew. In Ruckteschell's next attack, on the Arabistan, all but one of the 60-man crew perished. Two weeks later, aware of his continued successes, the Kriegsmarine promoted Ruckteschell to the rank of Kapitän zur See der Reserve.

As this voyage progressed, an interesting pattern evolved. Ruckteschell had full faith in his Executive Officer, Wolfgang Erhardt, and with Erhardt as a buffer, he developed a certain rapport with his senior officers, whom he called together frequently to plan their next moves, giving the men a sense of participation. Often in the middle of the night, however, following his instincts, Ruckteschell would alter the decision. His instincts were almost always correct and the new decisions brought success, so the others seldom criticized the process. For a veteran of the earlier cruise on the Widder like Konrad Hoppe, Hellmuth von Ruckteschell, while still stern and often furious, was a different man than the

Captain he had known on the first raider. This may have been Erhardt's positive influence, or the fact that with his Knight's Cross medal he didn't have to prove himself to anyone; but whatever the cause, Hoppe was content with the improved situation. For a new member of the wardroom like Jürgen Herr, who hadn't known the earlier Captain von Ruckteschell with his particularly ruthless abandonment of survivors and other excesses, the Ruckteschell he came to know was a skilled, professional naval officer who warranted his respect.

Ruckteschell's next attack, on the *American Leader,* was similar to the attack on the *Anglo-Saxon,* the raider heavily and indiscriminately mauling the freighter. While the heavy guns did their destructive job on the ship's structure and a number of her lifeboats, the smaller but deadly 37mm and 20mm rapid-fire guns swept the decks and sent sailors like Third Officer George Duffy scrambling for their lives. In an attempt to free one of the life rafts, Duffy courageously leapt into the rigging to cut away the lashings. Instantly, he was the target of fire from the menacing raider and had to spring to safe cover. In twenty-five minutes, the ship went down, and Duffy and 46 others on rafts in the water were picked up. Although apprehensive at being a captive, Duffy was relieved that she was a German ship rather than a Japanese vessel that had rescued them.

The brutal attacks continued, the next against the *Empire Dawn.* Since the fire did not cease when the *Empire Dawn*'s wounded Captain, W. A. Scott, signaled that the ship was being abandoned, Ruckteschell had another charge against him when he would be called to account for his actions. For the time, however, Ruckteschell continued with his assaults. He was moved to the Indian Ocean and then ordered by the SKL to the Antarctic, where they hoped he would swoop down on the whalers working there, as another raider, the *Pinguin,* had once done. However, the independent Ruckteschell refused the order, and once again his bosses allowed the successful Captain to make the decision. By the late fall of 1942, due to the sinking, scuttling, or conversion of raiders to other purposes, the *Michel* remained the only raider still at work at sea. Hellmuth von Ruckteschell and his crew were the last of their breed.

In contrast to the brutality of the attacks, those who were taken onboard as prisoners were treated decently. There was no abuse, sometimes good humor was exchanged between captors and captives, and the prisoners ate the same food in the same quantities as the German crew. By the time the *Michel* was ordered to the Indian Ocean, she had transferred most of her prisoners, including George Duffy, to supply ships, which then turned the prisoners over to the Japanese in Southeast Asia. The *Michel*'s prisoner accommodations would not remain vacant for long, however. On November 30, the *Michel* overwhelmed the American freighter *Sawokla,* and took 35 of her crew on board. A week later, the Greek freighter *Eugenie Livanos* became her next victim when she stumbled on the *Michel,* which was waiting for a storm to clear.

To lift morale in the time leading up to Christmas 1942, elaborate preparations were made to celebrate the holiday onboard the *Michel,* which give insight into life on the raider and her complex Captain. As his contribution to the festivities, Ruckteschell wrote a lengthy, five-act puppet play as a gift to his *erwachsene Kinder* (grown-up children), his sailors, which reveals his paternalistic approach to his crew. Even this play, intended to bring joy, provoked Ruckteschell's ire, when he became frustrated by the poor performance of his masterpiece during rehearsal. Konrad Hoppe volunteered to assume supervision of the rehearsals, which then went well. Hoppe, who had had a falling-out with the Captain, was now back in the good graces of his commanding officer.

The preparations for Christmas extended throughout the ship, to crew and prisoners alike. Christmas trees and decorations were fabricated out of whatever was available, and each person of the crew crafted a gift for another crew member chosen by lot. Festive food and drink, cakes, fruits, and beer, were provided to the prisoners, and each was given a special sack filled with items that would have been exceedingly rare at home—a large raisin cake, a pound of Dutch chocolate, cigarettes, and canned fruit. The highlight of the celebration was the successful performance of the puppet play, an elaborate production featuring a puppet theater and fine puppets purchased in Bavaria before the voyage. Some members of the crew worked the puppets, while others shifted the sets or provided the music.

The play was a drama set on board the *Michel*, with a flashback to the preceding Christmas when they had been at home. The central characters were two sailors, Michel and Kuddel, and the plot revolved around Kuddel going astray, in typical sailor fashion, stopping at a bar on his way to spend Christmas with Michel and his family. The play was laced with both religious and erotic allusions. Kuddel gave the gift he intended to give Michel's daughter to a prostitute, and the moral of the story was the inherent goodness and innocence of youth, symbolized by the child's forgiveness of Kuddel for giving her present to someone who had no other gift that Christmas. The complex drama, with its multiple layers, sacred and profane, reflects the multidimensional personality of Ruckteschell and also the influence of Rudolf Steiner and the religion he inspired.

Another highlight of that Christmas Day was the surprise presentation to Captain Ruckteschell of Oak Leaves for his Knight's Cross medal. This made him the 158th member of the German military to receive the treasured award. With this recognition from his country, Ruckteschell was elevated to high status among heroes of the Third Reich.

A few days later, the German crew and the prisoners jointly honored the prisoners' dead shipmates in a solemn ceremony, demonstrating once again the stark contrast of a Captain who could be so ruthless and violent in his attacks, and then so civil in his treatment of his prisoners.

As 1943 dawned, the *Michel* was back in the Atlantic, and everyone looked forward to completing their mission and returning triumphantly to occupied France, as the *Widder* had done. On January 2, the *Empire March* was shadowed and dispatched with the usual violence, and 26 additional prisoners were brought onboard. This was the *Michel*'s last conquest under Ruckteschell's command.

All hands and the prisoners onboard the *Michel* were eager to head back to Europe after ten months at sea, but it was clear that the war was not going well for the Germans and the possibility of returning safely was diminishing. On January 8, it was announced that the raider would not be returning home but would be going to Japan. For the officers and crew, this was a devastating blow, since it meant that they would not return to their homes and loved ones for the foreseeable future. It was also an ominous admission that Germany could no longer provide safe passage for her successful sailors. For the prisoners, their fate was sealed—they would become prisoners of the Japanese. They had received proper treatment on the *Michel,* but this would be a cruel change and some would die as a result.

The raider turned to the east, made her way past the Cape of Good Hope and across the Indian Ocean. After a brief stop in Bali, where the *Michel*'s former prisoner, George Duffy, witnessed the raider's arrival while laboring as a Japanese prisoner of war, the ship went on to Singapore, where she had to make her way through the mines protecting the harbor. There the *Michel*'s prisoners were turned over to the Japanese authorities, who put some of them to work on the infamous Pakanbaru railroad-building project on the island of Sumatra, which cost the life of one out of every four prisoners assigned to the incredible task. From Singapore, the *Michel* made her way to Japan, where she arrived on March 1, 1943, picking up a mooring in Kobe and ending her deadly cruise. The crew had been gone a year, and although they had fallen short of Ruckteschell's ambitious goal, they had sunk nearly 100,000 tons of Allied merchant shipping. The promise of their next cruise in the Pacific was before them.

While the ship entered the Mitsubishi Shipyard for a quick overhaul, the crew was given supervised liberty, and Ruckteschell attended to various ceremonial and administrative duties. It was clear, however, that he needed medical attention. His ship's doctor, Friedrich Wilhelm Schröder, and the medical staff ashore evaluated his condition. He continued to suffer migraines, an intestinal malady, and now problems with his heart. The stress of command had taken its toll, and he was urged to take three months for treatment and recuperation.

By this time in the war, both the Germans and the Japanese had experienced serious setbacks, and it was impossible to have a German warship sit idle in the Pacific for three months. The *Michel* was ordered back into battle, without Ruckteschell, who was replaced by Kapitän zur See Gunther Gumprich, whose raider, the *Thor,* had been destroyed by the explosion of the *Uckermark* while moored alongside in Yokohama Harbor. On his fifty-third birthday, March 23, 1943, Hellmuth von Ruckteschell relinquished command to Gumprich; he was finished as a raider Captain. His Executive Officer, Erhardt, Adjutant Jürgen Herr, and Flying Officer Konrad Hoppe stayed "on the beach" as the *Michel* got under way on March 31. The eager and irrepressible torpedo-boat skipper Malte von Schack was one of the original crew who stayed with the *Michel* for her cruise with the new Captain.

Those who were left behind were "distributed" to a variety of assignments throughout the Far East. Herr was assigned to a language school in Japan. Hoppe was sent to Batavia (now Jakarta). After his treatment in a hospital in Tokyo, Ruckteschell was sent to Penang, on the west coast of the Malaysian peninsula, to establish a submarine center there. He did not last long in this position, since the independent and often contrary Ruckteschell clashed with the senior Japanese officer to whom he reported.

As these officers adjusted to their new lives, their former shipmates quickly adapted to Captain Gumprich, a regular Navy officer who ran his ship effectively but with less rigor than his predecessor. He was a relaxed and approachable commanding officer, unlike the austere Ruckteschell. The *Michel*'s second cruise was not particularly effective. Only two ships were sunk in June and another in September before she was ordered back to Japan.

On October 16, the *Michel* was 100 miles away from the main Japanese island of Honshu, with only one more night before arrival in Kobe. Her crew was anticipating the pleasure that lay ahead. However, the hunter and her crew that had sent so many Allied ships and sailors to watery graves had become the hunted. In the *Michel*'s path lay the United States submarine *Tarpon*, under the command of Thomas L. Wogan. The *Tarpon* was operating on the surface when, in the first minutes of Sunday, October 17, an approaching ship was spotted at a range of 7.5 miles. As the ship came steadily on, Wogan and his crew positioned themselves for their attack. After forty-five minutes, the *Tarpon* silently submerged and moved forward on her electric motors, ready to fire her torpedoes at this prime target upon the Captain's order. To ensure success, Wogan launched four torpedoes of the size the *Michel* had used against her victims. Moments later, two of those torpedoes hit their target, and the seemingly invincible *Michel* took a sudden list and glided to a halt.

Onboard the *Michel,* her crew experienced the horror they had inflicted on so many other vessels. Gumprich got the engines functioning after only a few minutes, and the ship began to move again. Then another torpedo struck the ship in the aft aircraft compartment, which began to flood quickly. The auxiliary generators failed, and the ship was engulfed in darkness. Orders immediately followed to abandon ship as the last torpedo hit the raider. Malte von Schack dramatically dove from the top of the pilothouse, which still towered over the water, before the ship, with many of her crew trapped inside, slid out of sight. The stunned men in boats and in the water raised a cheer in salute to the doomed ship and their mates. The era of German surface raiders was over.

Some of the survivors set off for Honshu in several small boats and arrived after two nights on the ocean. Nearly 100 others crowded onto inflatable lifeboats and floating debris that had been gathered together to create a makeshift raft. Many who could not make it into the boats or onto the raft clung to it in the water. Schack, the senior officer in the group, sent an inflatable boat for help, staying behind with his men. The exhausted men in the inflatable were finally picked up seven days later. They were the last survivors from the *Michel* to reach safety. After eighteen months of destructive attacks on Allied merchant shipping, the *Michel* and most of her crew were gone—243 sailors and 16 officers were lost, including Ingrid Herr's fiancé, Malte von Schack.

Michel, the ship, was gone, but Hellmuth von Ruckteschell, the man who related so closely to the concept of Michel in both its symbolic forms, the warrior saint and the common man, was still alive. Although he was unwell, this man who had inflicted so much death and destruction through his U-boat exploits in World War I and the *Widder* and the *Michel* raider campaigns of World War II was about to settle into a comfortable life in China for the duration of the war.

Chapter 21

WAR CRIMINAL

During the two years that he spent in Shanghai and Peking, which were under Japanese control at the time, Ruckteschell had no official responsibilities. Little is known of his day-to-day life and the medical treatment he required, but the military paymaster who covered his expenses chafed at the cost. While the Allied forces fought their way across Europe and island-hopped through the Pacific, pushing the aggressors back toward their homelands, Ruckteschell was convalescing in China. Insulated from the strife, he was spared the destruction and deprivation the war brought to Germany.

War news did reach the German community in Peking, however, and they knew their armies had failed in Russia and Africa and were being defeated in Europe. The news of Hitler's suicide on April 30, 1945, and the unconditional surrender of Germany, signed by General Alfred Jodl on May 7 and ratified the following day by Field Marshal Wilhelm Keitel, reached Peking quickly. Once again, Ruckteschell was part of a defeated and humiliated Germany. Those events were followed in early August by the detonation of atomic bombs over Hiroshima and Nagasaki, and Emperor Hirohito's surrender of Japan on August 14. The Second World War was over. Germany and Japan were defeated, and Hellmuth von

Ruckteschell, weakened by gall bladder problems, migraine headaches, and heart problems, awaited his fate in Peking.

That wait lasted almost a year. He was placed under arrest by American forces and in June of 1946, Ruckteschell was transported to Shanghai, where he and other Germans being repatriated from Asia boarded the transport SS *Marine Robin* for the long voyage home. Some of the passengers were diplomats or civilian dependents, but many, like Ruckteschell, were military prisoners of war. Each POW was given work to do, and Kapitän zur See von Ruckteschell, the winner of the Knight's Cross with Oak Leaves, was reduced to working in the food service. He had the exhausting job of handing out three meals a day to the 1,000 people crowded on the *Marine Robin* as she steamed through the heat of the Indian Ocean and the Suez Canal. On August 4, 1946, the ship arrived in Bremerhaven, and Ruckteschell was overwhelmed with joy at seeing the meadows, farms, and churches of his native land for the first time in four and a half years. He hoped to be transferred to a reception camp and then released, but knew he must pass through "the sieve," the screening process for prisoners of war, which determined if there were alleged war criminals among them. His concern on this point was an indication that he was anxious that his actions would fall into this category.

In 1919, Ruckteschell had evaded prosecution by fleeing to Sweden until the war crimes issue died out in the mire of post–World War I politics. The debacle of those earlier war crimes tribunals was considered by the Allies in 1942 as they prepared to try war criminals at the end of World War II. The commitment to hold the trials was strengthened when confronted with the horrendous crimes, particularly the Holocaust, perpetrated by the Nazi regime. Within six months of the German surrender, the International Military Tribunal in Nuremberg was in session, trying the top twenty-three alleged Nazi war criminals. By the time Hellmuth von Ruckteschell reached Germany, the major cases were concluded, but they still sifted through the reports of crimes and atrocities to identify those responsible. By mid-August, Ruckteschell was in Internment Camp No. 76, in Asperg, near Stuttgart, only 80 miles from his home, where he enjoyed the somewhat relaxed atmosphere and opportunity to use carving tools in the craft programs. He was hopeful of a quick release, but that hope dissolved a week later when he was separated from the others, told to pack his gear, and was lead to a jeep, under guard. No one told him what lay ahead, but he caught a glimpse of the cover of his file, where in a bold red stamp it said "War Criminal."

Ruckteschell found himself in a small cell with a single light that stayed on all the time. He was given meager rations and was able to exercise only by marching in a long line of men around the prison yard for thirty minutes a day. During his ten-day stay in this British Military Command Interrogation Prison in Minden, he was interrogated but was unable to determine the offense for which he was being investigated. He suspected it might be the charge of attacking vessels without warning, since that was a tactic not extensively used by other raiders. The authorities, however, were investigating a much longer list of allegations, stemming from a number of his violent attacks. What they gleaned from him in those days in Minden convinced them that Ruckteschell's case needed far more investigation. On August 30, he began the journey, first by train to the Hook of Holland, and then by a Channel steamer to Harwich, on England's east coast.

For the next seven months, Ruckteschell was kept in England as the Allied investigators gathered information from official sources, shipping records, war diaries, witnesses, and interrogations of Ruckteschell himself. There is always the question of whether war crimes trials are simply "victor's revenge," but with the solid British commitment to the rule of law, that could not be said of this process. This was anything but a kangaroo court or a show trial. As was seen in the six English war-crimes prosecutions before the German High Court in Leipzig in 1921, the British cases were thoroughly investigated, precisely prosecuted, and the witnesses gave their evidence in a dispassionate manner. The result in 1921 was that the German court found five of the six Germans accused guilty of their crimes. The preparation of the charges brought against Hellmuth von Ruckteschell was as thorough as those prepared a quarter of a century earlier. There is no evidence that there was any knowledge of, consideration of, or reference to any war crimes allegations against Ruckteschell from World War I. The charges on which he was tried were purely related to his actions as the Commanding Officer of the *Widder* and the *Michel* during World War II.

Ruckteschell was imprisoned in London for three weeks, where he was interrogated further, filled out forms and biographical statements, and spent long hours of solitude in his cell. He then went back and forth between Prison Camp No. 17 in Sheffield and continued interrogation in London. Under the stress of these legal problems, he experienced more trouble with his heart and intestines. During the fall, resigned to whatever fate lay before him and girding himself to cope with it, he made the commitment to be as friendly as possible and exude "the most simple kindness of heart." By November, the trips to London had diminished, and he settled into the routine of prison life in Sheffield.

For a person who had a passionate love of classical music, its lack had been one of Ruckteschell's greatest deprivations. As the Christmas season approached, he was encouraged to discover that the prison camp had a number of competent musicians preparing an elaborate Christmas concert, which included Bach, Corelli, and Mozart. Even though he was not a participant, he attended every rehearsal to soak up as much of the treasured music as possible. In a letter to his wife, he reminisced about the Christmas of 1942 and the puppet play on the *Michel*. His circumstances reversed, he and his fellow prisoners cobbled together sparse Christmas decorations, as his prisoners in the *Michel* had done four years earlier.

It was not by happenstance that Hellmuth von Ruckteschell was identified while in Internment Camp No. 76 in Asperg during the summer of 1946 and transferred to the interrogation prison at Minden. The Allies had a long list of alleged offenses that might result in charges against German military personnel. In Ruckteschell's case, there were allegations by survivors of the sinking of the *Davisian,* the *Beaulieu,* the *Empire Dawn,* and, of course, the *Anglo-Saxon.* This last case was obvious, since it had received such wide press coverage at the time and was the subject of the book *Two Survived.* The Allied forces kept track of the outrages during the war and sought out those who had committed them. Ruckteschell's war diaries from the *Widder* and the *Michel* provided the investigators with the information they needed. He had taken great pride in his conquests and in the detailed accounts recorded in the diaries, which he worked hard to get to his superior officers so that his successes and how they were accomplished would be known. At the end of the war, those diaries were available to the Allied forces to read and analyze.

The investigators sought out and gathered evidence from George Jolly and others who had been aboard the *Davisian* and had experienced the fury of a daytime attack by the *Widder*. In cooperation with authorities in Norway, they worked with 5 survivors of Ruckteschell's first nighttime attack on the tanker *Beaulieu*. They also talked to Captain Scott and others from the crew of the *Empire Dawn,* the *Michel*'s tenth victim. The assault on the *Anglo-Saxon* presented a challenge for the investigators. The 7 men who survived the initial violent attack were absolutely convinced that the Germans were determined to leave no survivors to tell the tale of the brutal and prolonged attack, and they recorded this in their log. Bob Tapscott was the sole survivor now, and he was back at sea, once again serving England as a merchant seaman. It was difficult to track him down, and more difficult for him to be available to testify at trial. Tapscott's statement was critical, since one of the charges against Ruckteschell could bring the death sentence. The issue involved the firing at survivors in rafts and boats, as Tapscott and the other 6 in the jolly boat had witnessed.

Tapscott was serving on the SS *Langleetarn* on a voyage that took him through the Mediterranean, the Suez Canal, and down the east coast of Africa. While in Durban, South Africa, on November 5, 1946, Tapscott made a sworn written statement before George Palmer, a Commissioner of Oaths. It was upon this statement and Ruckteschell's war diary that the *Anglo-Saxon* charges would hang. Tapscott's statement is powerful, giving a horrifying account of the attack on the ship, his specific ordeal on deck, and his escape. With regard to the most serious allegation, he said, "After we had drifted past the raider about one to two hundred yards I saw the lights of two rafts come on. The raider immediately opened fire on them with tracers and continued firing until the two lights went out." In the final two paragraphs of the statement, he summed up the feeling he and the others in the jolly boat had had on that night more than six years earlier, saying: "I am quite sure that the Commander of the raider intended that there should be no survivors and I am sure that had we been spotted we would have shared the fate of our shipmates. The raider gave no chance for the launching of life boats or life rafts by keeping up a continuous stream of fire with tracer ammunition." He went on, "Normally we would have signaled to the attacking ship to pick us up, but his intention was so clear that we kept quiet and thereby got away." A great deal would depend on this statement.

As 1947 began and Tapscott continued his voyage, the full brunt of the English winter fell upon Camp No. 17, and the Nissen hut Ruckteschell shared with 39 other prisoners was constantly cold. The 100 yards from the hut to the latrine was either frozen or muddy, and each prisoner was allowed only one shower per week. Ruckteschell had a constant cold; he was discouraged and looked to his faith to give him the strength to face the consequences of his deeds. February brought even more severe weather, with so much snow that it was difficult to get the hut door open or reach the latrines. He found some cheer in another prisoners' concert and the gift of a small painting on glass from his stepdaughter, whose artwork he encouraged in letters. Ruckteschell and 156 other prisoners were moved to better facilities at a new camp at Quorn in Leicestershire, some 60 miles south of the Sheffield camp. During the move, while struggling to carry his belongings in the winter cold, Ruckteschell became dizzy and had "severe pressure on his heart." He was put in the prison infirmary and diagnosed with a defective heart valve. He had clean white sheets and blankets to provide a warmth he hadn't felt for some time, but his 6-by-9-foot room was still a cell, and from his bed he watched the winter sun through a barred window for five weeks. While he regained some health, he dreaded what was to come. He and the other war crimes suspects were referred to as "Londoners" because of the frequent trips made there for interrogation. In bitterness, he felt that all "Londoners" were viewed as murderers, and he had difficulty steeling his resolve for the next phase of the process.

That phase began at the end of March, less than a week after his fifty-seventh birthday. He was flown to Bückeburg in Germany and then taken by car to Compound Y at Munsterlager, where Kapitän zur See der Reserve, Hellmuth von Ruckteschell was discharged from the Navy on April 5, 1947. Severed from the Navy he loved, he became Herr von Ruckteschell, German citizen and accused war criminal.

Armed with Tapscott's sworn statement and information from numerous witnesses regarding other attacks, the authorities brought charges against Ruckteschell, and by mid-April he was moved to the investigative prison in the Hamburg district of Altona. He was back in the city where he was born and had spent his early youth, and only a short distance from Altona's Osterkirche, for which he had carved the altarpieces before the war. His sister, Hilde von Ruckteschell, still lived there and was able to visit him. His wife, who had been his faithful correspondent during the five years they had been apart, was notified that he was in Hamburg, where he would be placed on trial. She urgently desired to get to Hamburg, but the Ruckteschell home was in Freiburg, in the French zone of occupation. Hamburg was in the British zone. Passage between these zones was controlled by permits, and Margaret von Ruckteschell became entangled in bureaucracy. In a demonstration of fairness and compassion, the English sent a special liaison officer from Baden-Baden to Freiburg to assist Frau von Ruckteschell in getting the appropriate interzonal passport, and she was able to get to Hamburg by April 29, one week before the trial began.

By the time he returned to Germany, the roster of charges against Ruckteschell was established, and a competent German attorney, Dr. O. Zippel, was appointed to conduct his defense. In the days leading up to the trial, Ruckteschell spent long hours with Dr. Zippel preparing his defense. There were five charges, which involved his attacks on four ships. The first charge related to the *Davisian,* and alleged that the attack continued after the *Davisian* surrendered by signaling her willingness to obey orders from the *Widder.* The second charge was the attack on the *Beaulieu* in the open ocean, for making "no provision for the safety of the survivors of the crew." The third charge was the first of two relating to the *Anglo-Saxon,* the charge that could bring the death sentence. Here it was alleged that the *Widder* had "fired at members of the crew of the said ship who were on life rafts." The second charge relating to the *Anglo-Saxon* alleged that Ruckteschell again, "in violation of the laws and usages of war, made no provision to provide for the safety of the survivors of the crew of the said ship." The fifth and final charge related to the *Michel*'s attack on the *Empire Dawn,* alleging that the *Michel* continued to fire on the British ship after those onboard signaled that they were abandoning ship. It was a serious array of charges, and Zippel, a tall, thin man who conveyed an air of intelligence and confidence, had his work cut out for him.

In addition to meetings with Ruckteschell, Zippel gathered information from defense witnesses and also met with Frau von Ruckteschell in Hamburg. The prisoner and his wife were not allowed to meet prior to the trial, but Ruckteschell continued to write to her and revealed his fears as well as his resolve to face the consequences of the trial. In a letter written three days before the trial began, he told of his emotional ups and downs and commented on his weeping, saying it "eases the tension a little bit." While he longed for freedom, he realized he could possibly face the death sentence. In the same letter, he contemplated his past deeds, saying, "I always think: 'How many people did I frighten and make to suffer with my ship?'—and now it is my turn."

In a long letter to both his wife, Margaret, and sister, Hilde, the last written before his trial began, he demonstrated that he and his ship were one and the same, when he signed the letter, "Yours, Michel."

On Monday morning, May 5, 1947, the accused war criminal Hellmuth von Ruckteschell was placed in handcuffs and taken to a prison car for the trip through the streets of Hamburg to the University district near the Dammtor Station and the Curio Haus, where the trial would take place. This large, handsome structure, which dominates the block on which it stands, was designated "No. 1 War Crimes Court" and was the site of the drama that played out between May 5 and May 21. Ruckteschell's trial began in a large courtroom on the ground floor, which was entered from a central courtyard. Separate doors on the left-hand side admitted the Court officials, witnesses, and press to their area. Spectators went to another area, up stairs that lead to the balcony reserved for them.

The five Court members sat at a massive table facing the rest of the court-room, with large windows looking out into the garden on their right.

The earnest President of the Court was a bright, severe young Royal Artillery Lieutenant-Colonel, G. J. James. Flanking him were two ruddy-faced Majors, A. O. Mordaunt of the Somerset Light Infantry and H. D. P. Nicol of the Gordon Highlanders, resplendent in his tartan kilt. On each side of the Majors were two more English officers: Captain W. E. Donald of the Intelligence Corps, and the only naval officer on the panel, Lieutenant C. C. Anderson, Royal Navy. Also seated at the Court's table was the legal authority for the trial, the Judge Advocate, H. Sturge, Barrister-at-law. In his wig and robes, he was described in a letter by Frau von Ruckteschell as "an outstandingly intelligent and clear person in whose hand all threads were concentrated and who was almost always complete master of the situation."

Immediately in front of the Court was the stenographer. To the left was the Prosecutor, Major Reade, and the press gallery. To the right was the witness box and three interpreters, including one of extraordinary talent. Directly across from the Court officers sat the Defense Counsel, Dr. Zippel, and seated immediately behind him, within easy communication, was the defendant, Hellmuth von Ruckteschell, and his guard.

While the large, light, and airy courtroom created an appropriate environment for this solemn process, the acoustics were poor, which exacerbated the fact that the Prosecutor had a serious stammer. In this chamber the five charges were read, and to each Ruckteschell replied with an emphatic "Not guilty." Then began days and days of presentation of evidence, testimony, and examination and cross-examination of witnesses for both the Prosecution and the Defense. The 900-page record of this trial reveals that, despite being a military tribunal, this was a carefully conducted judicial procedure, with ample fairness and opportunities for the Defense. In one instance, the Defense wished to call another successful raider Captain, Admiral Bernhard Rogge, the former Captain of the *Atlantis*. The Admiral, however, had been viewing the trial from the spectators' gallery. He had not been isolated, as is normally the case for witnesses so that they are not influenced by the testimony of others. The

Court waived this practice and allowed Rogge to testify. This trial was not indiscriminate "victor's vengeance." None of the other raider captains, even those who exceeded Ruckteschell's tonnage sunk, were brought before war crimes courts; Ruckteschell's zeal and excesses had made him the single defendant.

As the Court addressed the first charge, the issue revolved around signals between the two ships. The two witnesses from the *Davisian* swore that the *Widder* had signaled them not to use their radio. They responded that they would not, and that it was their intention that this response constituted surrender. The *Widder* resumed firing, and in the process killed 3 sailors who were crossing the deck on the *Davisian*. Ruckteschell testified that he thought the sailors were going for the ship's gun. Using his war diary as a record, he said there was no entry that a signal to not use the radio had been sent, and therefore there was nothing to which the men of the *Davisian* could have responded. Several Defense witnesses, including Konrad Hoppe, Gunnery Officer Damschen, and Navigation Officer Rödel, could not remember the specifics of the incident and their comments worked against the Defense.

The second charge focused on Ruckteschell's failure to provide for the safety of the Norwegian crew of the *Beaulieu*. The Prosecution witness, a Royal Norwegian Air Force officer, Lieutenant Stannes, who was an officer in the *Beaulieu* at the time of the attack, described how, hoping to be recognized as an unarmed merchant ship so the attack would cease, the tanker turned on all her navigation and deck lights as soon as the attack commenced. When the firing continued, he and two-thirds of the crew launched one boat, while the rest of the crew worked to launch the other. In testimony that heightened the tension in the courtroom, Stannes described how his lifeboat came under direct machine-gun fire, and a number of men leapt into the sea to avoid being gunned down. Ruckteschell and others from the *Widder* testified that they did not have small machine guns of the type Stannes described and denied deliberately firing on the lifeboat.

It was on this point, during the Judge Advocate's summation, that Dr. Zippel asked for and received the exceptional opportunity to introduce

statements from 4 other members of the *Beaulieu* crew. This was controversial, but the Court was lenient and allowed the statements. While they
did not directly rebut Stannes's testimony, two of them simply did not
mention any firing on the lifeboats and the other two attributed the sense
of being fired upon to the ricocheting of other projectiles. These statements neutralized this aspect of Stannes's testimony, which allowed the
Court to focus on the actual charge of abandoning the crew. Ruckteschell
had recorded in his war diary that he had seen one loaded lifeboat and was
aware that another was being lowered. The fine point was: did the fact
that the Norwegians deliberately evaded the raider absolve Ruckteschell
of the responsibility to provide for their safety? Stannes's testimony established that those in the boats were convinced that if the raider found
them they would be annihilated. The Court would have to ponder the evidence.

The third charge, that the *Widder* had fired on the life rafts of the
Anglo-Saxon, was the next to be addressed. In the brutal and prolonged attack, the *Widder* had eliminated 34 possible witnesses. In the jolly boat, agonizing death and desperate acts eradicated 5 more people who had all
witnessed the firing and had recorded their perceptions in the jolly boat's
log. *U-69*'s sinking of the *Siamese Prince* had ended the life of Roy Widdicombe, who had told the story of the firing on the rafts to numerous journalists and others, and had made a signed statement regarding this before
Commissioner Gerassimos. Of all who had been on the *Anglo-Saxon* that
night, only one sailor remained alive, Bob Tapscott, who had made his
sworn statement in Durban six months before. Major Reade, the Prosecutor, was counting on its power to make the case. The attack was addressed in some detail, comparing the elements in Tapscott's statement
with the entries in Ruckteschell's war diary, with particular attention paid
to the excesses of the attack, and the fact that Ruckteschell admitted in
his war diary that the firing had gone on too long because a cease-fire
order was not heard by the gunners. He also affirmed a written statement
he had made earlier about night attacks, in which he said: "It was clear
that there was a loss of human life by this method, but it was not our intention to destroy human life, but to destroy enemy tonnage. The sever-

ity of this method of fighting was nevertheless necessary, for the opponent often tried to send out signals or even to fire." In this statement, he
admitted to the violence of his tactic, which was not used by other raider
captains. Ruckteschell had also stated that "the 2cm. AA had to rake the
entire deck of the opponent's ship. According to orders it did not fire on
fixed targets but 'sprayed' so as to prevent the crew from running to the
guns, or in order to hasten them taking to the boats." The indiscriminate
and continuous spraying of the ships with murderous 2cm fire "to hasten
them taking to the boats" was seen as excessive violence, and Ruckteschell's statements reinforced the brutality of the attacks in the minds
of the members of the Court.

The focus of this charge was the firing on the rafts. The Defense witnesses all testified that they did not see such firing and never heard of an
order to fire on boats and survivors in the water. Ruckteschell testified
that he had never given such an order. He did admit that in the heat of
battle a gunner might have swung his gun at lights in the water, but Ruckteschell emphasized that if he had become aware of it, "the row that
would have followed from me later if I had observed, that would have
been another story."

In an effort to explain how Tapscott might have thought the rafts
were being fired upon, Ruckteschell used his artistic ability to draw a
pencil sketch from Tapscott's perspective in the jolly boat. This fascinating document, Exhibit Y in the trial, attempted to show that from where
the people in the jolly boat were positioned, gunfire directed at the ship
might have seemed to be aimed at rafts in the water. While the defendant's hypothetical version of the incident was only partially successful, it
did introduce doubt. Against all the denials, there was only a lone piece of
paper, Tapscott's statement.

Citing the severity of the charge, Dr. Zippel argued that he could not
properly defend Hellmuth von Ruckteschell without cross-examining
the sole witness. Tapscott was serving on the *Houston City*, which had departed New York five days before the trial began and would not arrive in
Haifa until the day the trial ended. The key witness, the only British witness, was unavailable. No effort was made to introduce the jolly boat's log,

of which only Captain Millar's transcript existed, or newspaper accounts of statements made by Widdicombe, or the statements made by Tapscott and Widdicombe to Commissioner Gerassimos or Guy Pearce Jones. With only Tapscott's sworn statement to consider, midway through the trial the Court acquitted Ruckteschell on the most serious charge against him. If First Officer Denny, Second Radio Officer Pilcher, Third Engineer Hawks, Gunner Penny, Assistant Cook Morgan, and Able Seamen Roy Widdicombe and Robert Tapscott had been at the trial to testify under oath what they were certain they saw, the trial would likely have had a different outcome. It is possible that Ruckteschell did not give an order to fire on the rafts, but seven men were convinced that this occurred. If it did, the responsibility would ultimately lie with the raider's Captain.

Crucial pencil sketch made by Ruckteschell during his trial and submitted as "Exhibit Y," drawn from the perspective of Tapscott (labeled "Tascott" in the drawing). Ruckteschell used the drawing to illustrate how Tapscott and those in the boat might have perceived gunfire aimed at the *Anglo-Saxon* as being aimed at rafts in the water. *Courtesy Public Records Office, Kew, UK.*

This most serious charge was dropped, and the next question concerned whether Ruckteschell had failed to provide for the safety of the *Anglo-Saxon* survivors. Again, the issue of the jolly-boat crew deliberately evading the raider was raised, but this was tempered by the undoubtedly ruthless and prolonged violence of the attack. In addition, unlike in the case of the *Beaulieu,* which had stayed afloat for several hours, during which time the *Widder* hovered nearby, Ruckteschell's war diary confirmed that he only circled the *Anglo-Saxon* as part of the attack and immediately steamed off. Noting that the Azores were only 800 miles away, he made no effort to search for survivors in boats. The callousness of this act, particularly when he had no knowledge of the condition of the men in the boat, or of the boat herself, or how she was equipped, was easily perceived by the Court.

The final charge once again involved the question of signaling surrender. The *Empire Dawn* was attacked during the day by Ruckteschell in the *Michel.* The merchantman's skipper, Captain Scott, was present to testify and described how, with serious wounds, he had made his way aft on his burning ship and signaled his surrender with a flashlight using Morse code. The attack continued and Captain Scott received further wounds as a result of his signaling. Ruckteschell and the other Defense witnesses denied that any signal had been seen. In an effective courtroom drama, Dr. Zippel produced a light similar to the one used by Captain Scott and asked him to demonstrate his signal to the Court. The flashlight was only about 10 inches long, with a lens 3 inches in diameter. When the Court saw its weak light and considered the chaos, the daylight, flashes from firing guns, and flames from the burning ship, Zippel had made his case.

On the third day, the trial had been moved to a smaller courtroom with better acoustics. Ruckteschell found this a bad omen, for the two previous defendants in that courtroom were concentration camp staff members who were sentenced to death. Despite the fact that the third charge against him had been dropped, the specter of a death sentence was still before him. After their testimony as Defense witnesses, the defendant's former officers were in the spectators' gallery, along with his wife, as the trial neared its end. There must have been a sense of relief for

Ruckteschell and his supporters when the Prosecutor, Major Reade, began his final argument with a conciliatory statement. He said: "Now, the accused does not appear before you in the same kind of capacity as some of the S.S. commandants of concentration camps and figures of the Gestapo, who have appeared before these courts. He comes before you as a man on whose integrity no previous reflections have been cast and he is entitled, while his case is being judged, to enjoy the same presumption of innocence as any accused before any English court."

There is no doubt about the presumption of innocence required by justice; however, it is clear from Ruckteschell's description "as a man on whose integrity no previous reflections have been cast" that the Prosecutors had not discovered or read the contents of the twenty-six-year-old file bearing the bold inscription "German War Criminal Lt. Ruckteschell, U-54, Drowning of Crew of Sailing Vessel." If that information had been known to the Prosecutor, it is extremely unlikely that he would have been so sympathetic as to offer the generous opening statement. The damning accusations concerning Ruckteschell in the First World War were not admissible in court because they were simply allegations. But it was possible that Master's Mate Otto Wiedemann was alive in Poland and could have been called to testify about the character of the Ruckteschell he knew. Ruckteschell could not have been tried for his World War I actions in the Hamburg tribunal, but an awareness of this most serious allegation of murder and his escape to Sweden, which he told a journalist was made to avoid prosecution, would, indeed, have cast reflections on his integrity.

After all the evidence had been given and the Prosecution and the Defense had made their closing arguments, the Judge Advocate gave his summation, which took significant portions of two days and was approximately 20,000 words in length. It included thorough instructions to the Court and a charge-by-charge summary of the cases presented by both the Prosecution and the Defense. Although the rules for these trials did not permit it, the Judge Advocate gave Ruckteschell the opportunity to make the final statement to the Court. The officer made the point that he was acting as a soldier with a good conscience and admitted that "Undoubtedly I made mistakes but not from malice." The final words from the philosophical Hellmuth von Ruckteschell were, "I have learned that my highest duty as a soldier is not to shoot but to keep the peace. My years are counted [numbered] but if I am able to contribute to this wherever it may be, I shall be very glad to do so." He was clearly making a plea that his life be spared.

On that note, the Court was closed, while its members considered the findings. That night, resigned to his fate, Ruckteschell wrote, "I have erred, and now they are erring; we both did it on orders and in the belief in justice and now both are wrong." The following morning, at 10:30, the Court reconvened and delivered its findings. The Court had considered the case carefully.

The first charge, firing after the signal of surrender on the *Davisian*— guilty.

The second charge, not providing for the safety of the crew of the *Beaulieu*—guilty.

The third charge, firing on the *Anglo-Saxon* rafts—not guilty.

The other *Anglo-Saxon* charge, not providing for the safety of the crew—guilty.

The final charge, firing after the *Empire Dawn* signaled surrender—not guilty.

Ruckteschell had been found guilty on three charges and not guilty on two. The Court then withdrew to determine the sentence, returning at one point to clarify how long Ruckteschell had been in prison since his arrest in China, obviously taking that into consideration. After deliberating for almost two hours, at shortly after noon, the Court returned. Ruckteschell stood and the Court announced its sentence: "Hellmuth von Ruckteschell, you are sentenced to ten years in prison."

Midway through the trial, Ruckteschell wrote his wife, "I think: If they sentence me now, then it may mean that such conventions of sea warfare will be renounced, and that there will be less suffering at sea. I suppose that my sentence will be used as a warning example, and if that is so, then I shall accept it gladly."

The press greeted the news with partisan reaction. The Hamburg newspapers, with the exception of the communist *Hamburger Volkszeitung*, felt Hellmuth von Ruckteschell should not have been tried and that the sentence was severe. The *New York Times* and *The Times* of London both reported that it was appropriate. The thin, weakened man who was old beyond his fifty-seven years had won the sympathy of many around him, including his English guards. His commitment to project an air of friendliness had achieved its goal.

The day after the trial, the convicted war criminal spent time with his wife for the first time in five years. The next day, Ruckteschell was transferred to the penitentiary in the Hamburg suburb of Fuhlsbüttel to begin serving his sentence. His wife and the Defense Counsel, Dr. Zippel, came the following day to discuss the review of the trial. By the end of May, Frau von Ruckteschell resigned herself to the future she and her husband would lead, and returned to her home in Freiburg. Ruckteschell attempted to settle in to life in the penitentiary. As a master cabinetmaker, he hoped to work in the penitentiary's carpentry shop, but after three weeks realized this was too strenuous for him and he was assigned to less demanding work. His visitors were primarily his sister, his stepchildren, a nephew, and several pastors, who brought spiritual support to the prisoner with deep religious convictions.

On August 22, 1947, Ruckteschell's case was submitted for review by the General Officer, Commanding-in-Chief, of the British Army of the Rhine, who a week later confirmed the findings relating to the *Davisian* and the *Anglo-Saxon* offenses but did not confirm the charge of abandoning the *Beaulieu* crew. Apparently, the facts that Ruckteschell had lingered long in the area and the crew had deliberately avoided the raider influenced the reviewing officer. As a result of the review, Ruckteschell's sentence was reduced from ten years to seven. He was informed of this on September 22, but it still seemed a lifetime, and the monotony of life in the penitentiary stretched interminably before him. Fall wore on into winter, and the spring of 1948 brought a serious decline in Ruckteschell's frail health. Dr. Zippel made the case that he was too ill to be treated in the prison hospital and should be released from prison or transferred to a civilian hospital. The prison physician, Dr. Frommer, insisted that he could be treated in the prison facility and there was no need to declare him unfit for imprisonment. Frau von Ruckteschell returned to Hamburg to visit her ill husband on April 23, 1948, a month after his fifty-eighth birthday. Two months later, at 10:30 in the morning of June 24, Hellmuth von Ruckteschell died of a sudden heart attack.

He died in the same community where his family gravesite is located. Within the towering trees and luxuriant rhododendrons of the famous Ohlsdorf Cemetery, in a forest-glen setting of pines, with stones memorializing his parents and many of his siblings, lies a rough natural stone bearing the names of both Hellmuth von Ruckteschell and his older brother Walter, who died seven years before.

At age fifty-eight, this extraordinary and complex character was gone. During his life, he had lived as a simple master craftsman as well as one of the most highly decorated heroes of the Third Reich. The contrasts in his life are stark. At one moment, he was the kind and concerned father figure for his crew, and at another the furious, incensed taskmaster, demeaning his officers. He was sometimes the cunning and ruthless U-boat or raider Captain leading a violent attack, and at others the pious and religious person holding a funeral service over the body of an enemy sailor he had just killed. Hellmuth von Ruckteschell was all these people and more, and his life left evidence of this in his treatment of friends and enemies, in the record of his artistic endeavors, and in the record of death and destruction he meted out to his victims.

In the end, the simple stone, amid others of his family, marks Ruckteschell's life. For so many of those merchant seamen who died as a result of his actions, there is no grave and no stone amid those of their family members. The grave for all but one of the *Anglo-Saxon*'s officers and crew members is the Atlantic Ocean, and their names are clustered, as shipmates in life and shipmates in death, on the bronze tablets of the Merchant Marine Memorial at Tower Hill in London.

Chapter 22

HAUNTED HERO

Bob Tapscott was in Australia when the Germans surrendered in early May 1945. After a three-month voyage on the *Moreton Bay,* he had jumped ship in Tasmania. The ship sailed on without him, and six weeks later he signed on to the *DeBrett* in Melbourne, serving as a member of her crew for almost a year, until May 1946. He spent two weeks at home in Cardiff before joining the *Langleetarn* for the voyage that took him to Durban, where he made the sworn statement used in Hellmuth von Ruckteschell's trial. The *Langleetarn* went through the Gulf of Suez and the Red Sea in July of 1946, passing the *Marine Robin,* which carried Ruckteschell as a prisoner of war.

Working up and down the east coast of Africa through the summer and into the fall, the *Langleetarn* transported "dirty" cargo of phosphates from Quṣeir, Egypt, south to Durban, and coal north to Aden or Suez. Phil Hayden was on that voyage with Bob Tapscott and remembers him as a good sailor who was liked by the officers and men. He also describes him as sometimes moody and a loner. The *Langleetarn* was a Cardiff ship, so Tapscott was among friends. Nevertheless, Hayden recalls that while at times Bob was affable and enjoyed a joke, at others he was morose and depressed. The crew knew only vaguely of Tapscott's ordeal. When Hayden tried to learn more, Tapscott would not be drawn out and told him to shut up and leave him alone. Hayden was just beginning his career at sea and was in awe of strong, silent men like Tapscott who had been through hardships during the war years and somehow seemed to take it in stride. Despite his stoic facade, however, it was a struggle for Tapscott to put his past behind him and lead a normal life.

Two months after giving his statement in Durban, he signed off of the *Langleetarn* in Lourenço Marques, now Maputo, Mozambique, a favorite recreation port for sailors on that coast, with its bars and the Hotel Polana's shark-protected beach. It was not for recreation that Tapscott left, however, for on the following day, January 4, 1947, he signed on to the *Fort Covington,* departing immediately for England. His motivation must have been high, because Able Seaman Tapscott signed on as a fireman-trimmer, and had to work in the engine room on his homeward voyage.

Ruckteschell's trial took place during Tapscott's next long voyage, on the *Houston City,* which left Cardiff on March 25, 1947. Calling first at Philadelphia and New York, the ship then worked her way eastward around the world. The trial was conducted as Tapscott crossed the Atlantic and continued into the Mediterranean, through the Suez Canal to Singapore, and on to Yokosuka, Japan; Coos Bay, Oregon; Los Angeles, and finally through the Panama Canal and home to the River Tyne, where he signed off after six months. This voyage seemed to go smoothly for Tapscott, but was followed by a period of instability, with premature departures from his next two ships, and a series of short voyages on a number of different vessels.

In the late 1940s, the handsome twenty-eight-year-old mariner met Norma Louise Michalitsianos, whose Greek father and Scots-Irish mother had endowed her with good looks and an agile mind. Her father, a ship's chandler, died when she was only thirteen. One of four children, she was not able to stay in school and develop her academic talent. She was immediately attracted to the tall, bright sailor, whom she describes as "a perfect gentleman," and it was not long before they were engaged, and then married. Good things were happening to Tapscott, a step toward the normal life he sought. He did not tell his new wife about his harrowing World War II experience. In November 1950, Tapscott signed off of the

MV *Naranio* in Lagos, Nigeria, because of illness. As a "distressed British Seaman" in a foreign port, he was transported back to England on the MV *Accra*. On the bright side, the very bright side, in the early fifties, Bob and Norma Tapscott added a new member to their family, with the birth of their daughter, Diane.

The life of a sailor is difficult for families because of the long absences. Diane recalls that it seemed her father was always gone. It appears that Tapscott was content while at sea, but that he was often depressed and moody ashore. He had trouble sleeping both at sea and ashore. He was also sensitive about wasting food, having nearly starved to death. His daughter remembers that he always ate everything served to him and urged her to do the same, reminding her, "You never know when you'll get your next meal." The 1950s passed without Norma knowing what Tapscott had endured and was still coping with.

Those who sailed with Tapscott were also conscious of his moodiness and often found him gazing vacantly out to sea. He rolled his own cigarettes, and spent sleepless hours on deck at night. He earned the respect and friendship of his shipmates, and was known as a man who was not afraid to stand up for what was right, even if that involved a fight. On the *Anglo-Saxon* and on a later vessel, he had taken the crews' complaints about the food to the higher authorities, and on at least one occasion when one of his shipmates was being discriminated against in a Newport News, Virginia, bar, he stood up for his shipmate and physically took on the other man. On another occasion, a man in a pub who had heard something of his jolly-boat voyage called him "Lifeboat Billy." Tapscott's response was immediate and violent.

In the late 1950s, Tapscott stopped going on voyages to foreign lands and worked locally on small coastal vessels, including serving as the Bosun on an excursion boat out of Swansea. This was a far cry from his travels to exotic ports around the globe, and the adjustment was difficult. Occasionally, he put his sailor's skills to work ashore, as when Chipperfield's Circus came to Cardiff and called on his skills as a rigger to assist with the raising of the big top.

The symptoms of people suffering from post-traumatic stress disorder often seem to increase in intensity at middle age, and this appears to have been the case with Tapscott. The diagnosis by the Canadian Army doctors, at the 1st Neurological Hospital in Basingstoke in 1942, that Bob Tapscott suffered from "Anxiety Neurosis," was inadequate because of the lack of medical knowledge at the time. Today PTSD is recognized as a severely debilitating disorder. Tapscott had all of the symptoms. He had endured a life-threatening trauma, the first criteria in assessing the disorder. Avoidance of the issue is another symptom, illustrated by his refusal to talk about his ordeal. Hyperreactivity and emotional extremes are other key indicators. Tapscott worked hard to remain steady and lead a normal life, but his periods of stability alternated with occasional "rage responses," as in the Newport News bar and the "Lifeboat Billy" incident. Insomnia is a common element in the lives of those dealing with PTSD, an effort to avoid the haunting dreams of reexperiencing the trauma.

The final component of the disorder is that it "is also associated with impairment of the person's ability to function in social or family life, including occupational instability." The effects of this aspect of the disorder are seen in the record of Tapscott's employment, with uncompleted voyages and the variety of jobs he held in the late 1950s and early '60s. He was often gripped by deep depression.

The maritime hero did not get the ongoing medical support and counseling he needed and deserved. The Canadian Army doctors had recommended both psychotherapy and occupational therapy for him, but there was a prevailing sense in the military that psychotherapy applied during World War I had actually created more neurosis than it cured, and there is no evidence that he was ever treated. Instead, he was discharged from the military in Canada to cope on his own. This he did, remarkably well, for twenty years. When he reached midlife, however, his problems compounded.

Tapscott's depression mounted. In 1962, he finally told his wife and young daughter about the ordeal he had experienced two decades before. In the spring of 1963, he had difficulty finding employment after work for the sand and gravel company of F. Bowles & Sons was completed. Apparently, it grew to be too much for him. He had witnessed several suicides while in the jolly boat, and he and Widdicombe had made halfhearted attempts themselves. That June, he was found in a gas-filled room. Tapscott's apparent attempt at suicide was unsuccessful, and he was taken to Cardiff's Whitchurch Hospital, highly respected for its mental health expertise. This was an opportunity for him to get the specialized care he needed to deal with what was described as "paralytic depression." Tapscott spent seven weeks in the hospital, where under the care of the specialists it is probable that the barbiturate sodium amytal was used in his treatment. The drug had been developed by the Eli Lilly company in the late twenties and was experimented with in the early 1940s by Dr. William Sargant. Sargant was assigned not to the Army, but to the British Emergency Medical Service, where he used the drug with considerable success in easing the trauma of civilian victims of the blitz, but his approach had not filtered through to help Tapscott while he was in the Canadian Neurological Hospital. Given in controlled therapeutic settings, the drug helps the patient relax and talk about issues that have been bottled up and assists the therapist in drawing out the deep anxieties of the traumatized patient. Sodium amytal is also used as a sleeping pill, and it is likely that Tapscott was prescribed a supply of these when he was released from the hospital.

It is known today that the depression associated with post-traumatic stress disorder is not always relieved by antidepressant drugs. Apparently, this was the case for Tapscott. Within a matter of weeks of his release from Whitchurch Hospital, he wrote and mailed a cogent, well-written letter to the South Wales Echo newspaper and then took advantage of the fact that his wife and daughter were out of the house visiting Norma's mother. As described in the South Wales Echo, he seems to have accidentally set the sofa in the parlor of his home on fire with a cigarette or match and then moved to another chair in the room. There, Robert George Tapscott, age forty-two, consumed three boxes of sodium amytal tablets and ended his tortured life.

As Norma and Diane recall the grim time, they arrived at their South Clive Street residence and realized the windows were hot and soot-covered. Knowing something was wrong, Norma summoned Cardiff Police Constable Raymond Hopkins. Disregarding his own safety, Hopkins forced his way into the smoke-filled house. He stumbled over the body of Bob Tapscott, which he immediately dragged out into the back garden. He realized that Tapscott was dead and raced back into the house, where he beat down the flames and got the situation under control. On September 10, 1963, the *South Wales Echo* carried a front-page story under the headline "War Hero Found Dead in City House Blaze." In death, Tapscott's wartime heroism, which he had suppressed for so long, was once more front-page news.

Within a day or two, the editor of the newspaper received Bob Tapscott's letter explaining his suicide. With appropriate respect and restraint, the paper did not publish the full contents of the letter, but rather gave it to the Coroner, Gerald Tudor, responsible for investigating the death. On October 3, 1963, the paper reported the results of the Coroner's Inquest, which were that Bob Tapscott had committed suicide and that his death had been caused by a combination of sodium amytal and carbon monoxide poisoning. Coroner Tudor commended Constable Hopkins for his bravery in attempting to rescue Tapscott and also thanked the editor of the newspaper, Mr. Geoff Rich, for promptly forwarding the letter.

The full contents of the letter were not released, but the two key points were made public. Tapscott had said he was going to kill himself but asserted that he was not insane. The last point was emphasized by the Coroner. Bob Tapscott used the same logical reasoning that those in the jolly boat had. In evaluating his situation, he had apparently concluded that the depression brought on by that ordeal was too difficult to bear. Just like those earlier compatriots in the boat, there seemed to be three motivations for Tapscott's act; first, wanting to end the continuing torment; second, the inability to envision a positive future and wanting to take control of life and end it on their own terms rather than face a decline they could not tolerate; finally, making a gift to those around them by removing a burden in their lives. As with the others, those who cared for Bob Tapscott, particularly Norma and twelve-year-old Diane, would not have wanted such a gift from Bob. In the mind of this strong man who had endured so much, however, it is doubtful that he could see anything but a dark future, which he didn't want to inflict on those he loved.

The day after the paper covered the Coroner's report, it ran a major story with the headline "War Hero's Death Was Grand Design in Irony." The intent of the article was to encourage the people of Cardiff to consider Tapscott as not simply a man who committed suicide, but as the merchant mariner who had risked his life and suffered horrendously in doing his part to keep England and her cause alive during the worst time of the war, England's finest hour. The article must have been of consolation to Tapscott's widow and daughter. His funeral was private, and Norma was grateful that the expenses were covered by the Canadian War Veterans Association, in appreciation for Tapscott's voluntary service in the Canadian Army twenty years earlier. There was no time for Norma to collapse in her grief, as she had to get a job to provide for herself and her daughter. Diane had burdens of her own with which to cope during the three weeks between her father's death and the Coroner's report. Thoughtless and insensitive schoolmates dwelled upon the rumored suicide, which at the time carried a social stigma, and Diane felt the sting.

Bob Tapscott's death was caused by the wound he carried for over twenty years. In the aftermath of the war, people frequently encountered those visibly maimed by their wounds and felt respect, sympathy, and indebtedness. Bob Tapscott's wound was invisible and he did all he could to keep it that way, but it was no less real. His wound could not heal but instead festered during those decades, allowing its poison to surge through his system just as lethally as gangrene had spread through Roy Pilcher, until it killed him. Ultimately, his country would come to recognize his heroism, suffering, and sacrifice.

On September 10, 1963, fifteen years after his own death, Hellmuth von Ruckteschell had claimed his final victim from the *Anglo-Saxon*.

Chapter 23

SURVIVORS

With the death of Bob Tapscott, the *Anglo-Saxon* and all who were onboard that August night in 1940 were gone. The story of that ship and those men remains alive through the families and friends who survived them and through those who work to carry the story of those brave sailors forward for future generations. Many mothers and fathers lost their sons in the sinking, thirteen wives lost their husbands, and a number of children had their fathers taken from them.

Captain Paddy Flynn left his wife, Monica, but no children, behind. Monica Flynn, who became somewhat reclusive in her home in Sutton, Surrey, after the war, had carried on with her teaching during the war years. She also continued in her role as the Captain's wife and attempted to console the wives of officers from the *Anglo-Saxon*. In 1941, she wrote to Ethel Milburn giving sympathy, inquiring after the Milburn boys, and offered encouragement by saying, "Take courage, dear Mrs. Milburn, in the consoling thought that they gave their lives for all that is right and good. . . ."

Ted and Derek Milburn left their mother and home to attend the Royal Merchant Navy School. In 1947, at age sixteen, Ted was awarded the "Norisian Prize for manliness and honour" by his future Queen, then Princess Elizabeth. The Milburn family was again touched by the Royal

Family when an envelope containing an illuminated scroll arrived at Ethel Milburn's home. It was one of many that were sent "by Command of the King," and it commemorated "E. E. Milburn, Chief Engineer Merchant Navy, held in honour as one who served King and Country in the world war of 1939–1945 and gave his life to save mankind from tyranny. May his sacrifice help to bring the peace and freedom for which he died."

Both Ted and Derek pursued full careers in the Merchant Navy, Ted as a Radio Officer and Derek completing his career as a Master. Since his retirement in 1989, Ted has created a remarkable archive on the *Anglo-Saxon* and has developed friendships with others who share his interest. Through Derek's three sons, another generation of Milburns carries forward the family memories of Eddie Milburn and the *Anglo-Saxon*.

Jim Fowler's niece, Betty, never forgot her favorite uncle. The rosary that she purchased for him, which he left in her care as he boarded the *Anglo-Saxon,* remained her most treasured possession, which she always carried with her. When her purse was stolen, the two things most dear to her were gone: her husband's Navy cap band bearing the name HMS *Venerable,* which she had kept since their first meeting, and Jim Fowler's rosary. Two days later, a builder called to say he had found her purse at a construction site and would bring it back to her. With her husband, Mac McAteer, hovering over her, she searched the purse and found her treasures.

In 2001, Betty McAteer booked a cruise from England to the Mediterranean in the P&O Line ship *Victoria* and confided in the Cruise Director that this was not simply a pleasure cruise for her; she had a mission. At 7:50 P.M. on Sunday, July 1, 2001, the Cruise Director interrupted Betty's dinner and discreetly led her out of the dining room and aft toward the stern of the ship, where the ship's officers and a clergyman who was on board had assembled. Amid the honor guard of merchant mariners, Betty McAteer let the rosary slide over the side into the Atlantic to rejoin her Uncle Jim, sixty-one years after his death. Betty, her son Niel, daughter Lesley, and Lesley's son Jamie, who carries his great uncle's name, carry on the memory of Jim Fowler.

The ship's First Mate, Barry Denny, inspired the men in the jolly boat until his own health severely deteriorated. His leadership and sacrifice is remembered by his brother, Desmond Denny, a member of a British Army tank regiment during the war, who worked most of his life near Tower Hill and the Merchant Marine Memorial that bears his brother's name, along with the others who perished with the *Anglo-Saxon*. Desmond and his wife, Joan, have regularly attended the memorial service there on Remembrance Day, while most of the nation's attention is directed toward the extensive ceremony at the Cenotaph, with the Monarch and other dignitaries present. Barry Denny was not married, but his memory is carried on by a niece and nephew living in Australia.

When approached by the *Evening Chronicle* of Newcastle, in November 1940, Lionel Hawks's parents were described as "prostrate with grief" and "too overcome to make any statement." They and his sister, Margaret, carried his loss with them for the rest of their lives.

Nothing is known of the reaction of the family of Leslie Morgan, Widdicombe's neighbor on Lewis Street in Newport, Wales, whose story seems to have been overwhelmed by Widdicombe's survival in the jolly boat and subsequent death in the sinking of the *Siamese Prince*. It is thought that a sister still survives.

Roy Pilcher's sister, Beryl, came to the United States while working in the British diplomatic service in the 1950s, and made the pilgrimage to Mystic Seaport to see the boat in which her brother suffered and died. Roy's good friend Cliff Walder married his sweetheart, Daphne, and together they never forgot their friend Roy. Cliff kept the letter Roy had written to him, which survived the jolly-boat voyage in Pilcher's attaché case. Recently, Cliff Walder donated the letter, stained by seawater, to the Imperial War Museum in London, where it rejoins the jolly boat. With the death of Roy Pilcher, Marion Wastell lost her sweetheart. She later married and emigrated to Canada, where she lives today.

Royal Marine Francis Penny had retired in the 1930s to the naval town of Portsmouth, where the great traditions of the Royal Navy have been present since before the time of Henry VIII. It was at his Reginald Street home there that his wife, Edith, received the news that her "retired" Marine, who had been serving his country in his second global conflict, had been lost. He was mourned by Edith and his children, and his memory is carried on today by his daughter-in-law, Emily Penny, her son, Kevin, and her daughter, Ros.

For most, the tragic figure of the story of the *Anglo-Saxon* is Roy Widdicombe's young bride, Cynthia, symbolic of the countless war widows, not only of World War II, but of all conflicts. After she and Roy courted and married, she had only four months with him before he headed back to sea to be lost, then found, and lost again. Cynthia's spirit survived, and in August of 1945 she married Ronald C. Gill, a widower who was completing his wartime service in the Royal Navy, and they had a son and daughter. Cynthia has passed away, but her daughter, Sue Irvine, sustains family interest in their heritage, which includes Cynthia's marriage to Roy Widdicombe. Sue's three children carry his story on to future generations.

Bob Tapscott's widow, Norma, lives in Cardiff, where she and Bob spent their years together. Norma has been an active participant in keeping the story of the *Anglo-Saxon* alive. Their daughter, Diane, would be a point of pride to Bob, who didn't live to know the fine woman she has become. Diane works for NATO and lives near Brussels with her husband and two sons, who know the story of the heroism, suffering, and sacrifice of their grandfather.

As a youth during the war, Anthony Smith read Guy Pearce Jones's book *Two Survived,* which made a lasting impression on him. Anthony went on to a life of adventure, ballooning, motorcycling across Africa, and writing many books, while also being heard on the BBC. In 1990, commemorating the fiftieth anniversary of the sinking of the *Anglo-Saxon,* he broadcast the story on the radio, which was heard by tens of thousands, including Desmond Denny, the brother of the First Mate. A correspondence began, which led to contact with Ted Milburn, who had begun his own search for information on the event. Working together, the three men attempted to find out what had happened to the jolly boat herself and locate as many of the relatives of the *Anglo-Saxon* mariners as possible.

They found relatives and friends of 13 of the *Anglo-Saxon* crew. Through leads in Nassau, they discovered that the boat had survived and was being preserved at Mystic Seaport in Connecticut. Joined in the effort by Norma Tapscott, they approached the museum with the request that the boat be returned to England. Mystic Seaport, whose mission had evolved to be the Museum of America and the Sea, was willing to transfer the boat, a process that took several years to carry out. Eventually, the issues of ownership, title, transportation, and which museum would receive the boat were settled. In 1997, the P&O Nedlloyd Lines sent a 20-foot container to the Preservation Shipyard at Mystic Seaport, where the jolly boat was carefully eased into the container for the completion of a voyage that had begun fifty-seven years before. A few weeks later, on November 17, 1997, Ted Milburn stood at the port in Felixstowe as the container was opened and he saw the carefully cradled jolly boat for the first time since 1939, when he was a child on board the *Anglo-Saxon*.

Anthony Smith championed the cause, Ted Milburn instigated the search and moved the effort along, and Norma Tapscott played a persuasive role in the jolly boat's becoming the key object in the Imperial War Museum's exhibition on the Merchant Navy in the Second World War, entitled "Survival at Sea." Anthony Smith has chronicled this story, with all the details of searching for the relatives and the boat itself, in his book *Survived*, which he published in 1998.

The *Anglo-Saxon*'s adversary, the *Widder*, survived the war as a supply ship and was first turned over to Britain as a war reparation before transferring to Greek ownership as part of the war settlement. In 1947, she began three years of work for the Ionian Maritime of Piraeus as the *Ulysses*. In 1950, she was sold back into German hands and named the *Fechenheim*. For the next five years, she operated as a tramp, until she went aground off Bergen, Norway, on October 3, 1955, and was broken up the following year, ending a twenty-six-year career.

George Duffy was one of the many men who had been prisoners aboard Ruckteschell's ships and turned over to the Japanese. He survived his three-year ordeal of imprisonment and forced labor. No news of his fate reached his family until ham radio operators around the United States picked up a Japanese broadcast that mentioned George Duffy as a POW. On postcards, they sent his mother the news that her son, who had been missing at sea, was alive. After Duffy was liberated and returned to the United States at the end of the war, he renewed his merchant marine career and was in Hamburg, Germany, in May of 1947, when he read in a German newspaper that Hellmuth von Ruckteschell was on trial for war crimes there.

Forty years after the end of the war, on July 19, 1985, George Duffy visited Germany and the home of Konrad Hoppe, whom he had met while a prisoner on the *Michel*. Hoppe expressed his "deep regret for the distress and torture inflicted by the *Michel* to the crews of the sunken merchantmen," and expressed his "great delight that the fateful enmity has changed into sincere friendship," a friendship that has deepened over the years.

After leaving the *Michel* in Japan, Konrad Hoppe spent the rest of the war in Batavia, in the former Dutch colony of Indonesia, where he married a European woman, Louise Mathus, who had been born there. As a German citizen and former officer in the Kriegsmarine, he spent time in a prison camp before he was sent back to Germany aboard the troopship *Sloter Dyck* in 1946 and was then released into civilian life. Because his wife was born abroad, and with the postwar political changes, she was declared stateless. Given the choice of Indonesian or Dutch citizenship, she chose Dutch and was able to join Konrad in West Germany, where, as the decades passed with peace and prosperity, they established a good life for themselves and their son and daughter. Although his wife has died, Konrad continues to lead a very active life, visiting the United States and Canada every year and sustaining his friendship with George Duffy.

A fellow officer from the *Michel* remains in contact with Hoppe and shares the friendship with George Duffy. After leaving the *Michel*, Adjutant Jürgen Herr spent the remainder of the war assigned to a language school in Japan. There he met a German woman, Margaret (Gretl) Steinbeiss, employed at the German Embassy in Tokyo. They were married on May 10, 1945, and after the war were interned in Japan. Their treatment was anything but harsh, as they were assigned to an idyllic Japanese house in the hills above the resort community of Hakone, which had a view of Mt. Fuji from the bedroom. This peaceful existence was short-lived, and in March of 1947 they were returned to Germany by ship. A baby girl was born to the Herrs two years after their return, but tragically Gretl died during childbirth. Fortunately, it was not long before Herr met Liesl Drotl, who became his wife and the only mother his daughter, Ute, has ever known. Jürgen Herr faced the difficulties experienced throughout war-torn Europe, eventually finding work in the automotive industry. Jürgen and Liesl have been married for over fifty years, during which time the family has sustained close ties to the United States, where his two grandsons attended Kent School, as he did in the 1930s. A meticulous archivist, he has methodically chronicled the history of his family and gathered copious information about Hellmuth von Ruckteschell, including this curious detail.

Sometime after Ruckteschell's death, a German naval officer named Hellmuth Drews approached his widow and other members of the family and presented his "family credentials." He asserted that he was Hellmuth von Ruckteschell's son with the dancer Agnes Schmidt. The von Ruckteschell family concluded that he was indeed a son that Ruckteschell did not know existed and accepted him as part of the family. At his death in 1995, a stone was placed next to his father's, which reads "Hellmuth Drews von Ruckteschell, 1918–1995."

Through the efforts of Ted Milburn, Anthony Smith, Norma Tapscott, and others, and the Imperial War Museum in London, the single surviving British relic of that August night in 1940 is preserved and displayed for all to experience. It is a reverential experience to be in the presence of this powerful object. The small boat radiates history. It is not enough to approach her, read the label, and move on to the rest of the exhibit. Stand and contemplate all that is embodied in this vessel. In looking at the boat, think about the boatbuilders on the Tyne who crafted this classic ship's jolly boat. Think about the design and strength of the boat that enabled her and the men in her to cross the ocean and contend with the destructive force of an Atlantic cyclone. Consider her size and envision seven men, three of them seriously wounded, trying to find comfort in the crowded confines of the small space. Study the notches carved by Barry Denny in the rail at the port quarter and realize what each of those notches represents: a day full of hopes and fears for the men struggling for survival on the open ocean. The notches were Denny's personal mark on history and mark the last days of his life.

One must stand in awe and contemplate what happened within the space that this boat represents. Think about the horror the men witnessed as they saw the lights on the distant rafts snuffed out. Honor the stoic, heroic, gentle man, Roy Pilcher, and remember his suffering as gangrene took his life in the boat. Salute the thrice-wounded Royal Marine, Gunner Penny, as he acknowledged his grim future and ended his life, leaving a bit of extra water for the others. Reflect on the fateful conversations that led the ill and weakened Denny and young Hawks to go over the side together, sharing the final act. Consider the deranged Morgan and the muddled story of his demise. And finally ponder the raw instinct to live that provided the fortitude for Tapscott and Widdicombe to complete the remarkable voyage, with the boat coming to rest on the sands of Eleuthera.

The *Anglo-Saxon*'s jolly boat represents all this and more. It is right that she has an honored place in a distinguished museum where hundreds of thousands of visitors will be touched by her power. She stands in tribute to all those who sailed in the *Anglo-Saxon* so many years ago and who gave their lives in the service of King, Country, and the World.

Afterword

The story of the men from the *Anglo-Saxon* lives on and will not be forgotten. The *Anglo-Saxon* was but one of thousands of ships of the Allied merchant navy during World War II. Among the more than 3,000 ships that were lost during the war and the tens of thousands of merchant mariners who died, there were many whose stories will never be known. Hundred of ships disappeared without a trace, and each of them undoubtedly had her own tale of heroic acts, self-sacrifice, desperation, suffering, and a trail of tears shed by those left behind who would never know what happened to their loved ones.

The *Anglo-Saxon* could have easily been one of those ships that simply vanished, but her story lives and stands as a tribute to all lost ships and all brave sailors.

S.S. *Anglo-Saxon* Crew List
Final Voyage — August 1940

NAME	CAPACITY	PLACE OF BIRTH	AGE
FLYNN, Philip R. L.	Master	Plymouth	53
DENNY, Barry C.	Mate	London	31
DUNCAN, Alistair St.C	2nd Mate	Stromness	28
PICKFORD, Walter M.	3rd Mate	Wallasey	30
O'LEARY, Michael	1st Radio Off.	Killarney	48
PILCHER, Roy H.	2nd Radio Off.	Durham	21
HANSEN, Oscar W.	Carpenter	Denmark	47
MAHER, Thomas F.	Bosun	Duncannon	34
ELLIOTT, Stanley G.	A.B.	Nantyglo	22
WIDDICOMBE, Roy W. C.	Sailor	Totnes	21
BRESLER, Aldolphus	A.B.	Russia	45
SMITH, Alfred E.	Sailor	Grimsby	41
SAVORY, Robert	Sailor	Grimsby	33
ALLNATT, Walter R. T. L.	A.B.	Fleetwood	28
GORMLEY, James J.	Sailor	Monaghan	24
PROWSE, William F.	O.S.	Newport	18
TAKLE, Philip J.	O.S.	Cardiff	16
PENNY, Francis G.	Gunner	Mortimer	44
TAPSCOTT, Robert G.	A.B.	Bristol	19
MILBURN, Edward E.	Chief Engineer	North Shields	39
HOUSTON, John I.	2nd Engineer	Lisburn	55
HAWKS, Lionel H.	3rd Engineer	Dudley	23
RICE, Thomas A.	4th Engineer	South Shields	20

NICHOLAS, Alfred J.	Donkeyman	Plymouth	37
FOWLER, James	Greaser	Newport	37
WILLIAMS, Charles H.	Greaser	Barry	29
WILLIAMS, David J.	F/Trimmer	Barry	20
GREEN, Verdun C.	F/Trimmer	Barry	24
ELEY, Albert	F/Trimmer	Swansea	26
TENOW, Frederick	F/Trimmer	Estonia	58
RASMUSSEN, Lars C.	F/Trimmer	Denmark	53
STUART, Charles	F/Trimmer	Newport	44
PEASTON, John D.	F/Trimmer	West Ham	29
WALLACE, Charles J.	F/Trimmer	Newport	21
OLIVER, Andres	F/Trimmer	Unknown	26
TOBIN, M.	F/Trimmer	Unknown	35
WILLIS, Harry A.	Chief Steward	Newport	40
WARD, George W.	Asst. Steward	South Shields	19
BEDFORD, George	Cook	Newport	21
MORGAN, Leslie J.	Asst. Cook	Newport	20
KEYSE, Trevor	Mess Room Steward	Newport	19

Notes for crew list:

Abbreviations: A.B. – Able Seaman; O.S. – Ordinary Seaman; F/Trimmer – Fireman/Trimmer

Charles Williams and David Williams were brothers who were lost on the *Anglo-Saxon*.

This list was compiled from the original ship's articles and other documents by Ted Milburn, son of E. E. Milburn, Chief Engineer.

Appendix A: Comparable Naval Ranks

In comparing the ranks of officers in the German, United States, and British navies below the flag ranks, there are slight variations in the insignia designating the ranks but for the most part they are equivalent. The British use the one rank of Sub Lieutenant to cover two ranks of the German and United States navies.

The ranks are designated as follows:

GERMAN	UNITED STATES	BRITISH
Kapitän zur See	Captain	Captain
Fregattenkapitän	Commander	Commander
Korvettenkapitän	Lieutenant Commander	Lieutenant Commander
Kapitänleutnant	Lieutenant	Lieutenant
Oberleutnant zur See	Lieutenant Junior Grade	Sub Lieutenant
Leutnant zur See	Ensign	Sub Lieutenant
Fähnrich zur See	Midshipman	Midshipman

Appendix B: The Log of the *Anglo-Saxon* Jolly Boat

Nassau, N.P.
November 2nd 1940.

Enclosure to A. & W. I. submission No. 938/629/7
Of R. M. Millar to the Secretary of the Admiralty.

Commander in Chief,
America & West Indies Station,
Bermuda.

Sir,

Acting upon instructions received from the Colonial Secretary of the Bahamas, I have the honour to enclose copy of a report covering the sinking of the S.S. Anglo Saxon by an armed enemy raider on August 21st 1940,

2. The Colonial Secretary has I believe, cabled you that a full report is being sent by mail, this is the report to which he refers.

3. After a report of the landing of these two men had been received, the Colonial Secretary took charge of the matter and released the information to the Press, under the circumstances I considered it unnecessary for me to incur further expense by cabling.

I have the honour to be,
Sir,
Your obedient servant,

R. M. Millar

Reporting Officer.

Nassau, N.P.

November 2nd 1940

Commander in Chief,
    America and West Indies Station
        Bermuda.

Sinking of S.S. Anglo Saxon by armed German raider on
<u>August 21st 1940 at Lat. 26. 10 N. Long. 34. 09. W</u>

Sir,

On Wednesday October 30th a ships boat containing two men came ashore on the Island of Eleuthera. The men were discovered lying on the beach in an advanced state of exhaustion, by a farmer named Martin who was working in a field nearby and had seen the boat approaching. He obtained help and the men were removed to Governors Harbour and the resident Commissioner reported the circumstances to the Colonial Secretary at Nassau, who issued instructions for their removal to the hospital in Nassau by aeroplane, the Chief Medical Officer went with the plane from Nassau and they were brought back and placed in hospital the next day, although in a very weakened and emaciated condition every hope is entertained of a rapid recovery.

2.   The men, Wilbert Roy Widdicombe and Robert Tapscott were able seamen on the S.S. Anglo Saxon, 5000 tons, of the Lawther Latta line, bound from Newport, Mon to Bahia Blanca with a cargo of coal, they are apparently, the sole survivors of a crew numbering about 40.

3.   They had with them in the boat, three pocket books containing papers, the property of the junior wireless Officer Pilcher, these were delivered to the Colonial Secretary who turned them over to me for examination. Among these papers I found a rough log kept by the Chief Officer B. C. Denny from the time the boat was launched up to a short time before his death, a few entries were made subsequently by Widdicombe, A.B. As the events recorded therein tell the story of this frightful outrage by the German raider, I give it in full as follows: -

<u>August 21st 1940.</u> At 8.20 p.m. in Lat 26. 10 N. Long. 34. 09 W. attacked by German raider assumed by crew to be S.S. Weser or Weber, Hamburg America line. Vessel was not sighted until she had steamed to

318

within a mile of us. Pitch black night. First sent four shells 4 inch crashing into poop and gun platform aft. Many of crew in fo'castle were killed. She then steamed to within 3 cables and raked the decks with incendiary machine gun bullets coloured red, yellow, white and blue. Then a shell hit engine room starboard side and main boiler burst. The bridge and wireless room were raked with Pom-pom shells and machine gun bullets. Some of the crew went to boats on boat deck but were mowed down by machine gun fire. The two big boats were badly damaged. Senior wireless operator reported wireless installations smashed, unable to send S.O.S. On reporting to Master found him presumed shot down by machine gun bullets in his cabin, saloon amidships was wrecked, poop by this time blazing and the crew few in number were told to take to the boats. The port gig under my orders was lowered and contained seven of the crew comprising, Chief Officer C.B. Denny, 3rd Engineer H.L. Hawkes, 2nd W/T Officer R.H. Pilcher, A.B. Widdicombe, W.R., A.B. Tapscott, R.G., Gunlayer F. Penny, Assistant Cook L. Morgan, of whom the 2nd operator was badly injured in the left foot by gun fire and 2nd cook in right foot, while gun layer was shot through right forearm and right leg.

When gig pulled away from the vessel the raider was lying off a half mile to port and a few minutes later fired tracer bullets in to two life rafts launched from vessel. The vessel sunk stern first and shortly disappeared altogether. Raider headed off to the eastward. Assumed that Germans wanted no members of the crew left alive and were fortunate in this boats crew escaping observation. We lay hoved to all night with sea anchors out and at dawn could see no trace of any description. Having no instruments for navigation except boat compass we set sail dipping lug and course started west to make W.S.W time, trusting to God's good grace to either finding a vessel en route or striking somewhere in the Carribean Sea.

<u>Thursday August 22nd 1940.</u> Wind N.E. 3. slight sea, slightly confused easterly swell. Course by compass W. All's well. Medical treatment given.
<u>August 23rd Friday.</u> Wind E.N.E 3. slight sea, slightly confused easterly swell, partly cloudy. Half a dipper of water per man 6 a.m. also half a biscuit with a little condensed milk. Sighted a vessel showing no lights at 11 p.m. showed sea flare, she cruised around but was of opinion she was a raider as she was heading N.N.E. We were about 100 miles from our original position. Kept quiet and let her go off.
<u>August 24th Saturday.</u> 85´ Crews spirits cheerful, wind N.W. 3/4 cloudy,

stering S.W. time. Issued half a dipper of water to each man and half a
biscuit, hoping for rain showers.

August 25th Sunday. 24′ 12′ 36′. Crew all well though 2nd cook and 2nd
W/T wounded feet very painful and starting to swell. Rations half a dipper of water at 6 a.m. and again 6 p.m. with one biscuit per man per day,
with a little condensed milk, hoping for rain showers but none around
yet. Wind N.N.W 2 cloudy, slight sea. D/L sail set. Course W.S.W true.
Nothing sighted and becalmed all day long. 6 p.m. opened 6 pound tin of
boiled mutton, crew ate half which greatly improved their morale which
is splendid. No signs of giving up hope. Sun set at 6.35 A.T.S. on leaving
ship estimated distance covered 225 miles W.S.W true.

August 26th Monday. Bosun bird flew overhead. Sun rose at 6.52 a.m.
A.T.S. Becalmed occasional fitful gusts. Glaring sun rays. Bale out 24
buckets daily. 6 a.m. issued meat rations out from day previous, wrapped
up in canvas, little taken, half dipper of water per man, little drop of condensed milk, spirits of whole crew keen, no murmur from wounded
men. Hoping to sight vessel soon but praying for squalls and a decent
wind. During a.m. medical treatment given by 3rd Engineer and myself.
W/T operators left foot which is badly crushed bathed with salt water
for an hour and last linen bandage applied, well covered up but swelling
badly. 2nd cooks right foot swollen badly, ankle badly strained with bullet wound just above ankle, bathed with salt water and well bandaged.
Gunlayers right forearm washed first in fresh water, then iodine applied
and bandaged. All day long blinding suns rays and cloudless, becalmed.
During afternoon first officer, 3rd engineer, gunlayer, A.B.'s Widdicombe and Tapscott dipped their bodies in water overside, taking care to
keep their faces out of water, result greatly invigorating. Rations still half
dipper of water per man at 6 a.m. and 6 p.m., only eat half a biscuit per
day, no need for more, and a little condensed milk. The boiled beef kept
in canvas still good and the fat is appreciated. Although the W/T is
weak, everyone else in good spirits and very cheerful. Keeping two
watches, one myself other 3rd engineer, two A.B.'s, four on and four off.
Having no nautical instruments or books on board can only rely on the
compass and stars at night. Trusting to make a landfall in vicinity of Leeward Islands, with God's will and British determination. 10.30 p.m.
wind freshening from eastward skimming along fine at about 5 knots.

August 27th Tuesday. Wind E.N.E 3 to 4, partly cloudy, no rain yet. 6
a.m. ration given, half a dipper of water, no one felt hungry. Managed to
give each man a cigarette made out of newspaper and half a can of to-

bacco, but only 8 matches left so this luxury will soon be stopped. On
Port tack heading S.W. true making about four knots and throughout
night, held a lottery in evening as to who gave nearest date of being
sighted or making landfall. Sun set 6.42 p.m. A.T.S.

August 28th Wednesday. 160´ During afternoon Chief Officer, 3rd Engineer, Widdicimbe and Tapscott had a dip over side felt greatly improved as body absorbed the water leaving salt on the skin, saliva came to
the mouth which previously parched. Moderate to fresh E.N.E trade,
heading S.W. true. Bosun bird and ordinary black seagull flying around.

August 29th Thursday. On our eight day in the boat, crews spirits extremely cheerful. W/T operator weak owing to left leg going dead. Ration still half dipper of water per man 6 a.m. and p.m. Noon half a biscuit
with light condensed milk. Wind E.N.E 4, moderate sea and swell. Gig
running free or Port tack heading S.W. true. High hopes of picking up a
ship or making landfall shortly, we are all putting our trust in God's
hands, everyone is fit except a weakness in legs and of course great loss in
weight. Do not feel particularly hungry but suffer from parched throat
owing to low water ration, pity we have no lime juice or tins of fruit,
which would ease matters considerably, but no one is complaining. All
day long strong E.N.E wind with strong swell, shipping a little water
everywhere.

August 30th Friday. 50´ Moderate N.E. trades and swell, course W.S.W
true, rationed half a dipper of water at 6 a.m. and again at 6 p.m. now a
1/4 biscuit per man, hardly touched now owing to slim issue of water,
small issue of thin condensed milk, crews spirits cheerful but W/T op
getting weaker, during evening becoming becalmed, W/T op delirious
kept everyone awake at night with moans.

August 31st Saturday. 30´ Becalmed, partly cloudy, nothing sighted whatsoever, have not had one speck of rain yet but living in hopes. 6.15 a.m.
water issue half a dipper also at 6.30 p.m.. Opened our second tin boiled
mutton (six pounds) have one left, also five tins condensed milk and 3/4
case hard biscuits, water breaker half full, nine days in boat.

XXXXXXXXSeptember 1st, Sunday. 30´ During Saturday night crew
felt very thirsty, boiled mutton could not be digested and some felt sick,
doubled the water issue that night. 6.15 a.m. half a dipper of water per
man and same in p.m. Wind S.S.W 2 slight nrtly swell, steering West
true. W/T op failing slowly, hope to see something soon. 8 a.m. W/T operator R.N.Pilcher passed peacably away. Committed his body to the
deep with silent prayer.

Sept 2nd Monday. 6.15 a.m. issued half a dipper of water per man and same in the evening with a little condensed milk diluted with it. Wind E. 2 slight sea, steering W. true. Crew now feeling rather low, unable to masticate hard biscuit owing to low ration of water.

Suggestion for life boat stocks. At the very least two breakers of water for each boat, tins of fruit such as peaches, apricots, pears, fruit juices and lime juice, baked beans etc. Our stores consisted of:

> one tank filled with dry biscuit.
> 11 tins condensed milk.
> 3 tins each 6 pounds of boiled mutton.
> One breaker of water, XXXXXXXXXXXXXX half filled.

Note by R.O., at this point the writing is visibly much weaker and subsequent entries in different hand.

Sept 3rd Tuesday. 120′ One dipper of water per man at 7 a.m. and again in evening. Things going from bad to worse, 1st mate who wrote this diary up to this point going fast. Good breezes from E.S.E.

Sept 4th. 100′ Everybody very much weaker. The mate is going fast now. 1.30 p.m. Sunday, Penny very much weaker slipped overboard. From 10 p.m. tonight 14 days out, tried to make the Leeward Islands or Porto Rica, Hayti, but the German raider given none the right to take a sextant, chronometer, extrer water, tin fruit or bottled fruit, no rum or brandy for wounded crew. Evidently intended to smash all life boat gear to kill all inquiry, but we got the small gig, seven of us by wind somewhere in vicinity of Leeward Islands.

Sept 5th. Chief mate and 3rd Engineer go over the side no water.

Sept 9th. 2nd cook goes mad dies. Two of us left.

Sept 12th. A cloud burst gave us water for 6 days.

Sept 20th. Rain again for four days. Getting very weak put trusting in God to pull us though.

R. Widdicombe.

R. Tapscott.

Sept 24th. All water and biscuits gone but still hoping to make land. R.W..

   This concludes the entries in the log or diary which are corroborated by Widdicombe and Tapscott, who explain the fact that no entries were made after September 24th by saying that there was nothing to report, they simply drifted and sailed as best they could and that they were too weak to bother about keeping a log, a fact easily appreciated. There was an occasional shower of rain and once they succeeded in capturing a flying fish which landed in the boat.

Widdicombe was at the wheel and the 3rd Mate on the bridge when the ship was attacked, they had no idea that another ship was in the vicinity until the raider opened fire without any warning. According to Widdicombe the master Flynn was struck in the chest by machine gun bullets while in the act of dumping the ships papers overboard, he also said that the raider was the Hamburg American cargo liner Weser which he said he had seen before in the River Plate and he was able to identify the silhouette of the ship.

Both the men are without clothing or possessions of any kind, there was no time to collect anything before getting away in the boat, but arrangements are being made to provide them with whatever is necessary. They have given the names of their next of kin, who on the instructions of H.R.H. the Governor, were notified immediately by cable through the Secretary of State for the Colonies.

I have the honour to be,

Sir,

Your obedient servant,

<u>R.M. Millar</u>

Capt.
Reporting Officer.

Notes

PART I

1: ATTACK

The attack of the *Widder* on the *Anglo-Saxon* is documented in a number of sources. Primary among these are:

The War Diary of *Schiff 21 (Widder)* for the dates of Aug. 21 and 22, 1940. This was the official deck log kept onboard the *Widder* at the time of the engagement.

Hellmuth von Ruckteschell, "Operations and Tactics, Analysis of Important Events in Sea Warfare, Booklet 8, The Voyage of the Hilfskreuzer 'Ship 21' [*Widder*]," Berlin, May 1943. This is the Captain's summary and analysis of his entire cruise in the *Widder,* prepared after the completion of the voyage.

Testimony of Ruckteschell and a number of other witnesses during his war crimes trial in Hamburg in 1947. The 900-page record of that trial is preserved in H. M. Public Records Office in Kew, London.

Exhibit "A.F." from the above trial record, which is Ruckteschell's reconstruction of the courses and speeds of the two ships from the moment of first sighting, through the attack, and up to the *Widder*'s departure from the scene.

Exhibit "Y" from the trial record, which is a drawing by Ruckteschell from the perspective of the witnesses in the jolly boat, showing the *Anglo-Saxon* and the *Widder*.

Exhibit "Z" from the trial record, which is Ruckteschell's reconstruction of the relative positions of the two ships, the rafts, and the jolly boat during the time of the alleged firing upon the rafts.

The log maintained onboard the *Anglo-Saxon* jolly boat during its voyage, typescript copies of which can be found in several repositories, including the Public Records Office, Kew, and Mystic Seaport, Mystic, CT (see Appendix B).

Guy Pearce Jones, *Two Survived* (New York: Random House, 1941). This is a book that the journalist Jones published based on extensive interviews with the survivors of the jolly-boat voyage.

Numerous newspaper and magazine articles that appeared on both sides of the Atlantic in the months following the rescue of the survivors.

See notes for chapter 8 for specific references.

2: THE CATALYST

21 *When later asked what:* Ruckteschell War Crimes Trial Record, p. 753.

22 *When this stealthy weapon:* Corbett, *History of the Great War,* vol. 2, p. 393.

23 *Before the war, in 1913:* Churchill, *The World Crisis,* vol. ii, p. 280.

23 *There were instances in:* Slader, *The Red Duster at War,* p. 22.

24 *In the spring of 1916:* Hough, *The Great War at Sea,* pp. 176–77.

24 The descriptions of the activities of the three U-boats in which von Ruckteschell served are drawn from Spindler, *Der Krieg zur See.* Translated by Olaf Griese.

27 *During the spring of 1917:* Knowledge of this relationship comes from the author's visit to the von Ruckteschell family grave site in the Ohlsdorf Cemetery, in Hamburg, and from personal correspondence with Jürgen Herr.

28 *"Still at a depth of 30 meters":* Spindler, *Der Krieg zur See,* p. 293.

32 *He states that after the capture:* The following is the full text of Otto Wiedemann's statement in File TS 26/51 in the Public Records Office, Kew:

Translation of written statement by Otto Wiedemann, concerning German submarine atrocities during the war.

AMSTERDAM, May 26th 1921

Account of the treatment of prisoners of war by the German U. boat commander, 1st Lieut. von Ruckteschell, in command of the S.M.U. 54.

———————————

One afternoon during the last operations before the revolution of September–October 1918, in the western limit of the English Channel (indicated as point X), shortly after coming to the surface, having previously in the morning been obliged to submerge by a British airship, we sighted a small sailing vessel (? French).

As far as I can recollect we fired a warning and hoisted the international signal M N (stop immediately). The sailing vessel, however, did not stop but commenced to tack and disappeared behind a smoke screen, upon which the commander ordered us to open fire. Our shots were replied to by the small calibre guns of the sailing vessel and after about 15 rounds her foremast was shot away and she ceased to resist, her crew taking to their boat. Having made sure that there was no one left on the sailing vessel we approached the small boat and took the crew on board the submarine. After having blown up the sailing vessel our crew returned. As a heavy sea was now running the prisoners were kept aft behind the conning tower. The commander asked me, as former helmsman, whether under the circumstances I considered it possible to close the conning tower hatch. This question strengthened me in the belief that the commander intended to abandon the prisoners to the sea without any attempt at saving life. The commander detecting in my answer strong objections to his plan covered me with a loaded pistol and ordered me to descend. Immediately afterwards giving the order to submerge. When the 'ready to submerge' was sounded he closed the conning tower hatch under cover of the pistol in his hand and ordered 'complete submerging'.

When after about half an hour we rose to the surface again no trace of the prisoners was to be seen.

Other occurrences which I cannot now recollect are entered in the log of S.M.U.54.

Former Master's Mate,

S.M.U.54.

(Signed)   Otto Wiedemann,
                 Boatswain poksadowy,
                 O.R.P. LWOW Gdansk.

34 *The von Ruckteschell family had:* During the turbulent early months of 1919 Ruckteschell rallied to the call of Germany's most successful submarine commander, who had sunk more than 400,000 tons of shipping. He joined the Naval Brigade von Lowenfeldt lead by the submarine "ace" with the un-Germanic last name, Arnauld de la Periere, and then became an artillery officer in the Freikorps Lettow-Vorbeck. Both these anti-Communist groups, made up mainly of former officers, sought, with other Freikorps contingents, to put down the attempt to seize power that had been launched by the Communist "Spartacist" movement. During the spring, the Freikorps, in bloody fighting, eradicated a Communist revolt in Bavaria, and the fledgling government, which had been elected in January 1919, began meeting in Weimar.

34 *Throughout the war:* Willis, *Prologue to Nuremberg,* pp. 113–16.
35 *Erich Raeder chose to:* Raeder, *My Life,* pp. 109–10.
35 This account is drawn from the Gothenburg and Stockholm newspapers of the time and other sources such as hotel registers, Gothenburg police records, and Swedish government records. These were obtained for the author and translated by Christer Johansson.

3: THE BRITISH

40 *These losses, of course:* Grove, *The Defeat of the Enemy,* table 3.
41 *Philip Limpenny Flynn is the classic:* Flynn information comes from the author's interview with Dr. Desmond Flynn and information provided by Ted Milburn.
43 *Serving with him:* Barry Denny information provided by Ted Milburn with assistance from Desmond Denny.
43 *It was he who drew:* Southey, *The Life of Nelson,* p. 278.
44 *This young man, Edward Ernest Milburn:* E. E. Milburn information provided by Ted Milburn.

45 *Lionel Henry Hawks was:* Hawks information drawn from the Family Records Center, London, and the *Newcastle Evening Chronicle,* Nov. 11, 1940.

45 *Roy Hamilton Pilcher was:* Pilcher information from the Family Records Center, London; Cliff Walder; Marion Wastell Blake; Ted Milburn; Frank and James Bacon.

46 *While Pilcher was refined:* Widdicombe information from the Family Records Center, London; Jones, *Two Survived;* Sue Irvine; records of the *Conway* and the *Indefatigable.*

47 *In Roy Widdicombe's case:* Records of the *Conway* at the Merseyside Maritime Museum, Liverpool.

47 *Nor does he show:* Records of the *Indefatigable* at the Liverpool Central Library.

48 *The near opposite of Widdicombe's:* Tapscott information is from the Family Records Center, London; Jones, *Two Survived;* Tapscott's Canadian Army Record in the National Archives of Canada; Tapscott's merchant seaman's packet at the Public Records Office in Kew; Norma Tapscott and Diane Tapscott Terrazino.

50 *Francis Penny was not:* Penny information from Ted Milburn; Emily Penny; Jones, *Two Survived.*

4: THE GERMANS

This chapter is informed primarily by "Kurz-Biographie von Hellmuth Max von Ruckteschell" ("A Short Biography of Hellmuth von Ruckteschell") by his former shipmate Jürgen Herr and by the author's conversations and correspondence with Jürgen Herr and Konrad Hoppe. Other key sources include: information from Swedish sources gathered by Christer Johansson and Grossadmiral Erich Raeder's autobiography, *My Life.* The issue of the war crimes is covered in two fine books, Willis's *Prologue to Nuremberg* and Horne and Kramer's *German Atrocities, 1914,* as well as articles in the *New York Times* and *The Times* of London for February 1920.

52 *The official blessing on:* Reichswehrministers PA 7413 of Nov. 24, 1919.

52 *In July, as his first:* Landskansliet Goteborg och Bohus Lan, Forteckning, July 29, 1919.

53 *Hermann Baron, one of:* Landskansliet Goteborg och Bohus Lan, Ansokan om Uppehallsbok, Tyska undersatar, 1918–1926.

53 *When asked about giving: Göteborgs-Posten,* June 27, 1919, "Tyska Flytingar i Goteborg."

53 *Ruckteschell's first employment:* Herr, *Short Biography,* entry for 1919.

54 *In that same year:* Kitchen, *The Cambridge Illustrated History of Germany,* p. 239.

54 *That huge list of:* Willis, *Prologue to Nuremberg,* pp. 118–25.

55 *It was just as the Leipzig trials:* Letter from R. Graham to Lord Curzon of Keddleston in File TS 26/51 in the Public Record Office, Kew.

56 *The Attorney General checked:* Admiralty letter of July 7, 1921, in File TS 26/51 in the Public Record Office, Kew.

56 *Since it had been such:* Letter from H.M. Procurator General's Department to the Attorney General, dated July 9, 1921, in File TS 26/51 in the Public Record Office, Kew.

56 *The charge against the:* New York Times, Feb. 5, 1919.

56 *It is perhaps outlandish:* Ruckteschell letter of May 10, 1947.

57 *At age thirty-two, he began:* Herr, *Short Biography,* entries for 1922–1932 and correspondence with Jürgen Herr.

58 *In 1932, Hitler had:* Kitchen, *The Cambridge Illustrated History of Germany,* p. 249.

59 *Following the election, the:* Ruckteschell War Crimes Trial Record, p. 781, and author's correspondence with Olaf Griese, Oct. 23, 2002.

59 *That same year, Master:* Herr, *Short Biography,* entry for 1934.

60 *The oldest of these:* Author's correspondence with Jürgen Herr.

61 *Konrad Hoppe did not:* Author's conversations with Konrad Hoppe.

61 *Jürgen Herr, several years:* Author's conversations and correspondence with Jürgen Herr.

63 *Apparently at this point:* Author's conversations and correspondence with Jürgen Herr.

63 *In 1938, he married:* Herr, *Short Biography,* entry for 1938.

5: RAIDER!

67 *This Confederate plan involved:* deKay, *The Rebel Raiders,* pp. 53–62.

67 *The CSS* Alabama *was the:* Ibid., pp. 96–107.

68 *The Second Hague Peace Conference:* Schmalenbach, *German Raiders,* p. 13.

68 *In World War I, both:* Muggenthaler, *German Raiders of World War II,* pp. 5–7.

69 *By the terms of:* Ruge, *Der Seekrieg,* p. 29.

70 *The conversion of the* Neumark: Lloyds Register of Shipping, 1931.

71 *Instead, the* Neumark, *after:* Schmalenbach, *German Raiders,* p. 24.

75 *While it is difficult:* Muggenthaler, *German Raiders of World War II,* pp. 56–58.

75 *On the business side:* Schmalenbach, *German Raiders,* p. 71.

6: THE *WIDDER* AT SEA AND AT WAR

This chapter has several primary and several secondary sources. The Operations and Tactics report by von Ruckteschell outlines all of these activities, as does the *Widder*'s War Diary. There are also numerous reviews of aspects of the voyage contained in the verbatim trial record of the war crimes trial of von Ruckteschell. Fritz-Otto Busch's brief biography of von Ruckteschell, published as part of Der Landser's series on recipients of the Knight's Cross, contains details and personal insights from interviews with shipmates. Muggenthaler's book on German raiders has valuable information on *Widder*'s operations and the operations of others for comparison.

77 *smaller vessels were:* It is an interesting point that after the sinking of the *Admiral Graf Spee,* the German naval authorities were so concerned about the potential of having their proud ship the *Deutschland* sunk and the morale connotations because of that name, they took the unprecedented step of changing the name of an active warship from the *Deutschland* to *Lützow.*

77 *There were questions about:* Muggenthaler, *German Raiders of World War II,* p. 48.

78 *On Sunday, May 5, 1940:* Busch, *Kapitän,* p. 7.

79 *Equally as important, it:* Ruge, *Der Seekrieg,* p. 42.

83 *English and German seamen, comrades!:* This speech and the one quoted below were ob-
    tained by the author from Konrad Hoppe who served with von Ruckteschell in
    both the *Widder* and the *Michel.* Five weeks later, Ruckteschell held another funeral
    service, this time for Thomas Lavelle of the *Davisian,* who died on board the *Widder*
    from wounds received in the attack. It contains many of the same Steiner sensibil-
    ities.

    Ruckteschell's speech is as follows:

    Comrades, Seamen!
    All medical skill and carefulness was not able to save the life of this young man,
    whose mortal frame is lying before us. He died of the heavy wounds inflicted by one
    of our bullets.
    If the war shall have any sense it is necessary that we look at his face with all at-
    tention we are able to maintain. We recognize, engraved on his face, the great dis-
    tress and the pains and the destruction and the misery and the sorrow which the
    peoples inflict on each other.
    The people should be awakened by the war, so that they long for peace.
    And if this comrade, whom we now want to give the last company, had done
    nothing else in this world but wait for the bullet in order to die aboard this ship, we
    should thank him for his sacrifice, because we learn anew to long for peace.
    His soul is free and returns to his creator.
    On the rays of the morning sun, past the wide horizon which surrounds us, our
    affectionate thoughts and wishes follow him in his new world which is full of
    friendliness.
    On the way, we have shown to our comrade that we are looking into the holy
    sun and pray that her rays may beam the power and the will for peace into our
    hearts.
    So the death of our comrade will bring blessings to himself and us.
    Yes, so be it.

    This speech was held in honor of:

    Thomas Lavelle, born 4-10-1913, died 7-24-1940
    By Korvettenkapitän Hellmuth von Ruckteschell

    Commander of the German auxiliary cruiser *Widder*

    This fascinating glimpse of the civil Ruckteschell is in contrast to the brutal attack
    on the *Anglo-Saxon* less than a month later.

87 *Attention turned back:* Muggenthaler, *German Raiders of World War II,* p. 49.
88 *They learned that all: Wartime Instructions to Merchant Ships,* vol. 3, p. 106, spells out the of-
    ficial usage of these signals as: "RRRR—on sighting or when attacked by an enemy
    warship; QQQQ—on sighting or when attacked by an armed merchant ship
    raider; SSSS—on sighting or when attacked by a submarine or on striking a mine;
    and AAAA—when attacked by aircraft." However, in practice there seems to have
    been some variation in usage of the "RRRR" and "QQQQ" codes as accounts from
    ships under attack from raiders such as the *Widder* used either the "Q" or the "R."
89 *Other raider captains, like:* Muggenthaler, *German Raiders of World War II,* p. 62.

7: PATHS TO WAR

See notes for chapter 4 for sources of information on the *Anglo-Saxon*'s officers and crew.

92 *The Anglo-Saxon nestled:* Report on Ocean Convoy SL III, File ADM 199/218, at the Public Records Office, Kew.
94 *Jim Fowler, now thirty-seven:* Author's conversation with Betty McAteer.
95 *The fiancée of one:* Author's conversations and correspondence with Ted Milburn and Ella May Sim.
95 *On the way back:* Statement made by Ellis on visit to Mystic Seaport, n.d.
97 *On her last voyage:* Slader, *The Red Duster at War*, p. 51. It should be noted that Jones's *Two Survived* has a different version of the attack on the *Orford*, but it does not correspond with Slader's well-researched version or the two partial accounts cited in the next note.
97 *The ship was apparently:* Tapscott's "Case History Sheet," 1st Neurological Hospital, Basingstoke, p. 1, and *South Wales Echo*, Nov. 1, 1940, p. 1.
98 *The Anglo-Saxon was part:* Report on convoy OB 195, File ADM 199/23, at the Public Records Office, Kew.
99 *The complicated job of:* The captains of the convoys were given the height of the masts above the water of all the other ships in the convoy. This figure could be set into a simple instrument know as a stadimeter, which through a split mirror allowed the top of the mast to be matched with the waterline. When that had been done, a dial on the instrument would tell the distance from that ship. In the days before radar, this was an essential for station keeping.
101 *In the sailors' fo'c's'le:* Jones, *Two Survived*, p. 43.
102 *Widdicombe, a friend of the:* Ibid., pp. 42, 43.

8: THE RAIDER STRIKES

The portions of this chapter that relate to the *Anglo-Saxon* have as their major sources:

The log maintained onboard the *Anglo-Saxon*'s jolly boat during its voyage, typescript copies of which can be found in several repositories, including Mystic Seaport, Mystic, CT. (See Appendix B.)

Guy Pearce Jones, *Two Survived*. This book is based on extensive interviews with the survivors of the jolly-boat voyage.

Numerous newspaper and magazine articles that appeared on both sides of the Atlantic in the months following the rescue of the survivors.

This chapter also draws on several primary and several secondary sources relating to the *Widder*. The Operations and Tactics Report written by von Ruckteschell outlines all of these activities, as does the *Widder*'s War Diary. There are also numerous reviews of aspects of the voyage contained in the verbatim trial record of the war crimes trial of von Ruckteschell. Fritz-Otto Busch's brief biography of von Ruckteschell, published as part of Der Landser's series on recipients of the Knight's Cross, contains details and personal insights from interviews with shipmates. Muggenthaler's book on German raiders has valuable information on the *Widder*'s operations and the operations of others for comparison.

104 *He found the officer of the watch*: Leutnant Scharnberg was one of an unusual group of officers on the raider. In addition to the regular allocation of officers, the raiders each carried several officers who were designated "prize" officers. Normally, these were former merchant marine Captains who had relatively little naval training, but had the ability to command a captured merchant ship and take the prize to a German controlled port. These men had the designation of *Sonderführer,* meaning "special leader," and had naval commissions at the lowest rank. While assigned to the raiders they stood watches on the bridge, easing the workload for the regular officers. In the case of the *Widder,* she initially carried four such officers, but by August, one of them had already been sent off to France in the prize tanker *Krossfonn.*

104 *The incensed Ruckteschell wanted*: Ruckteschell, War Diary, entry for Aug. 20, 1940.

104 *On a number of occasions*: Author's conversations with Konrad Hoppe.

105 *Rather than awarding a*: Ruckteschell, War Diary, entry for Aug. 20, 1940.

105 *Once the British ship was*: The details of the *Widder*'s shadowing of the *Anglo-Saxon* are drawn from Exhibit "A.F." from the Ruckteschell War Crimes Trial Record.

106 *It had been so stressful*: Ruckteschell, Operations and Tactics, p. 17, entry for Aug. 11, 1940.

107 *Swinging a boat out*: The boats weigh thousands of pounds, so the task of shifting them from the deck to the water required a number of men to haul on the falls to first hoist the boat up off the deck. Then, since the davits were not far enough apart for the boat to be pushed out over the side, it had to be swung forward so the stern could be pushed out past the aft davit. The boat was then pushed out and back so the bow of the boat would clear the forward davit as it moved out. The boat was then out over the water. One last critical point concerns lowering the boat. If the ship was still moving forward, it was important for the stern to hit the water first, keeping the bow up, so the boat moved along with the ship. Once ready to set off, the aft boat fall was released first and then the forward fall.

109 *The crew of the Anglo-Saxon*: Jones, *Two Survived,* p. 49.

110 *Just before the first shots*: Ruckteschell, War Diary, entry for Aug. 21, 1940.

110 *On the bridge, Roy Widdicombe*: It is unclear precisely what the initial sequence of events was since there are conflicting versions from two credible sources, G. P. Jones's *Two Survived* and the official log, or war diary, of the *Widder.* The initial differences are slight, but Jones reports that Widdicombe first heard the explosion, saw the raider, and then put the helm over to port on his own initiative. Ruckteschell's war diary states that before he opened fire; "They must have seen us, but instead of turning to starboard they turned to port." Ruckteschell has them turning before he opened fire and Jones after. Since Jones got his information from Widdicombe and since Widdicombe had demonstrated a tendency to enhance stories, this could have been an attempt to enhance the perception of his role.

Ruckteschell's surprise at the *Anglo-Saxon*'s turn to port comes from the normal procedure for meeting ships to each alter course to starboard, passing each other port side to port side. In this case, assuming the *Anglo-Saxon* did see something, it would have been difficult to instantly determine its course and speed since it showed no lights, and Widdicombe's instinct took over as he turned away from the then unknown danger.

It is also fascinating in retrospect to think of what would have happened if, instead of turning away, the *Anglo-Saxon* has steamed straight for the *Widder* and attempted to ram her. She would have presented a smaller target by heading directly for the *Widder,* and it would have taken only a matter of minutes to close the 1.4 miles between the ships.

111 *When the First Mate:* Denny et al.,"The Log of the *Anglo-Saxon* Jolly Boat," entry for Aug. 21, 1940.

111 *The force of the blast:* Tapscott's Statement, Exhibit "H," Ruckteschell War Crimes Trial Record.

111 *The guns swept the decks:* Ruckteschell's statement of September 1946, Ruckteschell War Crimes Trial Record, p. 100.

112 *He never reappeared:* Jones, *Two Survived,* p. 57.

112 *In the midst of this:* Ibid., p. 77.

113 *The First Mate made:* Denny et al., "The Log," entry for Aug. 21, 1940.

114 *Other faces, possibly Eddie Milburn:* Milburn's son, Ted, today often reflects on the possibility that his father was at this location and watched the jolly boat slip away. Eddie Milburn's widow apparently said later that she was glad, in a sense, her husband didn't get into the jolly boat, because at his age, it is doubtful that he would have survived and he would have suffered enormously.

114 *It was, in fact:* Ruckteschell, War Diary, entry for Aug. 21, 1940.

115 *On his ship, the* American Leader: Author's interview with Captain Duffy, 2002.

115 *Their optimism was abruptly:* Denny et al., "The Log," entry for Aug. 21, 1940, and Tapscott's Statement, Exhibit "H," Ruckteschell War Crimes Trial Record.

PART II

The portions of this part that relate to the *Anglo-Saxon* have as their major sources:

The log maintained on board the *Anglo-Saxon* jolly boat during its voyage, typescript copies of which can be found in several repositories, including Mystic Seaport, Mystic, CT. (See Appendix B.)

Guy Pearce Jones, *Two Survived.* This book based on extensive interviews with the survivors of the jolly-boat voyage.

Douglas F. Storer, *The Most, Amazing but True,* which contains a chapter devoted to the jolly-boat story. Storer was an associate of Robert Ripley and interviewed the jolly-boat survivors prior to their Ripley radio broadcast.

Numerous newspaper and magazine articles that appeared on both sides of the Atlantic in the months following the rescue of the survivors.

9: SPECK IN THE OCEAN

120 *Once the raider disappeared:* Denny et al., "The Log," entry for Aug. 21, 1940.

120 *He thought his foot:* Jones, *Two Survived,* pp. 64, 65.

127 *Other items in the case:* The letter to Cliff Walder was eventually delivered to him and is in the collection of the Imperial War Museum.
130 *While in the process:* Jones, *Two Survived*, p. 88.
130 *Realizing the need to:* Denny et al., "The Log," entry for Aug. 25, 1940.
131 *Although the remaining mutton:* Ibid., entry for Aug. 26, 1940
131 *When blood is no longer able:* Dorland's *Illustrated Medical Dictionary* (2000 edition), p. 728.
132 *In his log that day:* Denny et al., "The Log," entry for Aug. 26, 1940.
133 *After they lighted up:* Ibid., entry for Aug. 27, 1940.
133 *Their fortitude was reflected:* Ibid., entry for Aug. 26, 1940.

10: DRASTIC CHOICES

135 *Modern scientists assert:* The Encyclopedia of Human Nutrition, dehydration section.
135 *The daily minimum fluid:* Critchley, *Shipwreck-Survivors*, p. 24.
135 *Its source was Pilcher:* Jones, *Two Survived*, p. 101.
136 *This was the beginning:* Denny et al., "The Log," entry for Aug. 30, 1940.
137 *They had to amputate:* Jones, *Two Survived*, p. 103.
138 *The ax was cleaned:* Storer, *The Most*, p. 102.
138 *In this forlorn moment:* Denny et al., "The Log," entry for Aug. 31, 1940.
139 *A minimum of 2 pints:* Robertson, *Sea Survival*, p. 41.
139 *With his usual decisiveness:* Denny et al., "The Log," entry for Sept. 1, 1940.
139 *When they looked at:* Jones, *Two Survived*, p. 105.
141 *There were no words:* Denny et al., "The Log," entry for Sept. 1, 1940.
142 *Although it is difficult to create:* Critchley, *Ship-Wreck Survivors*, p. 30.
142 *In 1965, the Marine Division:* Robertson, *Sea Survival*, p. 34.
142 *Studies show that coherent:* Ibid., p. 35.
143 *This was fortunate, because:* Storer, *The Most*, p. 109.
144 *The efficiency and order:* Jones, *Two Survived*, p. 113.

11: DESPERATE DECISIONS

147 *When the boat suddenly:* Jones, *Two Survived*, p. 116.
147 *By going over the side:* The three objectives accomplished by Penny match those of Captain Oates of the ill-fated Robert Falcon Scott expedition of 1910–12.
148 *He simply recorded, "Penny":* Denny et al., "The Log," entry for Sept. 4, 1940.
150 *Out of this lassitude:* Jones, *Two Survived*, p. 121.
153 *They noted that gross:* Critchley, *Ship-Wreck Survivors*, p. 50.
153 *Sea survival manuals urge:* Robertson, *Sea Survival*, pp. 68, 69.
154 *"Do you think you're":* Jones, *Two Survived*, p. 131.
155 *As other shipwrecked sailors:* Critchley, *Shipwreck-Survivors*, pp. 25, 26.
156 *The futility of the situation:* Jones, *Two Survived*, p. 137.
157 *The decision made itself:* Ibid., p. 141.

12: WATER!

160 *The men scrambled out from:* Jones, *Two Survived*, p. 143.

162 *While Tapscott and Widdicomb had ceased:* Denny et al., "The Log," entry for Sept. 12, 1940.

163 *Documented cases show:* Critchley, *Shipwreck-Survivors*, p. 45.

164 *Two days later, a:* Jones, *Two Survived*, p. 153.

165 *In actuality, they were:* This estimate is derived by an analysis of the log notations of course and winds along with the current's effects plotted on a modern chart.

165 *The two species of floating:* Author's consultation with Dr. Jim Carlton, Director of the Williams College/Mystic Seaport Maritime Studies Program, Apr. 18, 2002.

166 *Suddenly, keenly awake, with:* Jones, *Two Survived*, p. 156.

167 *The tropical waters in:* Robertson, *Sea Survival*, pp. 28, 29.

167 *The men were remarkable:* Ibid., p. 35.

167 *To their joy they:* Author's consultation with Dr. Jim Carlton, Apr. 18, 2002.

169 *He then looked toward:* Jones, *Two Survived*, pp. 162–63.

13: FORTITUDE

170 *The letters were from:* This text is drawn from letters sent by The Shipping Federation to Mrs. E. E. Milburn and Mrs. C. H. Williams.

171 *The Battle of Britain still raged:* Dear, *The Oxford Companion to World War II*, p. 108.

172 *Eddie Milburn's pay was:* Articles of Agreement and List of Crew for *Anglo-Saxon*, July 25, 1940.

173 *Denny's decision had been:* Robertson, *Sea Survival*, pp. 24, 25.

174 *There is a clockwise sweep:* K. A. Neumann et al., *Tropical Cyclones*.

175 *The current throughout September:* Ibid., pp. 8–11.

176 *The average person can:* Sadler et al., *The Encyclopedia of Human Nutrition* (online, starvation and dehydration section, Academic Press).

176 *The body goes through:* Van De Graaff and Fox, *Concepts of Human Anatomy*, p. 94.

176 *A landmark study was:* Guetzkow and Bowman, *Men and Hunger*, pp. 11–16.

177 *Because of their timing:* K. A. Neumann et al., *Tropical Cyclones*, p. 102.

178 *For days, they were:* Bowditch, *Bowditch for Yachtsmen*, chapter 36.

178 *After several days of:* Jones, *Two Survived*, pp. 164, 165.

179 *As the tropical storm:* K. A. Neumann et al., *Tropical Cyclones*, p. 102.

179 *Well into the night:* Jones, *Two Survived*, pp. 165–70.

182 *To quell the ravenous:* Time, June 9, 1941, p. 34.

183 *In October, an unusual:* K. A. Neumann et al., *Tropical Cyclones*, p. 10.

184 *Widdicombe had been on:* Jones, *Two Survived*, p. 175.

186 *They spotted a break:* Ibid., pp. 179–80.

14: WARRIOR WIDDER

This chapter draws primarily on Ruckteschell's War Diary and his Operations and Tactics report, as well as the Ruckteschell War Crimes Trial Record.

187 *In the* Widder's *war diary:* Ruckteschell, War Diary, entry for Aug. 21, 1940.
187 *It is unlikely he:* Ruckteschell War Crimes Trial Record, p. 799.
188 *At midday on August:* Ruckteschell, Operations and Tactics, p. 18.
190 *He felt that by:* Ibid., p. 19.
191 *There was little mercy:* Ibid., p. 20.
193 *When the cruiser HMS* Cornwall: Muggenthaler, *German Raiders of World War II*, p. 164.
194 *It is difficult to:* When later questioned on this point during his trial, Ruckteschell simply said it was the limitation of the *Rekum.*
195 *The* Widder *hoisted a Norwegian:* Maloney, *Chapman Piloting*, p. 66.
196 *On the night of:* Ruckteschell, Operations and Tactics, p. 22.
198 *Later that night, with:* Ibid., p. 23.

PART III

15: RESCUE

This chapter primarily draws on *Two Survived* by Guy Pearce Jones, numerous newspaper and magazine articles that appeared on both sides of the Atlantic in the months following the rescue of the survivors, and interviews with numerous individuals in the Bahamas and in England who were aware of the events and knew Tapscott and Widdicombe.

203 *With his wife a:* The term "cutlass," relating to machetes, is a fascinating holdover from the days when cutlass-wielding pirates controlled many of the Bahamian islands.
204 *Once back on the road:* Author's interview with retired Constable Elijah Mackey, Eleuthera, 2002.
205 *With no hospital or clinic:* Young, *Eleuthera*, p. 106.
205 *They took the men to:* Author's interview with Loraine and Joy Pyfrom, and Rev. Samuel B. Pinder, Eleuthera, 2002.
206 *The first hint of media:* Recollections of the editor recorded in her book review of *Two Survived, Nassau Guardian,* Aug. 9, 1941, p. 3.
207 *The statements are one-page:* Statements by Tapscott and Widdicombe in the possession of Dr. Michael Gerassimos, Nassau, Bahamas. Copies of these documents are held by the author.
207 *However, with the number:* Colonial Office File CO 23/681.
207 *Dr. Kline, referred to as:* Author's interviews with Loraine and Joy Pyfrom and Rev. Samuel B. Pinder, Eleuthera, 2002.
208 *Their skin had:* Dorlands, p. 1342, and *Professional Guide to Diseases,* pp. 881 and 882.
209 *At 12:14 P.M. on October 31:* Colonial Office File CO 23/691, p. 42.
209 *On Lewis Street in Newport: South Wales Argus,* Nov. 1, 1940, p. 1.
209 *She told reporters: South Wales Echo,* Nov. 1, 1940, p. 1.
210 *Betty McAteer, the ten-year-old:* Author's interview with Betty McAteer, Cardiff, 2002.
210 *In his entries in:* Denny et al., "The Log," pp. 3, 4.
211 *Tapscott's signed statement says:* Statements made by Tapscott and Widdicombe and transcribed by Commissioner Michael Gerassimos.

211 *In this telling, Morgan:* Jones, *Two Survived,* p. 134.
211 *In his first, with Edwin Brownrigg: Nassau Guardian,* Oct. 31, 1940, p. 1.
211 *That same day, October 31: Nassau Daily Tribune,* p. 1.
212 *The Nassau reporter for the: New York Sun,* Nov. 1, 1940. The story appeared around the
world, including the *South Wales Echo,* Nov. 1, 1940, p. 1, and the *Winnipeg Tribune,*
Nov. 1, 1940.
212 *The following day, the Nassau Guardian: Nassau Guardian,* Nov. 1, 1940, p. 1.
213 *Widdicombe later said: The Lookout,* March 1941, p. 5.

16: RETURN, REDEMPTION, AND REWARD

This chapter draws primarily on the following sources:

Kapitän z.S. v. Ruckteschell, Hilfskreuzer-Gespensterschiffe auf den Weltmeeren by Fritz-
Otto Busch, a biography of von Ruckteschell.

The "Comparing Timetable" by Konrad Hoppe. As an officer serving on both
the *Widder* and the *Michel,* Hoppe had keen insight into his commanding officer and
the events that took place. In this timetable, which he gave to the author, he develops a timeline that begins with the return of the *Widder* from her voyage and continues until April 16, 1942, with the *Michel* at sea and about to commence
operations.

Author's interviews with Konrad Hoppe.

Author's interview and subsequent correspondence with Jürgen Herr, and information supplied from his remarkable archive that documents his career, his
father's career, and von Ruckteschell's career.

214 *It totaled ten ships:* Schmalenbach, *German Raiders,* p. 139, and Ruge, *Der Seekrieg,* pp. 70
and 71.
215 *Soon after they dropped anchor:* Busch, *Kapitän,* p. 32.
216 *For two weeks, the ship lay at anchor:* Hoppe, entry for Nov. 14, 1940.
216 *The Captain was singled:* www.wehrmachtawards.com.
217 *When the war erupted:* Busch, *Kapitän,* p. 32.
217 *The Captain held a:* Hoppe, entry for Nov. 20, 1940.
217 *The Executive Officer:* Busch, *Kapitän,* p. 32, and Hoppe, entry for Nov. 20, 1940.
217 *The rejection of the Chief:* Hoppe correspondence, Feb. 25, 2003.
218 *Hermann Göring, with the:* Griese, footnote 75, to translation of Busch.
218 *With the decisions about:* Hoppe, entry for Dec. 1, 1940.
219 *In the thick of:* Ruge, *Der Seekrieg,* p. 89.
220 *Two German destroyers were:* Author's interview with Jürgen Herr.
220 *His first destroyer shot:* Author's interview with Jürgen Herr and e-mail correspondence of Mar. 16, 2003.
221 *In a somewhat similar:* Raeder, *My Life,* pp. 260 and 261.
221 *When the Captain explained:* Ruckteschell Trial Record, p. 781.
222 *The modern 15cm guns:* Busch, *Kapitän,* pp. 33 and 34.
222 *Ruckteschell also wanted improved:* Ibid., p. 34.
222 *Remembering the constant frustration:* Ibid., p. 33, and Hoppe, entry for Aug. 25, 1941.
224 *As the time for Shiff 28's commissioning:* Busch, *Kapitän,* pp. 34 and 35; Muggenthaler,

German Raiders of World War II, p. 206; and Griese, footnote 78 of translation of Busch.

224 *Once again selecting a name:* There is a naval tradition that associates the identity of the ship with its Captain, where the Captain is sometimes referred to by the ship's name. For example, when the Captain of the destroyer USS *DeHaven* arrived at his ship, he would be announced as "*DeHaven* arriving." In the case of Ruckteschell, he had the opportunity to tailor the names of his ships to his particular image.

225 *There were a few mishaps:* Hoppe, entries for Oct. 10, 1941, and Nov. 1941.

17: CELEBRITY

228 *He endured long periods:* Jones, *Two Survived*, p. 191.

228 *According to retired Constable Elijah Mackey:* Author's interview with Elijah Mackey, 2002.

228 *Since it appeared in:* The Harlingen, Texas, *Valley Morning Star,* Feb. 24, 2003, "Tale of the Nameplate," p. 2.

228 *The boat was moved:* Nassau *Daily Tribune,* Nov. 30, 1940, "Ripley Forerunner Expected Monday," p. 1.

230 *The evening edition of the:* Nassau *Guardian,* Dec. 2, 1940, p. 1; and Nassau *Magazine,* January 1941, "Believe It or Not."

231 *The task of making:* Nassau *Daily Tribune,* Dec. 7, 1940, "Radio History Made in Nassau," p. 1.

232 *He commented on the miraculous:* Nassau *Guardian,* Dec. 7, 1940, "Vast Radio Audience Listens . . . ," p. 1.

232 *Regarding Tapscott and Widdicombe's voyage:* Script for radio broadcast, signed by "Ripley," dated Dec. 6, 1940, Registrar's Office of Mystic Seaport.

233 *At the conclusion:* An amusing coincidence is that just prior to introducing His Royal Highness, there was a commercial announcement for Royal Crown Cola, the program's appropriate sponsor.

233 *The Duke continued:* Nassau *Daily Tribune,* Dec. 7, 1940, "Radio History Made in Nassau," p. 1. In commenting on the minesweeping responsibilities, the Duke is referring to the Reserve Naval Patrol Service, which was made up of fishermen from the home fishing fleets and their small boats.

234 *Among the eager bidders:* Letter from Cora Mallory Munson to Carl Cutler, Apr. 7, 1941, Registrar's Office of Mystic Seaport.

234 *One of the formidable bidders:* Nassau *Guardian,* Dec. 7, 1940, "Vast Radio Audience Listens . . . ," p. 1.

235 *The drama of the sailors' tale:* The Joneses were an interesting couple who for a number of years had spent their winters in exclusive Lyford Cay, 13 miles west of Nassau, where Constance Jones had owned several properties during the thirties. Guy Jones had begun his journalistic career in the city of his birth, San Francisco, and then moved to Springfield, Ohio, when he took a job as managing editor of one of the Crowell Publishing Company magazines. He also said, "I was in on the organization of the North American Newspaper Alliance of which I became the managing editor during the heyday of transatlantic flying and cosmic monkeyshines of the late twenties." At some time in those twenties, he and his adventuresome wife

spent more than a year traveling in the exotic Far East, including a 700-mile trek on horseback from the Vale of Kashmir into the Himalayas. This formed the basis of Mrs. Jones's first book, *Thin Air*, published under her maiden name, Constance Bridges, in 1930. Her own background was centered on Cambridge, Massachusetts, where she was born and graduated magna cum laude from Radcliffe College of Harvard University in 1917. In 1933, a play by Constance Jones entitled *Fidelity Insured* was produced at the famous Pasadena Playhouse in Los Angeles. By 1940, the Joneses had settled down to a pattern of spending their winters in Lyford Cay and the remainder of the year in "Summerhill," their home in Old Lyme, Connecticut. It appears as if they had sufficient resources to lead this comfortable life, without regular employment. *Nassau Guardian*, Dec. 9, 1940, "Winter Visitor to Write Book for Seamen," p. 2; book jacket notes by Guy Jones and Constance Jones for their book *There Was a Little Man*; and information drawn from *Thin Air* by Constance Bridges.

235 *Widdicombe's return to Governor's:* Author's interview with Richard Rolle, 2002.

235 *He visited and had tea:* Author's interview with Dr. Michael Gerassimos, Jr., who related information told to him by his father.

235 *Mrs. Percy Lightbourn: Nassau Guardian*, Nov. 2, 1940, "The Rescued Seamen," p. 4.

236 *Widdicombe took full advantage:* Author's interview with Gwen French, 2002.

236 *Nassau's Imperial Order of:* Ibid.

236 *How he made this acquisition:* Note on Nassau services in *The Nassau Magazine*, January 1941.

237 *There was an indication: Nassau Daily Tribune*, Dec. 23, 1940, "Accident, p. 1."

237 *Both men were still hospital patients: Nassau Daily Tribune*, Dec. 12, 1940, "Widdicombe Visits Landfall," p. 1.

237 *The message read: "I suggest":* Ministry of Shipping letter, Dec. 9, 1940, File CO 23/691, p. 38, in the Public Records Office.

237 *The strong response from:* From draft of response by the Colonial Office to the Ministry of Shipping letter, Dec. 9, 1940, File CO 23/691, pp. 36–37, in the Public Records Office.

238 *The letter to Ethel Milburn read:* Letter from Nitrate Producers Steam Ship Co., Nov. 14, 1940, copy in possession of author, provided by Ted Milburn.

238 *Her in-laws lived nearby:* Author's interview with Ted Milburn, 2002.

238 *Throughout the war:* "Lord Haw Haw" was the sobriquet for William Joyce and his predecessor, probably Norman Baille-Stewart, who broadcast regularly from Germany to England feeding pro-German propaganda with the purpose of demoralizing their listeners. Joyce had been born in America but lived in the UK from an early age in 1922 until he fled to Germany in 1939. After the war he was tried for treason, found guilty, and executed. *The Oxford Companion to World War II*, p. 503.

239 *Tapscott would require extended: Nassau Guardian*, Jan. 11, 1941, "Widdicombe and Tapscott to Join Up," p. 4.

18: HOMEWARD BOUND

241 *A few days after: Nassau Guardian,* Jan. 11, 1941, "Widdicombe and Tapscott to Join Up," p. 4.

242 *Plans were being made:* Letter dated Jan. 7, 1941, from Ronald Cross, Minister of Shipping, to Lord Lloyd, Secretary of State for the Colonies, File CO 23/691, p. 29, in the Public Records Office.

243 *The Institute wanted:* Foreword by the Rev. Peter Larom to *Anchored Within the Vail.*

244 *The Institute maintained a supply: The Lookout,* March 1941, p. 4.

244 *It was a stirring occasion: New York Times,* Jan. 31, 1941, "Ball Tonight Assists Scottish War Relief."

244 *In that interview, he: New York Herald Tribune,* Jan. 31, 1941, "British Tar Tells of 70 Days at Sea in Lifeboat."

245 *A message sent from:* Text of telegram from the Governor of the Bahamas to the Colonial Office, Feb. 18, 1941, File CO 23/691, p. 26, in the Public Records Office.

247 *On February 7, 1941:* Middlemiss, *Pride of the Princess,* p. 96.

247 *As the days passed at sea:* Colonial Office letters, Mar. 8, 1941, File CO 23/691, p. 23, in the Public Records Office.

248 *For added security:* Metzler, *The Laughing Cow,* p. 37.

248 *For several days, a sinister black:* Ibid., pp. 32–43.

250 *On Lewis Street in Newport: South Wales Argus,* Feb. 27, 1941, "Brave Hopeful Wife."

251 *At the Seamen's Church Institute: New York Sun,* Feb. 27, 1941, "On the Sun Deck," p. 8.

251 *Wartime security slowed the news: Nassau Guardian,* Feb. 27, 1941, "Roy Widdicombe Said to Be Passenger on Missing Freighter," p. 1.

19: WOUNDED WARRIOR

253 *In 1980 a new term:* Friedman, *Post-Traumatic Stress Disorder,* p. 1.

253 *There are descriptions of:* The National Center for Post-Traumatic Stress Disorder, "What Is Post-Traumatic Stress Disorder? Understanding PTSD."

254 *A passage from the:* The National Center for Post-Traumatic Stress Disorder, Fact Sheet, p. 1.

254 *The seventh edition of the:* Campbell, *Psychiatric Dictionary,* p. 552.

255 *The Governor's Office had:* Telegram from the Governor of the Bahamas to the Colonial Office, February 18, 1941, in File CO 23/691, p. 26, in the Public Records Office.

255 *The Colonial Office replied:* Draft message dated March 4, 1941, from the Colonial Office to the Governor of the Bahamas, in File CO 23/691, p. 24, in the Public Records Office.

255 *In mid-March, when:* Telegram from the Governor of the Bahamas to the Colonial Office, in File CO 23/691, p. 21, in the Public Records Office.

255 *In a later medical report:* Case History Sheet, R. G. Tapscott, by Maj. J. C. Richardson, Canadian 1st Neurological Hospital, Basingstoke, U.K., in Personnel Record of R. G. Tapscott, National Archives of Canada.

256 *Remington said of Tapscott: The Lookout,* March 1941, p. 3.

NOTES

256 *Nassau attorney Andrew McKinney:* Author's interview with Andrew McKinney, 2002.

256 *The medical staff had:* Ministry of Shipping letter, Apr. 7, 1941, in File CO 23/691, p. 16, in the Public Records Office.

257 *Influenced by his ordeal:* Case History Sheet, R. G. Tapscott, by Maj. J. C. Richardson, Canadian 1st Neurological Hospital, Basingstoke, U.K., May 1942, in Personnel Record of R. G. Tapscott, National Archives of Canada.

257 *These were affected by:* Nassau Daily Tribune, Apr. 7, 1941, "Clifford Mallory Dies in Miami," p. 1.

257 *Ten days after the report:* Nassau Guardian, Apr. 17, 1941, "Historic Jolly Boat to Be Placed in Museum," p. 2.

258 *On May 29, page 2:* Nassau Guardian, May 29, 1941.

258 *His first stop was New York City:* The Lookout, July 1941, "Lone Survivor," p. 9.

258 *Like Widdicombe, Tapscott enjoyed:* New York Times, June 12, 1941, "British Seaman Safe Ashore After 70 Days in Open Boat"; and Time, June 9, 1941, p. 34.

258 *Photographs taken at the Institute:* The Lookout, July 1941, "Lone Survivor," pp. 9–10.

258 *Tapscott settled in at:* Enlistment Documents, in Personnel Record of R. G. Tapscott, National Archives of Canada.

259 *Within six weeks of his enlistment:* Record of Service of R. G. Tapscott, in Personnel Record of R. G. Tapscott, National Archives of Canada, p. 1.

259 *The book was featured:* New York Times Book Review, July 27, 1941, p. 1; New York Herald-Tribune Books, July 20, 1941, p. 3; The New Yorker, July 19, 1941, pp. 54–56; The Christian Science Monitor, Dec. 27, 1941, p. 12; and The Saturday Review of Literature, July 19, 1941, p. 12.

260 *The book was on the:* Nassau Guardian, Aug. 12, 1941, p. 2.

260 *He requested and received four days:* Record of Service of R. G. Tapscott, in Personnel Record of R. G. Tapscott, National Archives of Canada, p. 1.

260 *American sympathy was growing:* Letter from Mr. T. C. P. Brook, Headmaster, The Royal Merchant Navy School, Oct. 7, 1941.

261 *Ethel Milburn received:* Card from Buckingham Palace, in possession of Ted Milburn.

262 *These easily meet the:* Friedman, Post-Traumatic Stress Disorder, p. 1.

262 *Tapscott told of the anxieties:* Case History Sheet, R. G. Tapscott, by Maj. J. C. Richardson, Canadian 1st Neurological Hospital, Basingstoke, U.K., May 1942, p. 2, in Personnel Record of R. G. Tapscott, National Archives of Canada.

263 *Dr. Richardson wrote:* Ibid.

263 *The Commanding Officer of the:* Hospital Discharge Notification, May 27, 1942, Canadian 1st Neurological Hospital, Basingstoke, U.K., in Personnel Record of R. G. Tapscott, National Archives of Canada.

263 *The court showed its understanding:* Field General Court-Martial, June 19, 1942, Headquarters, 3rd Canadian Division, in Personnel Record of R. G. Tapscott, National Archives of Canada.

264 *Finally, on October 2:* Record of Service of R. G. Tapscott, in Personnel Record of R. G. Tapscott, National Archives of Canada, p. 2.

264 *On December 7, 1942:* Proceeding of Discharge, Dec. 7, 1942, in Personnel Record of R. G. Tapscott, National Archives of Canada.

265   *Harry Griffin, who now:* Author's interview with Harry Griffin, 2002.
266   *During the remainder of the war:* R. G. Tapscott's Merchant Marine Discharge Book, Imperial War Museum, London.
266   *And from a grateful Canadian government:* Awards—Canadian Army (Active) in Personnel Record of R. G. Tapscott, National Archives of Canada.

20: *MICHEL*—THE SHIP AND THE MAN

267   *As Bob Tapscott struggled:* Muggenthaler, *German Raiders of World War II,* p. 208.
267   *A special team of:* Busch, *Kapitän,* p. 41. "B-Dienst" is the abbreviation for Beobachtungsdienst.
267   *When they got under way:* Hoppe, p. 10.
268   *Just after midnight:* Muggenthaler, *German Raiders of World War II,* p. 209.
268   *Using his uncanny ability:* Hoppe, p. 10.
269   *In what was regarded:* Ibid., p. 11.
269   *At Ruckteschell's direction:* Author's interview with Konrad Hoppe, 2002.
269   *Ruckteschell had also created:* At least one other raider commander, Bernhard Rogge, had earlier created the first such "holiday space" for the benefit of the crew.
270   *The ship arrived in her area of operation:* Muggenthaler, *German Raiders of World War II,* pp. 210 and 211.
270   *Ruckteschell launched his special:* Roskill, *A Merchant Fleet at War,* p. 89.
271   *He assembled his crew:* Busch, *Kapitän,* p. 50.
272   *In a synchronized attack:* Muggenthaler, *German Raiders of World War II,* pp. 223 and 224.
272   *As this voyage progressed:* Author's interview with Konrad Hoppe, 2002.
273   *For a new member of the:* Author's interview with Jürgen Herr, 2002.
273   *In an attempt to free:* Author's interview with George Duffy, 2002.
273   *Since the fire did not cease:* Charge Sheet, Ruckteschell War Crimes Trial Record.
273   *He was moved to the Indian Ocean:* Busch, *Kapitän,* p. 59.
274   *To lift morale in the:* Ruckteschell, *O Tannenbaum,* title page.
274   *Konrad Hoppe volunteered to:* Author's interview with Konrad Hoppe, 2002.
274   *The preparations for Christmas extended:* Muggenthaler, *German Raiders of World War II,* p. 254.
275   *The play was a drama:* Ruckteschell, *O Tannenbaum.*
275   *Another highlight of that:* Busch, *Kapitän,* p. 61.
275   *A few days later:* Muggenthaler, *German Raiders of World War II,* p. 255.
275   *On January 2:* Ibid., p. 256.
275   *On January 8:* Busch, *Kapitän,* p. 62.
276   *After a brief stop:* Author's interview with George Duffy, 2002.
276   *His ship's doctor:* Busch, *Kapitän,* p. 62.
277   *His Executive Officer, Erhardt:* Muggenthaler, *German Raiders of World War II,* p. 266, and author's interviews with Konrad Hoppe and Jürgen Herr, 2002.
277   *Those who were left behind:* Author's interviews with Konrad Hoppe and Jürgen Herr, 2002.
277   *As these officers adjusted:* Muggenthaler, *German Raiders of World War II,* p. 266.

277 *On October 16, the Michel was 100 miles:* Vermehren, "Der Untergang," p. 1.

277 *In the Michel's path lay:* Muggenthaler, *German Raiders of World War II,* p. 271.

278 *Onboard the Michel:* Vermehren, "Der Untergang," p. 2.

278 *Nearly 100 others crowded:* Ibid., p. 7.

278 *Schack, the senior officer:* Ibid., p. 10.

21: WAR CRIMINAL

279 *During the two years:* Author's interviews with Jürgen Herr and Konrad Hoppe, 2002.

280 *That wait lasted almost:* Ruckteschell letter, July 21, 1946.

280 *On August 4, 1946:* Ruckteschell letter, Aug. 5, 1946.

280 *The debacle of those:* Gilbert, *Nuremberg Diary,* p. 3.

280 *By mid-August, Ruckteschell was:* Ruckteschell letters, Aug. 14 and 29, 1946.

281 *What they gleaned from him:* Extradition Order from the Headquarters, U.S. Forces, European Theater, Aug. 19, 1946, von Ruckteschell Prison Record.

281 *As was seen in the:* Mullins, *The Leipzig Trials,* pp. 39–42.

282 *Under the stress of:* Ruckteschell letter, Oct. 28, 1946.

282 *During the fall:* Ruckteschell letters, Nov. 3 and 16, 1946.

282 *As the Christmas season approached:* Ruckteschell letters, Dec. 1, 8, and 16, 1946.

283 *The investigators sought out:* Ruckteschell War Crimes Trial Record, p. 801.

283 *Tapscott was serving on:* Statement of Tapscott, Exhibit "H," von Ruckteschell War Crimes Trial Record, p. 49.

284 *As 1947 began and:* Ruckteschell letter, Jan. 9, 1947.

284 *During the move, while:* Ruckteschell letter, Feb. 26, 1947.

284 *He and the other war crimes suspects:* Ruckteschell letter, Mar. 28, 1947.

284 *That phase began:* Mrs. von Ruckteschell's letter, June 30, 1947.

285 *He was flown to:* Certificate of Discharge, Apr. 5, 1947, in Ruckteschell Prison Record.

285 *She urgently desired to:* Mrs. von Ruckteschell's letter, June 30, 1947, p. 2.

285 *There were five charges:* Charge Sheet—Military Courts for the Trial of War Criminals, Ruckteschell War Crimes Trial Record, p. 10.

286 *In a letter written:* Ruckteschell letter, May 2, 1947.

286 *In a long letter to both:* Ruckteschell letter, May 4, 1947.

286 *Ruckteschell's trial began in:* Mrs. von Ruckteschell's letter, June 30, 1947, p. 2.

287 *In one instance, the Defense:* Ibid., p. 11.

289 *He also affirmed a written:* Ruckteschell War Crimes Trial Record, p. 783.

290 *He did admit that:* Ibid., p. 799.

292 *He said: "Now, the accused":* Ibid., p. 656.

292 *There is no doubt:* Treasury Solicitor's Department, File TS 25/51.

293 *The officer made the point:* Ruckteschell War Crimes Trial Record, pp. 210, 211.

293 *That night, resigned to:* Ruckteschell letter, May 14, 1947.

293 *The first charge:* Charge Sheet—Military Courts for the Trial of War Criminals, Ruckteschell War Crimes Trial Record, p. 10.

294 *Midway through the trial:* Ruckteschell letter, May 10, 1947.

294   *The Hamburg newspapers: Hamburger Freie Presse,* May 7, 1947, p. 3; May 17, 1947, p. 3; May
      21, 1947, p. 2; May 24, 1947, p. 3. *Die Welt,* May 6, 1947, p. 3; May 8, 1947, p. 3; May 20,
      1947, p. 2; May 22, 1947, p. 2. *Hamburger Echo;* May 6, 1947, p. 3; May 9, 1947, p. 3; May
      17, 1947, p. 3. *Hamburger Volkszeitung,* May 7, 1947, p. 3; May 24, 1947, p. 3.

294   *The New York Times and: New York Times,* May 22, 1947, p. 55. *The Times* of London,
      May 6, 1947, p. 3; May 7, 1947, p. 3; May 22, 1947, p. 5.

294   *The day after the trial:* Mrs. von Ruckteschell's letter, June 30, 1947, p. 18.

294   *The next day, Ruckteschell:* Cover of Ruckteschell Prison Record.

294   *On August 22, 1947:* Letter of submission from the Judge Advocate General's Office to
      the General Officer, Commanding-in-Chief, British Army on the Rhine, August
      22, 1947, Ruckteschell War Crimes Trial Record, pp. 903–5.

295   *As a result of the review:* Charge Sheet—Military Courts for the Trial of War Crimi-
      nals, Ruckteschell War Crimes Trial Record, p. 10.

295   *Dr. Zippel made the case:* Letter from Dr. O. Zippel, Apr. 16, 1948, and reply to Dr. Zip-
      pel from Dr. Frommer, May 27, 1948, Ruckteschell Prison Record.

295   *Two months later:* A Report on a Case of Death in the Central Hospital, June 24,
      1948, Ruckteschell Prison Record.

22: HAUNTED HERO

297   *Working up and down:* Author's correspondence with Phil Hayden, 2002 and
      2003.

298   *Two months after giving:* Ibid., and information provided by Ted Milburn.

298   *In the late 1940s:* Author's conversations with Norma Tapscott, 2002.

298   *In November 1950, Tapscott:* R. G. Tapscott Merchant Marine Record, File BT372/
      0121 in the Public Records Office.

299   *Diane recalls that it:* Author's conversations with Diane Tapscott Terrazino, 2002.

299   *He had trouble sleeping:* Author's conversations with Phil Hayden and Harry Griffin,
      2002.

299   *On the Anglo-Saxon and on:* Jones, *Two Survived,* p. 43, and author's conversations with
      Norma Tapscott, 2002.

299   *The symptoms of people:* Consultation with Dr. A. Matsakis, Apr. 11, 2003.

300   *Avoidance of the issue:* Case History Sheet, 1st Neurological Hospital, Major J. C.
      Richardson, Royal Canadian Army Medical Corps, in Tapscott Personnel Record.

300   *The Canadian Army doctors had:* Medical History of an Invalid, May 25, 1942, Capt.
      A. E. McReicher, Medical Officer, Royal Canadian Army, in Tapscott Personnel
      Record.

300   *In the spring of 1963: South Wales Echo,* Oct. 3, 1963, p. 10.

301   *That June, he:* Ibid.

301   *The drug had been developed:* Shephard, *A War of Nerves,* pp. 207–9.

301   *It is known today:* Consultation with Dr. A. Matsakis, Apr. 11, 2003.

301   *As described in the* South Wales Echo: *South Wales Echo,* Oct. 3, 1963, p. 10.

301   *As Norma and Diane recall:* Author's conversation with Norma Tapscott, 2002, and
      correspondence with Diane Tapscott Terrazino, 2003.

302   *Disregarding his own safety: South Wales Echo,* Oct. 3, 1963, p. 10.

303   *The day after the paper:* Ibid., Oct. 4, 1963, p. 12.
303   *His funeral was private:* Author's conversations with Norma Tapscott, 2002.
303   *Diane had burdens of:* Author's conversations with Diane Tapscott Terrazino, 2002.

23: SURVIVORS

The information in this chapter was provided by the survivors who have generously shared their memories.

Bibliography

Basnight, Bobby L. *What Ship Is That?* New York: Lyons & Burford, 1996.

Bennet, Glin. *Beyond Endurance.* New York: St. Martin's/Marek, 1983.

Blanning, T. C. W., ed. *The Oxford History of Modern Europe.* Oxford: Oxford University Press, 2000.

Bourne, Randolph S. *War and the Intellectuals: Collected Essays, 1915–1919.* New York: Harper Torchbooks, 1964.

Bowditch, Nathaniel. *Bowditch for Yachtsmen. Piloting: Selected from American Practical Navigator.* New York: David McKay Company, c. 1980.

Bridges, Constance. *Thin Air.* New York: Brewer & Warren, 1930.

Bridgland, Tony. *Sea Killers in Disguise.* Annapolis: Naval Institute Press, 1999.

Burrell, David. *The Nitrate Boats.* Kendal: World Ship Society, 1995.

Busch, Fritz-Otto. *Kapitän z.S. v. Ruckteschell, Hilfskreuzer-Gespensterschiffe auf den Weltmeeren.* Baden: Erich Pabel Verlag, n.d.

Campbell, Robert J. *Psychiatric Dictionary,* 7th ed. New York: Oxford University Press, 1996.

Churchill, Winston. *The World Crisis, 1914–19.* 2 vols. London: Odhams Press, 1939.

Committee on Alleged German Outrages. Appendix to the *Report of the Committee on Alleged German Outrages.* London: Eyre & Scottiswoode, 1915.

Corbett, Sir Julian S., and Sir Henry Newbolt. *History of the Great War: Naval Operations.* 8 vols. London: Longman, Greene & Co., 1920–31.

Course, A. G. *The Deep Sea Tramp.* London: Hollis & Carter, 1960.

Critchley, Macdonald. *Shipwreck-Survivors: A Medical Study.* London: J. & A. Churchill, 1943.

Crystall, David, ed. *The Cambridge Encyclopedia.* Cambridge: Cambridge University Press, 1990.

Cunliffe, Tom. *Coastal and Offshore Navigation.* Arundel: Fernhurst Books, 1993.

Dear, I. C. B., ed. *The Oxford Companion to World War II.* New York: Oxford University Press, 2001.

Dorland's Illustrated Medical Dictionary. Philadelphia: W. B. Saunders, 2000.

deKay, James T. *The Rebel Raiders: The Astonishing History of the Confederacy's Secret Navy.* New York: Ballantine Books, 2002.

DeKerchove, Rene. *International Maritime Dictionary.* 2nd ed. New York: Van Nostrand Reinhold, 1961.

Denny, Barry C., Lionel Hawks, and Roy Widdicombe. "The Log of the *Anglo-Saxon* Jolly Boat." Transcription by Capt. R. M. Millar, Admiralty File 199/725, Public Records Office, Kew, London, U.K.

Domergue, Jean Gabriel. *The Crimes of Germany.* New York: American Defense Society, 1918.

Edwards, Bernard. *Beware Raider!* Annapolis: Naval Institute Press, 2001.

Fedden, Henry R. *Suicide: A Social and Historical Study.* New York: Arno Press, 1980.

Friedman, Matthew J. *Post-Traumatic Stress Disorder: An Overview.* Web site of the National Center for Post-Traumatic Stress Disorder, U.S. Dept. of Veterans Affairs, www.ncptsd.org.

Garraty, John A., and Peter Gay, eds. *The Columbia History of the World.* New York: Harper & Row, 1981.

Gilbert, G. M. *Nuremberg Diary.* New York: Da Capo Press, 1995.

Grove, Eric I. *The Defeat of the Enemy Attack on Shipping, 1939–1945.* Navy Records Society, vol. 137. Aldershot: Ashgate Publications, 1997.

Guetzkow, Harold S., and Paul H. Bowman. *Men and Hunger.* Elgin: Brethren Publishing, 1946.

Guy, John. *30s & 40s Britain.* Tunbridge: Ticktock, 1998.

Haws, Duncan. *Merchant Fleets in Profile.* vol. 4. Cambridge: Patrick Stephens, 1980.

Hocking, Charles. *Dictionary of Disasters at Sea During the Age of Steam.* London: Lloyd's Register of Shipping, 1969.

Horne, John N., and Alan Kramer. *German Atrocities, 1914: A History of Denial.* New Haven: Yale University Press, 2001.

Hough, Richard. *The Great War at Sea, 1914–1918.* Oxford: Oxford University Press, 1983.

Hoyt, Edwin P. *Guerrilla, Colonel von Lettow-Vorbeck and Germany's East African Empire.* New York: Macmillan, 1981.

Jamison, Kay Redfield. *Night Falls Fast: Understanding Suicide.* New York: Vintage Books, 2000.

Jones, Guy Pearce. *Two Survived.* New York: Random House, 1941.

Jones, Guy Pearce, and C. B. Jones. *There Was a Little Man.* New York: Random House, 1948.

Keegan, John. *The First World War.* New York: Alfred A. Knopf, 1999.

Kitchen, Martin. *The Cambridge Illustrated History of Germany.* Cambridge: Cambridge University Press, 1996.

Koch, Hannsjoachim W. *Der Deutsche Burgerkrieg.* Berlin: Ullstein Verlag, 1978.

Leach, John. *Survival Psychology.* New York: New York University Press, 1994.

Lettow-Vorbeck, Gen. Paul Emil von. *Heia Safari! Deutschland Kampf in Ostaafricka.* Leipzig: K. F. Koehler, 1920.

Lloyds Register of Shipping. Several editions, 1931–1956.

Lund, Alfred. *The Raider and the Tramp.* Self-published. 1992.

Maloney, Elbert S. *Chapman Piloting, Seamanship, and Small Boat Handling.* 61st edition. New York: Hearst Marine Books, 1994.

Masefield, John. *The Conway.* New York: Macmillan, 1933.

Matsakis, Aphrodite. *I Can't Get over It: A Handbook for Trauma Survivors.* Oakland: New Harbinger Publications, 1992.

———. *Trust After Trauma.* Oakland: New Harbinger Publications, 1998.

McKenna, Robert. *The Dictionary of Nautical Literacy.* Camden, Maine: International Marine, 2001.

Metzler, Jost. *The Laughing Cow.* London: W. Kimber, 1955.

Middlemiss, N. L. *Pride of the Princes: The History of the Prince Line Ltd.* Newcastle-upon-Tyne: Shield Publications, 1988.

Miller, David. *U-boats.* Washington: Brassey's, 2000.

Minois, Georges. *History of Suicide.* Baltimore: Johns Hopkins University Press, 1999.

Muggenthaler, Karl August. *German Raiders of World War II.* London: Robert Hale, 1978.

Mullins, Claud. *The Leipzig Trials.* London: H. F. & G. Witherby, 1921.

Neumann, Charles J., et al. *Tropical Cyclones of the North Atlantic Ocean, 1871–1980.* Ashville: National Oceanographic and Atmospheric Administration, 1978.

Neumann, Inge S. *European War Crimes: A Bibliography.* New York: Carnegie Endowment for International Peace, 1951.

Paine, Lincoln P. *Ships of the World.* Boston: Houghton Mifflin, 1997.

Pallud, Jean P. *Les U-Boote.* Bayeux: Editions Heimdal, 1988.

Poolman, Kenneth. *Armed Merchant Cruisers: Their Epic Story.* London: Leo Cooper, 1985.

Professional Guide to Diseases. 7th ed. Springhouse: Springhouse, 2001.

Pye, Michael. *The King over the Water.* New York: Holt, Rinehart and Winston, 1981.

Raeder, Erich. *My Life.* Annapolis: United States Naval Institute, 1960.

Ray, John. *The Battle of Britain.* London: Cassell & Co., 2000.

Reisenberg, Felix. *The Men on Deck: Masters, Mates and Crew, Their Duties and Responsibilities.* New York: D. Van Nostrand Co., 1918.

Robertson, Dougal. *Sea Survival: A Manual.* London: P. Elek, 1975.

Roskill, Captain S. W. *A Merchant Fleet at War: Alfred Holt & Co., 1939–1945.* London: Collins, 1962.

———. *The War at Sea, 1939–1945.* vols. 1 and 2. London: Her Majesty's Stationary Office, 1954 and 1956.

Rousmaniere, Leah Robinson. *Anchored in the Vail.* New York: The Seamen's Church Institute, 1995.

Ruge, Friedrich. *Der Seekrieg: The German Navy's Story, 1939–1945.* Annapolis: Naval Institute Press, 1957.

Sadler, M.J., J. J. Strai, and Benjamin Caballero, eds. *The Encyclopedia of Human Nutrition.* 3 vols. San Diego: Academic Press, 1998.

Salter, J. A. *Allied Shipping Control.* Oxford: Clarendon Press, 1921.

Scheer, Admiral Reinhard. *Germany's High Seas Fleet in the World War.* London: Cassell and Company, 1920.

Schmalenbach, Paul. *German Raiders: A History of Auxiliary Cruisers of the German Navy, 1895–1945.* Cambridge: Patrick Stephens, 1979.

Schmidt-Pauli, Edgar von B. *Geschicte der Freikorps, 1918–1924.* Stuttgart: R. Lutz, 1936.

Sereny, Gitta. *The Healing Wound.* New York: W. W. Norton & Co., 2001.

Shephard, Ben. *A War of Nerves.* Cambridge, Mass.: Harvard University Press, 2001.

Shneidman, Edwin S. *Comprehending Suicide.* Washington: American Psychological Association, 2001.

Slader, John. *The Red Duster at War.* London: William Kimber, 1988.

Smith, Anthony. *Survived.* London: Quintin Smith, 1998.

Southey, Robert. *The Life of Nelson.* Annapolis: Naval Institute Press, 1990.

Spindler, Arno. *Der Krieg zur See: Handelskrieg mit U-Booten.* Vols. 3, 4, and 5. Berlin: Mittler & Sohn, 1934.

Storer, Douglas F. *The Most, Amazing but True.* New York: Fawcett, 1966.

Tischer, Heinz. *Die Abanteuer des letzten Kapers.* Bad Hersfeld: Glockdruck, 1983.

Tutorow, Norman E. *War Crimes, War Criminals and War Crimes Trials.* New York: Greenwood Press, 1986.

Van De Graaff, Kent M., and Stuart Ira Fox. *Concepts of Human Anatomy and Physiology.* Dubuque: Wm. C. Brown, 1992.

Williamson, Gordon. *German U-boat Crews, 1914–45.* Oxford: Osprey Publishing, 1999.

Willis, James F. *Prologue to Nuremberg.* Westport: Greenwood Press, 1982.

Woodward, David. *The Secret Raiders.* New York: W. W. Norton & Co., 1955.

Young, Everild. *Eleuthera: The Island Called "Freedom."* London: Regency Press, 1966.

NEWSPAPERS AND PERIODICALS

SWEDEN

Goteborgs-Posten: June 27, 1919, Tysks flyktingar i Goteborg; June 28, 1919, De tyska flytingarna; June 30, 1919, De tyska flytingarnas ode; July 10, 1919, Tsykarna fa stanna.

Goteborg Morgonpost: June 27, 1919, Ett mystiskt besok i Molle; June 28, 1919, De unga tyskarnas odysse!

Stockholms-Tidningen: June 26, 1919, Tysk u-batsforstorare pa visit; June 26, 1919, Flyktingarna pa U Z 21 pa vag till Sydamerika; July 7, 1919, Flyktingarna fran U Z 21.

UNITED KINGDOM

The Literary Supplement, (London) *Times,* October 2, 1919.

Newcastle Evening Chronicle, November 11, 1940.

South Wales Argus, various editions, 1940 and 1941.

South Wales Echo, various editions, 1940 and 1941.

The Times (London), September 6, 1918; October 4 and 22, 1918.

BAHAMAS

Nassau Daily Tribune, various editions, 1940 and 1941.

Nassau Guardian, various editions, 1940 and 1941.

Nassau Magazine, various editions, 1940 and 1941.

UNITED STATES

Cosmopolitan, August 1941.

The Lookout of The Seamen's Church Institute, New York, December 1940 to June 1941.

New York Herald-Tribune, January 31, 1941.

New York Times, June 30, 1919; February 2, 4, 5, and 9, 1920; November 1, 1940; December 7, 1940; January 31, 1941; and June 12, 1941.

New York Sun, November 1, 1940; February 27, 1941.

Reader's Digest, September 1941.

Time, June 9, 1941.

GOVERNMENT DOCUMENTS

SWEDEN

Ansokan om uppelhallsbok, tyska undersatar, EVf: 2.
Forteckningar over avresta utlanningar, 1918–1919, EVd.
Goteborg poliskammare.
Landskansliet Goteborgs och Bohus lan.
Utlanningsavdelningen.
    Liggare enligt Kungl. Stadgan angaende hotell och pensionat, Continental Hotel, DXIV:96.
    Skrivelser till K B och Kungl. Utrikesdepartementet 1919-06-11 to 1919-10-17, Blb: 2.

UNITED KINGDOM

Admiralty Files ADM 199/23 and ADM 199/218, Public Records Office, Kew, London.
Anonymous, *German War Trials, Report of the Proceedings Before the Supreme Court in Leipzig,* His Majesty's Stationery Office, London, 1921.
C.b. 01292 Reported Destruction of Enemy Submarines: Summary of Cases, London: Admiralty, 1916–1918.
Colonial Office Files CO 23/681 and CO 23/691, Public Records Office, Kew, London.
German War Criminal Lt. von Ruckteschell, Treasury Solicitor's File TS 26/51, Public Records Office, Kew, London.
Ministry of Information, *Merchantmen at War,* His Majesty's Stationery Office, London, 1944.
Ruckteschell War Crimes Trial Record, War Office File WO 235/364, Public Records Office, Kew, London.
Wartime Instructions for Merchant Ships, WIMS 3, BR. 1012, vol. 3, Radio Procedure, London, Admiralty, n.d. and Washington, Navy Department, n.d.

CANADA

Personnel Record of R. G. Tapscott, National Archives of Canada.

GERMANY

Prison Record of Hellmuth von Ruckteschell, Document Group 242-1 II, Gefangnisver-waltung, Room MEG, Shelf 122B, Staatsarchiv Hamburg, Germany.
Reichswehrministers PA 7413 of November 24, 1919.
Ruckteschell, Hellmuth von. Operations and Tactics: Analysis of Important Events in Sea Warfare. "The Voyage of the Hilfskreuzer 'Schiff 21' ('*Widder*')," Kriegsmarine High Command, Berlin, 1943.

UNITED STATES

National Center for Post-Traumatic Stress Disorder, Fact Sheet.
National Center for Post-Traumatic Stress Disorder, "What Is Post-Traumatic Stress Disorder?"

OTHER DOCUMENTS

ENGLAND

Articles of Agreement and List of Crew for *Anglo-Saxon,* July 25, 1940.

Conway Records, Muster Rolls, Wages Book and Register of All Cadets, Merseyside Maritime Museum, Liverpool.

Register Books, *Indefatigable,* Liverpool Record Office, Liverpool Central Library.

UNITED STATES

Registrar's Office Files, Mystic Seaport, Mystic, CT.

PERSONAL WRITINGS

Herr, Jürgen. "Kurz-Biographie von Hellmuth Max von Ruckteschell." Olaf Griese, translator.

Hoppe, Konrad. "Comparing Timetable (Synchronopsy)." This document lists the events that took place in relation to the *Michel,* the German Navy, and the world, from October 28, 1940, to April 16, 1942.

Ruckteschell, Hellmuth von. "Prayers for the Burial of English Sailors, C. Carrington and T. Lavelle." Courtesy of Konrad Hoppe.

———. Letters written between July 21, 1946, and May 14, 1947. Courtesy of Konrad Hoppe. Olaf Griese, translator.

———. *Notizen zu den Ausfuhrungen unseres Kommandanten, Kapitan z. S. d. R. Hellmuth von Ruckteschell im Japanischen Marine-Klub in Tokio am 11 Marz 1943.* Courtesy of Jürgen Herr. Olaf Griese, translator.

———. "Oh Christmas Tree: A Christmas Play with Music Written for the Puppet Stage of the Hilfskreuzer *Michel.*" Courtesy of Konrad Hoppe. Olaf Griese, translator.

Ruckteschell, Margaret von. Letter, written June 30, 1947. Courtesy of Konrad Hoppe. Olaf Griese, translator.

Vermehren, Werner. "Der Untergang des Handelsstörkreuzer *Michel,* am 17 Oktober 1943." Typescript, copy provivded to the author by Jürgen Herr. Olaf Griese, translator.

Index

Munson, Frank C., 229
Munson steamship lines, 229, 242
Mystic Seaport, Connecticut:
    jolly boat exhibited in, 2–3, 257, 306, 307
    Marine Historical Association and, 232, 234, 257
    Museum of America and the Sea, 308

Nagasaki, atomic bomb in, 279
Napoleonic Wars, 43
Naranio, 299
Narvik, 11–12, 80, 87; *see also Widder*
Nassau:
    flight from Eleuthera to, 209, 210, 241, 244
    fundraising in, 234–35
    jolly boat in, 228–29
    Lucerne Hotel in, 240
    media stories in, 206, 211–12, 229–34, 237, 240
    medical care in, 207–8, 210, 227, 228, 239
    radio broadcast from, 230–34, 237, 259
    Royal Victoria hotel in, 229, 230, 232, 234, 240
    social life in, 229, 236, 239
Nassau Daily Tribune, 211, 231
Nassau Guardian, 206, 211, 212, 230, 240, 252, 258
National Center for Post-Traumatic Stress Disorder, 254
National Maritime Museum, Greenwich, England, 1–2
naval ranks, 314
Nazi Party, 54, 58–59, 207, 213, 216, 221, 280
Negenborn, Doctor, 89–90, 107, 217
Neger, Karl August, 69
Nelson, Horatio, 2, 43
Neumark, 66, 70–74; *see also Widder*
New York:
    Tapscott in, 258–60, 266
    Widdicombe in, 242–45, 251
New York Sun, 212
New York Times, 212, 295

Nicol, H. D. P., 287
Nitrate Producers Steam Ship Co., 172, 238, 248
Nordmark, 82
North German Lloyd Lines, 217
Norton, S. B., 258
Norway:
    invasion of, 79–80, 220
    neutrality of, 79
Nuremberg, International Military Tribunal, 280

Oakes, Sir Harry, 232, 234
Oakes, Lady, 232, 234, 257
O'Leary, Michael, 100, 112
Oostplein, 90, 197
Operation Cerberus, 267
Operation Sealion, 220
Orford, 96–97
Orion, 74, 76, 89, 217

P&O Nedlloyd Lines, 308
Pacific Ocean, German boats in, 265, 275–78
Pakanbaru railroad, Sumatra, 276
Palmer, George, 283
Pan-American Neutrality Zone, 85, 86, 229, 242, 247
Patzig, Oberleutnant, 35, 55
Paxton, 26
Peg Leg, 256
pellagra, symptoms of, 208
Penny, Edith, 50, 306–7
Penny, Francis:
    age of, 121
    on *Anglo-Saxon,* 95, 96, 101, 108
    death of, 147–48, 150, 210, 211, 311
    injuries of, 122, 124, 132, 134, 135, 136, 141, 142, 147
    and jolly boat launching, 114
    rowing the jolly boat, 119
    and Royal Marines, 50
    and *Widder* attack, 112, 113, 114
    and World War I, 50
Penzel, Kapitänleutnant, 106, 191, 217
Perière, Lothar von Arnauld de la, 34

in World War I, 22–24, 28–33, 35, 40, 84
in World War II, 10–11, 69, 78
Uckermark, 276
Ulysses, 308
United Kingdom, *see* England
United States:
  Civil War, 66–67, 90, 253
  flag of, 1
  impact of World War I in, 39
  and *Lusitania* sinking, 23
  merchant marine in, 4
  naval ranks of, 314
  neutrality of, 239
  protests against U-boats by, 24
  in World War II, 4, 230, 239
UZ-21, 34, 35–38, 53, 77

Vanoc, 98
Venerable, 305
Victoria, 305
Victory, 2
Vietnam War, 253
Von der Tann, 22

Walder, Cliff, 45, 93, 127, 306
Walder, Daphne, 46, 93, 306
war:
  laws of, 23, 24, 25, 68, 69, 286
  post-traumatic stress in, 253–55, 262–63
  see also specific wars
war criminals:
  of concentration camp staff, 292
  death sentences for, 285, 286, 292
  English investigations of, 55–56, 281–84
  Leipzig tribunals, 55–56, 281
  Nuremberg tribunals, 280
  Ruckteschell's defense, 285–86, 288–90, 291–92
  Ruckteschell's trial, 286–95, 297, 298, 309
  Ruckteschell's verdict and sentencing, 291–95
  victors' revenge on, 281, 288

of World War I, 24, 31–32, 34–38, 51, 54–56, 280, 292–93
of World War II, 85–86, 88, 280–95
Warspite, 220
Wastell, Marion (Blake), 46, 93, 306
Werner, Wilhelm, 32, 56
Weserwerft shipyard, Bremen, 24
Weyher, Kurt, 89
Widder:
  Anglo-Saxon approached by, 13–16, 88, 105–7, 109–10
  Anglo-Saxon attacked and sunk by, 16–18, 90, 110–16, 119, 127, 187–88, 197, 207, 210
  arrival in France, 198, 214–16
  awards to crew of, 216, 218
  "bloodless" conquests of, 191–92
  breakout of, 81–82
  in Brest, 216
  British attacks on, 81
  character of, 18–19, 65, 311
  commander chosen for, 73–74, 77–78
  crew members of, 60–63, 73, 217–19
  design of, 70–73, 75–76, 247
  as *El Neptuno,* 12–16, 88
  engine problems of, 85, 106–7, 189, 191, 192–96, 214, 215, 217
  entertainment on, 75, 219, 269–70
  heading for home, 196–98, 215
  ice damage to, 82
  as *Narvik,* 11–12, 80, 87
  as *Neumark,* 66, 70–74
  postwar existence of, 308
  preparation of, 74–76, 78
  prisoner accommodations on, 71, 83–85, 86, 190, 191, 193–94
  as raider, 67, 70–74, 107, 188–89, 192, 195, 219
  raiding territory of, 78–79, 82–83, 129, 188, 191, 194–95
  refueling of, 81–82, 83, 190, 193–94
  as *Schiff 21,* 77
  seaplanes of, 85, 106, 222
  ships attacked and sunk by, 12, 16–18, 83, 85–90, 110–16, 189–90, 191–92, 194, 214, 216, 270, 276, 292

Widder (cont.)

survivors abandoned by, 18, 89–90, 187–88, 190, 192, 194, 217, 283, 285, 289, 291–92

survivors shot by crew of, 115, 119, 283–84, 286, 288, 289–91

tactics used with, 12–16, 26, 67, 88–90, 106, 191, 271, 289–90

under way, 78–80

and war crimes trials, 282, 285–91

war diary of, 106–7, 110, 114, 187–88, 189, 192, 194, 197, 282–83, 288, 289

weapons on, 72–73, 75–76, 106, 222

Widdicombe, Cynthia Pitman:

engagement and marriage of Roy and, 48, 93–94, 307

and Gill, 307

notice of lost ship, 170–71

and other crew families, 210, 251

and Roy's death, 250–51, 255

and Roy's return, 242, 245, 248

and Roy's survival, 209, 237

Widdicombe, Roy (Wilbert Charles):

on *Anglo-Saxon*, 48, 94, 101, 102, 108, 109, 110

automobile of, 236–37, 241, 242

bond of Tapscott and, 155–58, 182–84, 252

and Canadian Air Force, 241–42

as celebrity, 229–30, 235, 236, 243, 245

clothing of, 48, 209, 236, 241, 244

death of, 250–52, 255, 257, 289, 307

early years of, 46–48, 93, 243–44

in Eleuthera, 201–6, 213, 316

engagement and marriage of, 48, 93–94, 307

first sinking, 93

and fish, 167, 168

gifts to, 209, 234–36, 256

and hurricane, 178–82

injuries of, 122

and jolly boat landing, 185–86, 201, 203

and jolly boat launching, 113–14

and jolly boat log, 210–11

on jolly boat watch, 120, 128, 165, 175

and Jones's book, 235, 241

and leadership, 144, 151, 152

leaving Nassau, 242–43

media stories about, 206, 209, 210, 211–12, 227, 229–34, 237, 243, 244–45, 251–52, 291

medical condition of, 208, 210, 227

new lifestyle of, 235, 236–37, 241, 242–43, 244, 256

in New York, 242–45, 251

official statements by, 206–7, 211, 289, 291

ordeal of, 161, 207, 227, 232–33, 243

personal traits of, 101, 102, 143, 144, 154, 184, 213, 228, 235, 241, 244, 251

physical deterioration of, 164–65, 175–76, 182–83, 203, 204, 208–9

radio broadcast about, 230–34

and rain, 159–61, 168–69, 181

recovery of, 205–8, 212, 227–28, 236, 237, 239, 240–42

return to England, 237, 242, 244, 245, 247–50

return to the sea, 238

and sea anchor, 120

on *Siamese Prince*, 245, 247–50, 251, 252, 289, 306

steering, 143, 149, 152, 168, 180–84, 186

stories told by, 46, 47, 127, 210–12, 227, 244–45, 246

and survival, 141, 143, 150, 152–53, 163–69, 173–86, 211, 227–28, 311

talkativeness of, 206, 207, 210, 211–13, 227, 246, 248

and *Widder* attack, 110, 112, 113–14, 187

youth of, 121

Wiedemann, Otto, 32–33, 55–56, 292

Wilhelm II, Kaiser, 33, 35, 55

William F. Humphrey, 272

Willis, Harry, 112–13

Willkie, Wendell, 206

Wilson, Woodrow, 33, 34

Wimmel, Adolf, 217

Windsor, Duchess of, 213, 227, 231, 255

Windsor, Edward, Duke of, 207, 213, 227, 231, 232, 233–34, 255